BANNING LANDMINES

Rebecca,

Girls rule!

Jody Williams

BANNING LANDMINES

Disarmament, Citizen Diplomacy, and Human Security

Edited by
Jody Williams,
Stephen D. Goose, and
Mary Wareham

ROWMAN & LITTLEFIELD PUBLISHERS, INC.
Lanham • Boulder • New York • Toronto • Plymouth, UK

ROWMAN & LITTLEFIELD PUBLISHERS, INC.

Published in the United States of America
by Rowman & Littlefield Publishers, Inc.
A wholly owned subsidary of The Rowman & Littlefield Publishing Group, Inc.
4501 Forbes Boulevard, Suite 200, Lanham, Maryland 20706
www.rowmanlittlefield.com

Estover Road
Plymouth PL6 7PY
United Kingdom

British Library Cataloguing in Publication Information Available

Library of Congress Cataloging-in-Publication Data

Banning landmines : disarmament, citizen diplomacy, and human security / edited by
  Jody Williams, Stephen D. Goose, and Mary Wareham.
    p. cm.
  Includes index.
  ISBN-13: 978-0-7425-6240-0 (cloth : alk. paper)
  ISBN-10: 0-7425-6240-9 (cloth : alk. paper)
  ISBN-13: 978-0-7425-6241-7 (pbk. : alk. paper)
  ISBN-10: 0-7425-6241-7 (pbk. : alk. paper)
  1. Arms control. 2. Land mines. 3. Land mines (International law) I. Williams, Jody,
1950– II. Goose, Stephen D. III. Wareham, Mary, 1970–

JZ5645.B36 2008
327.1'743—dc22   2007044224

Printed in the United States of America

∞™ The paper used in this publication meets the minimum requirements of American
National Standard for Information Sciences—Permanence of Paper for Printed Library
Materials, ANSI/NISO Z39.48-1992.

Contents

Acknowledgments

THE EDITORS WOULD LIKE TO THANK the donors who have supported the production of this publication: the Canadian Department of Foreign Affairs, the Royal Norwegian Ministry of Foreign Affairs, and the Swiss Federal Department of Foreign Affairs.

We are grateful to Next Step Productions for its management of this project and indebted to Rachel Good for her assistance in preparing this publication.

We would like to thank the contributors to *Banning Landmines*, who all participated in their personal capacities. Please note that the views expressed in this book are those of the contributors and do not reflect the opinion or position of their respective organizations and/or governments.

Foreword

Archbishop Desmond Tutu

THE DAY HAS NOT YET COME when people everywhere can walk in a world without fear of stepping on landmines. But as I come from Africa—the most mine-contaminated continent of our planet, I can say that our people never thought for a moment that we would be as close to that goal as we are today. In too many decades of the twentieth century, wars raged on our continent and in most of those wars landmines seeded our earth with death and destruction. Who would have imagined that before the end of that century, the world would be given the gift of a treaty banning antipersonnel landmines? Who would have anticipated the force of the movement that brought about that treaty and the ongoing impact on our world?

Of course, the scourge of landmines has not been limited to Africa. Those "eternal soldiers" are found on most of the world's continents. Still a lethal legacy in some seventy-eight countries in the world, they claim new victims every year and will continue to do so until the valiant struggle to eliminate landmines reaches its inevitable conclusion—a world free of antipersonnel landmines.

Millions of voices have been raised around the world to support the efforts of the thousands of men and women who have worked to achieve a mine-free world. I am blessed to be able to say that as the landmine campaign gained momentum in the 1990s, Africa played a leadership role in bringing about the Mine Ban Treaty. I recall clearly addressing the first government-sponsored continent-wide landmine conference in Kempton Park, South Africa, in May 1997 and calling upon my African brothers and sisters to continue their leadership and demonstrate that despite the many problems plaguing our countries, we could and must be a leader of hope—a leader demonstrating new ways to address old problems in this very difficult world we share.

My own government of South Africa was one of the "core group" of countries that helped guide the Ottawa Process through the successful negotiations of the Mine Ban Treaty—in fact, it was our Ambassador Jackie Selebi who presided over those historic negotiations. However, after heightened public attention about the landmine issue throughout that year culminating with the signing of the treaty by 122 nations in Ottawa, Canada, on December 3–4, 1997, came decreased coverage of the landmine issue. Much of the world seemed to believe—or wanted to believe—that somehow simply the words of the treaty alone magically resolved the problem. But of course that simply is not the case.

If the Mine Ban Treaty has made a difference in the world, it is because the partnership between governments and civil society forged through the process that created the treaty has continued to this day. Not only was the Ottawa Process itself unique, but the means developed to press for the full implementation of and compliance with the treaty, as well as civil society's monitoring of that compliance, are reflective of the ongoing work of governments and nongovernmental organizations (NGOs) after 1997.

The determination and creativity shown by NGOs and governments in bringing about the Mine Ban Treaty are held up as shining examples of arms control and humanitarian law in an otherwise very bleak landscape of attempts at disarmament. Such examples offer us hope and inspiration, but we must be very clear that they are the result of determination and hard work—not just our dreams of a better world. Such examples must be analyzed and studied so that we learn from the lessons they have to offer.

In this book, individuals active in the landmine movement offer their perspectives about different aspects of the continuing work to ensure that the Mine Ban Treaty was not just an historic document, but that it actually makes a difference in the lives of those communities that have had to endure the daily terror of living with landmines. Others from the movement share their insights into the broader impact that this effort has had on how we think about tackling old problems in new ways despite concerted efforts to keep us chained to a Cold War mentality of clashing global enemies. In that world, the specific and nebulous enemies can only be met with the fervent determination of the national security state bristling with new and more lethal weapons. These chapters of part two of the book consider how we might better approach our global problems in an increasingly intertwined world where overlooking even the most basic needs of the many threatens the security of us all.

Even though we are facing huge challenges today—global problems that perhaps seem insurmountable—we cannot give way to despair. We cannot give up hope of the promise of a better world. We must look to those examples of change and progress that demonstrate what each and every individual can contribute when we work together for a common good. But just admiring these agents of change is not the answer—we must learn from those successes to be able to strengthen our own work and enhance our contributions to creating a better world for us all. This book offers many such lessons for us to consider and is an invaluable addition to the continued chronicling of the landmine ban movement and its impact in today's world.

1

Banning Landmines and Beyond

Stephen D. Goose, Mary Wareham, and Jody Williams

CREATING A NEW LAW IS EASY; getting everyone to obey it is the hard part. This adage is sometimes applied to the international stage: achieving a new treaty is easy; getting everyone to join and to comply is the hard part.

In truth, achieving the 1997 Mine Ban Treaty[1] was not easy, as the editors and many of the contributors for this book can attest from deep personal involvement. With the passage of time, a myth has formed about how a potent combination of civil society and like-minded governments steamrolled the rest of the world into a ban treaty and the Nobel Committee into a Peace Prize with barely a bump in the road. But the odds were very long, the obstacles immense, the process fragile, and the outcome extremely uncertain throughout.[2]

Many view the Ottawa Process—launched by Canadian Foreign Minister Lloyd Axworthy's October 1996 challenge to negotiate a ban treaty in one year—and 1997 as the "glory days" of the effort to eradicate antipersonnel landmines.[3] The yearlong whirlwind of treaty preparatory meetings and constant activity by the International Campaign to Ban Landmines (ICBL), the exhilarating (though often tense) formal negotiations in September in Oslo, the pomp and circumstance of the signing ceremony in Ottawa in December (with 122 nations participating, many at the foreign minister level), and the beauty and honor of the award of the Nobel Peace Prize to the ICBL and its coordinator Jody Williams one week later in Oslo, captured the attention of the public and the media. The treaty was called a "gift to humanity" and the Nobel Prize was characterized as a "victory" for civil society—ordinary people doing extraordinary things. For the first time in history, a weapon in widespread use for decades had been comprehensively banned.

But the old adage is correct. The greater achievement has been the effective implementation of and compliance with the treaty over the past decade and the success in universalizing the treaty and establishing a new standard of behavior rejecting antipersonnel mines—a standard observed even by many that have not yet joined the treaty.

This book is the story of the successes—and the failures—of the first ten years of what might be called the "Mine Ban Treaty Process," building on the Ottawa Process. The story is told by the practitioners, by many of those who have been key to making the treaty a reality, both inside and outside government. In the second part of the book, the authors consider the broader impact of the treaty and the process, with an eye to the future. This book picks up from where a 1998 publication documenting the process leading to the establishment of the Mine Ban Treaty left off.[4]

Getting Started: From the Negotiations to the First Meeting of States Parties

When the Mine Ban Treaty negotiations were gaveled closed in Oslo on September 18, 1997, ICBL campaigners cheered wildly and more than a few diplomats joined in the celebrations. The treaty was not perfect, but it was better than anyone had believed would be possible. The text became stronger instead of weaker during the negotiations, a phenomenon almost unheard of in multilateral affairs, where narrow national interests seem inevitably to chip away at the greater good.

Even before the final gavel came down, the ICBL, key governments, and other partners had been contemplating how to make the treaty a reality and how to make sure the beautiful words on paper made a difference in mine-affected communities. There was a shared understanding that this was still the start of the effort to eradicate antipersonnel mines, and not the end—even if the treaty constituted an excellent beginning to the end!

On the final day of negotiations, the ICBL presented delegates with its post-Oslo plan of action that campaigners had developed during the talks. With the plan, the ICBL was not only demonstrating its view that the open partnership must continue, but was also challenging governments to step up to the plate with their own plans. The campaign made it completely clear that its members intended to work as hard to make the treaty succeed as they had to get states to the negotiating table. While the Mine Ban Treaty—a unique mix of arms control based on humanitarian concern—provided a framework for a world without landmines, unimplemented it would be worthless to the millions of people living with landmines and would also undercut the credibility of international law. As Liz Bernstein details in her chapter on campaigning, the ICBL was in this process for the long haul.

While the ICBL's determination was welcomed by its true partners, this was not a sentiment shared by everyone. Indeed, it may be that most governments thought, and perhaps wished, that with the successful treaty negotiations, the "victorious" ICBL would disband after the signing ceremony in Ottawa in December 1997 and leave treaty implementation and compliance to governments.

The mine ban movement received an incalculable boost when three weeks after the negotiations, on October 10, the Nobel Committee announced that the 1997 Peace Prize would be awarded jointly to the ICBL and its then-coordinator Jody Williams. Global awareness of the issue skyrocketed, not to mention the prestige of the ICBL. It instantaneously became much more difficult for governments to stay away from the treaty.

Eighty-nine governments participated in the negotiations in Oslo, several of which (including the United States) indicated at the end that they likely would not sign the treaty.[5] Less than three months later, 122 nations did sign the treaty in Ottawa on December 3–4, 1997. The stunning total can be attributed in part to the Nobel notoriety, but also to the intense "get out the signatures" activities carried out by the ICBL, the International Committee of the Red Cross (ICRC), and a number of governments in that period.

The leaders in the "core group" of governments that took responsibility for the Ottawa Process in 1996 and 1997 were Canada, Norway, Austria, and South Africa. Other highly active states included Belgium, the Netherlands, and Switzerland with additional contributions from Colombia, Germany, Mexico, New Zealand, and the Philippines. Most of these same countries continued to provide leadership for the next decade, none more so than Norway and Canada. But important new players also emerged, such as Mozambique, Nicaragua, Thailand, Croatia, and Jordan, all of which hosted annual Meetings of States Parties, and others such as Kenya (site of the First Review Conference) and Cambodia.

The partnership of the ICBL, key governments, the ICRC, and United Nations agencies (most notably UNICEF) wasted no time in setting about to make the treaty work. Just as the ICBL put a future action plan on the table in Oslo, the Canadian government organized a number of workshops during and after the treaty signing to identify what had made the Ottawa Process work to date and what was needed to fully implement and universalize the treaty, as well as to monitor compliance (both progress and problems).

The ICBL launched an "Entry into Force before the Year 2000" campaign, focusing on "The First Forty"—the number of ratifications needed to trigger entry into force and make the treaty binding international law. States became caught up in the "competition" to be among those forty states. UNICEF and the ICRC mobilized their field offices to press for rapid ratification, and Canada and other core group countries instructed their embassies to make this a priority.

Burkina Faso deposited the fortieth ratification with the UN on September 16, 1998, a mere nine months after the signing ceremony, and the treaty entered into force on March 1, 1999.[6] The Mine Ban Treaty thus became international law more quickly than any other major multilateral treaty in history.

The sense of urgency that resulted in the treaty being developed, negotiated, signed, and entered into force in record time continued to prevail. With the core group of governments as well as the ICBL pressing the issue, states decided to hold the first annual Meeting of States Parties just two months later, in May 1999 (even though it was not required to be held until March 2000).[7] In a bold, even radical, initiative strongly urged by the ICBL, they decided to hold the meeting in a mine-affected country, Mozambique, instead of in the typical UN venues in Geneva or New York. Nontraditional diplomacy continued to carry the day, as governmental representatives came to Maputo and were constantly reminded of the realities of living with mines, instead of being holed up in a sterile diplomatic setting doing business as usual. This did not make many UN bureaucrats happy, especially in the Department of Disarmament Affairs, which for a number of years appeared to resent the Mine Ban Treaty Process for its insistence on doing things differently.

This approach also meant that some States Parties would have to take on roles and burdens usually carried out by UN staff or others. For the First Meeting of States Parties, Canada in particular provided extensive financial, logistical, and substantive assistance to the government of Mozambique with its host responsibilities. The meeting, attended by representatives of 108 countries and more than 100 nongovernmental organizations (NGOs), ended up being held inside a giant tent on the grounds of a hotel—and one Canadian diplomat went so far as to personally help construct the tent!

Making a Difference: Ten Years of Achievements

As described by Alex Kmentt in chapter 2 looking at the treaty since its signing, the achievements have been nothing short of remarkable. The Preamble of the Mine Ban Treaty states that it was created "to end the suffering and casualties" caused by antipersonnel mines. While suffering and casualties certainly continue at levels that no one finds acceptable, there can be no question that the treaty and the mine ban movement have made tremendous progress. The number of new casualties each year has likely been halved from the common estimate of twenty-six thousand in 1997. More than 2,000 square kilometers (equating to two *billion* square meters) of land has been cleared. The number, quality, and sophistication of mine clearance, mine risk education, and survivor assistance programs have grown markedly.

The tide has been irrevocably reversed: many more mines are coming out of the ground every year than are being laid. In 2006, government forces used antipersonnel mines in only two countries—Burma (Myanmar) and Russia—and rebel forces in only eight. When antipersonnel mines have been used in the past decade, it has usually been on a relatively small scale.[8] Many of those using mines (both governments and rebels) have been reluctant to admit to it.

States Parties to the Mine Ban Treaty have destroyed more than forty million stockpiled antipersonnel mines—a crucial preventive means of stopping suffering and casualties in the future. Trade in antipersonnel mines has for the past decade consisted of only a low level of illicit, unacknowledged transactions—even those not part of the treaty have ceased export of the weapon. Fewer than ten countries still actively produce antipersonnel mines, compared to more than fifty before the ban movement was launched.[9]

In Shannon Smith's chapter, she explains how collective efforts to universalize the Mine Ban Treaty have paid off. As of September 2007, there were 155 States Parties to the Mine Ban Treaty, about 80 percent of the world's nations. More countries join every year, and many others have indicated their intention to join in the future. Some governments stress that they are *de facto* in compliance with the treaty, some already have national prohibitions on production and trade, and, as noted, almost none are using the weapon. Several countries outside the treaty are major donors to mine clearance programs worldwide. In December 2006, twenty states not yet party to the treaty voted for the annual UN General Assembly resolution calling on all states to join and fully implement the Mine Ban Treaty. The treaty has clearly had a powerful impact even on those not yet ready to be formal members.

For armed nonstate actors, the impact of the stigmatization of the weapon is less vivid. Today, the most significant use of landmines is by armed nonstate actors. Yet, as Yeshua Moser-Puangsuwan describes in chapter 10, through consistent and creative political intervention an increasing number of nonstate armed groups feel obliged to abide by, or answer to, the global norm that the mine ban movement and the Mine Ban Treaty are putting in place.

The Mine Ban Treaty has proven not only to be the disarmament vehicle for stopping new use, production, and trade in antipersonnel mines, and destruction of existing stockpiles, it is also accepted as a crucial humanitarian vehicle for ensuring the clearance of contaminated land and assistance to affected communities. As Bob Eaton shows in chapter 8, the Mine Ban Treaty has become the focal point for mine action and for the eradication of antipersonnel mines.

These impressive achievements have only been possible because of the continuation of the "new diplomacy" launched with the Ottawa Process that led to the Mine Ban Treaty. Above all, the new diplomacy has been characterized by the close working partnership among the ICBL, key governments, the International Committee of the Red Cross, and United Nations agencies.

These achievements have also only been possible because of bold and great ideas that were then well executed and because of the goodwill, dedication, and commitment of so many individuals, putting humanitarian aims and protection of civilians above all else.

Great Ideas, Well Executed

The "Mine Ban Treaty Process" has been sustained by the key elements of the Ottawa Process, such as the government-civil society partnership, nontraditional diplomacy with an extensive role for NGOs, a focus on shared humanitarian aims and not narrow national interests, and the intense dedication of numerous individuals inside and outside of government.

But the success of the treaty over the past ten years has also been propelled by several "great ideas" that were then expertly implemented. Perhaps chief among these have been the Intersessional Work Programme, the Implementation Support Unit, and the ICBL's Landmine Monitor initiative.

The Intersessional Work Programme was established at the First Meeting of States Parties in 1999 to facilitate work carried out during the year between the annual meetings required by the treaty. As discussed in chapter 6 by Kerry Brinkert, the notion itself was not radical, but the manner in which it was conceived and put into effect reflected the best of the Ottawa Process traditions. It has succeeded in the original stated aim of organizing the work within the framework of the treaty "in a way which promotes continuity, openness, transparency, inclusiveness and a cooperative spirit."[10]

States Parties established Standing Committees for key aspects of the treaty (including mine clearance, victim assistance, and stockpile destruction, as well as "general status and operation"), which would meet twice a year to identify areas of concern and develop plans to ensure effective implementation of the treaty: to mark, measure, and stimulate progress toward a mine-free world. This relatively heavy schedule of three weeks of Mine Ban Treaty meetings each year not only kept governments focused on the issue, but also provided a means of engaging a wide range of States Parties in leading roles through the positions of cochairs and corapporteurs for the Standing Committees.

Over the years, the meetings have been conducted with a refreshing air of informality. The ICBL and the ICRC have been afforded complete access and given a prominent role. Indeed, the ICBL has been consulted on the agendas for the various Standing Committee meetings and frequently has made more interventions than any State Party. ICBL and ICRC recommendations have been regularly taken up and acted upon.

Clearly, the Intersessional Work Programme has been a collaborative process conducted in the Ottawa Process tradition of inclusivity, partnership, dialogue, openness, and practical cooperation. It has fulfilled its intended purposes of helping to maintain a focus on the landmine issue, of becoming a meeting place for all key mine action players, of promoting the Mine Ban Treaty as a comprehensive framework for mine action, and of stimulating momentum to implement fully the treaty.

Another important development from the First Meeting of States Parties in 1999 was agreement on a specific format for annual Article 7 (Transparency Measures) reports, and agreement that the UN, which receives the reports, should make them publicly available.[11] Transparency reporting has been a notable element in the success of the Mine Ban Treaty, serving not just to keep States Parties informed about progress in implementation, but also as a means of keeping countries engaged, and more importantly, a way for states to communicate their needs with respect to mine clearance, victim assistance, and stockpile destruction.

In 2000, States Parties created a Coordinating Committee to promote a high degree of interaction among the Standing Committees and to further facilitate successful implementation of the treaty. The Coordinating Committee is chaired by the president of the annual Meeting of States Parties, and members include the cochairs of the Standing Committees; the ICBL and ICRC also participate in the meetings.

In 2001, States Parties agreed to establish an Implementation Support Unit (ISU), which then began operations in January 2002. While still avoiding the concept of a "do everything" secretariat, the ISU has proven to be invaluable in making the treaty function at a consistent and high level. It has contributed significantly to ensuring better preparations and follow-up by States Parties and ensuring the sustainability and continuity of the Intersessional Work Programme. It has also notably helped to engage a wider range of States Parties in the treaty's work on a regular basis, especially those mine-affected countries with limited resources.

The establishment of a Sponsorship Program, funded on a voluntary basis by individual States Parties, to bring other States Parties to Mine Ban Treaty meetings, has also been key in getting and keeping numerous countries involved in the treaty's operations. This has often included those with daunting implementation tasks, such as heavily mine-affected states or big stockpilers, and sometimes has included nations that might join the treaty with some extra encouragement.

The practice of having the annual Meeting of States Parties in a mine-affected country every other year (rotating with Geneva) is another example of creative, inclusive, humanitarian-based thinking so prevalent in the Mine Ban Treaty experience.

A final innovation that deserves highlighting related to the Intersessional Work Programme has been the establishment of "Contact Groups," most notably on universalization and on transparency reporting. These informal groups have again shown the effectiveness of the partnership of dedicated governments, the ICBL and ICRC, as the various actors have worked together closely to bring additional countries on board the treaty and to promote an extraordinary rate of compliance with the Article 7 reporting requirement.

On the NGO side, the "greatest idea" has likely been the ICBL's Landmine Monitor project, which it describes as an "unprecedented civil society-based initiative . . . that marks the first time that non-governmental organizations have come together in a sustained, coordinated and systematic way to monitor and report on the implementation of an international disarmament or humanitarian law treaty."[12] Mary Wareham's chapter shows how the system looks not just at implementation of and compliance with the treaty, but also at "the response by the international community to the global landmines crisis."

From 1999–2004, Landmine Monitor reported on every country of the world in its typically one thousand-page annual volume, and on a somewhat smaller number of countries since that time. It looks at landmine policy, use, production, trade, stockpiling, mine clearance, mine risk education, casualties, survivor assistance, and mine action funding.

Landmine Monitor quickly became accepted as the most comprehensive and authoritative source on the global landmine situation, utilized by governments, campaigners, the media, and mine action practitioners alike. It has been the ICBL's primary means of holding governments accountable. Since 1999, Landmine Monitor reports have almost always formed the basis for engaging states on difficult issues related to compliance with the Mine Ban Treaty.

Failures and Challenges

While progress has been undeniably impressive, the authors of this book make clear that the Mine Ban Treaty has not been an unqualified success and that future challenges may be more daunting than those faced thus far. Not surprisingly, some of the biggest problems have been encountered in the most ambitious areas of the treaty: the requirements to clear mined areas within ten years and to provide victim assistance. But failures have been documented in many other areas as well.

Perhaps the most challenging issue of all is how to meet the complex needs of landmine survivors, a task made even more difficult by virtue of the fact that assistance to survivors is not a strict treaty obligation as mine clearance is, for example. As Sheree Bailey and Tun Channereth detail in chapter 9, most mine-affected states still lack the capacity, resources, and in some cases political will, to meet the needs of mine survivors and their communities. Significant progress has been made at the international level to develop a better understanding of the key issues facing mine survivors, but much more needs to be done at the national level. How to achieve this in countries lacking all but the most basic medical infrastructure is a daunting challenge indeed.

While the first clearance deadlines loom in 2009 and 2010, more than one dozen states are not on track to finish in time. In the case of some heavily affected countries this is understandable—and was expected by the treaty drafters, who made provision for extension of the deadline if necessary. But other states clearly have not made sufficient effort to meet the deadline and some, as pointed out in chapter 7 on compliance by Steve Goose, may still be utilizing emplaced mines for military purposes—a serious violation of the Mine Ban Treaty.

Goose also describes worrisome developments concerning stockpile destruction. Four countries have missed their four-year deadline for stockpile destruction, and several others will likely soon join them. There is also concern that there is widespread abuse of the treaty's exception allowing states to keep some antipersonnel mines for demining training and development purposes—but only the "minimum number absolutely necessary." It appears that many countries are retaining far more mines than can be justified and that many are not utilizing the mines at all, just maintaining them in storage.

While there have been no confirmed instances of use or transfer of antipersonnel mines by States Parties, there have been a small number of serious allegations—and none of those allegations have been vigorously pursued by other States Parties. Moreover, States Parties have not taken any formal steps to prepare for the need to deal with any serious violations of the treaty in the future and have rejected suggestions to create an informal mechanism or process to ensure that compliance concerns are addressed in a systematic and coordinated fashion. Additionally, fewer than half the States Parties have adequately fulfilled their obligation to undertake legal measures to implement the Mine Ban Treaty domestically, including penal sanctions. Such national measures are of key importance given the overall "cooperative" approach to treaty implementation and compliance.

Mine Ban Treaty members have failed to resolve important issues of contradictory interpretation and implementation of certain provisions of the treaty by different states. These include such fundamental matters as differing views on what landmines are banned by the treaty—with most states believing that antivehicle mines with sensitive fuses that function like antipersonnel mines are prohibited, but a few are disagreeing and continuing to stockpile such mines, for example those with tripwires, breakwires, or tilt rods.

In addition, States Parties have not been able to reach a common understanding on what acts are permitted and not permitted under the treaty's ban on assisting with any prohibited acts—a concern that arises especially in the context of States Parties engaging in joint military operations with forces that are not party to the treaty and may use antipersonnel mines. There are also some states that believe it is permissible to allow the transit of antipersonnel mines across a State Party's national territory, contrary to majority opinion.

While difficult to characterize as a "failure," there is still a perception in many quarters, including among some States Parties, that the Mine Ban Treaty cannot truly be considered a success until at least some of the "biggest powers" are on board, most notably the United States, Russia, and China. Some would include India and Pakistan on that list as well, especially given their status as major stockpilers and recent users of the weapon. On the other hand, optimists point to the steps that even those states have taken that are consistent with the Mine Ban Treaty, and some realists express concern that if those states were party to the treaty, their presence and methods of operation would severely disrupt and alter the open, inclusive, and cooperative nature of the Mine Ban Treaty Process.

Many of the authors in this volume, while detailing the important strides made in the past decade, have concluded that it will be hard to sustain the success. The formidable challenges of completing mine clearance and of providing adequate victim assistance may be mountains that are too high to climb. The mine action community may be turning its attention to other related issues, such as explosive remnants of war and cluster munitions, which are not directly addressed in the Mine Ban Treaty. Compliance issues, including those related to the core prohibitions on use, transfer, and stockpiling, seem to become more prevalent and worrisome, rather than less. While more states will undoubtedly join the treaty, we may be approaching the saturation point, with many of the remaining states likely to be permanent holdouts, as Shannon Smith postulates in chapter 5.

Terms like "donor fatigue" and "burnout" are heard more often. It would not be unusual for both governments and NGOs to emphasize new priorities after a decade or more of focused, intense work. It becomes ever more difficult to keep governments and civil society engaged and energized. There is also the fear that as a second, third, and even fourth generation of diplomatic leaders comes into play, the special stature and feeling of the Mine Ban Treaty will increasingly get lost and will become more formal and more like diplomatic business as usual.

Clearly, future challenges loom large. The perception on the part of much of the general public that the work was done with the signing of the treaty in 1997 could not have been more wrong, but the even more widely held opinion now that there is little left to do is also far off the mark. The strongly stated commitment from the ICBL, the ICRC, and key governments to continue and even redouble their efforts in the coming years provides reason for optimism, as does the very solid foundation of a decade of creative and cooperative ideas and practices and well-honed implementation structures.

Beyond Landmines

While many of the chapters in part one of this book mention the "new international norm" against antipersonnel mines, it is a debatable proposition as to whether or not the prohibition has reached the level of customary international law. In chapter 12, Peter Herby and Kathleen Lawand examine the norm-making process to draw insights into how such international law develops.

While those working in the mine ban movement have always stressed that the true measure of the treaty is the difference that it makes on the ground, many have also recognized the potential broader impact of the movement and the effect that it might have on international law, humanitarian assistance, and approaches to international security. Indeed, the ICBL received the Nobel Peace Prize not just for its role in bringing about the Mine Ban Treaty, but because it was able to "express and mediate a broad range of popular commitment in an unprecedented way. . . . As a model for similar processes in the future, it could prove to be of decisive importance to the international effort for disarmament and peace." Steve Goose and Jody Williams explore these issues in chapter 11 that examines the model.

The mine ban movement showed that nongovernmental organizations could put an issue—even one with international security implications—on the international agenda, provoke urgent actions by governments and others, and serve as the driving force behind change. It showed that civil society can wield great power but, more importantly, demonstrated the power of partnerships, and of common and coordinated action by NGOs, like-minded governments, the ICRC, and UN agencies.

It proved that it is possible for small and medium size countries, acting in concert with civil society, to provide global leadership and achieve major diplomatic results, even in the face of opposition from bigger powers. It showed that it is possible to work outside of traditional diplomatic forums, practices and methods, without consensus rules, and still achieve success multilaterally. It demonstrated that there is not just room for, but a need for the voice of civil society in international affairs and international security.

As seen in various chapters in this book, the ICBL and the mine ban movement have clearly had a significant impact apart from the landmine issue, notably in serving as a model for and therefore helping to bring about the new legal instruments on the International Criminal Court, child soldiers, explosive remnants of war, and disability rights. In chapter 13 on cluster munitions, Steve Goose discusses the weapons as well as the exciting launch in February 2007 of the "Oslo Process," which closely mirrors the process that brought about the Mine Ban Treaty and is expected to produce a new international convention on cluster munitions in 2008.

And in chapter 14 on the rights of people with disabilities, Jerry White and Kirsten Young provide a firsthand account of how a huge gap in international human rights law has been filled with the conclusion in 2006 of the Disability Rights Convention. As with landmines, this process benefited enormously from the expertise and participation of civil society and other stakeholders, in particular key actors from the ICBL who applied lessons they had learned in banning landmines to the process that brought about this new treaty.

Other initiatives have not reflected the landmine model, and while some traditional diplomatic forums have been changed somewhat as a result of the mine ban experience, the reality is likely that none have been fundamentally altered. Yet, as discussed by John Borrie, the limited progress in the disarmament and arms control domain over the last decade has only been achieved when these issues are approached through a humanitarian lens. Jody Williams argues in her concluding chapter that the terrorist attacks of September 11, 2001, and the "global war on terror" resulted in retrenchment on many issues, including budding efforts to redefine security in terms of what makes individuals secure—"human security"—rather than simply the security of the state, or traditional "national security." She also argues that the need for a human security approach is greater than ever.

It remains to be seen if the success of the Mine Ban Treaty can be sustained, and if the model can continue to be applied and expanded in other efforts and issues. But after a decade, there is undeniably an excellent track record and many well-drawn lessons to follow. Many government officials and nongovernmental activists know what it takes—and as with a new treaty or new law—they just need to implement the lessons they have already learned in banning landmines.

Notes

1. The formal name is the Convention on the Prohibition of the Use, Stockpiling, Production and Transfer of Anti-Personnel Mines and On Their Destruction. The negotiations were concluded on September 18, 1997, in Oslo, Norway, and the treaty was opened for signature in Ottawa, Canada, on December 3–4, 1997. Other short titles in use include the Mine Ban Convention, the Antipersonnel Mine Ban Convention, the Ottawa Treaty, and the Ottawa Convention. The editors have chosen to use "Mine Ban Treaty," a term initiated and popularized by the International Campaign to Ban Landmines (ICBL).

2. There was virtually uniform opposition from governments at first due to the widespread deployment of antipersonnel mines, considered by most as common and acceptable as bullets, an integral part of in-place defenses and war plans, training, and doctrine. About 125 nations had stockpiles of antipersonnel mines and the weapon had been used in about 90 countries. Antipersonnel mines were not only considered a cheap and reliable substitute for soldiers, but were also the focus for future high tech research and development for richer nations. These were incredible difficulties to overcome, not to mention the opposition of major powers such as the United States, Russia, and China.

3. The best source on the mine ban movement from its origins through the treaty signing in December 1997 is Maxwell Cameron, Robert J. Lawson, and Brian W. Tomlin (eds.), *To Walk Without Fear: The Global Movement to Ban Landmines* (Toronto: Oxford University Press, 1998).

4. Cameron, Lawson, and Tomlin, *To Walk Without Fear.*

5. In addition to the eighty-nine participating governments, there were thirty-two observer states.

6. In Article 17, the treaty states that it "shall enter into force on the first day of the sixth month after the month in which the 40th instrument of ratification, acceptance, approval or accession has been deposited."

7. The ICBL noted that the decision to hold the meeting as soon as possible instead of waiting a year, as permitted by the treaty, "was not only consistent with the crisis nature of the landmine problem, but also a demonstration of the importance attached to the Mine Ban Treaty by the international community and the commitment of many governments to rapidly and effectively implement the treaty." ICBL, "Report on Activities, First Meeting of States Parties, Maputo, Mozambique, May 3–7, 1999," September 1999, p. 1.

8. The exceptions to this were the widespread use of antipersonnel mines by India and Pakistan on their borders during a period of tensions from December 2001 to mid-2002, by Ethiopia and Eritrea during their border war from 1998 to mid-2000, and by Russia in Chechnya in 1999 and 2000. Government forces in Burma (Myanmar) have

used antipersonnel mines extensively throughout the past ten years. Rebel forces have used mines in large numbers in Burma (Myanmar) and Colombia.

9. The ICBL's Landmine Monitor has cited thirteen producers, but a number of them are not actively producing, although they retain the right to do so in the future. The ICBL's producer list includes Burma (Myanmar), China, Cuba, India, Iran, Nepal, North Korea, Pakistan, Russia, Singapore, South Korea, the United States, and Vietnam. Those stating that they have not produced in a number of years include Cuba, Iran, Nepal, the United States, and Vietnam.

10. Final Report of the First Meeting of States Parties, APLC/MSP.1/1999/1, Annex IV, Intersessional Work, May 20, 1999, p. 27.

11. This subsequently spurred the decision by States Party to Amended Protocol II on landmines of the Convention on Conventional Weapons to make their annual reports public as well.

12. ICBL, *Landmine Monitor Report* 2006 (Ottawa: Mines Action Canada, 2006).

I

BANNING LANDMINES

2

A Beacon of Light:
The Mine Ban Treaty Since 1997

Alexander Kmentt

I N THE PUBLIC PERCEPTION, the fight against landmines reached its peak in December 1997 with the signing of the Mine Ban Treaty by 122 countries and the awarding of the Nobel Peace Prize to the International Campaign to Ban Landmines (ICBL) and its coordinator Jody Williams. These arguably constituted the most high profile moments for the landmine issue. But the intense and creative work over the subsequent decade of making the treaty a reality is a fascinating and illuminating story in its own right.

Since 1997, governments from mine-affected and nonaffected states, landmine survivors, representatives of civil society, and international organizations have worked together—usually out of the limelight and often bucking other trends on the international scene—to shape the global fight against landmines through the legal framework of the Mine Ban Treaty.

Remarkable progress has been achieved in realizing the treaty's key humanitarian and disarmament objectives. This success story is largely the result of a focus and determination rarely seen in international affairs. As a result, a diplomatic process has evolved demonstrating that international cooperation can effectively address global problems. At a time when multilateralism finds itself increasingly under threat, this is an outstanding achievement.

Nevertheless, many challenges remain, and there is still a long way to go on the path to a mine-free world. There are some doubts that the dynamism that has characterized the early years of the Mine Ban Treaty can be maintained for as long as it will take to solve the landmine problem.

This chapter provides an overview of the main successes and challenges to the treaty since its signing. It assesses the treaty both in terms of reaching its humanitarian and disarmament objectives and in the development of the diplomatic process. It considers whether the objectives set forth in the treaty have remained somewhat "lofty words on paper" or whether the agreement has actually changed things on the ground.

In the end, the importance of the Mine Ban Treaty has to be judged on this basis: has the agreement saved lives and limbs, improved the lives of survivors, brought cleared land back into productive use, led to the destruction of antipersonnel mine stocks, and reduced the use, production, and transfer of antipersonnel mines? The answers are overwhelmingly positive.

Moreover, against an overall bleak disarmament background, the Mine Ban Treaty has been and continues to be a "beacon of light." It is the only process where real and tangible progress is being made and where work without deep political divisions between the main protagonists is possible.

Banning Antipersonnel Landmines

The Mine Ban Treaty entered into force on March 1, 1999. Thus it became binding international law more quickly than any other multilateral disarmament or humanitarian law instrument.[1] This was the result of an extensive and coordinated ratification campaign carried out by the key "partners" that brought about the treaty: a core group of governments, the ICBL, the International Committee of the Red Cross (ICRC), and United Nations (UN) agencies, especially UNICEF.

By 2007, more than three-quarters of the world's states had joined the Mine Ban Treaty.[2] This speed—also probably a record for international treaties—is a reflection of the urgency with which the international community has sought to address the landmine problem. No doubt the humanitarian goals on which the treaty is largely based provided the overarching motivation for most states to join. But the large number of adherents also reflects the fact that the military utility of antipersonnel mines has been widely questioned, particularly when weighed against the weapon's disastrous long-term effects on the lives of civilians.

Another key element in the success of the "universalization" of the treaty—that is, the effort to get all countries to join—has been the positive momentum created by the Ottawa Process that led to the development and signing of the treaty. Many states, which might not have joined because they perceived the issue was of little or no direct concern to them, decided to join because it had become politically attractive to be associated with the mine ban movement.

Indeed, the stigma against antipersonnel mines has affected even those who are not party to the treaty. One can argue that a new standard of behavior—a new norm—against antipersonnel mines is now widely observed. Clearly, state behavior has changed significantly.[3]

States Parties to the Mine Ban Treaty have had an admirable record of compliance with the key provisions. Perhaps above all, they have observed the core prohibitions on use, production, and transfer of antipersonnel landmines. This certainly is a huge success, which even supporters of the treaty may not have expected. To date there is no proven case of States Parties using antipersonnel mines.[4] Similarly, no state sanctioned transfers of antipersonnel mines are definitively known to have occurred.[5] There have been no allegations of continued production of antipersonnel mines by a State Party.

The obligation to destroy stockpiled antipersonnel landmines constitutes another key disarmament provision of the treaty. State Parties are given four years to complete this undertaking that for some can be costly, technically challenging, or vast.[6] To date, only a very few State Parties have not fulfilled their stockpile destruction obligation within the four-year deadline.[7] Collectively, States Parties have destroyed about forty million stockpiled antipersonnel landmines. As of September 2007, eighty States Parties had completed stockpile destruction, and ten still have to complete their stockpile destruction programs (the remaining sixty-five did not hold operational stocks upon joining the treaty). This is disarmament in its truest form: the prevention of the use of a weapon through its destruction and, hence, the prevention of casualties.

While compliance by States Parties has been very good, it is also important to look at the behavior of states that have remained outside the treaty. Here some significant developments have taken place as a positive "spillover" from the Mine Ban Treaty. At one time, there were more than fifty states producing antipersonnel landmines. That figure has now fallen to thirteen, and several states not party to the treaty have stopped production.[8] Until the mine ban movement took hold, legal trade in antipersonnel mines was widespread, but it has now virtually ceased, even among those not party to the treaty. Many outside the treaty have formal bans or moratoria on export.[9] While small-scale illicit trade still occurs, the international market for antipersonnel landmines has all but disappeared.

The use of antipersonnel mines has also fallen sharply. In recent years, only a handful (or fewer) of governments have actively laid antipersonnel mines, including Burma (Myanmar), Georgia, Nepal, and Russia. The United States, whose decision not to join the treaty put it at the receiving end of often very harsh criticism, has not used antipersonnel mines since 1991. Arguably, the global drop in use has been caused by exactly the kind of political pressure and stigmatization of the weapon that the Treaty Community has been able to generate. The political price to be paid in terms of public criticism has perhaps been too high compared to the actual military value of antipersonnel landmines.

Clearly the norms established by the Mine Ban Treaty have led to a significant change in the behavior of states outside the treaty. On the other hand, moral authority, a key strength of the treaty, does not seem to have the desired effect in some countries. Some states that apparently are not as susceptible to humanitarian arguments or public opinion have continued to use the weapon. The behavior of armed nonstate actors, some of whom are responsible for widespread use of antipersonnel mines, is also a great cause for concern.[10] Because those groups are beyond the scope of the treaty, we are challenged as to how best to address this important issue.

Outside of the treaty's membership, states still hold large stocks. Although the numbers are not known exactly, it is believed that over 140 million antipersonnel mines are stockpiled by China, Russia, and the United States. India, Pakistan, and others hold millions more. This is, of course, a major challenge to the global disarmament objective of the Mine Ban Treaty. However, if the aim of the treaty is to have an impact on the lives of affected people, destroying stockpiles in those countries which have until recently deployed them (for example, States Parties like Angola, Bosnia and Herzegovina, Cambodia, Democratic Republic of Congo, and Sudan) has more significance than the stocks still held in big countries.

A total ban on use, production, trade, and stockpiling of antipersonnel mines has not yet been achieved, but progress is impressive, and even the behavior of some hold-out states has clearly altered for the better.

Clearing Mines

The parties to the treaty have an obligation to clear mined areas under their jurisdiction or control. For this task, the treaty foresees a deadline of ten years, which can be extended upon agreement of the other State Parties. Even with the first deadlines approaching in 2009, assessing progress in this area is not as straightforward as it might seem. The situation varies greatly from country to country. For example, in some States Parties such as Afghanistan, Angola, Bosnia and Herzegovina, and Cambodia, the landmine contamination is of such a scale that large parts of the population are directly and severely affected. In other countries only remote parts of a territory may be mined with little or no impact on people's daily lives. But the same ten-year deadline applies in all cases.

There are seventy-seven countries worldwide with mine-contaminated area, and fifty-three are party to the treaty. Since 1997 significant progress has been made not only in getting mines out of the ground, but also in the way that mine clearance is conducted. Although undertaken before the treaty came into existence, *humanitarian demining* has only been put on a solid and systematic footing since then. This is undoubtedly due to the treaty and the framework that it has provided for the range of mine action activities (clearance, risk education, and victim assistance) as well as for banning the weapon.

As a starting point, we now know much more about the extent of the landmine contamination in most affected countries. Systematic landmine impact surveys have been conducted, and information about where mines are located as well as where they have the greatest impact has increased dramatically. Internationally recognized mine action standards have been developed and disseminated and, consequently, the performance of demining operators has improved significantly. In most cases, mine clearance is now carried out much more effectively and efficiently than was the case not that long ago.

States Parties have focused most (but not all) of their funding and other assistance for mine clearance on the treaty's mine-affected countries. These affected states have, by joining the treaty, foresworn the use of antipersonnel mines. This provides donors with a degree of assurance that once the mines have been cleared, the land will not be mined again in the future.

Some states define mine clearance as a national priority and have set up mine action oversight bodies, with international assistance, and have made significant progress. Among these are Afghanistan, Cambodia, Croatia, and Mozambique. Yet other mine-affected countries have not achieved similar progress. This may be due to administrative or bureaucratic reasons or shortage of funding, but the most critical factor in many cases is a lack of political will to devote the necessary attention and priority to the issue. For some of the affected countries, this lack of determination at the national level may be fueled by an expectation that international assistance should take care of the landmine problem.

Six States Parties have already fulfilled their mine clearance obligations.[11] The majority of the remaining mine-affected States Parties have established detailed national demining plans that they are in the process of implementing. As a first step, some heavily mine-affected State Parties have secured their mined areas with fences or other means to ensure that civilians do not enter. Similarly, many are undertaking mine risk education programs to educate the population about how to deal with the dangers of mines.

Nevertheless, it is increasingly clear that meeting the ten-year deadline will be a very difficult challenge for a number of State Parties, and some may need to apply for an extension. In some countries, the magnitude of the problem may be so great that the job simply cannot be finished in ten years, despite best efforts. Unfortunately, some states may request an extension even though they are not in a position to demonstrate that they have made serious efforts to meet the clearance obligation within the first ten years. From a political point of view, denying a request for an extension would be a difficult and hence un-likely event. How State Parties handle such requests could be a test for the credibility of the treaty.

At the same time, meeting mine clearance deadlines may not be the best in-dicator of the success or failure of the treaty. When assessing progress in this area, it is important to consider what has been achieved as well as at how much land has been cleared and returned to productive use. According to the ICBL's Landmine Monitor, more than 2,000 square kilometers (two billion square meters) of land were cleared from 1999 to 2005. Without the treaty and its focus on mine clearance, we would not be as far down the road toward a mine-free world as we are today.

Victim Assistance

The Mine Ban Treaty exists in large part because of the plight of mine victims and the determination to put an end to the casualties and suffering caused by antipersonnel mines. This goal is translated into a treaty obligation to assist mine victims.[12] Measuring progress in this area is perhaps even more complex than that of mine clearance as it is not a "one-off" action but a comprehensive approach that aims to improve the lives of people victimized by landmines as long as they live.

There are now significantly fewer new mine victims annually compared to a decade ago. As of 2006, the best estimate was that fifteen thousand to twenty thousand people are killed or injured by landmines each year, compared to twenty-five thousand to thirty thousand per year when systematic attempts to record them began.[13] Although every year many thousands are added to the hundreds of thousands of existing landmine survivors, the declining figure of new mine victims is certainly a success in the collective effort in the fight against landmines.

But who do we mean when we talk about victims? Naturally, the survivors of mine incidents must be our main concern. However, work within the framework of the treaty has broadened our understanding of who can be con-sidered a landmine victim. It is now generally accepted that victims include those "who either individually or collectively have suffered physical or psy-chological injury, economic loss or substantial impairment of their funda-mental rights through acts or omissions related to mine utilization."[14] This general definition includes the families of victims as well as the communities whose lives are affected by landmines. In light of this, it is accurate to say these weapons have victimized millions of people.

With this approach has come the realization that in addition to being a humanitarian problem, landmines are a very real and serious obstacle to development, hindering the socioeconomic potential of many of the poorest countries in the world. In an important evolution, States Parties have tried increasingly to address the developmental dimension of the landmine problem.

The past decade has also seen a significant increase in awareness of the specific rights and needs of landmine survivors in terms of medical and psychological care. The treaty has provided the framework for landmine victims to discuss and highlight rights issues for people of weapons-inflicted disabilities, in particular, and those with disabilities in general as well. Survivors have gained recognition, and the devastating impact of those weapons on their lives and the challenges they face are addressed in serious forums.

As a result, much more is now known, not only about mine victim specific problems and challenges, but also about the situation of other people with disabilities in those countries. This too constitutes major progress and a significant achievement of the work of the treaty. The experience of the Mine Ban Treaty had a major impact on the development of the Disability Rights Convention (see chapter 14).

It has become apparent that most of the problems that mine survivors face are comparable to those of other people with disabilities. Therefore solutions need to be found in the broader context of the public health and social policies of the countries concerned. It is also clear, however, that mine victims require special medical assistance for as long as they live. Physical rehabilitation is a crucial element in achieving social and economic reintegration, which is the aim of all mine survivors. Empowering them through education and employment opportunities is what is ultimately required. This will remain a serious challenge for the future particularly in developing countries.

Cooperation and Assistance

Some of the core goals of the treaty—including victim assistance, mine clearance, stockpile destruction, and universalizing the ban—require significant financial resources. The primary responsibility for achieving these goals lies with the individual states that are party to the treaty. However, each State Party "in a position to do so" has an obligation to provide assistance.[15]

It is not a "hard" legal obligation because states decide for themselves whether or not they are "in a position" to provide assistance. But it is an obligation—albeit a political one—nonetheless. It is not known with precision how much money has been allocated for mine action since 1997, but approximately US$3 billion. Nor is it possible to establish a figure of how much money will be required to "finish the job" because different aspects of the problem vary widely from state to state.

But, it is clear that despite all the progress achieved so far, efforts to address mine clearance, victim assistance, and stockpile destruction need to be increased both by the affected states themselves and by donor states. It is a positive sign that funding levels have increased relatively steadily over the past decade. But in some states that are "in a position to do so" there is a discrepancy between the apparent political importance given to the landmine issue and their willingness to provide assistance. This is an issue that has the potential to hurt the integrity of the treaty. International support is necessary to ensure that mine-affected states continue to give political importance to this issue and devote their own scarce resources to mine action. And, it is a good investment. With the necessary cooperation and support, the landmine problem can be solved in a relatively short period of time and with comparably limited resources.

Disarmament's "Beacon of Light"

To understand and appreciate fully the "overall performance" of the Mine Ban Treaty, it is necessary to look beyond its actual scope and subject matter. The treaty is a remarkable phenomenon when put into the wider context of international affairs and multilateral diplomacy. The innovative diplomatic process created within the framework of the treaty deserves to be examined more closely.

Although the motives behind the Mine Ban Treaty are largely humanitarian, in the international context it is also a disarmament treaty, banning an entire category of weapons. It was negotiated primarily by disarmament diplomats who still follow and largely shape the implementation process. To better understand the treaty's impact, one should look at the overall situation in the disarmament sector in the years since the treaty was negotiated. This has been and continues to be a very difficult period for multilateral disarmament, nonproliferation and arms control efforts. After a brief interlude following the end of the Cold War, the international community has again become bitterly divided on these issues.

There are a variety of reasons for this, and this chapter is not the right place to discuss them. However, one key element that must be highlighted is a shift in the approach by the United States toward the entire multilateral treaty-based disarmament system. Much of this system was shaped largely by the United States, which has increasingly appeared to question its effectiveness. As a result, its uncompromising position often opposes courses of action supported by the overwhelming majority of other states. The result tends to be paralysis of disarmament processes—with the most notable exception being the Mine Ban Treaty. The Mine Ban Treaty process is probably the only one in the disarmament sector that has been able to progress without the involvement of the United States, and at times despite its opposition and efforts to undermine the success of the treaty.

In the bleak global disarmament context, the Mine Ban Treaty stands out as a "beacon of light." No other disarmament forum makes such concrete progress and in no other forum is there such an absence of political divisions between the main actors. This has resulted in disarmament diplomats throwing themselves into the work of the treaty as a "breath of fresh air" compared to the deep frustration and unproductive stagnation that characterizes other disarmament issues.

The Mine Ban Treaty therefore has a political significance that goes beyond the issue of landmines. Many states, and certainly many diplomats at a personal level, see that the treaty is actually having an impact on the lives and the security of people, which contrasts starkly with the classical state-centered security approach that drives most multilateral disarmament processes.

The Mine Ban Treaty has become a counter model—an example of a multilateral treaty and international cooperation effectively addressing a global problem at a time when the multilateral system is being called into question. It also has become a counter model to the typically unproductive debate that dominates the disarmament sector.

Progress within the framework of the treaty has been possible in part *because* some of the so-called big countries that rigidly adhere to the state-centered approach have not participated in the treaty. Hence, the Mine Ban Treaty has become almost an ideal process for states that want to show how multilateralism and international cooperation can work when unimpeded by the bigger states. The treaty is seen by many of its supporters as an avant-garde process, and one that many passionately want to succeed.

The Dynamic Process that Makes the Treaty Work

The work of the Mine Ban Treaty has been and continues to be driven by both state representatives and civil society. Nongovernmental organizations, nearly all under the banner of the ICBL, have been able to assume a prominent role in the work of the treaty that far exceeds their involvement in other disarmament processes—in many cases from which they have been excluded or barely tolerated. These two "Mine Ban Treaty constituencies" vigorously defend the treaty and put a lot of effort and ingenuity into making it work. Indeed, over the years a dynamic process has developed that in itself is different from other forums.

First, it is important to mention the consensus rule. Multilateral disarmament treaties, being closely linked to national security issues, tend to work on a consensus basis under which all decisions need to be reached unanimously. In political terms, this is to enable the major military countries to agree on international rules in the first place. In practical terms, however, consensus is often a recipe for stagnation. As desirable as reaching a consensus may be, the consensus obligation is, in fact, a veto rule. It provides states with a tool to ensure that nothing moves in any direction they may not wish. The procedural stagnation in the Conference on Disarmament is but one case in point. The Mine Ban Treaty on the other hand has always operated on the basis that voting is possible. It is true that in the treaty context, there are no major political issues that have the potential to create deep rifts between the State Parties. Nevertheless, the mere fact that issues ultimately could be decided by a vote has brought about consensus. Simply put, the consensus rule leads to veto, while voting provisions facilitate consensus.[16]

Second, the treaty has always operated through an informal work process, rather than the formal mechanisms that dominate the work of other disarmament treaties. This is apparent in a number of ways. The first annual Meeting of States Parties in Maputo, Mozambique, in 1999 established Standing Committees, devoted to addressing core elements of the treaty, and which meet during an Intersessional Work Programme. Since then, much of the work on the treaty has taken place in these "intersessional weeks," which initially met twice a year and now meet once a year.[17] These informal meetings are run by cochairs, generally one from a mine-affected state and one from a donor state. The meetings feature extensive participation by NGOs and international organizations that bring their practical experience and further contribute to an informal "hands-on" atmosphere.

Soon after the inception of the Intersessional Work Programme, it became clear that closely following these issues would be a challenge for many States Parties, especially the mine-affected states—whose meaningful participation is essential for the implementation of the treaty. States Parties created two crucial mechanisms to meet this need. An informal sponsorship program was set up and funded by voluntary contributions from a few states to enable mine-affected states to participate in meetings of the treaty. With this support, these states have usually been represented by people who are in charge of treaty implementation and/or mine action programs. A small but efficient Implementation Support Unit was established to provide guidance, support, and institutional memory for the work of the Mine Ban Treaty. It has greatly enhanced the opportunity for states, in particular mine-affected ones, to participate in the work of the treaty. The impact of the Sponsorship Program and the Implementation Support Unit on the successful implementation of the treaty cannot be overstated.

In addition to the Standing Committees, informal working groups have been established to identify practical ways to make progress in key aspects of the treaty. Most prominent among these is the Universalization Contact Group, where diplomats and NGOs discuss tactics and coordinate activities to approach states outside the treaty to convince them to join. It is another remarkable feature of the Mine Ban Treaty process that governments and NGOs combine their respective efforts to achieve a shared objective. Similar contact groups have been set up for other issues, including Article 7 transparency reporting and resource mobilization. Results from the work of these groups are forwarded as recommendations to the annual Meetings of States Parties, where formal decisions can be made. Other disarmament forums could certainly profit from such an approach.

Perhaps the key ingredient for the informal character of this process is the presence and prominence of NGOs at all levels of the treaty's work. One particularly remarkable aspect is the role of the ICBL's Landmine Monitor which tracks states' compliance with the treaty. The annual *Landmine Monitor* publication, a comprehensive report on the global landmine situation, is recognized as the main reference source and used by states and NGOs alike. Over the years, there have been several situations where States Parties found themselves confronted with unpleasant questions based on findings in the *Landmine Monitor* report. The verification of compliance with the treaty has in practical terms been "outsourced" to an NGO-based system, the Landmine Monitor research network. The very same NGOs are then permitted to participate in treaty meetings with governments whose performance they examine—a truly remarkable departure from "normal" diplomatic practice, especially in the disarmament sector.

The dynamism and unique approach of the Mine Ban Treaty process was again illustrated by the preparatory work for the Nairobi Summit on a Mine-Free World, the First Review Conference of the Mine Ban Treaty held in November 2004. Governments and civil society worked closely together to use this event marking the first five years of the life of the treaty to create positive political momentum. All the key players in the process recognized that key purposes of the conference would have to be to raise the profile of the landmine issue again and refocus governments on the implementation of the treaty. Thus, the Review Conference was designed to be a high-level political event with significant media attention.

The Nairobi Summit turned out to be the highest profile landmine event since the treaty signing in Ottawa in 1997. It produced very strong conference documents, most notably the Nairobi Action Plan, which provided a clear road map for the challenging years ahead. The close cooperation between governments and civil society organizations covered all aspects, including the preparation of documents, organization of the Summit itself and its side events, and a joint communications strategy to promote the Summit's main message: "Progress has been made, challenges remain." Without that partnership and close cooperation, the success of the Nairobi Summit would not have been possible.

At the same time, the experience of Nairobi also pointed to limitations of the government-civil society partnership. For NGOs, the importance of the Summit as an occasion to generate a positive political momentum for the future was somewhat in conflict with the wish to use the conference to voice some of their grievances and concerns. In the end the NGO community had to accept—albeit grudgingly—that not all of their positions and proposals would be accepted and taken into account. For some, this normal diplomatic decision-making proved to be difficult to accept, and they may have felt co-opted as "validators" for a governmental "feel good exercise"—a role which they did not like playing.

Conclusion

Looking at the future, there is a certain danger with respect to the close partnership between governments and NGOs. The Mine Ban Treaty process is *the* model that civil society and NGOs alike refer to as proof of the changing political power of civil society campaigns. Nowhere else have NGOs gained such a prominent and hence co-responsible role in what is—after all—a governmental undertaking. However, as in all matters, there are shortcomings and limitations to the process.

A great deal has already been accomplished toward meeting the treaty's objectives. But it is possible that in the future there will be significant disappointments and even failures, such as less than full implementation by some States Parties and missed treaty deadlines. In this process, especially, the public perception of success or failure of the treaty will ultimately be determined by civil society. How will civil society react to this? How far will NGOs push governments and what effect will this have on the partnership and on the treaty itself? Hopefully, in the end civil society and the entire Mine Ban Treaty process will not fall victim to their own high expectations.

Governments and NGOs alike will have to maintain their commitment to achieve a mine-free world in the context of the Mine Ban Treaty framework. It will require a great deal of work to ensure continued progress and meet recognized and new challenges for the treaty's implementation and the firm establishment of the ban norm.

The Mine Ban Treaty in large part came about because of the mine ban movement's insistence that the suffering of people must be given precedence over the perceived military utility of antipersonnel landmines. Applying this model beyond the relatively narrow issue of landmines will require a considerable amount of time and effort, but the mine ban experience has opened up the debate about how to properly balance humanitarian and military concerns. This is an important development that will shape future discussions and the way in which more and more states will approach such issues. What a remarkable success!

Notes

1. According to the terms of the treaty, entry into force takes place on the first day of the sixth month after forty ratifications by signatory states. The fortieth ratification came on September 16, 1998, just nine months after the treaty was opened for signature.

2. As of September 2007, 155 states had ratified or acceded to the treaty. Another two states, Poland and the Marshall Islands, have signed but not yet ratified.

3. Discussion and debate continues about whether a new legal norm has already been established, and whether the ban already constitutes part of customary international law and thus is binding on all states. See chapter 12.

4. There have been a small number of allegations, most seriously against the forces of Uganda and Rwanda operating in the Democratic Republic of Congo. See chapter 6.

5. Again, there have been allegations, more numerous than use allegations. Perhaps most notable have been allegations against Ethiopia and Eritrea by the UN Monitoring Group for the Somalia arms embargo. See chapter 6.

6. Italy destroyed 7.1 million antipersonnel mines, Turkmenistan 6.6 million, and Albania, France, Germany, Japan, Romania, Sweden, Switzerland, and the United Kingdom each destroyed more than one million antipersonnel mines. See International Campaign to Ban Landmines (ICBL), *Landmine Monitor Report 2004* (Washington, DC: Human Rights Watch, 2004), p. 13.

7. Afghanistan, Cape Verde, Guinea, and Turkmenistan did not complete destruction on time. Afghanistan, with a March 2007 deadline, was nearly done as of July 2007, and the other three finished destruction relatively soon after their deadlines.

8. The non-States Parties that have declared a halt to production include Egypt, Finland, Israel, and Poland. Taiwan has also stopped production. In addition, some of those still listed as producers have not done so in many years. See ICBL, *Landmine Monitor Report 2006* (Ottawa: Mines Action Canada, 2006), p. 10.

9. Among these are China, India, Israel, Kazakhstan, Pakistan, Poland, Russia, Singapore, South Korea, and the United States. In addition, representatives of Cuba,

Egypt, and Vietnam have stated their countries no longer export. See ICBL, *Landmine Monitor Report 2004*, p. 12.

10. *Landmine Monitor Report 2006* recorded use of antipersonnel mines by armed nonstate groups in at least ten countries, including three States Parties (Burundi, Colombia, and Guinea-Bissau). ICBL, *Landmine Monitor Report 2006*, pp. 7–8.

11. As of July 2007, Bulgaria, Costa Rica, Czech Republic, Guatemala, Honduras, and Suriname.

12. Article 6.3 of the treaty states: "Each State Party in a position to do so shall provide assistance for the care and rehabilitation, and social and economic reintegration, of mine victims and for mine awareness programs."

13. ICBL, *Landmine Monitor Report 2006*, p. 44.

14. See First Review Conference of the States Parties to the Convention on the Prohibition of the Use, Stockpiling, Production and Transfer of Anti-personnel Mines and on Their Destruction, "Final Report: Part II. Review of the operation of the statues of the Convention on the Prohibition of the Use, Stockpiling, Production and Transfer of Anti-Personnel Mines and on Their Destruction: 1999-2004," Nairobi, November 29–December 3, 2004, APLC/CONG/2005/5, February 9, 2005, p. 27, para. 64.

15. In addition to the victim assistance language cited above from Article 6.3 of the treaty, Article 6.4 states, "Each State Party in a position to do so shall provide assistance for mine clearance and related activities," and Article 6.5 states, "Each State Party in a position to do so shall provide assistance for the destruction of stockpiled anti-personnel mines."

16. There have been no recorded votes, either during the treaty negotiations or the formal annual Meetings of States Parties. The Mine Ban Treaty's culture of "no one state or small group of states can block" has discouraged putting issues to a vote.

17. The First Review Conference in 2004 reduced the frequency to one meeting per year.

3

Still Alive and Kicking: The International Campaign to Ban Landmines

Elizabeth Bernstein

WHEN THE DIPLOMATIC CONFERENCE on an International Total Ban on Anti-Personnel Landmines closed on September 18, 1997, and the Mine Ban Treaty was born, cheering campaigners hugged the diplomats who had made it happen. Moments earlier, members of the International Campaign to Ban Landmines (ICBL) had been handing out copies of their "Plan of Action" to secure the treaty's entry into force by the year 2000. Some 225 representatives of 130 nongovernmental organizations (NGOs) had put the plan together down the street at a meeting held parallel to the treaty negotiations.

This planning of the campaign's next phase of work is illustrative of how the ICBL activists have always refused to rest on their laurels in the aftermath of the Ottawa Process whirlwind, which culminated in the December 1997 signing of the Mine Ban Treaty and the high-profile awarding of the 1997 Nobel Peace Prize jointly to the ICBL and its founding coordinator Jody Williams. Instead campaigners have sought to continuously reaffirm their commitment and strategize to ensure the treaty is not simply beautiful words on paper, but that it makes a difference to those living with the daily scourge of landmines.

Perhaps many assumed the campaign would declare victory and disband, leaving governments to implement the treaty. But as Jody Williams has noted, the achievement of the treaty was viewed by the ICBL ". . . as the beginning of the 'real' work to eliminate landmines. Its members knew that if the treaty were to be fully implemented and complied with, the ICBL would have to continue its innovative strategies to sustain its partnerships and maintain the momentum."[1]

This chapter will look at some of the campaign's struggles, strategies, and successes in the period since 1997 as the ICBL has worked for the Mine Ban Treaty's ratification, implementation, and universalization.

1998: A Critical Year of Transition

From its very beginnings, the ICBL was truly a loose coalition of independent NGOs with no formal legal registration in any country, no common bank account, and no secretariat or headquarters.[2] While much remains the same, some changes were necessary for the campaign to move into the new, treaty-related phase of work. Late 1997 and into 1998 was a very tense and difficult period for the ICBL. Conflicting issues and personalities that had been kept mostly in check during the frenetic mobilization leading to the Mine Ban Treaty flared up in the lead up to and just after the awarding of the Nobel Peace Prize. At times it seemed very uncertain if the campaign would weather the storm.

Much of the ill will came to a head in discussions about what to do with the Nobel funds, since the ICBL "did not exist" (as one angry campaigner put it) and had no bank account. While not explicitly stated in the meetings at that time, some felt that whichever NGO became the custodian of the Nobel Funds for the ICBL would be somehow legitimized as "first among equals." Given the degree of animosity, the best solution was to incorporate the ICBL as an independent organization capable of receiving and spending funds for campaign activities.

The formal registration of the ICBL was a practical, as well as political, decision: campaigners wanted to incorporate as a nonprofit organization in a country which was party to the treaty, but with minimal bureaucratic and reporting requirements and while still meeting the essential legal needs of the coalition. Handicap International (HI), one of the ICBL's founders, was prepared to devote time and resources to assist with the process, so the ICBL registered in France in 1998.

Another pivotal change occurred in February 1998 when Jody Williams stepped down as ICBL coordinator and, for the first time, ICBL staff were hired to replace her and expand the campaign's work.[3]

The ICBL survived the ministorm and continued to thrive because of the intense commitment and focus of the overwhelming majority of the campaign on the goal of banning landmines. Some of the angriest campaigners withdrew from the work in practice if not immediately in name, while others moved on to different issues. A committed majority remained and the ICBL continued as a strong and vibrant coalition, attracting new and energized campaigners and working together to universalize and implement the Mine Ban Treaty.

Most of the changes and discussions outlined above took place at the ICBL's first "General Meeting" in Frankfurt, Germany, in February 1998. While the campaign met regularly and held activities all around the globe as it built momentum to ban landmines, the somewhat more formal General Meeting was a logical outcome of the stresses of the period.[4] At the same time, the ICBL remained a loose coalition, even as it sought to formalize some of its structures.[5]

The ICBL Steering Committee, originally composed of the six NGOs that founded the campaign in 1992, had expanded twice prior to securing the Mine Ban Treaty. In Frankfurt its membership was again expanded, its tasks somewhat changed, and the body was renamed as a Coordinating Committee.[6] Working groups were formed to focus on key campaigning issues—the treaty itself, mine action, and victim assistance.[7] These changes reflected new aspects of ICBL work now that there was a treaty and also sought to reflect more broadly campaign membership. As it always had, international leadership in the ICBL continued to emerge through the work undertaken by individuals to enhance the campaign, and not by fiat or design.

Despite the tensions and structural transitions, the ICBL never lost sight of its key function—campaigning to achieve its goals. The Frankfurt meeting was no different as it opened with a demonstration at the Rhein-Main Air Base to demand that the United States remove its antipersonnel landmines then stockpiled in Germany. The General Meeting's final statement laid out the key focus for ICBL in 1998, which was rapid achievement of the forty ratifications necessary to make the treaty binding international law, and also noted that the campaign would "explore a role for its members in monitoring the treaty."

No Lull in Campaigning

The ICBL was under no illusion that landmine problems would be resolved just by securing a treaty to tackle the weapon. This agreement had to take effect as quickly as possible, be universalized, and have sufficient resources for mine clearance, mine risk education, and mine victim assistance. The ICBL also wanted these programs to be integrated into long-term development programs.[8] The Mine Ban Treaty also needed to be fully implemented and complied with. Campaign discussions about what role, if any, the ICBL could play in treaty verification and compliance ultimately led to the creation in June 1998 of the Landmine Monitor, a ground-breaking civil society initiative to monitor the treaty.[9]

Ratification strategies involved national, regional, and international action, and countries committed to rapid treaty ratification were targeted first. Campaigners then drew up ratification targets by number per year, aiming for regional balance as well as mine-affected and nonaffected countries. Working with the International Committee of the Red Cross (ICRC), UNICEF, and concerned governments, the ICBL assisted governments with few resources by producing ratification kits and examples of ratification documents in various legal systems and languages.

Throughout 1998, activities were held in a number of signatory countries (including Australia, Cambodia, Italy, Japan, Jordan, Kenya, Sudan, and Thailand). Regional meetings took place in Hungary, South Africa, and parallel to the annual Organization of African Unity Summit in Burkina Faso, where campaigners engaged the media and lobbied governments to ratify the Mine Ban Treaty as soon as possible. At the OAU Summit in June 1998 and at the annual Non-Aligned Movement Summit held two months later in South Africa, Human Rights Watch issued reports documenting the treaty positions of member states, in effect launching a new campaigning tool that would later take the form of Landmine Monitor fact sheets.

All of this work bore fruit on September 16, 1998, when Burkina Faso became the fortieth country to ratify the treaty, triggering its entry into force on March 1, 1999, more rapidly than any other treaty of its kind in history. That ratification came almost one year to the day after the close of treaty negotiations in Oslo.

Similarly, the ICBL's universalization strategy involved setting targets and working in coordination with partner organizations and governments. For example, the Hungarian government, the ICRC, and the ICBL hosted a meeting in Budapest in March 1998 where treaty-related discussions were held with nineteen governments from the region, including several nonsignatories. Countries of the Commonwealth of Independent States (states of the former Soviet Union) were also a focus in May 1998, when the ICBL and member NGO International Physicians for the Prevention of Nuclear War held a conference in Moscow that resulted in the establishment of new campaigns in Armenia, Azerbaijan, Georgia, and Ukraine, where events were held soon after.

The ICBL also sent delegations to strategic countries, such as a May trip to Ukraine by Jody Williams and Steve Goose. Public activities remained a key tool of national campaigns, including events such as landmine week in Albania, a national day of action in France including shoe pyramids in twelve cities,[10] and mine action month in Afghanistan featuring a poster contests in schools and a signature campaign. In Japan, the landmine ban was the centerpiece of the Nagano Peace Appeal at the 1998 Winter Olympics, where landmine survivor Chris Moon carried the Olympic torch into the opening ceremony. On the December 1998 first anniversary of the treaty signing, campaigners organized landmine-related events throughout the world.

With the Mine Ban Treaty's rapid entry into force, the ICBL moved on to develop new goals and strategies to achieve them. At its General Meeting in Washington, DC in 2001, campaigners challenged themselves to increased activity and began to strategize and develop a "2004 Action Plan" for activities in the lead-up to the First Review Conference of the treaty, held in Nairobi, Kenya, in November–December 2004.

Tools for Advancing ICBL Work

Despite the perception that surrounds the almost "magical skill" of the ICBL, there really is not a lot of magic to good organizing. Effective advocacy and campaigning is about planning strategies and following through on them. It is about follow-up, follow-up, follow-up and communication, communication, and more communication. Planning, follow-up, and communication have remained the solid hallmarks of much of the success of the landmine campaign.

A primary function of the ICBL's coordinator (renamed executive director in 2005) has been to ensure regular communication throughout the membership. Campaigns share their individual political strategies and tactics and how they fit into the overarching planning of the ICBL. The ICBL has always recognized there is no "cookie cutter" model of campaigning that works in every country and context. Instead of trying to issue orders about what actions to take, campaigns share their own experiences, thus inspiring creativity and cross-fertilization of campaigning activities. Sharing information is about sharing power; it is also about respecting the importance of the contributions of all members of a campaign and giving everyone a sense of ownership and belonging.

To maximize communication, the ICBL has embraced new technologies as they emerge—whether the fax of the early years or e-mail starting in 1994. In 1998, the campaign launched its website and has continued to develop its use of Internet technologies and e-communication within and beyond the campaign. Without its experience and skill in global communication, it would have been virtually impossible to have a staff of seven living in five different countries on three continents, as the ICBL was doing by 2001. ICBL staff conducted virtual staff meetings online using Internet chat software and, by 2005, had started to use free computer-based "telephony" for such discussions.

This intense communication has helped foster a real sense of community among campaigners. When the ICBL carried out a survey among some 140 members in 2003 and 2004 to assess whether its work should continue following the First Review Conference, the responses were extremely heartening. About half of those surveyed said they had been campaigning against landmines since 1995–1996, demonstrating commitment not only to the treaty, but also to insuring its implementation in order to change lives on the ground. It was clear that the ICBL did not remain static but continued to attract new activists over the years. There was a healthy mix of old and new members.

In the survey, 92 percent said it was still challenging and enjoyable to be part of this coalition. One campaigner said, "This has been the most rewarding process I have ever been involved with. The enthusiasm of all members, their genuine sincerity, the lack of dissent/backstabbing, and our common focus make this overall a much better experience compared to other movements." And another reported, "I'm involved in several initiatives and I enjoy the community in ICBL. It includes a sense of ownership. I feel as if I'm important. I'm a stakeholder."

No matter how fabulous global communication systems might be, nothing could really replace face-to-face meetings to sustain and build the campaign. Some critics have complained about "too many meetings" and "wasted money" that could be "better spent in the field," but the ICBL has always believed that done well, at key times in strategic locations, meetings serve multiple and important functions. Often taking advantage of events hosted by others to hold campaign meetings, the ICBL's calendar has always been drawn up well in advance and in coordination with partners in government and the ICRC so events could complement rather than duplicate one another.

From the earliest days of campaigning during the Convention on Conventional Weapons (CCW) review process, the ICBL has used landmine meetings—often with more than one hundred governments present—as opportunities for capacity-building among its membership. For advocacy work to be successful, campaigners must be strategic and well organized. From the very beginning, wary of sponsoring numerous campaigners to come wander the halls of conference centers unaware of what to do—or worse, to go on shopping expeditions—ICBL began to hold orientation and organizational sessions for large meetings.

Even before leaving their countries, campaigners were asked to prepare by visiting their officials in capital to find out who would be representing the government at the meeting and what expectations they held, and then sharing that information with the ICBL. Upon arrival, campaigners participated in orientation sessions with working group cochairs, ICBL staff, and coordinating committee members to review key messages for governments as well as media. The messages are the easy part; making sure they are disseminated requires organization and an eye to detail. Together an overall work plan for each meeting was drawn up targeting governments to meet with; campaigners either volunteered or were assigned specific meetings. Report back forms were created to make sharing information from those individual meetings easier.

Because new campaigners were sometimes uncertain of their advocacy skills, they were often paired with more experienced activists. Similarly, for media outreach, campaigners were asked to inform their domestic media that they would be attending a landmine meeting and to try to set up interviews while at the meeting. At the meeting itself, they targeted media outlets and shared responsibility for outreach in various languages, as well as helping campaigners speak to their media at home. But the simple act of working together to organize ICBL activities at the various meetings has proved to be the best hands on capacity-building for everyone.

After 1997, a key series of ICBL meetings have been the regular regional and/or global Landmine Monitor meetings. Taking advantage of the Monitor's larger budget and need to bring together researchers to prepare for the annual *Landmine Monitor* report, landmine advocacy events were also built around these meetings. Sessions were organized about how to use the research effectively as an advocacy tool. The logistics of these meetings were shared by local organizers, as well as by Landmine Monitor and ICBL staff, with an eye to building on lessons learned from previous meetings. In the years building up to the 2004 Review Conference, a series of strategic meetings were held in significant mine-affected States Parties as well as universalization target countries.

The annual meetings of States Parties of the Mine Ban Treaty are also important. Since the first held in Maputo, Mozambique, in 1999 through the 2004 Nairobi Review Conference and beyond, the ICBL has used these meetings as focal points to galvanize action by campaigns and governments alike. They are a fixed opportunity for governments and activists to assess both the progress on the landmine issue as well as the challenges remaining to achieve a mine-free world.

Change with the Times or Disband:
ICBL Action after the Nairobi Review Conference

In February 2003, with the 2004 Review Conference on the horizon, the Coordinating Committee and ICBL staff began an extensive exercise to consider the future of the ICBL post-2004. The ICBL had always taken the position that it had come together to achieve a political goal, not to institutionalize itself in perpetuity. If its work was done, it would be time to disband.

In 2003 and into 2004, about 140 ICBL members were interviewed in person about the ICBL's work and its future; additional campaigners were reached via the Internet. A parallel consultation with Landmine Monitor researchers also fed into the process. Approximately 94 percent of those surveyed said the ICBL still had work to do post-Nairobi. As one member put it, "Now's the time the ICBL is needed the most. The easy part is over." Another stated, "We should stay together as a team, a group. I like the process, not just the outcome. We are a powerful group." But it was not just campaigners who felt this way, key government allies also surveyed in informal conversations during this period did not want the ICBL to disband.

Campaigners' opinions and suggestions were then crafted into a proposal for "ICBL Goals, Structure and Activities Post-2004," which was adopted at the ICBL's Fourth General Meeting, held immediately after the Meeting of States Parties in Bangkok in September 2003. This was the transitional strategy to take the ICBL forward after the 2004 Review Conference. While continuing with the same types of activities as in the past, gradually national campaigns and individual organizations were to play enhanced roles in the campaign's work. The Coordinating Committee was to be replaced by two bodies: a Management Committee of four to six people to handle daily oversight of ICBL work (such as fundraising, finances and reporting, as well as personnel management) and a larger Advisory Board board comprised of representatives of different aspects of landmine-related work, as well as geographic regions. The Advisory Board was tasked with providing strategic direction, input, and feedback to the Management Committee and staff.

When the transition was completed in 2005, ICBL staff would be reduced to four. Preparing for this transition became a significant part of their work as staff incorporated the process into their work plans during the end of 2003 and throughout 2004. Even as they were essentially transitioning themselves out of their jobs, ICBL staff gave the usual dedication and focus to the task that has always exemplified the work of ICBL members. At the same time, a concrete, strategic Plan of Action 2005–2009 was developed for campaigners to refine further in Nairobi.

The transition was not only about structure and staff, however. Campaigners stressed that increased attention and resources had to focus even more on mine action and on the even greater challenge of survivor assistance. More had to be done to make a real difference in the daily lives of mine-affected communities. This did not mean abandoning efforts to universalize the treaty, or promote timely stockpile destruction, or advocate on key (still controversial) issues of interpretation and implementation of the treaty but rather an enhancement of ICBL efforts on mine clearance and victim assistance.

Article 5 of the treaty requires mine-affected States to clear their minefields within ten years of joining the treaty. Prioritizing clearance became more starkly critical as the first clearance deadlines in 2009 and 2010 loomed closer.[11] This focus on clearance and more fully meeting the multiple needs of the survivors will remain ICBL priorities through 2009—the date of the second review conference of the treaty.

In December 2006, the ICBL decided to expand its work into cluster munitions. This was a major decision, representing the first time that the ICBL would undertake significant and sustained action on a weapon other than antipersonnel mines. In the past, ICBL leadership had on several occasions discussed the possibility of taking on new issues, including cluster munitions, antivehicle mines, and others, but decided that the coalition had to remain focused solely on antipersonnel mines in order to maintain its effectiveness and ensure continued progress in banning antipersonnel mines.

In explaining the decision, the ICBL Management Committee, Advisory Board, and staff said they "were unanimous in agreeing that the ICBL should now become more engaged in the cluster issue than in the past, and that there should be more cooperation and collaboration between the ICBL and Cluster Munition Coalition (CMC)." They went on to explain:

> The ICBL will not change its basic mandate or call, but we believe there is space for a more active role on clusters for the ICBL. The main reasons behind this approach of course are that cluster munitions inevitably end up leaving behind large numbers of what are essentially antipersonnel mines, that so many ICBL organizations are already working extensively on clusters, and that we are at a crucial point in trying to address cluster munitions, a point where we feel the ICBL can and should make a real difference in a closely related humanitarian issue. We do not envision that this will become the major focus of the ICBL's work. . . . We do not want the ICBL's work on mines to diminish or suffer from increased attention to clusters. But we also believe that combining work on mine and clusters could serve to invigorate some ICBL member activities, and even create new opportunities that would benefit progress on both fronts. [The ICBL can] help bring about a new treaty on cluster munitions that will—like the Mine Ban Treaty—make a huge difference in preventing more landmine-like contamination around the world, as well as promote expanded clearance of the existing mess, and assistance to affected persons and communities.[12]

The ICBL subsequently joined the Steering Committee of the Cluster Munition Coalition, hired a new staff person to work largely on cluster munition campaigning, and quickly began to engage its network on the issue, holding a training workshop for campaigners and Landmine Monitor researchers in Yemen in February 2007 and a regional seminar for NGOs and governments in Cambodia in March 2007.

A critical challenge facing the ICBL after 1997 was the perception that the landmine problem had been "solved." For some national campaigns, it was a challenge to maintain momentum, continue to interest the media, and raise funds adequately in the face of general "landmine fatigue" and the belief that simply having a treaty was enough to deal with the aftermath of landmines. But national campaigns have continued to change and grow as has the ICBL overall as shown by the examples below of campaigning by established campaigns in Canada and Italy as well as by a younger Lebanese campaign in a "difficult neighborhood."

Working in the Home of the Treaty: Mines Action Canada

This section is based on an interview with Paul Hannon, Executive Director, Mines Action Canada, Ottawa, March 3, 2006.

At the time of the treaty signing in Ottawa in 1997, Mines Action Canada (MAC), the coalition of organizations working for a ban in Canada, was legally and financially a project of Physicians for Global Survival, the Canadian branch of the International Physicians for the Prevention of Nuclear War (IPPNW).[13] When Paul Hannon joined MAC as its executive director in 1998, the campaign consisted of one and a half staff, two desks, an old computer, and about $145,000 in the bank that was anticipated to last about nine months. MAC became an independent NGO in 2001.

With Canada's immediate ratification of the treaty at the same time as the agreement was opened for signature, MAC's first post-1997 objective was to lobby for the government to establish a CD$100 million Canadian Landmine Fund. Its members wanted to ensure a strong campaign presence in Canada, "home" of the treaty, and hoped the government would provide resources—which it did when the fund was established in July 1998. Some campaigners worried that taking government funds might jeopardize MAC's independence, but most felt the Canadian campaign effort had to continue to make sure the treaty was implemented and that landmine funds were spent well.

Perhaps more challenging than accepting its funding was the change in MAC's relationship with the government. According to Hannon, "So much has been said about the government/NGO partnership and the new model. In implementing the treaty, it was important for MAC to prove we can continue this partnership. It's not unique to Lloyd Axworthy, Jody Williams, [Canadian diplomat] Jill Sinclair and Steve Goose. We can prove it works in other ways." But moving from the traditional campaign role of "opposition" to becoming Canada's partner in banning landmines was not an easy transition for many in MAC. Learning to treat government partners respectfully and still maintain independence and not "sell out" in the process was a significant challenge.

One of MAC's first joint initiatives with the Department of Foreign Affairs and the Canadian Red Cross was an outreach program called the Youth Mine Action Ambassadors Program (YMAAP). Among other things, it was challenging in Hannon's view because internationally "Canada seemed like gods, doing everything right, but we still had friction at home over some issues." For example, YMAAPers disagreed with the government not wanting to integrate mine action into larger development programming (now standard) and were deeply concerned about joint military operations with the United States if they were to use landmines. Everybody had to work out ways to address conflicts and disagreements and deal with different opinions, but the experiences resulted in a solid partnership. The YMAPP program has been a big success and key to keeping the landmine message alive in Canada. In Foreign Affairs polling, landmines turned up among the top five issues of concern, something MAC felt was due to YMAAP.

Despite the YMAAP outreach program in Canada, MAC was better known and respected internationally than at home. Hannon says, "Working internationally was a conscious decision. It was clear MAC could make a difference. We're not mine affected, we have no big assistance funds or clearance organizations. Why invest in parliament, MPs [Members of Parliament], outreach, when the work for us was international?" MAC played a leadership role in Landmine Monitor and the ICBL Coordinating Committee (and later ICBL Management Committee), seconded staff to ICBL, and, when scheduling conflicts arose, participated in international rather than national events.

In 2005, MAC created a new international capacity building project called the Leadership, Education, and Action Program (LEAP). MAC recruits young people for LEAP and places them with other campaigns to gain international experience. Once LEAP participants return home, they contribute nationally. MAC is also creating a new, separate charity and plans a more domestic focus to ensure strong and creative Canadian leadership.

Back on the international front, MAC took over the role of lead agency for Landmine Monitor in 2005, replacing Human Rights Watch after seven years. MAC is also among the most active NGOs working toward a new treaty on cluster munitions—part of MAC's overall concern with victim-activated weapons.

Prioritizing and Focusing:
The Italian Campaign to Ban Landmines

This section is based on a telephone interview with Simona Beltrami, then-co-ordinator of the Italian Campaign to Ban Landmines, March 13, 2006. In mid-2006, Beltrami assumed the position of ICBL Advocacy Director.

The Italian Campaign to Ban Landmines (ItCBL) began to wane after its initial successes. According to Simona Beltrami, "The number participating was very high until 1999, when bells were ringing all around Italy for the entry into force of the treaty. It was a real engagement of Italian civil society, with all the big NGOs, church groups and individual parishes, local institutions, and trade unions. It was a wide and diverse movement. Once the main goals in Italy were achieved—national legislation, to sign and ratify the treaty—it was as if much of the work was done, and others went back to their core business. On paper we still had 30 organizations saying they endorsed us, but actual numbers were lower."

As in Canada, the main ItCBL lobbying focus was to get the government to establish a trust fund for humanitarian demining, which it did in 2001. The Italian campaign has received some support from that fund, but since 2003 its main support has come from the European Commission through a joint project with the German Initiative to Ban Landmines, Landmine Action UK, and Pax Christi Ireland. Beltrami notes these campaigns forged strong links and organized joint lobbying initiatives. "Our biggest, most successful one was regarding the European Parliament resolution on cluster munitions, antivehicle mines and antipersonnel mines in October 2004. We prepared briefing documents, contacted our own MEPs, arranged meetings, and went to Strasbourg jointly. It was a good example of a regional lobbying initiative," she said.[14]

In 2003, Beltrami was hired as coordinator to reenergize the Italian campaign. After identifying work with youth as key to raising awareness, a youth coordinator was hired as well. The ItCBL started a peace education program in schools, which included the landmine issue, to encourage young people to be activists.

Although the particular approach was new and a key element of its post-1999 strategy, the ItCBL had always worked with young people. Schools acting as "loudspeakers" in the community with adults being sensitized by the kids had been instrumental in collecting signatures calling for national landmine legislation. Because of that earlier success, the campaign decided to replicate it. For the new effort, the ItCBL created an educational kit, adaptable for young people between the ages of ten to eighteen, and campaign staff and volunteers did the training sessions. Working with youth provided the ItCBL a tool to work with other national landmine campaigns, such as efforts with the Spanish campaign in 2006 on landmines in Morocco. The initiative has also brought the campaign in contact with local authorities who often support the ItCBL's other initiatives.

The Italian campaign has also supported small landmine projects in the field, including in Afghanistan in 1999 and a rapid response project with Intersos in Iraq. It has also worked with the Nepal Campaign to Ban Landmines on a project to send girls from mine-affected areas to school. In 2006, the ItCBL initiated a project to support demining of the Olympic complex in Sarajevo using funds provided by local and regional committees in Turin, home of the 2006 Winter Olympics.

One of its big challenges—as with many others—has been maintaining media interest with so many viewing the problem as "solved." Another has been how, as a small national campaign, to best participate internationally. Beltrami noted, "It is a huge source of richness, exchanging ideas, finding out how things are done in other countries, opening up opportunities and perspectives, taking on a more active role, such as hosting the annual, global Landmine Monitor research meeting in Rome in April 2003." But she also recognized that it takes a lot of time and can be a strain on resources.

One way the ItCBL surmounted its challenges was by prioritizing and focusing on a small number of clearly defined projects—at home, regionally, and internationally. The other was expanding its work to include cluster munitions, thinking it would help mobilize somewhat dormant public opinion and give the campaign a way to talk about landmines again—which worked. Another lesson was the importance of supporting concrete mine action projects. According to Beltrami, "We did it with small projects at first, but it worked well. For the Sarajevo project we received ten times as much funding as we asked for. It is a big contribution financially for demining, and good for our visibility." With the success of that project, the ItCBL plans to use it to raise awareness and also replicate the effort with other regional governments.

From the ItCBL experience, Beltrami counseled, "You must be very realistic about changing circumstances and the context you are moving in. There are risks that you keep operating in the same old way because it worked, but that's not necessarily good. Be open to new things, even if it's scary."

Younger Campaigns: Lebanon

This section is based upon a telephone interview with Habbouba Aoun, Coordinator, Landmines Resource Center, March 15, 2006. It took place before the war between Israel and Hezbollah. As a result of that fighting, the most significant threat to civilian populations trying to return home and reconstruct their lives are the cluster bombs that were dropped in the millions by Israeli forces, particularly in the final seventy-two hours before the ceasefire took effect. Of an estimated four million dropped on southern Lebanon, some one million were duds and now litter the landscape with lethal detritus of war.

There are also important experiences of campaigns formed after 1997. Two regions in particular experienced growth in national campaigns. One was in the Commonwealth of Independent States where new campaigns began after the May 1998 international conference in Moscow. The creation of new campaigns in this region (and others) was also greatly facilitated by the expansion of the Landmine Monitor research network, as most of the NGOs wore both campaigning and research hats. In countries with newly emerging civil society, many operated creatively in difficult circumstances, trying to build relationships with challenging governments. A few—such as the campaigns in Armenia and Azerbaijan—also worked cross-border in regional partnerships despite state-level conflict and inherent risks in such circumstances. But with a common language and similar experiences, these campaigns forged a cohesive group, supporting and encouraging each another.

Another region where campaigning activity began to develop during this period was the Middle East, and the experience in Lebanon is a particularly instructive one. Habbouba Aoun of the Landmines Resource Center in Beirut, Lebanon—now a member of both the ICBL Advisory Board and Management Committee—first started dealing with landmines while working as a consultant conducting a survey of war victims in 1996, funded by the World Rehabilitation Fund through the Ministry of Health. As she reported, "At the end of our analysis, we found 35 percent of the victims were landmine survivors." A national conference was held in March 1997 to publicize the results.

Aoun subsequently joined the Faculty of Health Sciences at the University of Balamand, which established the Landmines Resource Center. She helped organize the first landmine workshop in Lebanon in February 1998, which was cosponsored by the university, Rädda Barnen, and UNICEF and held in collaboration with the Lebanese Army. That June, the Army set up a national demining office and as Aoun said, "They did not know anything about humanitarian mine action so we held a workshop together to develop concepts."

From her perspective, civil society's role was to focus on mine risk education (MRE) and victim assistance, and not "interfere" with demining. Assisted by the Landmines Resource Center and supported by Rädda Barnen, NGOs developed a common plan and set up committees to work on MRE and victim assistance. With World Rehabilitation Fund financial support, the first humanitarian mine action money ever in Lebanon, more partners became involved in the campaign and also continued a nationwide survey to collect data on survivors and their families. Then, in February 1999 they hosted a regional conference in Beirut on "Landmines in the Middle East and North Africa."

As the campaigning effort grew, the first goals were to alleviate suffering caused by landmines in the country, to raise awareness, and assist victims—then work to have Lebanon forego antipersonnel mines and join the Mine Ban Treaty. A particular obstacle was the government's fear that investment would decline if the mine problem was publicized. To counter this, the campaign showed the results of the landmine survey and the impact of the mines on these communities. The mines themselves were an impediment to development.

Aoun said a crucial challenge is when decision-makers do not understand the Mine Ban Treaty and attempt to link it to regional political issues, especially to Israel and the United States. "We are working to safeguard our country. We only want to stop the harm of antipersonnel mines by pushing the treaty's goal that seeks to help all affected countries," she explained.

Another challenge was convincing the authorities to work with NGOs. Aoun said, "We had to prove it was a national problem in an international context. We had to convince them that NGOs should be working on MRE and victim assistance, and then we could establish a way of working that put them at ease, legitimized our work, and was coordinated with other NGOs. Sometimes we can talk about the Mine Ban Treaty, sometimes not; sometimes we have to restrain, sometimes push." She said it has been "not easy, with ups and downs" and has often depended on individuals at various levels in government, where there has been much turnover; building new relationships has not always been easy. But, she continued, "For us, international exposure and the role of experts was positive in terms of showing the army and stakeholders how things are being done."

From Aoun's perspective, the most important lessons are, "Be patient and don't give up easily. See the problem the way target communities see it. Don't impose, let it come from them. Be positive, listen carefully, [and] be culturally sensitive. They are the source of change, not us. If they abide by the message, they change, but you cannot make them change. Understand the point of view of the government and let it come from them. Sometimes they take credit for your work, let them. At first, it may be difficult to accept (your pride), but after a while it will show that it is your work; they cannot go ahead without you. As a woman, it is hard to make men of Arab countries accept you. They do not accept easily a woman with leadership or charisma."

Another lesson is to be aware of the political context. "Working on landmines in our part of the world, you cannot just talk development. We are a highly political society at all levels—with Israel, Palestine, Iraq, what is happening all around. We have to be careful and give context, so people will understand that ultimately we cannot build peace when landmines are there." Being part of an international network helped create neutral political space. "ICBL is our rescue. When we say NGOs, ICBL, peaceful movements, communities will accept us more. Otherwise they are afraid to talk. War, government, many factors that would hinder full cooperation. But we can see the impact at the village level. It has been helpful to be part of an international movement. I was lucky to be a pioneer in mine action in Lebanon, lucky to be member of ICBL."

Conclusion

The International Campaign to Ban Landmines is seen as a quintessential expression of the ability of committed civil society to play a meaningful role in resolving key issues of our times. ICBL activists have never rested on their laurels but constantly reaffirm their commitment to a mine-free world and are continuously forward looking, strategizing on next steps to bring the "utopian vision" of a mine-free world to complete reality through the framework of the Mine Ban Treaty.

Even in its most difficult moments at the end of 1997 and into 1998, the core of the campaign held firm and adjusted itself to its own new realities as well as to the reality of the newly negotiated Mine Ban Treaty and all the work it would take to ensure the treaty made a difference to those living with the daily scourge of landmines.

Staying focused on the goal in the face of fatigue and other demanding issues remains a critical objective a decade on. In 2007, as the Mine Ban Treaty entered into its tenth year of existence, the ICBL's Executive Director Sylvie Brigot described the treaty as ". . . a work in progress" and urged commitment by States Parties to ". . . continue providing the political leadership and financial resources to ensure we can declare final victory in the battle against landmines."[15]

The ICBL began as a coalition of NGOs determined to reach the goal of banning antipersonnel landmines and then disband and move on to other work. Disbanding remains an objective. Not abandoning the work until the job is done remains the focus. The ICBL has demonstrated that coalitions of independent NGOs can campaign together and achieve their goals. It has demonstrated an amazing ability to change with both the global context and as needed by its own membership.

At the same time, the campaign is really a transnational group of citizens who recognized a problem and took action to change it. Together we have proved that there is a place for "global citizen diplomacy." Together we have shown that individual action can and does make a difference—especially when those individuals number in the thousands and tens of thousands. ICBL activists exemplify those who work for human rights writ large by accepting their responsibility to act as global citizens working for a better world.

Notes

1. Jody Williams, "Eliminating Landmines in Wartorn Societies," in United Nations Development Programme, *Human Development Report 2002: Deepening Democracy in a Fragmented World* (New York: Oxford University Press, 2002), p. 103.

2. According to Williams: "Critical to the strength of the ICBL has been its loose structure, a phenomenon that is often misunderstood. The ICBL is a true coalition made up of independent NGOs. There has never been a secretariat or central office. The NGOs that comprise the ICBL have come together with the common goal of banning landmines, but there has never been an overarching, bureaucratic structure to dictate how members should contribute to the ICBL. The ICBL deliberately did not establish a central office; each NGO had to find a way to participate in making the campaign work. This structure helped to ensure that the ICBL 'belonged' to all of its members." Jody Williams, "Politics Unusual," http://www.icbl.org/campaign/ambassadors/jody_williams/.

3. The staff, all seasoned campaigners, included the new ICBL coordinator, Liz Bernstein, based first in Maputo, Mozambique, then in Washington, DC, and finally in Ottawa, Canada; advocacy officer, Susan B. Walker, based in Geneva, focused on government relations and treaty implementation; and Dalma Foeldes, a resources officer for the ICBL Resource Center in Oslo, Norway, which in 1999, moved to Sana'a, Yemen. The resource center served campaigns and the public by providing materials, documents, and other resources and support services to facilitate campaigns adaptation and development of their own resources. There were subsequent staff additions with Sylvie Brigot dealing with advocacy and universalization, Sue Wixley dealing with media and communications, Kjell Knudsen as webmaster, and Jackie Hansen as program assistant. Staff was reduced in a post-2004 ICBL transition period. A finance manager was added in 2006 and an advocacy and campaigning officer in 2007 to work mostly on cluster munitions. Anne Capelle served as Executive Director in 2005 and Sylvie Brigot as Executive Director since 2006.

4. At the Frankfurt meeting, composed of seventy representatives of national campaigns and international organizations from forty countries as well as a few individuals, it was agreed that annual or biennial general meetings would be held as funding and need permitted. Subsequent ICBL General Meetings were held in Maputo (May 1999), Washington, DC (March 2001), and Bangkok (September 2003).

5. Membership in the ICBL has never been based on formal agreements, and there are no dues. Members are organizations that publicly endorse the campaign's goals and agree to undertake at least one landmine-related activity a year.

6. The six founding organizations of the ICBL are Handicap International (France), Human Rights Watch (USA), Medico International (Germany), Mines Advisory Group (UK), Physicians for Human Rights (USA), and Vietnam Veterans of America Foundation (USA). For the changing makeup of the Coordinating Committee, see the ICBL website at: www.icbl.org.

7. In addition to the working groups related to these three key issues of concern to the campaign, a fourth working group, Legal and Moral Responsibility, was formed. Largely dysfunctional, it had folded by 1999. On the other hand, efforts begun in 1998 to focus on nonstate armed actors as the ban consolidated, and the Non-State Actors Working Group was recognized in 1999.

8. ICBL, "Report: NGO Forum on Landmines," Oslo, Norway, September 1997, Preface.

9. For detail on Landmine Monitor, see chapter 4.

10. To create these pyramids of shoes, citizens were asked to donate one shoe, representing a legless landmine survivor. One of the most impressive of the pyramids comprising countless thousands of shoes was near the Eiffel Tower in Paris. The French shoe pyramids became annual events and were duplicated by other country campaigns.

11. Country deadlines for mine clearance vary, depending upon when the treaty entered into force for the country.

12. E-mail to all ICBL campaigners from Steve Goose, Human Rights Watch, on behalf of the Management Committee, Advisory Board, and ICBL staff, December 20, 2006.

13. IPPNW is itself a recipient of the Nobel Peace Prize.

14. MEPs are members of the European Parliament; some of their meetings are held in Strasbourg, France.

15. ICBL news article, "The Mine Ban Treaty: A Success in Progress," March 1, 2007, http://www.icbl.org/news/march1_pr.

4

Evidence-Based Advocacy: Civil Society Monitoring of the Mine Ban Treaty

Mary Wareham

T HIS CHAPTER CONSIDERS THE UNIQUE ORIGINS and workings of the Landmine Monitor research system established by the International Campaign to Ban Landmines (ICBL) to promote universalization and implementation of the 1997 Mine Ban Treaty. It assesses the initiative's effectiveness in promoting compliance with the core provisions of the treaty prohibiting antipersonnel mines as well as its impact on increasing transparency, encouraging greater funding for mine clearance and victim assistance, and changing the behavior of actors regardless of their Mine Ban Treaty status. The chapter also looks at the extent to which Landmine Monitor has become an official part of the Mine Ban Treaty process and its relevance as a model for other endeavors.

An Unprecedented Initiative

Many discussions significant to the future of the mine ban movement took place on the sidelines of key Ottawa Process meetings throughout 1997 when it became apparent the Mine Ban Treaty would be successfully concluded. Some participants in the process (both governmental and nongovernmental)

The author is grateful to the United Nations Institute for Disarmament Research (UNIDIR) and the Institute for Applied International Studies (Fafo) for support provided to the author for earlier research on this subject that is reflected in this chapter. See: John Borrie and Vanessa Martin Randin (eds.), *Disarmament as Humanitarian Action: From Perspective to Practice* (Geneva: UNIDIR, May 2006) and Mary Wareham, *What If No One's Watching? Landmine Monitor: 1999-2005*, Fafo-rapport 550 (Oslo: Fafo, October 2006).

felt the compliance provisions in the treaty would not be strong enough and additional measures were needed—perhaps even including a system to monitor its implementation. Unlike other arms control agreements, the Mine Ban Treaty lacks a standing institutional structure to oversee implementation. There is no permanent inspectorate or secretariat capable of dealing with compliance matters, such as the Hague-based Organization for the Prohibition of Chemical Weapons of the 1993 Chemical Weapons Convention.

According to the treaty, States Parties commit to "consult and cooperate with each other" and "work together in a spirit of cooperation" in its implementation. Article 8 also lists five steps or stages of compliance actions, added during the last stage of the negotiations.[1] One diplomat at the center of the negotiations, Steffen Kongstad of Norway, noted that verification was not the highest priority because "the thinking at the time by the majority of negotiating states was that it should be politically so costly to breach the obligations of the treaty that it would deter anyone from doing it."[2]

Campaigners, deminers, and diplomats alike were also concerned about the lack of accurate and detailed information on various aspects of the landmine issue—most notably on the exact extent of landmine "crisis." ICBL members had long framed and shaped every aspect of the landmine issue through credible field research and reporting. Human Rights Watch (HRW), one of the six nongovernmental organizations (NGOs) that founded the ICBL, issued case studies on the landmine problem in affected countries as early as 1986, and by 1997 had built considerable capacity in tracking and publicizing the mine ban policies of governments in an effort to prove an emerging international consensus for the prohibition of antipersonnel mines.[3] Under Article 7 (Transparency Measures) of the new treaty, States Parties were obliged to provide regular reports detailing their implementation of the agreement. Yet independent data collection was also seen as necessary because, according to Peter Herby of the International Committee of the Red Cross (ICRC), the Mine Ban Treaty's transparency measures were "limited to that provided by governments and likely to lack analysis as to why some efforts are succeeding while others are not."[4]

ICBL members were considering how to play a role in monitoring the treaty, even as many worried the coalition might not even survive the heated internal debates and friction among members during the whirlwind period leading to December 1997. Many in the ICBL did not believe that the campaign could manage such an important monitoring function. There was "a very real concern" about the lack of NGO capacities to collect credible data for use in reporting on treaty implementation.[5] Canadian diplomat Bob Lawson recalls a "pretty decent fight" with Nobel Laureate Jody Williams in May 1998, where she candidly expressed her trepidation that, with a couple of exceptions, the ICBL campaigning network had no demonstrated ability to do in-depth research and writing.[6] There was concern that a "joke" of a product produced by a ragtag group of grassroots campaigners would weaken the ICBL structurally and do irreparable damage to the campaign's credibility.

At the same time, the campaign realized it would have to change gears quickly, shifting from work on securing the Mine Ban Treaty to work to ensure its implementation. In February 1998, at an ICBL General Meeting, campaign representatives reaffirmed the coalition's commitment to the objective of a total ban on antipersonnel mines, pledged to refocus efforts to include support for universalization and implementation of the Mine Ban Treaty, and announced that the ICBL would "explore a role for its members in monitoring the treaty."[7]

While many people have proven invaluable since, two individuals who played critical roles in the successful adoption of the treaty were also central to the establishment of Landmine Monitor: Bob Lawson of Canada's Foreign Affairs department and ICBL campaigner Steve Goose of Human Rights Watch. Together they laid the groundwork for the establishment of a civil-society based system to verify Mine Ban Treaty implementation—the Landmine Monitor, which was formally established at an ICBL meeting in Oslo in June 1998. The ICBL tasked five NGOs—which became known as the Landmine Monitor Core Group—with key decision-making responsibility for the initiative: Norwegian People's Aid had long field experience in mine action; Handicap International had years of work with landmine victims and also began mine action programs; while the rest—Mines Action Canada, Kenya Coalition Against Landmines, and HRW had considerable advocacy experience. As the preeminent research organization in the ICBL, Human Rights Watch was named the lead agency.[8]

As it developed, the Landmine Monitor proved to be of great benefit for the ICBL in many ways. In the sometimes tumultuous post-treaty signing, post-Nobel prize period, it gave the campaign new direction, focus, and unity. It also helped to expand the ICBL network into regions such as the Commonwealth of Independent States and the Middle East/North Africa. It also brought much needed financial resources to the ICBL and individual campaigners, who also served as researchers.

Producing the First Landmine Monitor Report

After Oslo the newly appointed Landmine Monitor Core Group returned home and began preparing the system for its first report. I joined HRW with the specific responsibility to get the Landmine Monitor system up and running. Initial tasks involved projecting the initiative's identity by producing a logo, a Land-mine Monitor section of the ICBL website, and a ten-page introductory book-let.[9] A call for researchers to contribute to the first report was issued and over the course of two days the Core Group approved most of the seventy-five re-search applications submitted. The resulting research network was not only made up primarily of ICBL campaigners, but also journalists, academics, and representatives of research institutions.[10] The Core Group agreed to try to pro-duce a report on every country in the world and drafted a set of mainly open-ended questions to guide research in each country. To facilitate the research and editing process, Core Group members divided regional and thematic coordina-tion tasks among themselves according to their expertise and geographic areas of operation.[11]

Goose recalls that when the researchers turned in their final reports in March 1999, "It was both impressive and depressing at the same time: im-pressive in that we did have an enormous amount of paper on the table com-ing from a huge range of sources, [but depressing because] very, very little of it was of publishable quality."[12] The detailed but, for the most part, poorly written reports nevertheless showed the potential of Landmine Monitor.

In an experience that is painful to recount, a five-person team in the Arms Division of HRW barely slept as they edited country entries, verified sources, drafted reports for countries where there was no research contact, summa-rized findings into thematic overviews with the assistance of thematic re-search coordinators, took care of all the production elements, and, in less than four weeks time, got the 1,071-page *Landmine Monitor Report 1999* to print.[13]

Turnaround time was so tight that the HRW team *literally* had to haul boxes of the report with them to Mozambique where the ICBL ambassadors pre-sented it to President Joaquim Alberto Chissano at the opening of the treaty's First Meeting of States Parties. The room fell silent as diplomats flipped through the pages to their country entry—each one curious to see how their country was portrayed on the landmine issue.[14] The cover featured a youth running swiftly on his prosthetic leg, conveying a positive message that worked well with the report's subtitle, "Toward a Mine-Free World." Many del-egates were surprised to see the report even though the ICBL had informed governments beforehand of the initiative.[15] According to Goose, "It stunned people. I don't think they had any notion that we were going to be able to pull together something that had so much information. The length itself shocked everybody and there was no 'filler' in it; it was very dense and filled with facts. People began to realize right away too that it wasn't a 'polemic.' It was in fact a very factually based approach to gathering information, a baseline for infor-mation from which to gauge progress."[16]

Measuring Landmine Monitor's Effectiveness

By 2006, the ICBL had issued eight annual Landmine Monitor reports as well as numerous fact sheets and briefing papers. While the initiative is inextricably linked with the ICBL and forms one of a number of innovative mechanisms designed to facilitate treaty implementation, it is possible to draw some conclusions as to its effectiveness, not least because it has functioned for nearly a decade.[17] Landmine Monitor has had an extensive influence on the actions and positions of the 155 States Parties as they have implemented major operational articles of the Mine Ban Treaty. The ICBL and Landmine Monitor have also been influential in changing the behavior of the forty non-States Parties as well as nonstate armed groups.

Increasing Transparency

The ICBL and Landmine Monitor have played an important role in improving the quality and quantity of information provided by States Parties in their Article 7 reports on actions they have taken to adhere to the treaty.[18] The campaign regularly disseminates Landmine Monitor fact sheets listing states with impending deadlines and those behind on their transparency reporting. Landmine Monitor researchers regularly inquire about the status of those reports and some approach government departments involved in the preparation of the reports. Since 2001 the number of States Parties submitting their initial reports has increased dramatically from 63 percent to an impressive 96 percent compliance rate.[19]

Transparency reporting has become more detailed since 1999. Landmine Monitor published its first report prior to the submission deadline for initial Article 7 reports and thus set the standard for comprehensive and detailed reporting. States Parties often "borrow" language from their Landmine Monitor country updates to include in their Article 7 reports. Officials sometimes share drafts of their reports with ICBL campaigners and Landmine Monitor researchers for their review and comment prior to submission. The campaign and Landmine Monitor also play an educational role by explaining the requirements of each form in the report and urging states to report in as much detail as possible. At the urging of ICBL, based on Landmine Monitor reporting about deficiencies, States Parties agreed in 2005 to a new expanded form for Article 7 reporting on mines retained for training purposes. Also at the urging of ICBL and Landmine Monitor, States Parties have agreed on the need for timely and detailed reporting on stockpiled mines newly discovered after the completion of formal destruction programs.

Even governments outside the treaty have become more transparent on the mines issue than ever before in part due to Landmine Monitor's influence. At the urging of the ICBL, several non-States Parties have voluntarily submitted Article 7 reports.[20] Previously confidential reports submitted by States Party to Amended Protocol II of the Convention on Conventional Weapons (CCW) have since been made publicly available, including on the Internet, in part because Landmine Monitor researchers were able to obtain, analyze, and publish this information.

Monitoring Core Prohibitions

Through careful and professional research, Landmine Monitor has identified confirmed cases of use of antipersonnel mines, and has also identified instances where there is compelling evidence, and other instances where there are strong allegations. The ICBL has used this information to engage in advocacy activities to stigmatize mine use and urge States Parties to act.

Landmine Monitor found no confirmed cases of use of antipersonnel mines by any State Party between 1999 and 2006. Landmine Monitor did, however, report compelling evidence of antipersonnel mine use in 2000 by Uganda, then a State Party, in the Democratic Republic of Congo (DRC), then a nonsignatory.[21] Uganda denied the reports, but at the Third Meeting of States Parties in September 2001 agreed with the ICBL's suggestion that a full investigation be carried out.[22] No result was ever announced, and States Parties chose not to pursue the matter forcefully with Uganda.

Landmine Monitor has investigated a number of allegations of use by other States Parties, but none have proven to be compelling. On the other hand, Landmine Monitor found strong evidence that several states used antipersonnel mines after signing the Mine Ban Treaty but before ratifying and formally becoming a State Party. This included Angola, Burundi, Ecuador, Ethiopia, Rwanda, Sudan, and Uganda.

Landmine Monitor closely scrutinizes States Parties that have previously used antipersonnel mines such as those listed above, as well as Afghanistan, Bosnia and Herzegovina, Cambodia, Nicaragua, and Mozambique. While it occasionally finds reports of mine use by civilians (as explosives for fishing or to demarcate property for example), no significant or systematic antipersonnel mine use has been detected in these countries since war fighting ceased. Landmine Monitor also follows current and ongoing conflicts for evidence of mine use. In West Africa, for example, there has been no antipersonnel mine use that Landmine Monitor can determine in the fighting in Côte d'Ivoire, Guinea, Liberia, and Sierra Leone.

While Landmine Monitor readily admits that research limitations some-times prevent it from accessing every piece of available or possible informa-tion on mine-laying, it is now more difficult than ever to conceal mine use or for it to go completely unnoticed. As with human rights violations, increased presence of NGOs and media in conflict zones together with improvements in information technology make it much harder for governments and even rebel groups to hide new antipersonnel mine use.

Landmine Monitor's research on the production of antipersonnel mines has uncovered previously unknown production activities carried out by States Parties before joining the Mine Ban Treaty. For example, the initiative was the first to report that Colombia had manufactured antipersonnel mines.[23] Other States Parties have been compelled to "set the record straight" by revealing past production activities after being cited by the Monitor. In September 2000, for example, Australia reported that it manufactured antipersonnel mines until the early 1980s.[24] Landmine Monitor has also revealed previously un-published information about production in non-States Parties, such as Burma (Myanmar), Nepal, and Russia.

Landmine Monitor has not documented any state-to-state transfers or ex-ports of antipersonnel mines since 1999 and believes that antipersonnel mine transfers have dwindled to a very low level of illicit trafficking and unacknowl-edged trade. However, it has occasionally reported on scandals triggered by in-vestigative researchers and reporters uncovering attempted sales of antiperson-nel mines, such as in the United Kingdom in 1999 by a Romanian arms company and by Pakistan Ordnance Factories.[25] Although Iran has denied ex-porting for many years, Landmine Monitor reported information obtained from mine clearance organizations in Afghanistan that they were removing and destroying many hundreds of Iranian YM-I and YM-I-B antipersonnel mines, date stamped 1999 and 2000, from abandoned Northern Alliance front lines.

Stockpile Destruction, Mine Action, and Landmine Survivor Assistance

The ICBL has challenged States Parties to declare and destroy their stockpiled mines in advance of the treaty-mandated four-year deadline for stockpile de-struction, setting certain events or dates as completion targets.[26] The campaign promotes greater transparency in stockpile destruction activities, including participation by civil society, mine survivors, and media in destruction events. By the end of 2005, every State Party had met their stockpile destruction dead-lines with the exception of Guinea and Turkmenistan.[27] After the ICBL repeat-edly criticized Turkmenistan's decision to retain 69,200 mines allegedly for training purposes as permitted by Article 3 of the treaty, in 2004 the government said it would destroy all the mines and invited the ICBL to witness the destruction.[28]

Landmine Monitor's compilations of data are continuously updated and regularly circulated to States Parties enabling them to identify problems and monitor progress in stockpile destruction. In addition to detailing best practices in stockpile destruction, the Monitor publishes other information on costs, environmental considerations, and destruction methods. It also identifies states that might have trouble meeting destruction deadlines and anticipates problems that they may encounter.

Much more is now known about the extent of the global landmine problem and efforts to remedy it, due in part to Landmine Monitor's provision of unique, global statistics on the mine problem through its annual report, fact sheets, statements and presentations.[29] Landmine Monitor is the only publication that independently develops and publishes each year a total for global spending on mine action, a total for global clearance of mined areas, and a total for global casualties, among other things.

Landmine Monitor's reporting has helped keep mine action on government agendas. Its research has charted and contributed to the greater sophistication seen in mine action today to show how mine clearance has evolved from a strictly military activity to a more sophisticated and systematic humanitarian and developmental enterprise. According to one observer, Landmine Monitor has achieved "a credibility which is amazing. I don't think there's been a better effort, in an environment that defies good data, to really rigorously get things right. The mine action content unfortunately reflects the status of mine action so it's weak in terms of the data that's gathered."[30]

As with mine action, the Mine Ban Treaty has proven a useful vehicle for the ICBL to raise awareness about the needs and rights of mine survivors and, by extension, people with disabilities. In support of this, Landmine Monitor has collected and presented detailed information that indicates a global decline in new mine victims since the treaty entered into force in 1999. Exact research findings are difficult, as precise numbers are hard to come by and the research encroaches into other areas, such as public health issues and disability rights. Nonetheless, Landmine Monitor has identified key trends and problems that enable donors and others to better understand the needs of mine survivors and to ensure that limited resources are used most effectively. It also lists significant gaps in victim assistance such as geographic coverage, affordability, and quality of available facilities, as well as a lack of resources to implement or maintain programs.

The tracking of financial support for mine action is a difficult task, despite greater transparency and better reporting mechanisms by states. This is in part because there is much variance in what donors report on, in what detail, and for what time periods. Nevertheless, Landmine Monitor has been able to provide an informative picture of the global funding situation. In-kind support has proven even harder to assess, but Landmine Monitor has also documented many examples of technical, material, and other forms of in-kind commitments to mine action and victim assistance as well as to stockpile destruction.

Landmine Monitor's reporting provides donors with a clear picture of needs, gaps, and available resources. According to one donor, Landmine Monitor "helps us formulate global policies, especially on mine action. It is comprehensive in that it tackles all aspects of the issue and generally gives us a feel for any one given country. It's a first port of call for information and we use it regularly on a country level. Most active donors have it [the annual Landmine Monitor report] on their desk."[31]

The ICBL's call for more resources for mine action is not targeted solely at States that are party to the Mine Ban Treaty. Since 1999, an increasing number of non-States Parties have made financial commitments in this area in part because of the awareness generated on the issue. Landmine Monitor's reporting on the lack of demining by some mine-affected non-States Parties with numerous mine casualties has helped spur action to remedy the problem.

"Issues of Concern"

The ICBL has consistently raised questions about how States Parties implement and interpret certain aspects of treaty Articles 1, 2, and 3, particularly on issues related to the prohibition on "assistance" with banned acts, joint military operations with non-States Parties, mines with sensitive fuses or antihandling devices, and the permissible number of mines retained for training. Landmine Monitor has become the principal collector and publisher of States Parties' policy and practice with respect to these articles.

The ICBL and Landmine Monitor have urged States Parties to reach a common understanding of what acts are and are not permitted by Article 1(c), under which each State Party undertakes to "never under any circumstances . . . assist, encourage or induce, in any way, anyone to engage in any activity prohibited to a State Party." While states have not been willing to reach a formal common understanding of how Article 1 applies to joint military operations, nonetheless a better view of the meaning of the word "assist" has begun to emerge as many States Parties agree on the need to address this issue and share their views on policy and practice. An informal understanding has begun to emerge. A total of forty-one States Parties have declared that they will not participate in planning and implementation of activities related to the use of antipersonnel mines in joint operations with a state not party to the Mine Ban Treaty, which may use antipersonnel mines.

Since the 1997 negotiations, the ICBL has emphasized that according to Article 2 any mine equipped with a fuse or antihandling device that causes the mine to explode from an unintentional or innocent act of a person is considered to be an antipersonnel mine and therefore prohibited. Many States Parties have agreed that this is their understanding, but a handful remain resistant and the campaign fears that a situation is developing whereby some states will keep a stockpile of such mines for future use or export while others will destroy the antipersonnel mines in question. Landmine Monitor has obtained and published States Parties' declarations and clarifications on measures they have taken to ensure that mines with sensitive fuses and antihandling devices are compliant with the Mine Ban Treaty. It has also urged States Parties to provide more information on certain types of mines that are designed to be capable of being both command-detonated and victim-activated. Twenty-seven States Parties have expressed the view that any mine, despite its label or design intent, capable of being detonated by the unintentional act of a person is an antipersonnel mine and is prohibited, while only a few have disagreed. In particular, there appears to be agreement, with some notable exceptions, that a mine that relies on a tripwire, breakwire, or a tilt rod should be considered an antipersonnel mine.

Efforts by the ICBL and Landmine Monitor to gain clarification from States Parties on their interpretation of Article 3 have resulted in considerable progress. With a couple of exceptions, during the 1997 Oslo negotiations and in Standing Committee discussions from 1999–2004, most States Parties agreed that the number of mines retained for demining training and testing purposes should be in the hundreds or thousands or less, but not tens of thousands. Landmine Monitor has documented the numbers of mines retained by States Parties in detail and draws special attention to those retaining more than ten thousand mines. About two dozen States Parties have responded to this negative publicity by reducing the number of mines retained from the high levels they had originally reported.[32] Several have decided to completely destroy their mines originally retained for training.

By profiling these "issues of concern," Articles 1, 2, and 3, "became topics of conversation," placed on the agenda of every intersessional meeting and Meeting of States Parties.[33] The ICBL and Landmine Monitor have helped remove ambiguities and preserve the integrity of the treaty by pointing out where individual States Parties diverge from predominant state practice.

Universalization

Landmine Monitor's researchers inquire after ratification and accession documents, the status of policy reviews, and other important information in a process that undoubtedly serves to bring on board new States Parties. Year after year the system provides constant reminders to States outside the treaty of pledges they have made in support of the eradication of antipersonnel mines. It reports on incremental yet encouraging policy developments in these states, identifies obstacles, and highlights successes and setbacks, making it a useful tool for those promoting universalization.[34] The campaign encourages non-States Parties to express their support for the ban by voting for an annual pro-Mine Ban Treaty resolution in the UN General Assembly (UNGA). While nonbinding, this builds support for the growing international norm against antipersonnel mines. The December 2006 UNGA Resolution was supported by twenty non-States Parties, while seventeen non-States Parties abstained, and none voted against. Among those supporting were some considered major holdouts such as Armenia, Azerbaijan, China, and Finland. This success is largely a result of the ICBL's advocacy efforts.

In addition to the ICBL's efforts to universalize the Mine Ban Treaty, Landmine Monitor documents how states outside the treaty and other actors are changing their behavior and practices toward eliminating antipersonnel mines. It has documented how antipersonnel mines are now being used by far fewer non-States Parties and in far lesser numbers than during the 1960s to the early 1990s, the period when the global antipersonnel mine crisis came into being. Some States have run counter to this trend such as Burma (Myanmar), Georgia, India, Nepal, Pakistan, and Russia. The overall decline in use cannot be attributed to the campaign's activities alone, but rather to the response by the international community as a whole in stigmatizing antipersonnel mine use and other factors, such as the cessation of hostilities in various countries.

Since its establishment, Landmine Monitor has reported in more detail on the landmine production activities of several non-States Parties. It was the first to publish extensive details on the locations of Russian mine-manufacturing factories.[35] Landmine Monitor uncovered evidence of antipersonnel mine manufacturing by Nepal that was subsequently acknowledged by the government, resulting in the country being the only new country added to the list of producers between 1999 and 2004.[36] It was largely responsible for obtaining formal public statements of policies renouncing production by four of these states (Egypt, Finland, Israel, and Poland), by repeatedly requesting these governments to formalize their position in writing and make it public.

Egypt, for example, claimed for years that it had ceased export of antipersonnel mines in 1984 and ended production in 1988 but refused to make that position formal and public until the Nairobi Review Conference at the end of
2004.[37]

Through Landmine Monitor reporting and various initiatives by ICBL
members and others, such as the Swiss nongovernmental organization Geneva
Call, much more is becoming known about nonstate armed groups (NSAGs)
and antipersonnel mines. According to Landmine Monitor, NSAGs now use
mines in more countries than government forces.[38] Monitor researchers have
collected more detailed information than any other data gatherer on NSAG
mine use in countries, including Burma (Myanmar), Colombia, India, Nepal,
Pakistan, Philippines, and Russia. Landmine Monitor has also reported in
more detail than ever before on the manufacturing of antipersonnel landmines
including victim-activated Improvised Explosive Devices (IEDs) and stockpiling of mines by NSAGs. Documenting NSAG activities on antipersonnel
mines, while difficult, is probably easier than convincing them to change their
behavior. Nevertheless, an increasing number of NSAGs appear to be embracing the antipersonnel mine ban. The ICBL has urged such groups to issue unilateral statements and enter into bilateral agreements, as well as commit to the
Geneva Call's Deed of Commitment to indicate their willingness to observe the
landmine ban.[39]

Other Civil Society Monitoring Endeavors

Landmine Monitor readily admits that it is "not a technical verification system
or a formal inspection regime." Rather, it describes itself as "an effort by civil society to hold governments accountable to the obligations that they have taken
on with regard to antipersonnel mines; this is done through extensive collection, analysis and distribution of information that is publicly available."[40]

The Monitor has become an accepted part of the process surrounding the
Mine Ban Treaty, but it remains unofficial since it is an initiative by the ICBL that
is carried out by NGOs and individual members of civil society. While it works
closely with governments and is funded in large part by them, it is not formally
recognized in the treaty text.[41] According to one observer, the Landmine Monitor reports carry "significant weight" because they come from the ICBL.[42]

Landmine Monitor claims that the initiative marks "the first time that nongovernmental organizations are coming together in a coordinated, systematic
and sustained way to monitor a humanitarian law or disarmament treaty."[43]
Civil society engagement in the monitoring of treaties and regimes is nothing
new, but Landmine Monitor does appear to be unique because it is the first

example of a coordinated coalition of NGOs (not a single NGO) systematically monitoring a multilateral treaty (and not only a humanitarian problem or other issue).[44] At the outset Landmine Monitor needed to be different from its predecessors because of the nature of the issue and the treaty it would monitor. Its in-country research network, coalition-comprised coordination structure, consistent donor support, and regular dissemination of credible research findings represent innovative practices.

There are multiple examples of NGOs engaging in and monitoring agreements in an unofficial capacity. The International Committee of the Red Cross (ICRC) is the most officially accepted civil society agency tasked with safeguarding and promoting international humanitarian law, such as the 1949 Geneva Conventions and their 1977 Protocols. Elsewhere, in the environmental realm in particular, civil society has been able to formalize links to official monitoring regimes.[45] The 1972 Convention on International Trade in Endangered Species (CITES) reflects a high-degree of formal engagement by NGOs. Official reporting by governments to the CITES Secretariat is supplemented by reports monitoring trade and transfers provided by the World Conservation Monitoring Center and the Trade Records Analysis of Fauna and Flora in Commerce (TRAFFIC).

Several federations or coalitions of NGOs monitor and regularly report on specific issues ranging from humanitarian aid and contemporary crises to access to health care and social services.[46] NGO coalitions have monitored and issued regular reports to influence issues that were in the process of becoming legalized through a treaty framework, such as the Convention on the Rights of People with Disabilities.[47]

Other NGO coalitions are now seeing the many benefits to having a monitoring system as well as a credible research product and are studying Landmine Monitor to establish similar mechanisms to monitor new agreements.[48] These include efforts to monitor the 2000 Optional Protocol to the Convention on Children in Armed Conflict and the 2001 UN Programme of Action on Small Arms and Light Weapons.[49] After the United States withdrew its support in July 2001 for a draft protocol to the 1972 Biological and Toxic Weapons Convention, effectively scuttling over six years of work to establish a verification mechanism, NGOs have set up their own initiative monitoring biological weapons with government funding and support.[50]

Conclusion

The effectiveness of the Landmine Monitor is sometimes difficult to demonstrate empirically. Its research informs and challenges other actors in the Mine

Ban Treaty process in complex and dynamic ways. The Monitor's findings are taken up by others, but often without attribution. Sometimes, Landmine Monitor's research prompts changes in posture or policy by governments that are not acknowledged in public. And, of course, many visible challenges remain for the achievement of the Mine Ban Treaty's goals—not least being the ongoing challenges of universalizing of the treaty, and the looming ten-year mine clearance deadlines for mine affected states.

While inevitably constrained by the evidence base, the capacity of its research network, and the extent to which governments and others make landmine-related information publicly available, Landmine Monitor has nevertheless flourished. Since its establishment, the initiative has constantly evolved, both in terms of quality of the product and functioning of the system. By 2007, most of its innovative mechanisms established a decade earlier were still functioning effectively. The research network has continued to gain in strength and expertise, with many original researchers still participating. The Core Group (since renamed Editorial Board) has remained intact, with Mines Action Canada taking over the lead agency role from Human Rights Watch in 2005.[51] Donor support for Landmine Monitor, while always a concern, remains strong.

Through Landmine Monitor and other means, the campaign has provided States Parties with a better understanding of what the Mine Ban Treaty requires of them, and it has helped to promote greater action to implement the treaty. Its independent evidence has proved a useful tool for States Parties to exert pressure on other states to comply with the Mine Ban Treaty. Even non-States Parties are changing their behavior as the Treaty gains strength, ever aware that the ICBL will not leave them alone as it constantly monitors their actions and encourages adherence to the antipersonnel mine prohibitions.

Landmine Monitor remains the foremost available source on the global landmine issue. Disseminated for free, its annual report and associated documents have become essential reading for diplomats, practitioners, donors, media, and others seeking to gain a better understanding of the mine ban movement's successes and setbacks. Its ability to regularly produce ever more detailed research is one of the hallmarks of the Monitor's success.

Landmine Monitor is an important factor in explaining why the ICBL continues to be accepted as an integral actor in the Mine Ban Treaty process. The ICBL remains a model for how an active, coordinated, and engaged civil society can play an integral role in realms traditionally reserved strictly for states such as negotiation, monitoring, and implementation of international agreements. Campaign members have forged long-term relationships with military officers, diplomatic representatives, political leaders, and government officials tasked with implementing the treaty, demonstrating the importance of continued partnership and cooperation on this issue.

According to academic Richard Price, the key source of NGO influence is authority, which can be derived from three principal sources: "expertise, moral influence, and a claim to political legitimacy."[52] Originating in part from civil society concerns in the field, the ICBL's claim to moral authority was clear from the outset. It gained political legitimacy through its participation in the process leading to the establishment of the Mine Ban Treaty. Landmine Monitor has strengthened and reinforced the ICBL's expertise, which was credible from the beginning, and a reliable Monitor is crucial to the ICBL's continued credibility.

Landmine Monitor has demonstrated that civil society-based verification is no longer just a concept but can be a practice and a model for other campaigns to consider when exploring similar initiatives.

Since governments and the ICBL broke away from the traditional mode of multilateral diplomacy to negotiate the 1997 Mine Ban Treaty, the historic break from "business as usual" diplomacy has continued with civil society endeavors, such as Landmine Monitor. Its impact has been unprecedented in adding credibility to advocacy in support of a multilateral process. Its work, primarily in support of the ICBL, has helped push humanitarian perspectives—which differ from orthodox national security-focused arms control approaches—to the forefront of the minds of multilateral practitioners.

But, perhaps most significantly, the initiative continues with the routine business of monitoring the eradication of a weapon that was once in widespread use. The Mine Ban Treaty might look very different today if the ICBL had folded after December 1997 and there had been no Landmine Monitor.

Notes

1. See chapter 6 on cooperative compliance.

2. Interview with Steffen Kongstad, Deputy Director General, Royal Norwegian Ministry of Foreign Affairs, Oslo, April 5, 2006.

3. Human Rights Watch, *Land Mines in El Salvador and Nicaragua: The Civilian Victims* (New York: Human Rights Watch, 1986), 120 pp. See also: Human Rights Watch and Physicians for Human Rights, *Landmines: A Deadly Legacy* (New York: Human Rights Watch, October 1993), 510 pp.

4. Letter from Peter Herby to Bob Lawson, Department of Foreign Affairs and International Trade, Canada, November 11, 1997. Three-page proposal attached. Copied to Steve Goose, HRW, and Jody Williams, ICBL.

5. Minutes of March 24, 1998, NGO Meeting, circulated by Celina Tuttle, Mines Action Canada (MAC), March 31, 1998.

6. Telephone interview with Bob Lawson, Director of Human Security, Foreign Affairs Department, Canada, February 23, 2006.

7. ICBL statement, "General Meeting of the International Campaign to Ban Landmines," February 22, 1998, www.icbl.org/news/archive/before_2001/statements_frankfurt/. The ICBL's Call to Ban Landmines is also published at the front of every annual Landmine Monitor report.

8. Mines Advisory Group (MAG) was named at the meeting, but one week later, following discussions at its headquarters, MAG indicated it would not be able to participate after all and Norwegian People's Aid accepted an invitation to fill its place. MAG indicated its decision was due mainly to its concerns over its capacity to participate and worries about potential conflicts of interest in countries where it was working.

9. HRW on behalf of the ICBL, *Landmine Monitor: An Introduction*, August 1998. From the outset, Landmine Monitor took care to ensure the initiative, as a project of the ICBL, did not overshadow the campaign itself.

10. The criteria for considering research proposals included their credibility, feasibility, methodology, timeline, geographic distance from its object of study, comprehensiveness, complementarity with other applications, relevance to Mine Ban Treaty, and connection to International Campaign to Ban Landmines. "Landmine Monitor Brussels Core Group Meeting," updated and circulated to ICBL by email, October 29, 1998.

11. NPA took on responsibility for mine action coordination as well as for European research. Handicap International became responsible for victim assistance and mine risk education coordination, as well as for the Asia-Pacific researchers. MAC agreed to establish the Landmine Monitor database and coordinate research in the Americas. The Kenya Coalition Against Landmines became research coordinator for sub-Saharan Africa. In addition to its global and production responsibilities, HRW agreed to take on thematic research coordination on ban issues (policy, use, production, trade, and stockpiling) and coordination responsibility for the Middle East/North Africa and the former Soviet Union.

12. Telephone interview with Steve Goose, Executive Director, Arms Division, HRW, April 11, 2006.

13. The team consisted of Steve Goose (chief editor), Mary Wareham, Alex Vines, Kathleen Bleakley, and Jody Williams (ICBL Ambassador and member of the Advisory Committee of HRW's Arms Division). Arms Division associate Jasmine Juteau was responsible for the final formatting and printing of the report.

14. The first two annual reports ordered country entries both regionally and by their status on the treaty (state party, signatory, nonsignatory, or other). In part this was intended for advocacy purposes: to make the government concerned understand their status. The front was a "good" place to be located because countries that had not banned the weapon were relegated to the back of the book. Later the regional groupings were dropped from the main report, but regional overviews added to the executive summary as another way of encouraging governments to "look good" on the landmine issue.

15. In addition to providing several progress reports, Landmine Monitor wrote to every foreign minister prior to publication to explain the nature and intent of the re-

port that was about to be released. Country campaigners also met with government officials to explain the initiative and present materials such as the "Introduction" booklet.

16. Telephone interview with Steve Goose, April 11, 2006.

17. See, for example, Kjell Erling Kjellman, "Norms, persuasion and practice: *Landmine Monitor* and civil society," Review in *Third World Quarterly*, 24:5, 2003, p. 958.

18. The ICBL participates in other initiatives aimed at improving the reporting compliance rate, such as the "Article 7 Contact Group," established in 2000 and led by Belgium. Moreover, the production of educational tools, such as a "Guide to Article 7 Reporting" prepared by the Verification Research, Training, and Information Centre (VERTIC), in cooperation with ICBL, have been useful.

19. The rate was 96 percent in 2005 and 2006. *Landmine Monitor Report 2006* reported that six States Parties were late in submitting their initial reports: Cape Verde, Ethiopia, Equatorial Guinea, Gambia, Guyana, and São Tomé and Principe. *Landmine Monitor Report 2005* also reported six late reports. The 2004 edition listed twelve; in 2003 the number was fifteen; in 2002, the number was thirty; in 2001, the number was thirty-seven; and in 2000, the number of late reports was thirty-six. ICBL, *Landmine Monitor Report 2006* (Ottawa: Mines Action Canada, 2006), pp. 15–16; ICBL, *Landmine Monitor Report 2005* (Ottawa: Mines Action Canada, 2005), pp. 15–16.

20. This includes in recent years Morocco, Poland, and Sri Lanka. Before becoming States Parties, Cameroon, Gambia, Latvia, and Lithuania submitted voluntary reports. A number of others have stated they intend to submit voluntary reports, including Armenia, Azerbaijan, China, and Mongolia.

21. See ICBL, *Landmine Monitor Report 2002* (Washington, DC: Human Rights Watch, 2002), pp. 501–502.

22. Uganda subsequently informed States Parties that a joint Uganda-Rwanda commission looking into the conduct of the fighting in the DRC would also investigate the allegations of landmine use. Two years passed and by the Fifth Meeting of States Parties in September 2003, the ICBL expressed disappointment that Uganda had made no further public statements regarding the allegations or the investigation. Using its right of reply, the Ugandan representative stated, "In the interest of the established mechanisms to ease the tensions, it was deemed inopportune to continue with the process that would jeopardize the healing process. In the interest of both parties involved, the report of the commission has not been made public." Statement entitled "Right of Reply," delivered by Captain Asingura Kagoro, Fifth Meeting of States Parties, Bangkok, Thailand, September 18, 2003.

23. ICBL, *Landmine Monitor Report 1999* (Washington, DC: Human Rights Watch, 1999), pp. 294–295.

24. Letter to Mary Wareham from Richard Maude, Assistant Secretary, Arms Control and Disarmament Branch, Department of Foreign Affairs and Trade, Australia, September 7, 2000. Also posted online in Landmine Monitor Comments section, www.icbl.org/lm/comments/australia/.

25. ICBL, *Landmine Monitor Report 2000* (Washington, DC: Human Rights Watch, 2000), pp. 747–748.

26. See for example, ICBL press release, "Landmines Campaign Challenges Governments to Complete Stockpile Destruction by September 2001," Buenos Aires, November 6, 2000.

27. Both completed destruction shortly thereafter. Information came to light in 2007 that Cape Verde and Afghanistan also missed deadlines.

28. ICBL, *Landmine Monitor Report 2004* (Washington, DC: Human Rights Watch), pp. 830–832.

29. Notably, the Landmine Impact Surveys by the Survey Action Center have provided a much more detailed understanding of the extent of the mine problem in heavily affected countries; see http://www.sac-na.org/.

30. Telephone interview with Bob Eaton, Director, Survey Action Center, February 10, 2006.

31. Telephone interview with Andrew Willson, Department of Foreign Affairs and International Development, United Kingdom, February 10, 2006.

32. This includes Argentina, Australia, Bulgaria, Chile, Croatia, Denmark, Ecuador, Italy, Lithuania, Macedonia, Mauritania, Moldova, Peru, Portugal, Romania, Slovakia, Slovenia, Spain, Thailand, Turkmenistan, Uganda, United Kingdom, Venezuela, and Zambia.

33. Telephone interview with Steve Goose, April 11, 2006.

34. The ICBL participates in the Canadian-led Universalization Contact Group, established in 1999. This group uses the Landmine Monitor report as a baseline document to track various universalization opportunities, efforts, and outcomes.

35. ICBL, *Landmine Monitor Report 1999*, pp. 805–807.

36. ICBL, *Landmine Monitor Report 2003* (Washington, DC: Human Rights Watch, 2003), pp. 8; 656.

37. Landmine Monitor removed Egypt from its list but has noted with concern that it is still not aware of any official decrees or laws by the government to implement prohibitions on production or export of antipersonnel mines.

38. *Landmine Monitor Report 2006* reported use by three governments (Burma (Myanmar), Nepal, and Russia), and use by NSAGs in at least ten countries, including three States Parties (Burundi, Colombia, and Guinea-Bissau) and seven non-States Parties (Burma (Myanmar), India, Iraq, Nepal, Pakistan, Russia/Chechnya, and Somalia). ICBL, *Landmine Monitor Report 2006*, pp. 7–8.

39. More information about Geneva Call, as well as its Deed of Commitment, is available at: http://www.genevacall.org/.

40. See the "About Landmine Monitor" introductory section contained in every annual report issued since 1999.

41. Oliver Meier and Clare Tenner, "Non-governmental Monitoring of International Agreements," in VERTIC, *Verification Yearbook 2001* (London: VERIC, 2001) p. 211.

42. Meier and Tenner, "Non-governmental Monitoring of International Agreements," p. 211.

43. See the "About Landmine Monitor" introductory section contained in every annual report issued since 1999.

44. The International Council of the Federation of Trade Unions (ICFTU) has monitored and issued annual reports detailing violations of the standards contained in the 1919 International Labor Organization (ILO), but this cannot be described as an NGO endeavor. See ICFTU, *Annual Survey of Violations of Trade Union Rights: 2005* (Brussels: IFCTU, 2005).

45. Meier and Tenner, "Non-governmental Monitoring of International Agreements," p. 208.

46. For example, as a self-described "independent transparency mechanism," the Small Arms Survey has reported annually since 2001 on all aspects of the problem of small arms and light weapons. See Small Arms Survey, *Small Arms Survey 2001: Profiling the Problem* (Oxford: Oxford University Press, 2001), p. 2; see http://www .smallarmssurvey.org.

47. In 2002, the Center for International Rehabilitation (CIR) formed the International Disability Rights Monitor (IDRM), together with Disabled Peoples International and other disability groups, to "document problems, progress, and barriers experienced by people with disabilities" in a report format to assist in the establishment of a UN convention on the rights of people with disabilities. See IDRM, *International Disability Rights Compendium 2003*, US: CIR, June 2003. See http://www.disability.ws.

48. The author has provided feedback to initiatives tackling biological weapons, disability rights, small arms, and tobacco control, among others. See also: Jenni Risseanen, "Comparative Survey on Civil Society Monitoring," unpublished evaluation prepared to inform the creation of the Bioweapons Project in 2002.

49. Coalition to Stop the Use of Child Soldiers, "Global Report 2004," November 17, 2004; International Action Network on Small Arms (IANSA) & Biting the Bullet, "Examining Implementation of the UN Programme of Action: 2005," July 2005.

50. The global civil society BioWeapons Prevention Project (BWPP) aims to strengthen the norms against using disease as a weapon by tracking compliance with agreements that outlaw hostile use of biotechnology. See: http://www.bwpp.org.

51. The Core Group was reduced by one member in its post-2004 structural reshuffle, the Kenya Coalition Against Landmines.

52. Richard Price, "Transnational Civil Society and Advocacy in World Politics," Review Article in *World Politics* 55:4 (July 2003), p. 387.

5

Surround the Cities with the Villages: Universalization of the Mine Ban Treaty

Shannon Smith

SURROUND THE CITIES WITH THE VILLAGES; isolated, the cities will fall. Thus was Mao Tse-Tung's phrase to sum up his strategy of revolutionary warfare. This was recalled, for more peaceful purposes, by a Thai Ambassador to describe ongoing collective efforts to universalize the Mine Ban Treaty. Universalization is shorthand for the goal of all states choosing to become legally bound by a treaty.[1] The rhetorical application of Mao's strategy has proven to be an apt analogy.

Due to persistent and creative efforts to convince more and more states to join the Mine Ban Treaty, a domino effect has occurred in certain regions, including Africa, the Americas, and Europe. A large number of small and medium powers, along with a few large ones, are in the process of "surrounding," both geographically and morally, many of the major military powers that have not joined (analogous to Mao's "cities") through the establishment of an international norm rejecting antipersonnel mines.

Progress to date is significant. As of September 2007, 155 states had ratified or acceded to the Mine Ban Treaty, and a good number of the states outside the treaty are still likely to join it.

The sustained and deep commitment of States Parties to universalization of the Mine Ban Treaty is highly unusual in the diplomatic universe, as is the level of coordination and cooperation to that end with each other and with nongovernmental actors, such as the International Campaign to Ban Landmines and International Committee of the Red Cross. Universalization is a key agenda point at virtually all meetings related to the Mine Ban Treaty. At the Fourth Meeting of States Parties of the Mine Ban Treaty in September 2002, universalization was formally recognized as one of the treaty's four "core humanitarian aims" and embraced as a key responsibility for all States Parties.[2]

But the antipersonnel landmine revolution is not likely to be complete for some time, as there are many obstacles and limits to universality of the Mine Ban Treaty.[3] Among some of the holdout states, the eventual eradication of these weapons may not be solely attributable to the treaty and campaigning efforts. The complete disappearance of the last stockpiled antipersonnel mines will likely be due to attrition and obsolescence arising from evolving weapons technology and changing military doctrines.

Universalization: The Basis and the Practice

First, a few words about technical language: six terms are commonly used in describing the status of the treaty vis-à-vis states. A state that has *signed* a treaty has indicated its intention to be bound by the treaty's legal obligations at a later date; but until then it is obligated to refrain from actions that *defeat the object and purpose* of the treaty.[4] *Ratification* constitutes the second step a signatory state must take to be legally bound by the treaty, which is completed through submission of the state's instrument of ratification to the treaty's depository (in this case, the Secretary-General of the United Nations).

A treaty *enters into force* on the date it takes legal effect after being ratified by a determined number of states, which varies from treaty to treaty. The Mine Ban Treaty entered into force on March 1, 1999, following its ratification by forty states. After entering into force, states could no longer sign; nonsignatory states can join only through accession. *Accession* refers to a one-step process through which a state becomes legally bound by a treaty. States that have ratified or acceded to a treaty are known as *States Parties*; those that have not are called *non-States Parties*.[5]

On the face of it, it is not clear why treaty universalization has come to share center stage with the Mine Ban Treaty's legally binding obligations. In the treaty itself there is only one reference to universalization, found in the preamble.[6] The preamble is not legally binding, although it does set out context and may be used in treaty interpretation.[7] Other results-based "core aims" of the treaty as identified by the States Parties—assistance to the victims of landmines, the destruction of stockpiled mines, and the clearance of mined areas—are treaty obligations.

At least in part, the activities and attention given to universalization reflect tradition arising from the process that led to the creation of the treaty. The fast-track Ottawa Process—and the multiple players, both governmental and nongovernmental that were instrumental in its emergence—has been well documented. The flurry of meetings and conferences that marked the process, in particular the regional meetings and groupings, played an important role in the creation of the Mine Ban Treaty.[8] The key architects and players in its establishment also planned for an immediate campaign of rapid ratification among treaty signatories.[9] In fact, the very number of ratifications for the treaty to enter into force—forty, or twice the number required for the Convention on Conventional Weapons—was set "with a view to rebutting the argument of [its] lack of universality."[10]

Thus, there have been definite political as well as humanitarian reasons for an ongoing, concerted universalization campaign, and States Parties from all regions have embraced the task. Regional organizations and institutions have also promoted the Mine Ban Treaty and supported the work of others. The Organization of American States (OAS), the African Union (AU), the Organization for Security and Co-operation in Europe (OSCE), and the European Parliament and Commission have all played different roles, for example. The UN "family" has also developed a universalization strategy involving relevant UN agencies (including UNICEF, UN Development Programme, UN Mine Action Service), and the Secretary-General has promoted the treaty on many occasions.

Nongovernmental organizations (NGOs), and especially the International Campaign to Ban Landmines (ICBL), have played a critical role in universalization successes. The ICBL has engaged the voices of civil society more broadly speaking and has worked to include landmine survivors, youth, and parliamentarians in universalization efforts. They continue to work in partnership with states and institutions and have become particularly adept at lobbying on the issue. The ICBL has tailored its own internal resources to promote universalization, including dedicating staff, a diplomatic advisor, and special ICBL ambassadors—importantly including landmine survivors.

The International Committee of the Red Cross (ICRC), one of the key actors from the outset, has continued this role including with respect to universalization. The treaty's Implementation Support Unit (ISU) has also played an active and important role.

In the early years of the treaty, a forum developed in which these "universalization actors" could come together to share information and strategize. The Universalization Contact Group was the first of a number of informal groups that have evolved to tackle different treaty-related issues. Launched by Canada, which has coordinated it since its inception in 2000, the Universalization Contact Group meets on the margins of other Mine Ban Treaty meetings (the Meetings of States Parties, Intersessionals, and so on).[11] With no official status and no specific minutes taken, the group provides a forum for frank, off-the-record discussions, which do not necessarily represent a

particular official position. Beginning with a very small number of participants, it remains an "informal" group where all are welcome.

Participation in the Universalization Contact Group has grown quite large,
with forty or more individuals attending some of its meetings. In addition, focused regional discussions are often organized that frequently attract further
region-specific participants. Canada maintains a distribution list to share information between meetings. The group also provides reports on activities,
priorities, and recommendations at meetings of the treaty. Individual states,
ICBL, ICRC, and others often report on their own universalization efforts.

In addition to Canada, among the States Parties most consistently leading
universalization efforts have been Australia, Austria, Belgium, Croatia, Japan,
the Netherlands, New Zealand, Switzerland, and Thailand. A number of other
States Parties have been very active at particular periods of time, for example
coinciding with a high-profile Mine Ban Treaty-related national or regional
event, or even simply as a result of a particularly dedicated ambassador or senior official being posted into a position with responsibility for the treaty.
These have included states such as Jordan, Mali, and Nicaragua.

The Universalization Contact Group has helped to raise the profile of universalization, providing a valuable collaborative forum to exchange information about various universalization "tools" and to identify new ones. These
range from the very basic to the more sophisticated. Some are Mine Ban
Treaty specific, but many need not be.

For example, a standard tool of diplomacy is a *demarché* or communication
through diplomatic channels from one government to another to advocate directly for an issue or complain about another state's position(s). The Universalization Contact Group developed a common set of Mine Ban Treaty-related
questions that should be asked about each non-States Party, and encouraged
governments to customize demarché instructions based on these questions. It
has also categorized the positions of these states according to types, which helps
prioritize universalization efforts. Most simply, these categorizations identify
those "most likely to join in the near future," those which "could join with some
effort," those with some stronger objections, and finally the hardliners.

The group has also categorized states according to certain characteristics,
which help identify possible obstacles to joining the treaty, and therefore possible avenues to explore to promote universalization. For example, one category is states that have never produced, stockpiled, or used antipersonnel
mines, and therefore where it is likely simply a matter of finding a way to
move the issue further up the political agenda. Other categories have included
those states where ministries of defense are clinging to old doctrine, perhaps
as a result of regional armed disputes now or in the past, even though they
have not used the weapons in some time; those states with a large stockpile or

mine contamination problem, or a large survivor population, which causes them to fear taking on time-bound obligations; or, those states which are simply preoccupied by other matters. Then of course there are those states that are still large stockpilers and those which still use or believe they must be able to use antipersonnel mines.

In addition, universalization proponents have developed lists of possible "interim steps" that a state might be encouraged to take in order to demonstrate good faith consideration of the treaty and agreement with its objectives. These include voting for the annual UN resolution on the treaty; adoption of a moratorium on production, export, or use; initiation of national legislation or other processes needed for accession or ratification; attendance at Mine Ban Treaty meetings; destruction of (at least some) stockpiled mines; implementation of a comprehensive victim assistance program; support for humanitarian demining; voluntary submission of a transparency report that is in accordance with Article 7 of the treaty, or publicly providing information on stockpiles. Such steps can help ease a state toward joining the treaty provided they are not used as a delay tactic or as a substitute for joining.

While an individual State Party, the ICBL, or other universalization actor has often taken the lead in encouraging a particular country to join the treaty, coordinated efforts have also been common, and effective. In many instances, the impact on a non-States Party increases a great deal if the same "target" country is contacted by multiple universalization actors. This is especially true if those efforts are coordinated and the universalization actors share information and analysis through the Universalization Contact Group or other means. Among the countries that have joined in recent years after consistent, coordinated efforts by States Parties, ICBL, ICRC, various UN agencies, and others include: Afghanistan in 2002; Belarus, Cyprus, Greece, Turkey, Serbia and Montenegro, and Sudan in 2003; Ethiopia in 2004; Ukraine in 2005; Brunei Darussalam, Cook Islands, and Haiti in 2006; and Indonesia, Iraq, and Kuwait in 2007.

A useful universalization "hook" in many cases is available in Article 6 of the treaty ("International Cooperation and Assistance"). This article provides the right to States Parties to "seek and receive assistance" to implement the Mine Ban Treaty and obliges States Parties "in a position to do so" to provide it. Some non-States Parties that are mine-affected or have large stockpiles of antipersonnel mines have softened their stance when educated about this article, realizing they could benefit from assistance to resolve their challenges. The offer of resources backed up by Article 6 helped some decide to join the treaty, providing greater confidence they could meet its obligations.

A review of the first five years of the Mine Ban Treaty found that "States Parties repeatedly have stated that assistance and cooperation for mine action

will flow primarily to those that have forsworn the use of anti-personnel
mines forever through adherence to, implementation of, and compliance with
the Convention."[12] Donor States Parties can feel more assured that their contributions to mine clearance, stockpile destruction, and survivor assistance
will be sustainable as beneficiaries that are also States Parties have committed
to never again acquire or use antipersonnel mines. Beneficiary States Parties
that are mine-affected and/or have stockpiles believe they should receive priority from donors since they have taken the step of adopting the treaty's legal
obligations, many of which are time-bound.

This was, for example, a key factor during years of discussions with
Ukraine, which required a precise agreement on financial support for the destruction of its large and volatile stockpile of antipersonnel mines. Once assistance guarantees were received from a donor—the European Commission
in this case—along with reminders that these funds could not be held indefinitely, Ukraine ratified. Belarus also joined as a result of similar engagement.
In another example, through high-level military and diplomatic dialogue, Serbia and Montenegro became convinced it would have support to destroy its
antipersonnel mine stockpiles.[13]

In other cases, technical assistance has helped assure states that are small or
otherwise have limited capacity that they will be able to meet treaty obligations. For example, both the ICRC and the Implementation Support Unit
offer assistance in drafting required national legislation and annual Article 7
transparency reports. The UN has assisted States Parties in developing mine
action plans. In the case of one very small country, assistance in couriering
ratification documents to the UN in New York even played a role!

The Sponsorship Program, established by a group of donors, provides financial assistance for government representatives from capitals to attend the
treaty's meetings. It is primarily available to States Parties "in need" and which
are mine-affected, have significant numbers of landmine survivors, or hold
stockpiles. However, some assistance is reserved for representatives of States
not Parties. Typically, the Universalization Contact Group has identified which
states should be offered this assistance based on factors including whether the
state is close to formally accepting the Mine Ban Treaty or if increased interaction will help move the issue up the agenda in that state. Representatives are educated about the treaty and its obligations and support systems, become familiar with its culture, and are usually lobbied on the margins of the meetings.
In some cases, representatives leave as personal champions of the treaty and
make a real difference in moving it forward in their countries.

Regional initiatives have been a mainstay of universalization efforts, most
notably regional conferences hosted by States Parties and/or regional organizations. The meetings typically include participation by the ICBL, prominent

personalities and donors, and have paid big dividends, as seen by the spread of States Parties across three continents in particular.

For example, in February 2001, Canada, France, and Mali teamed up to organize the "Seminar on Universalization and Implementation of the Ottawa Convention in Africa," attended by more than forty-five African countries, as well as regional African organizations, numerous NGOs, international organizations, and donor countries. The seminar was held because the organizers felt "the process of Universalization and Implementation of the Ottawa Convention was running out of steam," and to "ensure the continent's full participation" in the success of the treaty.[14] One of the priorities was to encourage African countries to join the Mine Ban Treaty before the Fifth Meeting of States Parties in September 2003. Within eight months, an additional eight African countries had completed formal acceptance. With some follow-up, by the time of the meeting a total of seventeen African countries had ratified or acceded since the Bamako seminar occurred, leaving only five on the entire continent outside the treaty.

Military-to-military dialogue and access to high-level former military officials have played a significant role in a number of countries' formal acceptances. This was particularly important in the cases of Estonia, Latvia, and Lithuania. Retired Canadian General Maurice Baril, the former Chief of the Defense Staff, has played an especially active role. One innovative "tool" is the Ottawa Convention Generals Support Team, a group of retired generals and other senior officers from a variety of countries, including non-States Parties who have worked together to promote the treaty. While these avenues hold a lot of promise, only a very small number of States Parties have conducted universalization initiatives from this angle; the positive results suggest others should follow suit.

Those pursuing universalization have promoted adherence to the Mine Ban Treaty as a confidence and security-building measure within peace processes. So far this approach has not been embraced by many non-States Parties, with one particularly notable example. In April 2001, the foreign ministers of Greece and Turkey announced their intent to join the treaty simultaneously, despite their cool relations in other areas. They fulfilled this promise and deposited their instruments at the UN together on September 25, 2003. Efforts to get others to follow this model, such as Armenia and Azerbaijan, or India and Pakistan, have not yet been successful.

At the First Review Conference of the Mine Ban Treaty in December 2004, the Nairobi Summit on a Mine-Free World, the official documentation reflected the work that had been ongoing since 1997. Now more than just a short reference in the treaty's preambular language, a formal document adopted by States Parties set out essential and specific universalization actions. The Nairobi Action

Plan, while not legally binding, is a strong statement of the States Parties' "determination" to "pursue a plan of action" guided by the strategies and steps detailed in the Plan. Its first section includes eight action points identified for achieving universalization.[15] It also includes a reminder that "the States Parties have made this a core task of their collective endeavours these past five years" and affirms that "universal adherence will remain an important object of cooperation among States Parties" for the 2005–2009 period (the years until the Second Review Conference is scheduled to meet). This "codification" indicates a widespread acceptance of universalization as a collective commitment.

The Measurements: Gauging the Extent of Universalization

Progress in universalizing the Mine Ban Treaty can be carved up a number of different ways, providing different but equal illumination.

Universalization by numbers. As of September 2007, there were 155 states party to the Mine Ban Treaty. One hundred thirty-three of these states had signed the Convention between December 1997 and entry into force on March 1, 1999. Of these 133 signatories, only two have yet to ratify (Poland and Marshall Islands). A significant number of the signatories have only completed ratification in the recent past and were a major target of universalization efforts.

In addition to the 131 ratifications, a total of twenty-four countries have acceded to the Mine Ban Treaty since entry into force (after signature was no longer possible).[16] Thus, more than three-quarters (79 percent) of the countries in the world are party to the treaty. Forty states, including the two signatories, have yet to join.

Universalization by region. As of September 2007, every state in Africa was party to the treaty except Egypt, Libya, Morocco, and Somalia. Every state in the Americas had joined except Cuba and the United States. All but two European states were members: Finland and signatory Poland.[17] Only two of the twenty-six members of the North Atlantic Treaty Organization (NATO) have not joined the treaty: Poland and the United States.

So far so good. But moving further east the story changes, and the neighborhoods become tougher for the antipersonnel mine ban. Of the twelve members of the Commonwealth of Independent States (CIS), only five have joined, and in the Middle East and North Africa there are only seven States Parties. Finally, in Asia only twenty-three out of forty states have joined the Mine Ban Treaty (see table 5.1).

Universalization and progress in the eradication of antipersonnel mines. What about questions of "quality" versus "quantity"? Or more to the point, what has

TABLE 5.1
Mine Ban Treaty Status (September 2007)

Region	States Parties	States Not Party
Africa	47	1: Somalia
Americas	33	2: Cuba, United States
Asia	23	17: Burma, China, India, North Korea, South Korea, Laos, Marshall Islands,* Micronesia, Mongolia, Nepal, Pakistan, Palau, Singapore, Sri Lanka, Tonga, Tuvalu, Vietnam
CIS	5	7: Armenia, Azerbaijan, Georgia, Kazakhstan, Kyrgyzstan, Russia, Uzbekistan
Europe	40	2: Finland, Poland*
Middle East	7	11: Bahrain, Egypt, Iran, Israel, Lebanon, Libya, Morocco, Oman, Saudi Arabia, Syria, UAE
TOTALS	155	40

*Signatories

been the impact of universalization in ameliorating the global landmine problem? How many State Parties were former users, stockpilers, producers, or traders in antipersonnel mines? How many are mine-affected countries with significant numbers of landmine casualties or survivors? By looking at universalization through this lens, a picture begins to emerge of progress in eradicating antipersonnel mines and addressing their impact and what the world might have looked like without the successful campaign for a legal ban.

According to the ICBL, at one time more than fifty countries were known to produce antipersonnel mines. Today thirty three of these, the vast majority of former producers, have joined the treaty and therefore are legally bound to never produce these weapons again. Another four non-States Party have declared an end to production (Egypt, Finland, Israel, and Poland). The ICBL identifies only thirteen countries that actually produce or *retain the capacity* to do so, and many of these states have not produced mines in years.[18] Arguably, the significant decrease in production can be partially attributed to the virtual elimination of demand through treaty universalization.

Some sixty States Parties are past users of antipersonnel mines. Today, antipersonnel mine use is not only absent among States Parties but ever more rare among those outside the treaty. The ICBL identifies just three governments using antipersonnel mines in 2005 and 2006: Burma (Myanmar), Nepal, and Russia.[19] About two dozen States Parties are past exporters of antipersonnel mines. Today, the export or trade of the weapon, as treaty actors are fond of saying "is virtually dead," as no country has acknowledged transfers in a decade, and many non-States Parties have official policies or laws against trade. Clearly, even for those outside the treaty, the stigmatization of the weapon through the successes of the mine ban movement has had an important impact.

Because antipersonnel mines were relatively inexpensive and in such widespread use during the twentieth century, many states held stockpiles—often quite large. As of September 2007, 145 States Parties had no stockpiles of antipersonnel mines and collectively had destroyed about forty million mines.[20] Another ten States Parties have an additional fifteen million mines left to destroy. Some of the biggest stockpilers from the past are now States Parties, including Italy, Turkmenistan, Ukraine, Belarus, and Turkey; fourteen States Parties held at least one million antipersonnel mines.

These are important results, particularly when one considers that many of the stockpiles destroyed or being destroyed are in the most mine-affected regions and countries in the world. However, the three biggest stockpilers by far historically are still not party: China (with an estimated 110 million mines), Russia (26.5 million), and the United States (10.4 million).[21]

Fifty-three States Parties have reported that they were mine-affected, of which seven have finished clearance operations.[22] Twenty-four States Parties report "significant numbers" of landmine survivors.[23] Not only do mines create a humanitarian hazard when left uncleared, they also make land unavailable for development. For these obvious reasons, States Parties have a treaty obligation to clear mined areas. They can seek assistance if needed, and the treaty obliges states "in a position to do so" to provide such help. The treaty not only spurs clearance by legally requiring it, the treaty also ensures that the clearance will be sustainable—unlike clearance that may occur in states outside the treaty which could be recontaminated with future mine use.

Treaty acceptance and UN bodies. Given their "major military power" status, and their position within the UN Security Council, questions are often asked about the status of the treaty among the Security Council's "Permanent Five." France and the United Kingdom, both of which ratified in 1998, are parties, while China, Russia, and the United States are among the staunchest holdout states, although it was not necessarily always so in the case of the United States.

Another way to analyze acceptance of the Mine Ban Treaty is to review the annual UN General Assembly resolution related to the treaty. Since 1997, the General Assembly each year has considered and voted upon a Mine Ban Treaty resolution that welcomes the treaty and calls for its universalization and full implementation.[24] While many UN General Assembly resolutions are adopted without vote (i.e., by consensus), every year a recorded vote is requested for this resolution; states can vote "in favor," "against," or "abstain."

There has been only one occasion when a state voted against the resolution, apparently mistakenly.[25] Seventeen states consistently abstain from the vote.

The abstentions are, for the most part, made by those most unlikely to join the treaty, at least in the foreseeable future.[26]

Some non-State Parties vote in favor of the resolution each year; twenty non-State Parties voted in favor of the resolution in 2006.[27] In many instances, this list indicates less about a state's position than does the list of abstainers. These votes are not indicators of *when* they might ratify or accede.

Non-States Parties that have consistently voted in its favor include some likely to accede in the next few years, but also others unlikely to join.[28] Of the eight states that have recently and suddenly voted "in favor," at least four are not likely to join in the near term.[29] The UN vote does not necessarily indicate a state's position on joining the treaty, and in a few cases it does not even necessarily signal a state's agreement with the Mine Ban Treaty's central goals. Nepal, for example, voted for the resolution at the same time its armed forces were using antipersonnel mines in its internal war.

Why have some states that are unlikely to accede in the foreseeable future voted in favor of the UN General Assembly resolution? For some, in particular those that have recently changed their vote, this is probably attributable to outreach and dialogue with the treaty's universalization actors. Voting for the annual resolution is often identified as one of the "interim steps" these states can do to show they are generally in support of the Mine Ban Treaty's humanitarian goals, or even their intention to "eventually" join. Taking this step is generally "safe" because it does not commit a state to actually do anything, either positive or negative. But it has a value to the "ban community" in that it helps to build the international norm against the weapon.

Reviewing the Ledger

Universalization has been placed at the center of treaty-related efforts, along with only a few other issues, in the belief that it will ensure the Mine Ban Treaty will truly have an impact in the real world. Have all the endeavors and innovations been worth it? Are the relatively few big "cities" being surrounded, and does this make a difference?

The collective campaign for treaty universalization has been a successful enterprise. In adding up the progress made to date, this is certainly borne out. The rapidity of ratifications meant the Mine Ban Treaty entered into force in less than half the time typical of multilateral treaties, and additional states continue to join each year. While more recently the rate of ratification/accession has declined to almost a trickle, this is perhaps not surprising and is comparable to rates experienced over the years by the 1994 Chemical Weapons Convention—a very successful example, with 182 member states (as of August 2007). In comparison to the 1980 Convention on Conventional Weapons, which has 102 States Parties (as of August 2007), ratification rates are very healthy.

The work on universalization has provided a sphere that sustains and further solidifies the partnership among states, NGOs, international and regional organizations, and civil society considered so unique to the Mine Ban Treaty. This collective focus has also resulted in universalization being relatively quickly transformed from a general "desire" into an officially recognized "core aim" of the treaty. The eight specific universalization "actions" agreed to at the Nairobi Summit provided a formal basis for action and for measuring progress at each subsequent annual Meeting of States Parties and the Second Review Conference in 2009.

The success of universalization is also demonstrated by the various states that have joined and the related impact on addressing the humanitarian impact of antipersonnel mines. The universalization net has been cast widely and has now captured the majority of former users, producers, exporters, and stockpilers of antipersonnel mines, as well as the majority of mine-affected countries and major donors. Universality is all but achieved in three of the major regions of the world, including those where mines have been used extensively in the past (Africa, Americas, and Europe). It is true that some of the major military powers remain outside the treaty, but virtually all of them have endorsed an eventual elimination of antipersonnel mines, and most are in *de facto* compliance with key provisions in the treaty.

Continued efforts are likely to lead to more States Parties. The Final Report adopted by the Sixth Meeting of States Parties in December 2005 included a document known as the "Zagreb Progress Report." It was "the first in a series of annual progress reports prepared by the States Parties in advance of the 2009 Second Review Conference" in order to "support the application of the *Nairobi Action Plan* by measuring progress made."[30] The universalization section of this document includes a (nonexhaustive) list of ten non-States Parties that "have indicated they could ratify or accede to the Convention in the near-term."[31] Of this list, Brunei Darussalam and Indonesia have subsequently completed ratification, and Kuwait and Iraq have acceded. In addition, three countries not even on the list formally accepted the treaty within a few months of the report being adopted (Cook Islands, Haiti, and Ukraine), and Montenegro joined shortly after it became independent.

It is notable that work in the Middle East region appears to be paying dividends. A few years ago, no states from the region were on anybody's list as a near-term State Party candidate. After a number of conferences, workshops, and missions in the region, the concentration of efforts seems to have planted some fertile seeds. Furthermore, fluidity in the political situation in some parts of the region has cracked open doors previously firmly shut to the Mine Ban Treaty. Thus, Bahrain, Oman, the United Arab Emirates, and even Lebanon are showing increased openness to the treaty. Jordan hosts the Eighth Meeting of States Parties in November 2007, which could provide further impetus in the region.

Beyond the Middle East, the greatest room for an increase in adherents is in Asia, where six or seven states are contenders to be officially inside the tent by the 2009 Review Conference. While past experience demonstrates that it is unlikely all of these would come on board within that time period, Indonesia's ratification in February 2007 could provide a "tipping point'" to greater inroads there. An important regional player, Indonesia is the most populous Muslim state, and its ratification means that the majority of the members of the Association of Southeast Asian Nations (ASEAN) are now members, potentially leading the way for the Mine Ban Treaty to be included as an agenda item at its meetings.

The possibilities for increased universalization in the CIS region, on the other hand, remain much murkier, with the positions and flexibility of some of those states unclear.

True universality is unlikely. Despite the successes, a number of "hard-liners" remain unlikely to join in the foreseeable future. Full universalization of the Mine Ban Treaty is highly unlikely at any point. The hard-liners all stockpile antipersonnel mines and reserve the right to use them in the future. Some continue to use mines regularly and to produce the weapon. Their stated rationales for not joining the treaty vary and are not always clear or even logical, particularly in the face of repeatedly confirmed arguments against the military utility of antipersonnel mines.

The end of the antipersonnel mine could come through continued stigmatization, including the "surrounding/isolating" processes of continued universalization. But there is always the possibility that a small group of states will not see themselves as "rogues" or out of step with modern times, but instead as part of a small, elite group that retains exclusive authority for these weapons that others should not have or use (in the same way nuclear weapons states may feel about their right to retain nuclear weapons).

It is perhaps more likely that antipersonnel mines will pass into the annals of history when they are considered by all as obsolete weapons that are no longer militarily useful, or when stockpiles become an expensive maintenance burden where the effort and costs outweigh any perceived need to keep them.

The number of States Parties consistently playing an active role has not increased much. While participation in the Universalization Contact Group meetings has grown, those making sustained and ongoing efforts have "plateaued." Arguably, those States Parties that have in the past consistently worked on a multitude of universalization efforts may have largely exhausted their sphere of influence; that is, non-States Parties for which they would have significant influence have already been engaged and have either joined or made their position clear. Some of those who have long played a leadership role on universalization have turned their focus at least in part to encouraging and offering support to other States Parties to take leading roles as "regional facilitators." To date, it seems this has only resulted in a few new actors, not all of which exercise strong influence with their neighbors or within their regional organizations. In some cases, a State Party has taken on a significant universalization project, but it turns out to be driven by one or two individuals within a ministry and once they have moved on, the effort has dried up.

In addition to regional approaches, two other areas that could use input by new actors are efforts at sustained military-to-military dialogue and those by mine action donors. Very few States Parties have participated meaningfully in military dialogue, and only one State Party, Canada, has placed any sustained and significant resources into it. Taking into account the profiles of many of those states yet to join, it is clear any door-opening will require engagement of the militaries and the ministries of defense and by States Parties with whom those institutions have particular relationships. Similarly, others could be influenced by frank approaches from donor states to make it clear why greater resources typically flow to States Parties.

Universalization may now detract from other important issues. At this stage of the treaty's life, it is reasonable to question whether universalization should receive the same level of prioritization and coordinated effort as it has up to now, particularly in light of the significant achievements already made in universalization. Other aspects of the treaty—especially issues associated with the ten-year mine clearance deadlines for many states, as well as ways to implement the more amorphous victim assistance requirements—have not benefited from similar coordination and collective energy over the years. It appears the collective attention of the States Parties may be starting to turn this way. With 155 States Parties, and clearance deadlines looming, the time is ripe for this reordering of the work.

Each individual universalization actor, be it a state or nongovernmental entity, should ask themselves if it makes sense to pay greater attention to other issues and how much added value they can provide to other areas of concern. And collectively, it should be determined if universalization efforts can be carried out more efficiently, or by fewer actors and using fewer vehicles, all more strategically chosen.

Conclusion

Clearly, universalization cannot be abandoned. The remaining non-States Parties present challenges to the goal of eradicating antipersonnel mines and their humanitarian impact. There are still important states that can be brought on board completely, and other states that can be convinced to take interim steps toward the treaty, and yet other states where there is a need to ensure no backward slippage even further away from the treaty.

One of the most useful developments would be for the States Parties that have the most influence with the remaining non-States Parties, regionally or through military and aid relationships, to play a more active and focused role in promoting universalization. Examples could include a joint approach by States Parties Kuwait and Qatar to the other four members of the Gulf Cooperation Council; intense efforts by the UK with Nepal, along with other donors to this country; a concerted and explicitly coordinated endeavor by all NATO members (minus the United States) to bring pressure to bear on signatory Poland; cooperative efforts by Jordan, Iraq, Tunisia, and Yemen toward Lebanon and even Egypt and Syria; and, coordinated steps by southeast Asian States Parties toward Laos, and even Singapore and Vietnam.

A challenge will be balancing the energy going into universalization efforts with the need to focus more on other issues coming to the fore. Ultimately, though, Mine Ban Treaty actors need to decide when they can declare victory regarding universalization. Even the most creative and dedicated actions of the Mine Ban Treaty's universalization actors are not going to bring all of the remaining holdout states into the treaty.

But it is already clear, in light of the success of the Mine Ban Treaty's universalization enterprise, that there are lessons to be learned and methods, actions, and tools that can be applied in other treaty forums. This has already occurred to some extent with respect to the Chemical Weapons Convention and the Convention on Conventional Weapons. It would be worthwhile to find a way to exchange lessons more systematically with other regimes. After all, the overall goal is the same: to spread greater and greater zones for human security across the world, leaving behind the very minimum of isolated "unsafe cities."

Notes

1. This chapter focuses on the status of the Mine Ban Treaty for states. The term "universalization" has usually been reserved to refer to a treaty's acceptance among states. The engagement of nonstate armed actors in the antipersonnel mine ban is addressed by Yeshua Moser-Puangsuwan in chapter 10.

2. Fourth Meeting of the States Parties to the Convention on the Prohibition of the Use, Stockpiling, Production, and Transfer of Anti-Personnel Mines and on Their Destruction, "Final Report," Geneva, September 16–20, 2002, APLC/MSP.4/2002/1, September 27, 2002.

3. This discussion of universalization focuses on the individual actions of states in ratifying or acceding to the treaty. The question of whether the treaty may be considered part of customary international law is addressed by Peter Herby and Kathleen Lawand in chapter 12.

4. For a discussion of signature, ratification, and entry into force, see Stuart Maslen, *Commentaries on Arms Control Treaties Volume I: The Convention on the Prohibition of the Use, Stockpiling, Production, and Transfer of Anti-Personnel Mines and on their Destruction* (Oxford: Oxford University Press, 2004), pp. 285–296.

5. For states joining the treaty after March 1, 1999, the agreement takes legal effect "on the first day of the sixth month" after the state's ratification or accession. In this chapter, states are described as States Parties as soon as they have deposited their instrument of ratification/accession.

6. The preamble states, "Emphasizing the desirability of attracting the adherence of all States to this Convention, and determined to work strenuously towards the promotion of its universalization in all relevant fora. . . . "

7. Stuart Maslen, *Commentaries on Arms Control Treaties Volume I*, p. 53.

8. See Maxwell A. Cameron, Robert J. Lawson, and Brian W. Tomlin (eds.), *To Walk Without Fear: The Global Movement to Ban Landmines* (Toronto: Oxford University Press, 1998); International Committee of the Red Cross, "Progress towards a Ban on Anti-Personnel Landmines: Measures by Countries and Organizations," Geneva, January 17, 1997.

9. Maxwell A. Cameron, "Global Civil Society and the Ottawa Process: Lessons from the Movement to Ban Anti-Personnel Landmines," in Andrew Cooper, John English, and Ramesh Thakur (eds.), *Enhancing Global Governance: Towards a New Diplomacy* (New York: United Nations University Press, 2002).

10. Stuart Maslen, *Commentaries on Arms Control Treaties Volume I*, Section 0.52, p. 28. The comparison to the 1980 Convention on Conventional Weapons (CCW) is especially relevant because CCW's Protocol II restricts the use of landmines.

11. Canada first brought the group together during the May 2000 meetings of the intersessional Standing Committees. The Universalization Contact Group was recognized and endorsed in the President's Action Program that emerged from the Second Meeting of States Parties in September 2000.

12. First Review Conference of the States Parties to the Convention on the Prohibition of the Use, Stockpiling, Production, and Transfer of Anti-Personnel Mines and On Their Destruction, "Final Report: Part II. Review of the operation of the status of the Convention Prohibition of the Use, Stockpiling, Production, and Transfer of Anti-Personnel Mines and on Their Destruction: 1999–2004," Nairobi, November 29–December 3, 2004, APLC/CONF/2004/5, February 9, 2005, p. 14, para. 15.

13. Accession to the treaty took place prior to Montenegro's referendum and decision to separate from Serbia. Serbia remained a State Party, and Montenegro joined on October 23, 2006.

14. Seminar on Universalization and Implementation of the Ottawa Convention in Africa, *Operational Conclusions and General Report*, February 16, 2001.

15. The action points commit States Parties to: (1) Call on those states that have not yet done so to accede; (2) or ratify as soon as possible; (3) Prioritize universalization challenges presented by states which "warrant special concern" (those that continue to use, produce, or possess large stockpiles of antipersonnel mines); (4) Accord particular importance to promoting adherence in regions where the level of acceptance of the treaty remains low; (5) Take all opportunities to promote universalization and adherence pending accession, including in bilateral contacts, military-to-military dialogue, peace processes, national parliaments, and the media; (6) Actively promote adherence in all relevant multilateral fora; (7) Condemn and take appropriate steps to end the use, stockpiling, production, and transfer of antipersonnel mines by armed non-state actors; (8) Encourage and support involvement and active cooperation in these universalization efforts by all relevant partners. First Review Conference of the States Parties to the Convention on the Prohibition of the Use, Stockpiling, Production, and Transfer of Anti-Personnel Mines and on Their Destruction, "Final Reports: Part III. Ending the suffering caused by anti-personnel mines: Nairobi Action Plan 2005–2009," Nairobi, November 29–December 3, 2004, APLC/CONF/2004/5, February 9, 2005, p. 95.

16. The twenty-four includes Montenegro, which technically deposited an instrument of "succession" on October 23, 2006, after it separated from Serbia and Montenegro. The other most recent accessions include Iraq (August 15, 2007) and Kuwait (July 30, 2007). The most recent ratifications include Indonesia (February 20, 2007).

17. For the purpose of this discussion, a European state is an EU Member State, an EU candidate country, or "other European country," according to the official website of the European Union, except for CIS member states Belarus, Moldova, Russia, and Ukraine. See http://europa.eu.int/abc/governments/index_en.htm.

18. International Campaign to Ban Landmines (ICBL), *Landmine Monitor Report 2006* (Ottawa: Mines Action Canada, 2006), p. 10.

19. ICBL, *Landmine Monitor Report 2006*, p. 7.

20. These figures are updated from *Landmine Monitor Report 2006*, p. 12. Of the 143, a total of eighty destroyed stockpiles, and sixty-three declared never possessing stocks.

21. ICBL, *Landmine Monitor Report 2006*, p. 13.

22. Geneva International Centre for Humanitarian Demining, "Background/Status of the Convention," http://www.gichd.ch/742.0.html.

23. ICBL, *Landmine Monitor Report 2006*, p. 1.

24. Since the 1999 entry-into-force of the treaty, the resolution has been known as "Implementation of the Convention on the Prohibition of the Use, Stockpiling, Production, and Transfer of Anti-personnel Mines and on Their Destruction."

25. Lebanon in 1999; the representative of Lebanon subsequently advised the Secretariat that Lebanon had intended to abstain, rather than vote against.

26. In 2006, the seventeen states that abstained were: Burma (Myanmar), Cuba, Egypt, India, Iran, Israel, Kazakhstan, Kyrgyzstan, Lebanon, Libya, Pakistan, Republic of Korea, Russia, Syria, the United States, Uzbekistan, and Vietnam. Two other non-States

Parties usually do not have a recorded vote on the resolution but are also among those unlikely to join in the foreseeable future: North Korea and Saudi Arabia.

27. The twenty non-States Parties were: Armenia, Azerbaijan, Bahrain, China, Finland, Georgia, Indonesia (which has since ratified), Iraq (which has since acceded), Kuwait (which has since acceded), Marshall Islands, Micronesia, Mongolia, Morocco, Oman, Palau, Poland, Singapore, Sri Lanka, Tonga, and the United Arab Emirates. Three non-States Parties that have voted for the resolution in the past were absent in 2006: Nepal, Somalia, and Tuvalu.

28. Those likely include Bahrain, Marshall Islands, Micronesia, Oman, Palau, Tonga, and the United Arab Emirates. Those unlikely are Armenia, Azerbaijan, China, Finland, Morocco, and Singapore. Others are unclear. In the case of Finland, in 2004 the government announced that instead of joining in 2006, it would put off accession until 2012.

29. Eight non-States Parties voted in favor of the resolution for the first time in 2004, 2005, or 2006: Azerbaijan, China, Iraq (subsequently acceded), Micronesia, Morocco, Somalia, Sri Lanka, and Tuvalu. It is unlikely that Azerbaijan, China, Morocco, or Sri Lanka will join the Mine Ban Treaty soon.

30. Sixth Meeting of the States Parties to the Convention on the Prohibition of the Use, Stockpiling, Production, and Transfer of Anti-Personnel Mines and on Their Destruction, "Final Report: Part II. Achieving the Aims of the Nairobi Action Plan: the Zagreb Progress Report," Zagreb, November 28–December 2, 2005, APLC/MSP.6/2005/5, April 5, 2006. The subsequent "Geneva Progress Report" by the Seventh Meeting of States Parties did not update this list, but reiterated the need for States Parties to implement the eight universalization actions contained in the Nairobi Action Plan. Seventh Meeting of the States Parties to the Convention on the Prohibition of the Use, Stockpiling, Production, and Transfer of Anti-Personnel Mines and on Their Destruction, "Final Report: Part II. Achieving the Aims of the Nairobi Action Plan: The Geneva Progress Report," Geneva, September 18–22, 2006, APLC/MSP.7/2006/5, January 17, 2007.

31. Bahrain, Brunei, Indonesia, Iraq, Kuwait, Micronesia, Oman, Poland, Somalia, and United Arab Emirates.

6

An Emphasis on Action: The Mine Ban Treaty's Implementation Mechanisms

Kerry Brinkert

MANY FAMILIAR WITH THE MINE BAN TREATY when it was adopted on September 18, 1997, might not recognize it now. Certainly the destruction of stockpiled antipersonnel mines and the clearance of mined areas were to be expected given treaty obligations. What would be unrecognizable, however, is the solid foundation of implementation mechanisms established since the treaty took effect on March 1, 1999. These include a flexible committee system, a unique support unit, and a set of informal structures to facilitate implementation. Largely unforeseen in 1997, these mechanisms are now viewed as essential to the treaty's functioning.

This chapter describes the mechanisms and how and why they came into being. The treaty's ambitious set of positive obligations and its cooperation and assistance provisions meant that a degree of support, follow-up, and monitoring was required to ensure success. However, the provisions contained within the treaty itself would not have been enough. Due to the applied commitment and creativity of states and nongovernmental organizations (NGOs), the Mine Ban Treaty now rests on a solid foundation of implementation machinery.

This chapter also examines the limitations of the implementation mechanisms and how their emergence has presented challenges to some key actors. Finally, it discusses how these out-of-the-ordinary mechanisms may have applicability to other treaties and issues.

Development of Mine Ban Treaty Support Mechanisms

The Mine Ban Treaty does not provide for a formal secretariat. This was a deliberate choice by those negotiating the treaty. According to one official central to the negotiations, "There were always sidebar discussions on implementation mechanisms" and "the issue of a secretariat came up in the context of compliance."[1] In the end, though, "it was argued that resources should be devoted to mine clearance and victim assistance rather than to set up new structures."[2] There was an additional concern that "the authority of States Parties might have been compromised by a separate institution capable of taking substantive decisions relating to the Convention."[3]

The lack of a secretariat did not prevent intensive discussions on the practicalities of implementation. At the same time as the treaty was opened for signature in Ottawa on December 3–4, 1997, Canada's Minister of Foreign Affairs Lloyd Axworthy convened a forum where he noted that "the Convention will be meaningless unless we implement it" and "that the challenges are clear: the universalization and entry into force of the Convention; the destruction of stockpiles; the clearing of mined areas; and the care, rehabilitation and reintegration of mine victims."[4] He was asserting that the treaty provided a framework for the emerging concept of *mine action.*

Three months later Axworthy convened a workshop to discuss a coordinated international effort to achieve the treaty's aims. These Ottawa gatherings became critical stepping-stones in the development of initiatives such as the Landmine Impact Survey (an important tool for many States Parties to define a landmine problem in terms of scale, type, location, hazard, and social/economic impacts) and the ICBL's Landmine Monitor (an indispensable means of NGO verification of states' efforts to implement the treaty).

In early 1998, the Quaker United Nations Office (QUNO) convened a Post-Ottawa Geneva Consultation Group to promote the treaty. Participants included representatives of Austria, Belgium, Canada, Ireland, Mexico, the Netherlands, New Zealand, Norway, the Philippines, South Africa, and Switzerland, as well as the ICBL, various ICBL member organizations, and the International Committee of the Red Cross (ICRC). In essence, it was a reconstituted Ottawa Process *core group*—the group of states central to the development of the treaty.

The group met regularly, focusing at first on ways to ensure the treaty's fastest possible entry into force. By August 1998, it was clear that it could happen in the first half of 1999, and thoughts turned toward a possible First Meeting of States Parties to the treaty. On September 16, 1998, Burkina Faso became the fortieth state to ratify the treaty, triggering entry into force on March 1, 1999.[5]

At that time there was no formal process to prepare for a Meeting of States Parties, which under Article 11 needed to be convened within one year. The Geneva Group sought to fill this void, demonstrating the same deep care for the treaty's functioning as individual group members did for the Ottawa Process that led to its establishment. Canada proposed to Mozambique—one of the first severely mine-affected to join the treaty—that it host the First Meeting of States Parties in Maputo. Mozambique agreed, and the meeting was held in May 1999. The symbolism of that meeting taking place in a mine-affected country, with the plenary session ultimately taking place in a giant tent, was powerful and indicative of the Ottawa Process culture.

The Geneva Group discussed other practical matters. As early as August 1998 it discussed the need to establish a transparency-reporting format. Seven months later it debated the establishment of the first implementation support mechanism: intersessional working groups. Robert Lawson of Canada and Steffen Kongstad of Norway, both veterans of the Ottawa Process, along with Tom Markram and Bennie Lombard from South Africa were key to the development of this idea.[6] During the First Meeting of State Parties, the idea became reality when States Parties established the Intersessional Work Programme, with "Standing Committees" which were to meet informally between the formal annual meetings of the States Parties.[7]

According to Lawson, the Intersessional Work Programme did not emerge in isolation but "flowed from the March 1998 Ottawa workshop's focus on the Convention as a framework for mine action."[8] It reflected an effort both to avoid the temptation for work to be carried out in isolated "pillars" and also to capture the synergies of a community working together to achieve a common purpose.

Resistance to such an approach did exist, for instance, within parts of the United Nations system and NGO community who felt that they had a mandate for mine action and that the treaty was a political matter that concerned only a ban on antipersonnel mines.[9] By providing an umbrella for taking practical steps to end the suffering caused by antipersonnel mines, the Intersessional Work Programme affirmed the idea that the treaty is a framework for mine action. In addition, it expanded the notion of a core group of states maintaining ownership and primary responsibility for treaty operations. If the treaty negotiators had established a traditional secretariat in 1997, the impetus for a state-led initiative may have been removed.

The Intersessional Work Programme involves four Standing Committees which focus on key elements of treaty implementation: the General Status and Operation of the Convention; Stockpile Destruction; Mine Clearance, Mine Risk Education, and Mine Action Technologies; and Victim Assistance and Socio-Economic Reintegration. Each is cochaired by two States Parties and assisted by two more serving as corapporteurs. At each Meeting of States Parties, the corapporteurs become the new cochairs and States Parties select new corapporteurs. States Parties also select a president each year with over-arching responsibility for the Convention during the intersessional period.

Through this Standing Committee structure, eight States Parties accept re-sponsibility each year to advance an aspect of the implementation process, and eight more assure a degree of continuity by serving as corapporteurs (and cochairs in waiting). In selecting cochairs and corapportuers, States Parties have traditionally sought a balance of mine-affected countries and donor countries, as well as a regional balance. In essence, the Intersessional Work Programme has institutionalized perhaps not *the* core group, but rather *a* core group of concerned States Parties. More importantly, it has allowed a large number of states to make a contribution. From its inception until 2007, forty-five States Parties have served as cochairs or corapporteurs. By sharing re-sponsibility so widely, the committee structure has contributed to avoiding the North-South and regional divisions that are prominent in other multilat-eral forums.

During the first intersessional period in 1999–2000, the Standing Commit-tees met independently with the cochairs working in isolation in preparing programs for their meetings. Coordination was limited and what did exist was largely led by the ICBL. The main vehicle for NGO-led coordination of what in essence is a state activity became known as the *20+2* gatherings of cochairs and corapporteurs, along with a few other invitees, convened on the eve of Standing Committee meetings by Susan B. Walker, the ICBL's Geneva-based representative.[10] The purpose was "to exchange views and have a discussion on the process to implement an intersessional work program between the an-nual Meetings of States Parties."[11]

ICBL representatives led substantive discussions and prepared meeting summaries, including understandings regarding the roles and responsibilities of cochairs and corapporteurs. The ICBL also helped many cochairs and corapporteurs prepare for Standing Committee meetings, write reports, and do follow-up actions. This secretariat-type of assistance extended to the ICBL developing contact lists and chasing down individuals from States Parties who had accepted positions of responsibility but had not translated this commit-ment into action. The ICBL viewed this role as important in part because it was helping "to make the treaty work," but also because it gave the ICBL ex-tensive input into substantive matters—and was seen as part of the spirit of partnership and cooperation that forms the cornerstone of the Mine Ban Treaty.

In addition to NGO-led informal coordination, in 1999–2000 the Canadian and South African cochairs of the Standing Committee on the General Status and Operation of the Convention periodically convened informal dinner meetings of the initial cochairs to discuss practical matters that had not been considered when the Intersessional Work Programme was established. These decidedly informal gatherings, consistent with the work style of the Ottawa Process, both reinforced a sense of group ownership and led to the understanding that there was a need to more systematically address the relationship between the more informal intersessionals and the treaty-mandated Meetings of States Parties.

At the Second Meeting of States Parties in 2000, the States Parties agreed that the Standing Committees would meet sequentially each year during two one-week sessions in Geneva. In addition, they established a Coordinating Committee of Co-Chairs, chaired by the treaty's president, with a mandate "to coordinate matters relating to and flowing from the work of the Standing Committees with the work of the Meetings of the States Parties."[12] While coordination on basic organizational issues improved, the president and cochairs received only ad hoc support from committed ministries of foreign affairs, permanent missions in Geneva, the ICBL, or other NGOs. However, the States Parties had no central point of contact or official information source.

Discussions continued with a group of representatives both of States Parties and organizations that had been central in the effort to establish the treaty who periodically met informally to talk about its implementation. These included some but not all of the actors involved in the original Post-Ottawa Geneva Consultation Group. Participating individuals personally cared deeply about the treaty's success and were concerned about the sustainability of implementation efforts, particularly the ongoing viability of the Intersessional Work Programme. Representatives of some mine-affected States Parties expressed the need for support to enable delegations like theirs to have an enhanced role in the work of the treaty. A consensus emerged in this group that a secretariat in the traditional sense was still not necessary, but some form of permanent substantive and logistical support was desirable.

Establishment of the Implementation Support Unit

In early 2001, Steffen Kongstad of Norway and Tom Markram of South Africa began to discuss a way forward with the Director and the President of the Geneva International Centre for Humanitarian Demining (GICHD). Their interest, and that of others such as Gustavo Laurie of Peru and Cecilia Sanchez of Nicaragua, in establishing a sustainable implementation support mechanism coincided with GICHD's desire to become more actively engaged in the work of the treaty. Since 1999, this organization established by the government of

Switzerland had already played a valuable role by providing logistical support to and a venue for the Intersessional Work Programme. However, as the GICHD's director at the time, Martin Dahinden, recalls reporting to his governing board on December 19, 2000, "the GICHD was interested in becoming a less exclusively administrative role and having a more comprehensive support role."[13]

In May 2001, Laurie presented a discussion paper on the issue to the Standing Committee on the General Status and Operation of the Convention. He noted that during the first two years since entry into force, "a handful of States, individual diplomats and personalities, host countries and the ICBL and GICHD have worked closely and tirelessly . . . to fulfill the functions a proper secretariat or organization would have undertaken to ensure the arrangements for Meetings of the States Parties and the implementation of the Convention."[14] He added that "governments change, budgets get new priorities, people are transferred and time marches on" and that it was difficult for States Parties like his, without permanent support, to carry out the responsibilities.

Laurie's paper suggested that a unit could be established within GICHD to support the Intersessional Work Programme and Meetings of the States Parties. The GICHD's role in establishing such a unique structure was logical at the time given the GICHD's support to the Intersessional Work Programme and that the GICHD is "an independent centre of excellence on mine action."[15] The paper formed the basis for a proposal to create an Implementation Support Unit, housed at GICHD.

As one might expect with such an unprecedented proposal, several States Parties raised questions and concerns about the Implementation Support Unit (ISU). Some expressed the need for clear accountability. Brazil, for instance, called for the Coordinating Committee to report frequently on the activities of the ISU.[16] Croatia raised the matter of the scope of responsibilities, indicating its understanding that the ISU would not be "entrusted with politically delicate matters" nor "able to make decisions independent of those made by States Parties themselves."[17] Some wondered whether the ISU would serve the interests of a few States Parties or the interests of all. The ICBL, while strongly supporting the proposal, argued that "the ISU mandate had to be clear, independent and answerable to the States Parties (e.g., not just Switzerland since the ISU would be in the GICHD)."[18] In addition, States Parties raised concerns about costs and who would pay for them.

At the Third Meeting of States Parties in Managua, Nicaragua in September 2001, States Parties agreed to mandate GICHD to establish the Implementation Support Unit. The ISU began its operations on January 14, 2002. The ISU is special because its existence is the result of a decision by the parties to the

Mine Ban Treaty. While it is technically part of GICHD, the GICHD's director is not responsible to GICHD's governing body for the unit's functioning. Rather, as is noted in the unit's foundation document, "the Director of the GICHD (is) accountable to the States Parties for the work of the ISU and will submit an annual report on its functioning."[19]

The ISU is also a unique part of GICHD in terms of its funding arrangements. The ISU's mandate indicates that a fund for voluntary contributions will be opened, that an annual budget will be established by mutual agreement between the Coordinating Committee and the GICHD, and, most significantly, that "States Parties will endeavor to assure the necessary financial resources for its functioning."[20] Since the establishment of the ISU Voluntary Trust Fund in 2001, more that thirty-five States Parties have contributed to it.[21]

Informal Implementation Mechanisms

A variety of other informal and voluntary mechanisms have emerged to promote implementation of the treaty. The first of these was the Sponsorship Programme, formed in July 2000 after lessons derived from the first year of the Intersessional Work Programme. Some countries had provided funds to facilitate the participation by others (e.g., states' representatives and NGO speakers) in Standing Committee meetings held in 1999 and 2000, but this ad hoc, uncoordinated approach did not meaningfully address barriers to participation; it also favored the entrepreneurial individuals who were adept at acquiring donor financing, some of whom did not actually represent a state or an NGO.

To address these concerns, an equally entrepreneurial representative of Canada, Peter Sagar, brought interested donors together to pool their resources and apply a uniform and strategic approach to sponsorship. This original group included Belgium, Canada, the Netherlands, Norway, Sweden, and the United Kingdom. It sponsored twenty representatives of thirteen states to attend the Second Meeting of States Parties in September 2000. By 2006, the donors' group had grown to sixteen, and sponsorship was regularly provided to bring forty to sixty delegates to each meeting. Just as the Intersessional Work Programme has benefited from administrative and logistical support provided at no cost to States Parties as a whole by GICHD, so has the Sponsorship Programme.

The Sponsorship Programme evolved in a complementary fashion to the Standing Committee meetings themselves. In the early days, these meetings were largely dominated by donor states, the UN, and western NGOs. Progressively, this shifted to an environment conducive for States Parties challenged by mine clearance and stockpile destruction obligations and victim assistance responsibilities to raise their voices. The Sponsorship Programme's donors began to refine their efforts by sponsoring delegates who were expected to provide updates on aspects of implementation rather than merely attend the meetings.

Another informal mechanism established in 2000—the Universalization Contact Group—was the brainchild of another Canadian, Bob Lawson, who wanted to convert into action one of the easiest throwaway lines in any multilateral forum, that "*we* must universalize the Convention." To Lawson, the "we" had to be specific and there had to be a deliberate strategy to make progress toward universal acceptance of the treaty. Certainly universalization efforts, principally led by Canada, the ICBL, and the ICRC, had been undertaken ever since the treaty was adopted in 1997. What Lawson sought to achieve, though, was a more regular interaction of all interested partners to coordinate efforts, develop systematic approaches to particular country cases, and support regional universalization leaders.

To achieve this, Canada invited a group to an initial gathering held on the margins of the May 2000 meetings of the Standing Committees. A follow-up meeting was held in September 2000 on the margins of the Second Meeting of States Parties. Participants in these initial meetings included representatives of Argentina, Australia, Belgium, Canada, Hungary, the Netherlands, Nicaragua, Norway, Slovakia, South Africa, Switzerland, the United Kingdom, the ICBL, and the ICRC. The idea that these informal meetings of the Universalization Contact Group should continue regularly was noted in the President's Action Program at the Second Meeting of States Parties.

The seed was planted for similar initiatives in other areas. Before the Third Meeting of States Parties, Jean Lint of Belgium brought together actors interested in promoting full compliance with the treaty's Article 7 transparency reporting obligations. Lint's initiative resulted in a second contact group—the Article 7 Contact Group—being recognized by the meeting.

The September 2002 Fourth Meeting of States Parties provided the launching pad for Norway to establish a third contact group. In a paper that Norway's Knut Langeland presented to this meeting, it was noted that "although the Convention is functioning well, we are still far from fully meeting its humanitarian objectives," and more resources and funding are required to fulfill mine clearance and victim assistance obligations.[22] Norway proposed that "it might be useful to set up an informal contact group consisting of donor countries, mine-affected countries, multilateral development institutions, NGOs, and the private sector."[23] The Resource Mobilization Contact Group was therefore born and, like its sister contact groups, has met regularly ever since its establishment.

Between 1999 and 2001, another informal group also met periodically to discuss ways to overcome challenges related to meeting stockpile destruction obligations. The Romano Group, named after a modest Italian eatery in Geneva where the group met, was initiated by Laszlo Deak of Hungary, one of the first cochairs of the Standing Committee on Stockpile Destruction, with the support of Canada's Ambassador for Mine Action, Daniel Livermore. This group differed from the others in that its membership was small and by invitation, and that it terminated its efforts after the work of the Standing Committee had ensured that sufficient attention was being given to the stockpile destruction obligations.

Explaining the Establishment of the Convention's Implementation Machinery

What led to this solid foundation of implementation mechanisms, both formal and informal? In part, the treaty itself provides the basis for their development, with its requirements for mine action and the emphasis on *action*. To logical-minded principals of the Ottawa Process such as Steffen Kongstad, it was obvious that "some kind of implementation support was needed to . . . address all the practical needs that the fairly concrete and extensive demands of the Convention required."[24] Moreover, the treaty formally in Article 6 places an emphasis on cooperation and assistance.[25]

However, it is unlikely that anything beyond treaty text would exist if it were not for a large dose of individual action. Perhaps not coincidentally, many of the individuals involved in the Ottawa Process since the beginning were central to the establishment of implementation machinery after its entry into force. For instance, Norway's Kongstad, South Africa's Markram, and Canada's Lawson were central in driving the Ottawa Process forward. Following the treaty's adoption, these individuals remained central figures driving the establishment of the Intersessional Work Programme, the Coordinating Committee, the Implementation Support Unit, and various informal mechanisms.

NGO representatives who also transcended the periods before and after the adoption of the treaty played a key role as well. David Atwood of QUNO and Susan B. Walker of the ICBL were at the forefront of efforts to advance implementation efforts. After entry into force, Atwood and Walker ensured a continuation of informal networks of individuals committed to banning antipersonnel mines and to taking action to implement the treaty. These informal processes led to concrete initiatives for establishing formal implementation processes and helped maintain the Ottawa Process work culture. The formally adopted implementation machinery in turn both advanced implementation and provided a basis for further transmitting accepted understandings of the landmine problem, the solution to it, and methods of work.

A concrete example concerns Atwood, who maximized the niche role of QUNO to bring together diverse actors for informal discussion. That forum provided Ottawa Process veterans like Kongstad, Markram, and Lawson with a setting to advance ideas on formally established implementation machinery. This formal machinery in turn provided the opportunity for post-Ottawa Process state representatives like Laurie, Lint, and Sanchez to learn how the Ottawa Process had worked and take action in their own right.[26] Their actions were then central to establishment of additional implementation machinery, such as the Implementation Support Unit and the Article 7 Contact Group.

Challenges and Limitations

States Parties have been well served by the implementation mechanisms described above. In contrast to other international treaties, a wide range of actors truly is involved in the implementation process and the general operations of the treaty. The large number of States Parties to this demanding treaty has strongly countered conventional wisdom that suggests the more stringent a legal instrument, the more difficult it is to attract adherents.

When issues have emerged, the combination of formal and informal activities at the root of the treaty's processes has resulted in practical minded rather than politically charged responses. However, the implementation machinery has its limitations, is far from perfect, and has to some degree challenged actors involved in treaty implementation.

Mechanisms such as the Intersessional Work Programme and contact groups have enabled an increased number of representatives of states and organizations to be engaged in an existing "mine ban culture," which in turn could result in their acceptance of that culture. However, it is also normal that newcomers to a group affect the culture. While the aim of the first generation of the treaty's leadership may have been to broaden ownership and responsibility for treaty operations, each new actor to the fold naturally changes the character and dynamics of working relationships. While it is undoubtedly beneficial that states from all regions are engaged in the implementation process, the participation by an increasing number of states from regions where diplomacy is conducted in a more traditional manner has challenged or surprised individuals who have a deep grounding in the Ottawa Process and its ways of doing business.

For instance, in 2000 Canada launched a dialogue on actions that would be needed to use the compliance mechanisms contained in Article 8 of the treaty. This article provides for States Parties to authorize fact-finding missions of qualified experts to assist in clarifying concerns about compliance. In the spirit of the practical-minded approach to the Ottawa Process, Canada sought to better understand matters, such as what might constitute a qualified expert, equipment requirements, logistical issues, and standard operating procedures.[27] However, since the treaty community had grown to include many states that are typically adverse to any form of intrusive compliance mechanism, it became clear that a practical approach to "operationalizing" Article 8 was not something desired by many.

Of course, alterations of common understandings and methods of work can have positive results. The contributions of post-Ottawa Process actors such as Cecilia Sanchez, Gustavo Laurie, Jean Lint, and Peter Sagar were key to the call in 2002 for intersessional work "to focus with greater clarity on those areas most directly related to the core humanitarian objectives of the Convention," including destruction of stockpiled antipersonnel mines, clearing areas containing antipersonnel mines, assisting the victims, and ensuring universal acceptance of the treaty.[28] Some, especially in the ICBL and ICRC, expressed concern that this could be used as a way of avoiding controversial matters left unresolved from the treaty's negotiations, such as what mines are prohibited by the treaty's definitions. However, most agree that this approach has been beneficial in keeping in the forefront what is most important to the success of the Mine Ban Treaty, while still permitting space for dialogue on issues of interpretation.

The institutionalization and professionalization of implementation machinery also challenged some of the first generation of leaders. As noted, the ICBL played an invaluable role in supporting States Parties during the first years of the Intersessional Work Programme. In doing so, however, it was subsidizing a state responsibility. The ICBL strongly supported the establishment of the ISU as necessary to the successful implementation of the treaty, but its work meant a displacement of the informal support function provided in Geneva by the ICBL and a need to reorient its activities there.

The expanding circle of those working on implementation also affected the role of the UN. According to some, "parts of the UN were clearly against the whole [Ottawa] process since October 1996."[29] This ambivalence and a commensurate ambivalence on the part of key States Parties about the UN playing a central role in the work of the treaty, lingered for at least three years after its entry into force. Over time, as individuals in the UN changed, particularly when Martin Barber was appointed Director of the UN Mine Action Service (UNMAS) and with more states becoming actively involved in the implementation process, there were increased efforts by and for the UN to be engaged.

Increased UN involvement has had its pros and cons. Barber brought an insistence that the UN unambiguously stand behind the treaty, but the UN understanding of what that meant differed from that of others. In particular, perhaps because not all UN members are party to the treaty, UN involvement has been characterized by a generic call for support for mine action at the expense of a clear emphasis on treaty implementation.

It is problematic that the UN's conception of mine action turns on its head the notion of the Mine Ban Treaty as a framework for mine action. The UN has defined mine action itself as the framework, an aspect of which concerns the treaty. For example, while the Intersessional Work Programme was intended to bring to life the treaty as a mine action framework, in part by avoiding work proceeding in discrete pillars, the UN explicitly defined pillars and sought to place the treaty in one of these, oddly labeled as advocacy.

It is also problematic for treaty implementation that the UN has occasionally lost sight of the end point. That is, Article 5, by calling for "the destruction of all anti-personnel mines in mined areas under [a State Party's] jurisdiction or control," defines an unambiguous end point. However, through its 2004 Completion Initiative in which it explicitly sought to "stay away from a strict Article 5 obligation," the UN deceptively defined something as completion that was short of the legal obligation freely accepted by three-quarters of the UN's member states (the Mine Ban Treaty States Parties).[30] By the end of 2006 the misleadingly named initiative had been modified through the persistence of the UNDP's Sara Sekkenes, but undoubtedly damage had been done in altering both mine-affected states' understandings and donors' perceptions of completion.

There are also limitations to the most innovative structure established—the Implementation Support Unit (ISU). A support unit for any international treaty could take one of three possible forms: part of the UN system, part of or attached to an organization other than the UN, or "stand-alone." Each has its benefits and disadvantages. For pragmatic reasons in 2001, the ISU was established as part of GICHD. According to Kongstad, there was no alternative. Given that the memory of some UN opposition to the Ottawa Process was still fresh in the minds of Kongstad and others, "the UN was out of the question." It was also felt that States Parties could not come up with the resources necessary to run an independent, stand-alone institution.[31]

Circumstances were also right for GICHD, particularly given the appointment in May 2000 of Cornelio Sommaruga as the president of its governing board and Martin Dahinden as its director. Sommaruga arrived after having taken the ICRC to new heights of activism during his term as its president. His leadership resulted in the ICRC surprising many by expressing the view in February 1994 that a worldwide ban on antipersonnel mines was the only truly effective solution to the problems caused by the weapon. For his part, Martin Dahinden, as the official in Switzerland's Ministry of Foreign Affairs responsible for conventional weapons policy, had recommended in the mid-1990s, albeit unsuccessfully at the time, that Switzerland adopt a policy in favor of banning antipersonnel mines.[32]

These points, however, do not diminish the fact that there are limitations to the arrangement. For instance, a contradiction built into the system is that while the ISU is part of GICHD, its activities serve the parties to a particular international treaty while the activities of the other parts follow a strategy agreed to by GICHD's governing board. This is compounded by the fact that strong-willed states that have rejected accession to the treaty, including the United States and Finland, are on GICHD's board. While that has not to date affected GICHD's strong support to the treaty, a contradiction exists and hence a risk remains.

Another potential limitation relates to the independence and neutrality of the ISU. While intended to serve all States Parties equally, the fact remains that it is part of an organization established by the government of Switzerland, which continues to be its predominant financial supporter. Moreover, the GICHD's director is a Swiss diplomatic appointee. Fortunately, GICHD directors Martin Dahinden and Stephan Nellen have been unequivocal in their support for the treaty and have permitted the ISU to respond to the needs and interests of all States Parties. However, when such committed individuals move on the potential would remain, as the ICBL expressed in 2001, that the ISU would be answerable to one State Party more than others.

The Implementation Support Unit's neutrality could be affected as well if the GICHD as a whole increased its engagement in the politics of matters that concern landmines and other explosive remnants of war. States Parties sometimes are on different sides of issues related to treaty implementation and on matters related to other explosive remnants of war. The ISU has steered clear of favoring one side over the other. However, instances have occurred when GICHD has expressed political views that are not universally accepted. For instance, in September 2006 during a sensitive debate on developing a process for requesting extensions on the treaty's mine clearance deadline, GICHD weighed in to forcefully tell States Parties what information they needed, ignoring the fact that it is up to each individual State Party to determine its information needs.[33] Moreover, GICHD has grown dramatically in recent years in both size and scope. As Gustavo Laurie, one of the initiators of the ISU has observed, taking on an increased role commensurate with increased size could result in concerns for the independence of the ISU.[34]

Notwithstanding risks and limitations to ensuring the neutrality, independence, and responsiveness of the ISU, perfection may not lie elsewhere. While the GICHD could be perceived to be under the influence of a predominant donor, an analogy exists within the UN system. Obviously the UN could receive pressure by its powerful member states, particularly those that are not party to the treaty. Moreover, should the ISU be part of the UN system, it would benefit from global recognition of and appreciation for the UN, but the ISU's performance no doubt would be affected by the costs, bureaucratic complexity, and slow pace which are well-known characteristics of the UN.

Lessons of the Convention's Implementation Mechanisms

Overall, the implementation machinery has worked well as an integrated set of mechanisms:

- The annual Meeting of States Parties provides a forum for taking decisions and making formal assessments of the treaty's operations.
- The informal Intersessional Work Programme drives progress on implementation that can be recorded at Meetings of the States Parties.
- The Coordinating Committee ensures effective coordination between what happens in the intersessional period and what takes place at Meetings of the States Parties.
- The ISU is a cost-effective way to provide ongoing support to the implementation process, particularly to ensure that all States Parties can engage in the work of the treaty.
- Contact Groups facilitate cooperation on specialized matters.
- The Sponsorship Program ensures that those States Parties with limited means, which are in the process of fulfilling key obligations, can participate in the work of the treaty.

Given the successes and unique nature of the implementation mechanisms, the treaty's operations have been seen as a model for other international instruments. In fact, stakeholders concerned with a broad set of instruments ranging from the Framework Convention on Tobacco Control, the Convention on the Rights of Persons with Disabilities, the UN Program of Action on Small Arms and Light Weapons, the Biological Weapons Convention (BWC), and the Convention on Conventional Weapons (CCW) have sought to learn from the Mine Ban Treaty's operations. Some have already drawn pertinent lessons and have acted on them. For instance, in December 2006, the BWC's Sixth Review Conference established an intersessional work program, primarily intended, as is the case with the Mine Ban Treaty, to enhance national implementation and international cooperation. In addition, the States Parties to that convention established their own Implementation Support Unit, within the UN.[35]

With the entry into force of the CCW's Protocol V on explosive remnants of war, interest has also turned to consider how lessons could be applied to the CCW. While mechanisms such as an intersessional work program and a support unit may seem attractive, their establishment would be pointless unless the parties to the CCW decided that there was something to implement. There is some optimism that the working culture of the Mine Ban Treaty could spill over to efforts to apply Protocol V—but only if parties to the Protocol adopt not only the Mine Ban Treaty's implementation mechanisms but also its practical minded working culture. The Mine Ban Treaty's implementation process has been well served by a resistance to institutionalization for the sake of institutionalization and has forsaken doing what might be considered traditional in exchange for doing what is optimal for the specific implementation challenges posed by that treaty.

Conclusion

The Mine Ban Treaty has been referred to as "an extraordinary measure of what is considered to be success within international diplomacy."[36] It would remain nice words on paper, however, if not acted upon and implemented. A variety of mechanisms have been established which have played an important role in ensuring a successful track record of implementation since its entry into force in 1999. These mechanisms did not simply emerge by chance.

The treaty provided a basis for the development of implementation machinery. Making it happen, though, required deliberate actions of individuals. These were people active from the early days of the mine ban movement and others who followed in their footsteps; they pursued treaty implementation largely by following the working practices of the Ottawa Process. These individuals helped shape the understanding that the treaty is more than simply a prohibition on the use, production, stockpiling, and transfer of antipersonnel mines. They advanced the view that, in addition to adhering to negative obligations, positive action, or an implementation culture, is required. And they did so by applying and emphasizing ways of doing business that were deemed to have contributed to the success of the Ottawa Process. These included the interrelationship between formal and informal activities, the need to promote acceptance of innovative ways of doing multilateral business, and an emphasis on developing means to achieve specific ends rather than developing means as ends in themselves.

The result is a unique set of implementation machinery and meaningful progress toward the fulfillment of the Mine Ban Treaty's obligations and its promise. This machinery is less than perfect, though. To assume perfection and not question its utility would be to act in a manner inconsistent with the practical-minded approach that has been central to success to date.

The role of individuals remarked on in this chapter is also a potential weakness. Individuals move on and if newcomers do not continue the unique and successful working practices there may be a return to traditional multilateralism that is flavored more by a culture of inertia than of action. There is the risk that institutional memory could be lost and that what at one time was considered a common understanding or practice could become distorted into something unrecognizable.

Additionally, the central role of individuals suggests the potential of individual (or individual state's) interest to dominate the interests of all. While the treaty's presidents and committee cochairs, and the GICHD's directors, habitually have placed the interests of the treaty above individual interest, this might not always be the case. Certain individuals could play make-or-break roles concerning the successful operation of the treaty, given dysfunctions built into the implementation machinery.

In the end, though, one must have faith in the potential for human beings to do good. The story of the Ottawa Process is one of individuals who put the betterment of others before narrow self, state, or corporate interest, in part by reshaping how individuals and institutions came to understand their interest. The treaty's implementation phase to date has seen demonstrations of those same qualities. With mechanisms that have been established in part to reinforce understanding of the value of the treaty's working culture, one can remain hopeful that there will be continued positive, meaningful energy directed toward the fulfillment of an end to the suffering and casualties caused by antipersonnel mines for all people for all time.

Notes

1. Telephone interview with Bob Lawson, April 20, 2006.
2. Stuart Maslen, *Commentaries on Arms Control Treaties Volume I: The Convention on the Prohibition of the Use, Stockpiling, Production and Transfer of Anti-Personnel Mines and on Their Destruction* (Oxford: Oxford University Press, 2004), pp. 262–263.
3. Maslen, *Commentaries on Arms Control Treaties*, p. 263.
4. Address by Hon. Lloyd Axworthy, Minister of Foreign Affairs, to the opening of the Mine Action Forum, Ottawa, December 2, 1997.
5. Article 17 states that "the Convention shall enter into force on the first day of the sixth month after the month in which the 40th instrument of ratification, acceptance, approval or accession has been deposited."
6. Telephone interview with Bob Lawson, April 20, 2006.

7. First Meeting of the States Parties to the Convention on the Prohibition of the Use, Stockpiling, Production, and Transfer of Anti-Personnel Mines and on Their Destruction, "Final Report," APLC/MSP.1/1999/1, May 20, 1999. Originally, five "Standing Committees of Experts" were established. At the Second Meeting of States Parties, it was agreed to drop the term "Experts" and reduce the number of committees to four by combining Technologies for Mine Action with Mine Clearance.

8. Telephone interview with Bob Lawson, April 20, 2006.

9. Telephone interview with Bob Lawson, April 20, 2006.

10. The "20" represented the then twenty States Parties that served as cochairs and corapporteurs of the five committees that existed between 1999 and 2000. The "2" represented the two additional States Parties—Austria and Norway—that the ICBL wanted involved in these meetings due to their historical role in the treaty and their role as Friends of the President during the First Meeting of States Parties. On this basis, most states represented in the Post-Ottawa Geneva Consultation Group continued to be involved in this new form of informal coordination. In addition, the ICRC and Geneva International Centre for Humanitarian Demining (GICHD) were invited to these gatherings.

11. Susan B. Walker, "Informal Summary – '20 + 2' Meeting to Discuss Intersessional Work," August 20, 1999.

12. Second Meeting of the States Parties to the Convention on the Prohibition of the Use, Stockpiling, Production, and Transfer of Anti-Personnel Mines and on Their Destruction, "Final Report," APLC/MSP.2/2000/1, September 19, 2000.

13. E-mail from Martin Dahinden, April 9, 2006.

14. Paper presented by Peru, "Implementation Support for the Convention on the Prohibition of Anti-Personnel Mines," to the Standing Committee on the General Status and Operation of the Convention, Geneva, May 11, 2001.

15. Paper, "Implementation Support," May 11, 2001.

16. Statement by Brazil on the Coordinating Committee and on the Establishment of an Implementation Support Unit (ISU) for the Convention, Third Meeting of States Parties, Managua, September 18–21, 2001.

17. Statement by Croatia to the Third Meeting of States Parties, Managua, September 18, 2001.

18. E-mail from Susan B. Walker, April 20, 2006.

19. Third Meeting of the States Parties to the Convention on the Prohibition of the Use, Stockpiling, Production, and Transfer of Anti-Personnel Mines and on Their Destruction, "Final Report," APLC/MSP.3/2001/1, January 10, 2002.

20. Third Meeting of the States Parties, January 10, 2002.

21. These include traditional donors such as Australia, Belgium, Canada, Germany, Italy, the Netherlands, and Norway, as well as middle and low income states such as Albania, Burundi, Chile, the Czech Republic, Cyprus, Hungary, Malaysia, Mexico, Nigeria, the Philippines, South Africa, and Turkey.

22. Non-paper presented by Norway, "Resources to Achieve the Convention's Aims," September 2002.

23. "Resources to Achieve the Convention's Aims," September 2002.

24. E-mail from Steffen Kongstad, March 19, 2006.

25. Each State Party ultimately is obliged to destroy its stockpiled and emplaced antipersonnel mines, however. Article 6 makes it clear that they are not on their own; it spells out the rights of States Parties "to seek and receive assistance, where feasible, from other States Parties to the extent possible" and the responsibilities of each State Party "in a position to do so" to provide such assistance.

26. Cecilia Sanchez served as the lead substantive advisor to the President of the 2001 Third Meeting of State Parties and was instrumental at that meeting in advancing the proposal that resulted in the establishment of the Implementation Support Unit. Following the Third Meeting of States Parties, Sanchez chaired the Coordinating Committee and oversaw the process of reviewing and subsequently enhancing the functioning of the Intersessional Work Programme.

27. Paper presented by Canada, "Draft Recommendations with Respect to the Implementation of Article 8 of the Mine Ban Convention," Standing Committee of Experts on the General Status and Operations of the Convention, Geneva, May 2000.

28. Fourth Meeting of States Parties to the Convention on the Prohibition of the Use, Stockpiling, Production, and Transfer of Anti-Personnel Mines and on Their Destruction, "Final Report—Annex II," APLC/MSP.4/2002/1, September 27, 2002.

29. E-mail from Steffen Kongstad, March 19, 2006.

30. E-mail from Charles Sharpe, UNDP, February 22, 2005.

31. E-mail from Steffen Kongstad, March 19, 2006.

32. E-mail from Martin Dahinden, April 9, 2006.

33. Ian Mansfied, Operations Director, GICHD, Comments on draft Article 5 nonpaper, September 4, 2006.

34. E-mail from Gustavo Laurie, February 20, 2007.

35. Sixth Review Conference of the States Parties to the Convention on the Prohibition of the Development, Production, and Stockpiling of Bacteriological (Biological) and Toxin Weapons and on Their Destruction, "Final Document," BWC/CONF.VI/6, December 8, 2006.

36. Robert J. Lawson et al., "The Ottawa Process and the International Process and the International Movement to Ban Anti-Personnel Mines," in Maxwell Cameroon, Robert J. Lawson, and Brian W. Tomlin (eds.), *To Walk Without Fear: The Global Movement to Ban Landmines* (Toronto: Oxford University Press, 1998), pp. 160–184.

7

Goodwill Yields Good Results: Cooperative Compliance and the Mine Ban Treaty

Stephen D. Goose

I N 1997, AS THE MINE BAN TREATY was being developed and negotiated, its opponents sometimes dismissed it as a "feel good" exercise that only a small number of relatively inconsequential "like-minded" states would join. Skeptics speculated that it would be an unenforceable treaty, one without teeth that states were likely to ignore.

Ten years later, the doubters have been proven wrong—at least thus far. With 155 States Parties, the global reach of the treaty is undeniably impressive, even without the participation of China, Russia, and the United States.[1] Moreover, the record of treaty implementation and compliance by the States Parties has been just as impressive, though not flawless. The combination of a large and ever-growing number of countries joining the Mine Ban Treaty together with effective implementation and compliance has contributed to a global stigmatization of antipersonnel mines and an emerging international norm against the weapon that is being heeded even by most of those still outside the treaty.

States Parties have successfully implemented and complied with the Mine Ban Treaty to a degree that few observers, even the treaty's strongest supporters, would have expected. It is a record that other multilateral treaties would envy. There have been no confirmed violations of the prohibitions on use, production, and transfer. Thus far, only four of eighty-one States Parties have missed their four-year deadline for destruction of stockpiles of antipersonnel mines. There is an amazing 96 percent compliance rate for initial transparency reporting.

But State Party compliance has not been absolute or uniform. There have been—and still are today—serious questions in some instances about compliance with core obligations on use and transfer. The stellar record for on-time stockpile destruction could be threatened by a number of upcoming cases. There is concern that many States Parties are abusing the exception permitting the retention of antipersonnel mines for training purposes. Less than half have enacted national measures, such as domestic legislation to implement the treaty, as required. It is increasingly clear many States Parties are going to miss their ten-year deadline for clearance of mined areas.

Moreover, the lack of agreement by State Parties on fundamental matters that affect compliance, such as what landmines are banned and what acts are banned under the prohibition on assistance, undercuts the credibility of the treaty and raises concerns for the future.

Mine Ban Treaty Compliance Provisions: Cooperative Compliance or Verification "Lite?"

At first glance, it would appear that compliance was a key concern for those drafting the Mine Ban Treaty in 1997. One of the three key preparatory meetings to develop the treaty was devoted entirely to the issue. It was among the most contentious issues during the negotiations. The outcome—Article 8, titled "Facilitation and Clarification of Compliance"—is the longest article in the treaty by far.[2]

The discussions on compliance and verification were undertaken in the context of the failed attempt to add such language to the Convention on Conventional Weapons (CCW) during its First Review Conference in 1995 and 1996. Some delegations, notably Germany, France, and (during the negotiations) the United States, were determined to incorporate key elements of the rejected CCW proposal into the Mine Ban Treaty. They promoted an arms control approach with an emphasis on verification procedures.

However, at the meeting on verification and compliance held outside Bonn, Germany, in April 1997, the dominant, but by no means universal, view was that it would be more appropriate to look to human rights or humanitarian law treaties for guidance.[3] Canada strongly promoted the concept of "cooperative compliance," an approach that assumes goodwill on the part of all States Parties and emphasizes resolution of issues in a nonconfrontational manner and assistance to help States Parties to meet their obligations rather than criticism for failing to do so.

At the September 1997 treaty negotiations in Oslo, most delegations had come to accept that an overly intrusive, arms control-type verification and compliance regime was neither necessary nor desirable for the Mine Ban Treaty. The lead Norwegian diplomat later commented that "the thinking at the time by the majority of negotiating states was that it should be politically so costly to breach the obligations of the treaty that it would deter anyone from doing so."[4] Yet, some states still insisted that, as a condition for accepting the entire "package" of the treaty text, some of the CCW-type language be included.[5]

The negotiators worked to strike a balance that would help bring as many countries on board as possible while still providing meaningful measures to gauge and induce compliance. The final language reflects the view that complete verification of prohibitions on antipersonnel mines is an impossible task, and therefore an unachievable regime should not be attempted. A less ambitious regime was accepted because the antipersonnel mine is not like a weapon of mass destruction, where states must be concerned about a sudden, militarily devastating attack.

The end result is a treaty that has a "light" regime in the arms control context but a "heavy" regime in the humanitarian context—a compromise between the disarmament model of intrusive verification and the international humanitarian law model of fact-finding.

The first clause of Article 8 contains the essence of the cooperative compliance approach under which States Parties agree to "consult and cooperate with each other regarding the implementation" of the Mine Ban Treaty and to "work together in a spirit of cooperation to facilitate compliance." Before taking more aggressive steps, States Parties are to "clarify and seek to resolve questions related to compliance" through the gathering of information.

But the article also contains a multistage system of verification procedures. One or more States Parties can issue a "request for clarification" regarding a potential violation to the State Party concerned through the Secretary-General. If there is no response or an unsatisfactory response within twenty-eight days, the matter may be taken up at the next annual Meeting of States Parties or a Special Meeting of States Parties may be convened. The meeting can authorize, by majority vote, a fact-finding mission by a team of experts to investigate and report back on potential violations. An unusual provision permits the State Party concerned—the alleged violator—to invite a fact-finding mission to its territory at any time.

States Parties may then ask the State Party concerned to take measures to address the compliance issue within a specified period of time and suggest ways and means to resolve the matter, "including the initiation of appropriate procedures in conformity with international law," by a two-thirds vote if consensus cannot be reached.

When the Mine Ban Treaty was being negotiated, signed, and entering into force, the verification and compliance provisions perhaps drew more criticism than any other aspect of the treaty. Arms controllers tended to consider the agreement as weak and unenforceable. Others viewed it as too strong and overly intrusive and argued that sensitive states (such as India) would stay away because it could compromise national sovereignty. The criticisms have largely died away with the passage of time and the impressive record of compliance. This could easily change, however, if the record is not sustained in the future.

Approaches to Compliance Since 1999

The tensions about and different approaches to compliance and verification that were evident during the negotiations have also been present at various times since the Mine Ban Treaty entered into force on March 1, 1999. But no matter the philosophical divide, the overriding reality is that no State Party has seen it necessary or desirable to invoke formally any of the Article 8 provisions, even though there have been times when resort to Article 8 would have been an entirely reasonable option.

Just as there is a stigma now attached to the use of antipersonnel mines, there seems to be a stigma attached to the use of Article 8. For better or worse, it appears that States Parties have decided that invoking the article would go against the aura of good feeling that surrounds the Mine Ban Treaty and its work program, and there is a reluctance to threaten that unique nature of the enterprise. Though it need not be seen as such, it seems Article 8 is viewed by most as an accusatory and hostile act. It could instead, particularly in the positive atmosphere of the treaty, be seen as a convenient, coordinated, and systematic method to clarify potentially contentious issues that inevitably arise— a method explicitly provided for in the treaty, rather than one devised outside of the treaty structure.

In practice, nearly all of the compliance issues that have emerged thus far have been addressed—and mostly resolved—in a manner consistent with the first clause of Article 8, even if it was not invoked: by seeking information and clarifications through consultation in a spirit of cooperation. This approach has not resulted in absolute clarity about whether a violation has taken place but has succeeded in changing states' behavior and bringing them into clear compliance with the treaty.

Thus one could argue that the system has worked. But the problem is that it is not a system. The truth is that compliance concerns have been handled in an extremely ad hoc, uncoordinated, and unplanned manner that has relied heavily on actions by nongovernmental actors, principally the International Campaign to Ban Landmines (ICBL) and the International Committee of the

Red Cross (ICRC), and on the willingness of a small number of individual States Parties, and often individual diplomats, to take action.

Most often, it has been the ICBL's Landmine Monitor network that has identified and publicized serious allegations and actual violations. Then, often in cooperation with the ICRC, the ICBL has had to encourage various States Parties to take the lead and/or to act together to address the issue. States Parties have then usually taken quiet, but effective, behind the scenes measures to engage those about whom there are compliance concerns, while the ICBL and ICRC carried out their own combination of public and private steps to seek resolution.

Over the years, States Parties such as Austria, Belgium, Canada, the Netherlands, Norway, and South Africa have regularly pursued compliance issues. Certain leadership positions have also been key in addressing such matters, notably the presidents of the annual Meetings of States Parties, and the cochairs of the Standing Committees (especially General Status and Operation of the Convention, and to a lesser extent, Stockpile Destruction). There has also been an effort to involve States Parties from the same region as the country of concern.

For some issues, such as transparency reporting, stockpile destruction, mine clearance, mine risk education, and victim assistance, the treaty's Implementation Support Unit, United Nations agencies (especially the UN Development Programme, UNICEF, and UN Mine Action Service), and regional organizations (especially the European Union and Organization of American States) have played an important role.

The cooperative compliance approach of course breaks down if there is willful disrespect by a State Party for the treaty's obligations. In order to prepare for such a possibility, Canada took the lead in 2000–2002 to try to get agreement on a document aimed at "operationalizing" Article 8. As Canada noted, it "is probably obvious to all of us, that resorting to the full procedures contained in Article 8 would be relatively rare . . . nevertheless, States Parties need to discuss implementation of Article 8 provisions to clarify a number of matters, including financial, procedural, logistical and administrative issues related to Special Meetings of States Parties and fact-finding missions."[6]

This effort was imminently reasonable. Violation of a core obligation, such as use of antipersonnel mines, would be a huge challenge to the Mine Ban Treaty, and states should not be caught unprepared to deal adequately with any serious future compliance issues.

Also as part of this process, the NGO VERTIC (Verification Research, Training, and Information Center) produced in 2002 a "Guide to Fact-Finding Missions under the Ottawa Convention," funded in part by States Parties. In a separate initiative, France carried out extensive consultations on the possibility of establishing a separate body that would be tasked with taking the lead on compliance concerns.

By 2003, however, it was clear that there would not be agreement on operationalizing Article 8, and new, even informal measures on compliance would not be accepted. Many states that had been reluctant to agree to fact-finding missions and other "intrusive" measures during the negotiations did not now want to see them pursued further. This included many States Parties from the "south," including from Latin America, Africa, and Asia. Some states also stressed that time and energy should be devoted to promotion of mine clearance and victim assistance, not Article 8.

The ICBL expressed its extreme disappointment and stated, "States Parties should put a high priority on operationalizing Article 8 and on finding a new mechanism or a new way of ensuring a more coordinated, systematic, and effective response to compliance concerns. This should be done by the 2004 Review Conference."[7] At the Review Conference, the ICBL again called for an effective informal mechanism to deal with compliance and implementation concerns short of invoking Article 8, noting that the ad hoc manner used thus far to deal with such concerns could not be relied upon to be effective in the future. States Parties did not then, and still have not, risen to this call.

Given the aversion to Article 8, States Parties have stressed since the First Review Conference that the treaty's Article 9 (National Implementation Measures) should be viewed as the primary compliance provision. The article requires each State Party "to take all appropriate legal, administrative and other measures, including the imposition of penal sanctions, to prevent and suppress any activity" banned by treaty. This approach that "burden is rightfully on each State Party at the national level" is only viable if the state itself is not willfully violating the treaty. Moreover, Article 9 cannot be counted on to deal effectively with all compliance concerns since, as of mid-2007, fewer than half the States Parties had put national implementation measures in place.

Survey of Compliance

The following section will look at compliance with key provisions of the Mine Ban Treaty, including the prohibitions on use and transfer, the stockpile destruction deadline, the exception for retaining a limited number of mines, national implementation laws, and transparency reporting, as well as the efforts to deal with problems of compliance. It also looks at controversial issues of treaty interpretation that have important compliance implications.

But first it is instructive to relate the case of Tajikistan. In 2002, the ICBL sounded the alarm on Tajikistan, not because of an alleged or confirmed violation, but because it was not clear that Tajikistan considered itself to be formally bound by the treaty.[8] According to UN records, Tajikistan acceded to the Mine Ban Treaty on October 12, 1999 (accession is a one-step process for formal adherence to a treaty). In January 2002, however, Tajikistan issued a statement that it had signed but not ratified the treaty and still required parliamentary approval. Other statements indicated that it was reviewing its status and decision to join. Moreover, Tajikistan had not undertaken any national implementation measures as required by Article 9, had not submitted any Article 7 transparency reports, had not participated in any Mine Ban Treaty meetings, and had not started the process of stockpile destruction.[9]

The alarm bells were answered due largely to the efforts of the Netherlands, supported by a few other States Parties, the ICBL, and the ICRC. Tajikistan came to the Fourth Meeting of States Parties in Geneva in September 2002, where it stressed that it was now taking all necessary steps to comply with the Mine Ban Treaty. Tajikistan has gone on to become an active member of the mine ban community.[10]

The story of Tajikistan follows a familiar pattern. The ICBL identified a compliance concern, and while States Parties said little to nothing publicly, they pursued the matter privately with success. An ad hoc approach worked but only through consistent efforts by the ICBL, ICRC, and, most importantly, a personal dedication to resolving the matter on the part of one Dutch diplomat.

Use of Antipersonnel Mines

By 2007, there had been no *confirmed* instances of States Parties using antipersonnel mines. However, there was compelling evidence that Ugandan forces used antipersonnel mines while fighting in the Democratic Republic of Congo (DRC) in 2000, as well as credible allegations that Zimbabwean forces had used antipersonnel mines there in 1999 and 2000. Both governments strongly denied the charges.[11] The chaotic situation in the DRC led the ICBL in 2000 to note, "Uncertainties about who is responsible for the use of antipersonnel mines in the DRC have continued for more than two years now. Landmine Monitor believes it has reached the point where States Parties to the Mine Ban Treaty should make detailed requests for clarification from Uganda, Rwanda, and Zimbabwe, and should make all other efforts to establish the facts regarding mine use in the Democratic Republic of Congo."[12]

Based on Landmine Monitor findings and its own information gathering regarding possible use of mines by Zimbabwe, Canada publicly raised concerns during the Second Meeting of States Parties in September 2000.[13] Zimbabwe denied the allegations in the strongest possible terms, claimed the ICBL had a "hidden agenda" against Zimbabwe, and declared that it had "stopped using antipersonnel mines upon ratification [of the Mine Ban Treaty] in 1998."[14]

While no State Party subsequently raised the issue again publicly, several privately informed the ICBL that they were engaging with Zimbabwe and stressing the importance that all commanders in the DRC understand their obligations under the Mine Ban Treaty. The ICBL was disappointed that the States Parties publicly let the matter drop, but the end result was as desired: Zimbabwe's behavior changed and there have been no further serious allegations about use by its forces in DRC or elsewhere. The combination of public revelation and private expressions of concern was effective.

The most serious mine use allegations involved Ugandan forces in the DRC, especially in the fighting around Kisangani in June 2000.[15] As with Zimbabwe, after presenting the evidence to Uganda and asking for comment, the ICBL reported the information in its Landmine Monitor report and called on States Parties to consult with Uganda and resolve the issue.

Uganda repeatedly denied the mine use allegations, but after the publication of additional, more compelling details in *Landmine Monitor Report 2001*, it expressed support for the ICBL's suggestion of a full investigation. In February 2002, Uganda said that a joint Ugandan-Rwandan investigative commission looking into the conduct of the fighting in the DRC would now also look at use of mines. States Parties and the ICBL expressed their appreciation for Uganda's spirit of cooperation in attempting to resolve the matter. However, Uganda never reported back on the findings of the commission, and when repeatedly pressed by the ICBL, finally stated in September 2003 that in order to ease tensions with Rwanda, a joint decision was made not to make the report public.[16]

Despite the seriousness of the allegations, States Parties remained largely silent, and to the ICBL's knowledge, few if any engaged in intensive behind-the-scenes engagement with Uganda on the matter. But the high level of attention brought to the matter by the ICBL appeared to have an impact.[17] There were no allegations of use of antipersonnel mines by Ugandan forces in the DRC or elsewhere after 2001.

Landmine Monitor has investigated charges of antipersonnel mine use by another handful of States Parties since 1999 but without finding sufficient evidence to merit further attention. Nearly every year there are allegations of State Party use that warrant at least some follow-up.

A related "use" issue has come to the forefront as some States Parties approach their ten-year deadlines for mine clearance. There appear to be several cases where States Parties rely on antipersonnel mines that they laid in the past to serve an ongoing military purpose. In particular, this applies to mines emplaced around military installations and prisons, and in border areas. States Parties using existing minefields for military benefit are in violation of the treaty. Their unambiguous obligation is to clear those minefields as soon as possible.

At an intersessional meeting of the Mine Ban Treaty in April 2007, Venezuela came under fire from the ICBL over this issue. The ICBL noted Venezuela's statement that it had not yet started clearing the mined areas around its naval bases, even though its deadline is October 1, 2009, because it has not finalized its search for alternatives that would provide early warning and protection of its bases from Colombian guerrillas. The ICBL went on to question "why this did not draw a response from any State Party. Does this not constitute 'use' of antipersonnel mines? Venezuela has in essence said that it is purposefully deploying antipersonnel mines in order to derive military benefit from them, and is refusing, as required by the treaty, to clear them as soon as possible, or possibly even by the ten-year deadline. It can be easily argued that this may constitute two treaty violations: of the Article 1 prohibition on use and of the Article 5 clearance requirements."[18] The ICRC concurred with the ICBL and expressed its concern, but States Parties did not intervene.

There is compelling evidence that a number of *signatories* to the Mine Ban Treaty used antipersonnel mines after signing but before ratifying the treaty and becoming States Parties. Angola admitted to using antipersonnel mines after signing the treaty, justifying it as necessary for the survival of the nation. Ecuador indirectly acknowledged using mines after signing when it indicated in its Article 7 transparency report when it emplaced minefields. Ethiopia used large numbers of mines in its border war with Eritrea from 1998–2000, after signing the treaty in 1997. Other signatories who likely used antipersonnel mines include Burundi, Guinea-Bissau, Rwanda, Senegal, Sudan, and Uganda.

While signatories are not fully bound by the Mine Ban Treaty, the use of antipersonnel mines by signatories can be considered a violation of international law. Under Article 18 of the Vienna Convention on the Law of Treaties, "a state is obligated to refrain from acts which would defeat the purpose of the treaty when . . . it has signed the treaty."

It is noteworthy, and a testament to the Mine Ban Treaty, that so many states which used antipersonnel mines in the recent past have joined the treaty and immediately halted use and continued to abide by its prohibitions. This applies not just to the signatories named above, but also to many states that laid mines in the years before signing, such as Bosnia and Herzegovina, Cambodia, Colombia, Mozambique, Serbia, and others.

Transfer of Antipersonnel Mines

For the past decade, global trade in antipersonnel mines has consisted solely of a low level of illicit and unacknowledged transfers, and there have been only rare, unconfirmed accusations of involvement by States Parties. However, in 2006 the UN arms embargo Monitoring Group on Somalia released two reports with detailed and specific allegations of transfers of antipersonnel mines by Eritrea and Ethiopia to warring groups in Somalia.

Both governments strongly denied the charges in the reports, first in general declarations about embargo-busting to the Monitoring Group, and then in response to Landmine Monitor inquiries specifically about antipersonnel mines. The ICBL brought these UN reports to the attention of individual States Parties and also highlighted them as matters of grave concern in the Seventh Meeting of States Parties in September 2006 and the intersessional Standing Committee meetings in April 2007.

During the April meeting, the president of the Seventh Meeting of States Parties, Ambassador Caroline Millar of Australia, expressed concern over the UN reports and said that she had written to the chair of the Monitoring Group to seek further information. The ICBL lamented the fact that States Parties had not vigorously pursued these serious and specific allegations as potential violations of the Mine Ban Treaty and strongly encouraged them to seek further information and clarification from both the UN Monitoring Group and the governments of Eritrea and Ethiopia. A number of countries, such as Austria, Canada, and Norway, indicated to the ICBL they were following up on the matter. Neither Eritrea nor Ethiopia has addressed the charges during a gathering of States Parties.

Meeting Stockpile Destruction Deadlines

Compliance with the four-year stockpile destruction deadline has, for the most part, been exemplary, though developments in 2006 and 2007 are cause for concern. By September 2007, a total of eighty States Parties had completed destruction of their stockpiles of antipersonnel mines, leaving only ten with stocks awaiting destruction. Combined, States Parties have destroyed some forty-two million stockpiled antipersonnel mines. The treaty obligation is to destroy the mines "as soon as possible" but no later than four years after entry force for the State Party, and many finished far in advance of the deadline, some by two years or more.

States Parties have put a good deal of effort into emphasizing the importance of meeting the stockpile destruction deadline in order to maintain the credibility of the treaty. The Standing Committee on Stockpile Destruction in particular has been used to build the necessary political will to get the job done, as well as to identify potential problems with compliance (whether technical, financial, or other), and find ways to overcome those problems.

Only four States Parties have missed their deadlines thus far: Turkmenistan, Guinea, Cape Verde, and Afghanistan. Neither Guinea nor Cape Verde had revealed that they possessed a stockpile of antipersonnel mines. This fact was discovered only when reports came out of the completion of destruction, in Guinea's case seven months after its April 2003 deadline, and in Cape Verde's case eight months after its November 2005 deadline.[19] Afghanistan was unable to meet its March 2007 deadline for stockpile destruction, telling States Parties in April 2007 that while it had destroyed 486,226 stockpiled antipersonnel mines (including 463,807 in 2006), two depots of antipersonnel mines still remained in Panjsheer province. The provincial authorities apparently did not make the mines available for destruction in a timely fashion. Afghanistan has indicated it expects to finish by November 2007.

The Turkmenistan situation is an interesting example of cooperative compliance. When it reported the completion of its stockpile destruction on February 28, 2003, just ahead of its deadline, Turkmenistan also reported that it would retain 69,200 antipersonnel mines for training purposes under the exception allowed in Article 3 of the treaty. The ICBL denounced this decision as "a violation of a core obligation of the treaty," calling it an "unacceptable" and "illegal" number of retained mines, and maintaining, "It is obviously NOT the minimum number absolutely necessary, as required by the treaty; it could constitute an operational stockpile."[20] The ICBL pointed out that it had been widely understood since the Oslo treaty negotiations that the acceptable number of retained mines should be in the hundreds or thousands or less, and not in the tens of thousands.[21] Six States Parties publicly chastized Turkmenistan at a meeting in May 2003, including Austria, which said the decision "cannot be accepted as state practice, as it would severely undermine the integrity of the Convention," and New Zealand, which noted such a large stock "could be seen as kept for future use in conflict."[22]

Despite widespread recognition that Turkmenistan's decision was not in keeping with the letter or spirit of the Mine Ban Treaty, no State Party gave consideration to invoking the procedures of Article 8. However, a small number of States Parties, the ICBL, and ICRC took the initiative to engage with Turkmenistan repeatedly, explaining the nature of the Article 3 exception and the degree to which Turkmenistan was out of step with accepted state practice. In a dramatic reversal announced in February 2004, Turkmenistan said it would destroy sixty thousand of the retained mines, and a four-person ICBL delegation accepted an invitation to witness the destruction two months later. Only then did it became clear that Turkmenistan had in fact been retaining 572,200 individual antipersonnel mines, as most of the retained mines were of the remotely-delivered type and Turkmenistan had been counting only the containers and not the mines inside! In June 2004 Turkmenistan announced that it would destroy the remainder of its retained mines later in the year.

While Article 8 was not invoked, in essence its initial stages were followed: States Parties (and in this case NGOs) consulted with each other "in a spirit of cooperation to facilitate compliance," seeking to clarify and resolve questions.

Potential stockpile destruction problems loom large on the horizon, as countries emerging from conflict and countries with extremely large stocks struggle to destroy those mines. Angola had to make a strong push at the last minute to meet its January 1, 2007, deadline with extensive help from UNDP and encouragement from the ICBL, and it has acknowledged that it expects to find additional stocks in the future. Sudan and Burundi are having trouble locating all of the stockpiles in their countries in order to destroy them. Iraq, which acceded to the Mine Ban Treaty on August 15, 2007, is likely to face extreme difficulties as well.

In Belarus, a project funded by the European Commission to provide technical and financial resources to destroy the country's 3.37 million PFM antipersonnel mines was abruptly cancelled in late 2006. Its collapse will most likely result in Belarus being unable to destroy its stockpiled mines by its March 1, 2008, deadline. A similar regrettable situation is also occurring in Ukraine, where in April 2007, the European Commission-funded project to destroy 5.95 million PFM mines was terminated by the contractor. Ukraine's June 1, 2010 deadline thus appears to be in serious jeopardy.

Retaining Unjustifiable Numbers of Antipersonnel Mines

Article 3 permits "the retention or transfer of a number of antipersonnel mines for the development of and training in mine detection, mine clearance, or mine destruction techniques," but, according to the article, "the amount of such mines shall not exceed the minimum number absolutely necessary for the above-mentioned purposes." As of mid-2007, of the 155 States Parties, 69 retained a total of almost 228,000 antipersonnel mines for research and training purposes.

The ICBL told States Parties in April 2007 that it "is increasingly convinced that there is widespread abuse" of the Article 3 exception. It said, "It appears that many States Parties are retaining more antipersonnel mines than 'absolutely necessary' and are not using mines . . . for the permitted purposes. It is time for States Parties to think about this as a serious compliance issue, and not just a reporting or transparency issue. . . . Some States Parties have yet to use their retained mines at all; they are simply sitting in storage—the equivalent to continued stockpiling. . . . Unless a State Party is clearly retaining the minimum number of antipersonnel mines, is actively utilizing the mines for the permitted purposes, and is being fully transparent about the process, there may rightly be concerns that the mines are in essence still being stockpiled and could be used for war fighting purposes."[23]

Some states, such as Norway and New Zealand, have insisted that there is no need for live mines for training purposes, a view shared by the ICBL. As a way of ensuring Article 3 compliance, the ICBL has long urged all states to declare the intended purposes and actual uses of retained antipersonnel mines. At the First Review Conference of the Mine Ban Treaty in November 2004, States Parties agreed to report in detail on the intended purposes and actual uses of retained mines. They subsequently agreed in December 2005 to adopt a new voluntary expanded reporting format to encourage and facilitate such reporting. However, only eleven States Parties made use of the new format in 2005 and eleven again in 2006.

On the positive side, at least two dozen States Parties have reviewed and decided to reduce their number of retained mines, or even eliminate the mines altogether (as Moldova and Macedonia did in 2006).[24]

Failure to Adopt National Implementation Measures

One of the most ignored implementation and compliance shortcomings is the failure of so many States Parties to enact national measures to implement the Mine Ban Treaty, as required by Article 9. As of mid-2007, only a third (fifty-three) of States Parties had passed new domestic implementation laws, while another twenty-seven States Parties reported that steps to enact legislation were underway.

Since the Mine Ban Treaty's entry into force, both the ICBL and ICRC have stressed that all States Parties should have legislation in place that includes penal sanctions for any potential future violations of the treaty and that provides for full implementation of all aspects of the treaty. The ICRC has taken the lead in promoting adoption of national legislation, including by disseminating an information kit translated into four languages. The ICBL has invested considerable energy in reporting, cajoling, and offering assistance to states on national legislation. States Parties have not been particularly active in this area. The "Article 7 Contact Group" was expanded to include work on Article 9, but it has remained largely an afterthought.

It is reasonable to question whether States Parties are in fact "preventing and suppressing" prohibited acts as called for in Article 9. There is a striking lack of information on the application of penal sanctions contained in the domestic landmine legislation in any country, including any specific instances of application of such sanctions—despite the fact that there have been many instances of possession and even use of antipersonnel mines by criminals, members of armed opposition groups, and others.

Meeting the Transparency Requirement

Article 7 of the Mine Ban Treaty requires States Parties to submit a report to the UN detailing steps taken to implement aspects of the treaty within 180 days after entry into force, and then to submit annual updates by April 30 each year.

As of mid-2007, the compliance rate of States Parties submitting initial transparency reports was an impressive 96 percent (compared to 63 percent in 2001). Six States Parties—Equatorial Guinea, Cape Verde, Gambia, São Tomé e Principe, Ethiopia, and Haiti—had not submitted their initial reports.[25] Unlike the success in getting more and more initial reports submitted, there was a decrease in the rate of annual updates for the third year in a row in 2007, with only 54 percent compliance, compared to the high water mark of 78 percent in 2004.

States Parties, ICBL, ICRC, UN agencies, and even regional organizations, such as the Organization of American States, have worked hard to ensure that states meet this obligation. The Article 7 Contact Group, under the leadership of Belgium, has been especially active and effective in improving compliance with this provision. Transparency reporting has been seen as an important obligation not just so that other States Parties are informed about progress, or lack thereof, in implementing the treaty, but also as a confidence-building measure, a means of ensuring engagement with the mine ban community, and, very importantly, a way for states to communicate their needs with respect to assistance with mine clearance, victim assistance, and stockpile destruction.

Clarifying Matters of Interpretation and Compliance

Since the treaty entered into force, the ICBL and ICRC have led the way in raising concerns about matters related to the interpretation and implementation of Articles 1 and 2, as well as Article 3 (mines retained for training) already discussed. For Article 1, the main issue is how the treaty's prohibition on "assistance" with banned acts is interpreted, especially in the context of joint military operations with a non-State Party who may use antipersonnel mines, and with regard to foreign stockpiling and transit of antipersonnel mines. The key concern with Article 2 is whether antivehicle mines with sensitive fuses or sensitive antihandling devices that cause them to function like antipersonnel mines are prohibited by the treaty.

Largely at the urging of the ICBL and ICRC, these issues have been placed on the agenda at every annual Meeting of States Parties and intersessional meeting, and the ICBL and ICRC have carefully documented the positions and practices of states. There has been progress toward what the ICBL would consider "compliance" on these issues over the years as more States Parties have made their views known and an ever increasing number have espoused interpretations championed by the ICBL and ICRC.

Over the years the ICBL has raised concerns about a number of States Parties assisting with the use of antipersonnel mines by others, including Rwanda, Uganda, and Zimbabwe with various forces in the Democratic Republic of Congo, and Namibia with Angolan troops before Angola became a State Party.

As a result of the ongoing discussions, a clear understanding of how Article 1 applies to joint military operations and the meaning of "assist" has begun to emerge. More than forty States Parties have declared that they will not participate in planning and implementation of activities related to the use of antipersonnel mines in joint operations with a state not party to the Mine Ban Treaty which may use antipersonnel mines.[26] Nearly all States Parties expressing views have agreed that transit of antipersonnel mines through the national territory (land, air, sea) of States Parties is not permitted, nor is foreign stockpiling of antipersonnel mines on the national territory of States Parties. U.S. mines were withdrawn from Italy, Norway, and Spain.[27]

With respect to Article 2, more than two dozen States Parties have expressed the view that any mine, despite its label or design intent, capable of being detonated by the unintentional act of a person is an antipersonnel mine and is prohibited. However, five States Parties (the Czech Republic, Denmark, France, Japan, and the United Kingdom) have said that the Mine Ban Treaty does not apply to antivehicle mines at all, regardless of their employment with sensitive fuses or antihandling devices. There appears to be agreement, with some notable exceptions, that a mine that relies on a tripwire, breakwire, or a tilt rod as its firing mechanism should be considered an antipersonnel mine. Several States Parties have destroyed these types of mines, but a small number still stockpile them, including the Czech Republic, Slovenia, and Sweden.

Despite these clarifications and emerging understandings, States Parties' interest in these matters has diminished in the past several years, and there is a definite impression that they would prefer to see the issues "go away." At the First Review Conference of the Mine Ban Treaty in November 2004, the ICBL expressed its deep frustration at the "inconsistent and contradictory" implementation of Articles 1, 2, and 3.[28] It noted that five years of discussion had brought much greater clarity, but "a small number of states have blocked common understandings and the majority of States Parties have not had the political will to push the issues." If the situation persists, the ICBL warned, the "credibility of the treaty will be threatened and ultimately its humanitarian impact could be undercut." The ICBL has since set its sights on the Second Review Conference in 2009, calling on States Parties to reach a formal common understanding on these matters before or by this important mark.[29]

Mine Clearance and Victim Assistance

Most observers would agree that, for mine-affected countries, the biggest implementation challenges are mine clearance and victim assistance. From a compliance perspective, it appears that many States Parties will have difficulty meeting their ten-year deadlines for mine clearance and that many will have to ask for an extension of the deadline, as is provided for in the treaty. This issue is addressed in detail elsewhere in this book (see chapter 8).

Victim assistance is not a "hard" obligation in the Mine Ban Treaty, as it calls for each State Party "in a position to do so" to provide assistance, but States Parties have emphasized victim assistance as essential to the successful accomplishment of the treaty's objectives. This issue is also addressed in detail elsewhere in this book (see chapter 9).

The Norm Takes Hold:
"Virtual Compliance" by Non-States Parties

There are forty states that are not yet party to the Mine Ban Treaty. But a new international norm rejecting the antipersonnel mine is taking hold, as more and more of those nations embrace the humanitarian and disarmament objectives of the treaty, including a widespread reluctance to use the weapon (see chapter 5).

Many of the states outside the treaty are in "virtual compliance" with its key provisions, in that they are not using, producing, exporting, or, in some cases, not even stockpiling the weapon. Even more are contributing to global mine action efforts. An increasing number of non-States Parties are attending the Mine Ban Treaty meetings and are voting in favor of the annual UN General Assembly resolution calling for universalization and full implementation of the treaty.[30] Some have even submitted voluntary transparency reports in accordance with Article 7 of the treaty.

Among the states that have publicly stressed that they are in *de facto* compliance with most of the treaty's obligations are Georgia, Finland, Morocco, Mongolia, Poland, and recently, Vietnam. Although the United States does not trumpet the information, it has not used antipersonnel mines since 1991, exported them since 1992, or produced them since 1997, and has destroyed more than three million stockpiled antipersonnel mines.[31]

As a result of the mine ban movement and the Mine Ban Treaty, the use of antipersonnel mines has decreased dramatically, production has fallen sharply, and export has virtually halted. Non-States Parties have also destroyed tens of millions of stockpiled antipersonnel mines, but that has usually been because the mines were obsolete.

Landmine Monitor Report 2007 cites compelling evidence of use of antipersonnel mines by just two governments from mid-2006 to mid-2007: Burma (Myanmar) and Russia. This contrasts starkly with the findings of the first *Landmine Monitor Report 1999*, which identified fifteen governments using antipersonnel mines in the previous year. It is noteworthy that only Russia and Burma (Myanmar) have used antipersonnel mines regularly, each and every year.

Several non-States Parties have stated that they have stopped producing antipersonnel mines, including Egypt, Finland, Israel, and Poland, as well as Taiwan. Only thirteen continue to produce, or indicate they may produce, antipersonnel mines: Burma (Myanmar), China, Cuba, India, Iran, Nepal, North Korea, Pakistan, Russia, Singapore, South Korea, the United States, and Vietnam. Of those, Iran, Nepal, the United States, and Vietnam have said they are not actively producing antipersonnel mines.

There has not been any significant trade in antipersonnel mines by any country since the mid-1990s, as a once booming business has been reduced to a trickle of unrecognized, illicit deals. Many non-States Parties have formal bans or moratoria on antipersonnel mine transfers, including China, India, Israel, Kazakhstan, Pakistan, Poland, Russia, Singapore, South Korea, and the United States. In addition, Cuba, Egypt, and Vietnam have made policy statements saying they do not export.

The states not party to the treaty that have submitted voluntary Article 7 transparency reports include Morocco, Poland, and Sri Lanka.[32] All have said that the reports should be seen as a sign of their commitment to the elimination of antipersonnel mines. Several other countries have stated their intention to submit voluntary reports including Armenia, Azerbaijan, China, and Mongolia.

It is also noteworthy that a significant and growing number of nonstate armed groups have indicated their willingness to observe a ban on antipersonnel mines, and that use of antipersonnel mines by such groups is also on the decline (see chapter 10).

Conclusion

Overall, State Party compliance with the Mine Ban Treaty has been exemplary. This is all the more notable in light of the large number of countries now party to the treaty, the number of countries that used the weapon in the not so distant past and had significant stockpiles, and the number of countries that are just emerging from conflict, or in some cases are still engaged in conflict. Though (not surprisingly) little remarked upon, the record of compliance is also all the more impressive because of the number of States Parties that have been criticized for their failure to obey other treaties and for their lack of regard for human rights and international humanitarian law.

The experience of the past decade has shown that a treaty with stringent disarmament requirements can succeed, even without an intrusive verification regime. Indeed, it can succeed even if the primary means for monitoring implementation of and compliance with the treaty is carried out by nongovernmental organizations, as in the case of the ICBL's Landmine Monitor initiative.

Cooperative compliance has worked for the Mine Ban Treaty in large part because of the sustained "like-mindedness" of States Parties and their shared commitment to the humanitarian goals of the treaty; the ongoing power and effectiveness of the partnership between states, the ICBL, ICRC, and UN agencies that has characterized the Ottawa Process from the beginning; the continued avoidance of "business as usual diplomacy" in carrying out the work of the treaty; and the open and inclusive atmosphere that dominates that work.

But, as this chapter has shown, compliance with the Mine Ban Treaty has by no means been 100 percent, even when looking at some of the core obligations. The major compliance challenges since entry into force in 1999 have for the most part been successfully addressed but only through somewhat scattershot, ad hoc, uncoordinated efforts, and only with heavy reliance on the ICBL and ICRC.

Compliance issues may intensify in the years ahead. In April 2007, the ICBL warned States Parties that "some very serious compliance concerns have arisen that must be acknowledged and dealt with. These are compliance concerns related to the fundamental obligations of the treaty: the prohibitions on use, transfer, and stockpiling, and the deadlines for stockpile destruction and clearance of mined areas. It is possible that looked at individually, each of these compliance issues can be explained away in some fashion, or dismissed as not posing any real threat to the integrity of the treaty. But taken as a whole, they can be seen as a very troubling indicator about the health of the treaty."[33]

The ICBL cited Venezuela's "use" of emplaced antipersonnel mines to continue to derive military benefit and noted the phenomenon is not limited just to Venezuela. It cited the reports of the UN arms embargo Monitoring Group for Somalia with specific details on shipments of antipersonnel mines from the governments of Eritrea and Ethiopia to groups in Somalia. It noted that Afghanistan had missed its stockpile destruction deadline, that Belarus is almost certain to miss its deadline, and that Ukraine is in danger of missing its deadline as well. It expressed concern about what appears to be widespread abuse of the exception in Article 3 allowing for the retention of mines for training and development purposes. Finally, the ICBL stated that it has become increasingly evident that a large number of States Parties will not meet their mine clearance deadline.

It does not appear that States Parties are vigorously pursuing clarification and resolution of this disturbing slate of compliance problems, even though they are among the most serious raised since the treaty came into existence.

A major weakness is the lack of a coordinated system to address compliance concerns. In addition to the practical need to take steps to be able to utilize the compliance provisions of the treaty (Article 8) in a worst case scenario, the ICBL has repeatedly called for the development of informal mechanisms or an informal body to ensure that matters of compliance are dealt with in a systematic and coordinated fashion.

This could involve past and present presidents of Meetings of States Parties, some or all of the cochairs of the Standing Committees, some variation of the Contact Group model, or another innovative approach. States Parties have thus far not given enough serious consideration to the need for this, much less creative thought about how to do it. For an international process that has been notable for great ideas (such as the intersessional work program and its Standing Committees, the holding of annual meetings in mine-affected countries, the Implementation Support Unit, the Contact Groups, and the Landmine Monitor), this remains the much needed great idea still waiting to happen.

Ten years after the successful negotiation of the Mine Ban Treaty, its doubters have been proven wrong at nearly every turn, not least in terms of the record of compliance. But if the treaty is still to be held up as a shining example of implementation and compliance in ten more years, States Parties—in cooperation with civil society partners—will likely have to undertake new steps and explore new ways to meet the current and potentially increasing challenges to compliance with *all* aspects of the Mine Ban Treaty.

Notes

1. The 155 States Parties (79 percent of the world's countries) include all of the Western Hemisphere except the United States and Cuba, all of the European Union except Finland, all of NATO except the United States, all of sub-Saharan Africa except Somalia, and key Asian countries such as Japan, Thailand, and Cambodia. Recent additions include Indonesia (the fourth most populous nation in the world), Iraq, and Kuwait.

2. It is one of twenty-two Articles, but comprises about 20 percent of the treaty text.

3. Although a very impressive 120 countries attended the meeting, showing rapidly growing interest in banning antipersonnel mines, the author's personal observation is that this meeting was notable for the lack of preparation on the part of vast majority of delegations, and the lack of energy and interest in the room.

4. Steffen Kongstad, Deputy Director General, Royal Norwegian Ministry of Foreign Affairs, Oslo, April 5, 2006, quoted in Mary Wareham, "What If No One's Watching? Landmine Monitor: 1999–2005," Fafo-rapport 550, 2006, p. 17.

5. For more details on state positions during the Ottawa Process and the negotiations, see Stuart Maslen, *Commentaries on Arms Control Treaties, Volume 1, The Convention on the Prohibition of the Use, Stockpiling, Production, and Transfer of Anti-Personnel Mines and on their Destruction* (Oxford: Oxford University Press, 2004), pp. 209–242.

6. Ambassador Dan Livermore, New York, November 3, 2000, quoted in Stuart Maslen, *Commentaries on Arms Control Treaties, Volume 1, The Convention on the Prohibition of the Use, Stockpiling, Production, and Transfer of Anti-Personnel Mines and on their Destruction* (Oxford: Oxford University Press, 2004), p. 225.

7. ICBL Statement, delivered by Steve Goose, Head of ICBL Delegation, to the Standing Committee on General Status and Operation of the Convention, Geneva, May 16, 2003.

8. ICBL, *Landmine Monitor Report 2002: Toward a Mine-Free World* (Washington, DC: Human Rights Watch, 2002), p. 472.

9. ICBL, *Landmine Monitor Report 2002*, pp. 472–473.

10. It submitted an initial transparency report in February 2003 (perhaps most notable in that it became the first and only State Party to report details on antipersonnel mines stockpiled by a non-State Party, in this case Russia, on its territory), and updates every year since. It began stockpile destruction in 2002 and completed in March 2004, just ahead of its deadline. In June 2003, Tajikistan established a mine action center to enable it to meet its ten-year mine clearance deadline. ICBL, *Landmine Monitor Report 2003*, pp. 450–452. See also, Tajikistan country report in subsequent editions of *Landmine Monitor*.

11. There were also more vague accusations that troops from States Parties Rwanda and Chad also used mines in the DRC.

12. ICBL, *Landmine Monitor Report 2000*, p. 200.

13. The sensitivity of possible use by Zimbabwe was heightened considerably because it was taking over an important leadership position—cochair of the Standing Committee on General Status and Operation of the Convention—as of the Second Meeting of States Parties.

14. For more on this issue, see ICBL, *Landmine Monitor Report 2001*, pp. 176–179.

15. Uganda ratified the Mine Ban Treaty in February 1999, and the treaty entered into force for it on August 1, 1999.

16. ICBL, *Landmine Monitor Report 2004*, p. 834.

17. In conversations with the ICBL, a key Ugandan military official acknowledged that, while Ugandan policy clearly prohibited any use of antipersonnel mines, it was possible that Ugandan troops in Kisangani were unaware of the ban and could have

helped to lay mines (provided perhaps by rebels or Rwanda). He agreed on the importance of ensuring all troops are aware of Mine Ban Treaty obligations.

18. ICBL Intervention on Compliance, delivered by Steve Goose, Head of ICBL Delegation, Standing Committee on General Status and Operation of the Convention, Geneva, April 27, 2007.

19. Guinea's mines were destroyed with the assistance of the United States, and Cape Verde's with the assistance of NATO.

20. ICBL Statement on Article 3, delivered by Steve Goose, Head of ICBL Delegation, Standing Committee on General Status and Operation of the Convention, Geneva, May 16, 2003.

21. The 69,200 was more than four times the total retained by any other State Party; only four states retained more than ten thousand, and only six more retained more than five thousand.

22. See ICBL, *Landmine Monitor Report 2003*, p. 475.

23. ICBL Intervention on Article 3—Mines Retained for Training, delivered by Steve Goose, Head of ICBL Delegation, Standing Committee on General Status and Operation of the Convention, Geneva, April 27, 2007.

24. States that decided to reduce their number of retained mines include: Argentina, Australia, Bulgaria, Chile, Croatia, Denmark, Ecuador, Italy, Lithuania, Macedonia, Mauritania, Moldova, Peru, Portugal, Romania, Slovakia, Slovenia, Spain, Thailand, Turkmenistan, Uganda, the United Kingdom, Venezuela, and Zambia. Nine of these originally intended to keep ten thousand or more mines.

25. Their respective deadlines were August 28, 1999; April 30, 2002; August 28, 2003; February 28, 2001; November 28, 2005; and January 28, 2007. The ICBL has said Equatorial Guinea, Cape Verde, Gambia, and São Tomé e Principe are "grossly noncompliant" in ignoring this requirement, particularly because they passed their four-year deadline for stockpile destruction without ever officially informing other States Parties of their compliance with that key obligation.

26. More specifically, many States Parties have agreed that States Parties should not participate in planning for use of antipersonnel mines, agree to rules of engagement permitting use of antipersonnel mines, derive direct military benefit from others' use of antipersonnel mines, train others to use antipersonnel mines, request others to use antipersonnel mines, or provide security or transportation for antipersonnel mines.

27. Germany, Japan, Qatar, and the United Kingdom have stated that U.S. antipersonnel mine stocks in their countries are not under their national jurisdiction or control.

28. ICBL Intervention on the Five-Year Review Document—The Challenges Ahead, delivered by Steve Goose, Director of Human Rights Watch Arms Division and Head of ICBL Delegation at Nairobi Summit on a Mine-Free World, November 30, 2004, http://hrw.org/english/docs/2004/11/30/global10233.htm.

29. ICBL Intervention on Article 1, delivered by Steve Goose, Head of ICBL Delegation, Standing Committee on General Status and Operation of the Convention, April 27, 2007.

30. UNGA Resolution 61/84 was adopted on December 6, 2006, by a vote of 161 in favor, none opposed, and 17 abstentions. This was the highest number of votes in favor

of, and equal to the lowest number of abstentions on, this annual resolution since 1997 when it was first introduced. Twenty states not party to the treaty voted in favor.

31. In 2006, the United States began low-rate production of a new munition system called Spider that may be incompatible with the Mine Ban Treaty. A decision on entering into full-scale production has not been made, and opposition has been expressed in the U.S. Congress.

32. While still signatories, a number of current States Parties submitted voluntary reports, including Cameroon in 2001 and Gambia and Lithuania in 2002. Then non-State Party Latvia submitted voluntary reports in 2003, 2004, and 2005.

33. ICBL Intervention on Compliance, delivered by Steve Goose, Head of ICBL Delegation, Standing Committee on General Status and Operation of the Convention, Geneva, April 27, 2007.

8

An Indispensable Tool:
The Mine Ban Treaty and Mine Action

Robert Eaton

T HE MOVEMENT TO BAN LANDMINES did not invent mine action.[1] But the inspired work of the International Campaign to Ban Landmines (ICBL) cat-
apulted a small-scale effort to assist victims and underfunded work to locate
and destroy mines in the ground into a major global effort with broad public
support and significant funding. This chapter examines the historically unprecedented effect that the 1997 Mine Ban Treaty—in large part a disarmament treaty—has had on the humanitarian and development sector committed to attacking the problem of antipersonnel mines.

Virtually all recognize that the Mine Ban Treaty came about largely as a result of the ICBL's work. But less noticed is the impetus that the political organizing and agitation of the ICBL gave to mobilizing global support for mine
action, and the role that the treaty has played. The Mine Ban Treaty has been
an indispensable element in creating the mine action sector over the past
decade.

In the preamble to the Mine Ban Treaty, States Parties pledge "to do their
utmost to contribute in an efficient and coordinated manner to face the challenge of removing anti-personnel mines placed throughout the world, and to
assure their destruction." By any measure, the success of the treaty in generating funding for mine action is clear. Roughly one-third of a billion U.S. dollars was spent on mine action in 2006, and some $3 billion over the ten years
since the treaty was signed in 1997. In that same period, victim rates have
dropped by more than half.

While many factors contributed to this humanitarian triumph, it is largely
the result of the unorthodox relationship of the Mine Ban Treaty, campaigners

under the banner of the ICBL, and the larger mine action community of national authorities, donors, field operators—especially nongovernmental organizations (NGOs) —and United Nations (UN) agencies.

Yet, the treaty may have reached a point of diminishing returns as the global struggle to address the landmine issue reaches its end game, and the humanitarian and development sector moves beyond landmines to the broader concern of explosive remnants of war (ERW).[2] This has important implications for all of the actors, governmental and nongovernmental, who have put so much into this effort over the past decade and more.

The Beginnings of Mine Action:
From Laos to Afghanistan to Cambodia to Ottawa

When the war in Indochina ended in 1975, the Mennonites and Quakers in Laos began work to mitigate the negative social and economic impact of large areas of unexploded ordnance (UXO) and landmine pollution on rural populations. The border areas with Vietnam were awash in the blood of victims in the first five years after the conclusion of the war, as eastern Laos was one large *de facto* minefield, albeit filled largely with cluster bomblets. These efforts contributed significantly to recognition of mine clearance as a humanitarian and development concern. This change in consciousness helped fuel the campaign to eliminate these weapons.

The next big event in the evolution of mine action took place in Afghanistan. After the Soviets withdrew from Afghanistan in early 1989, the international community mobilized to help rebuild the country, and mine clearance was an essential part of the planning. For the first time, mine clearance was recognized as a humanitarian obligation and not simply an unfortunate and untreatable consequence of war. At first the UN took the approach of training refugees to carry out clearance when they returned home, but as post-Soviet Afghanistan slid into a violent civil war this became untenable. The UN moved toward creating well-trained Afghan NGOs to conduct clearance activities throughout the country.[3] The early effort was funded by Germany, the United States, and Japan, but by 1995 mine clearance by Afghan NGOs was being funded through the UN by twelve donor countries and the European Commission.

Meanwhile, on the other side of Asia, NGO activities in Cambodia were leading to a sea change in mine action. With the civil war and exodus of refugees to the Thai border in 1979, Handicap International began to assist landmine amputees in 1980. Through this early work with landmine victims, the humanitarian community began to take notice of the horror produced by these weapons.

In 1991 the Vietnam Veterans of America Foundation and Medico International of Germany began cooperation to provide medical assistance for amputee war victims inside Cambodia. These two organizations decided that in addition to helping victims of landmines there was an obligation to "go upstream" and stop the use and production of these weapons. In October 1992, Handicap International, Human Rights Watch, Medico International, Mines Advisory Group, Physicians for Human Rights, and Vietnam Veterans of America Foundation convened the founding meeting of the International Campaign to Ban Landmines.

With the creation of the ICBL and the process leading to the treaty five years later, mine action was changed forever. Rebuffed in traditional disarmament forums, the ICBL and its allies in several capitals and the International Committee of the Red Cross (ICRC) produced a fascinating stew of themes and approaches seldom seen before. It was a rich and bubbling brew of civil society, diplomats, disarmament advocates, crisis mitigation groups, and others. This was a glorious and opportunistic response to a humanitarian crisis and diplomatic deadlock that ultimately produced the treaty signed in Ottawa in December 1997.

The campaign raised global awareness and the treaty provided a legal framework, and mine action exploded onto the world stage.

The Mine Ban Treaty: Mine Action Will Never be the Same

The Mine Ban Treaty was conceived in the framework of "human security" and was viewed as much a humanitarian and development initiative as a disarmament one. The treaty is highly unusual in that it brings together disarmament and humanitarian objectives and requirements. It not only bans use, production, trade, and stockpiling of the weapons, it requires states to deal with the *effects* of the weapon. In keeping with the humanitarian impulses that gave birth to the mine ban movement, the treaty is responsive to the needs of communities already affected by mines, by mandating clearance of minefields and other forms of mine action, including assistance to victims.

Canada invited many of the participants from the treaty signing ceremony in late 1997 to return to Ottawa in early 1998 to get down to the task of coordinating the actual work to assist victims and clear mines. A rich mix of NGOs active in mine action on the ground, donor states, and diplomats attended this conference, as they did a similar meeting convened by the United States, a nonsignatory, to continue and further the coordination and planning effort.

Just as the Mine Ban Treaty had been created by a vital alliance of civil society and governments, it became increasingly clear in the years following its

signing and entry into force that it would be implemented with the same unorthodox combination of forces. This was not wholly accepted by everyone.
Some NGOs were content to ignore or even argue against the treaty and continue their mine action work independently. There were those within the UN
system that assumed that the humanitarian and development aspects of mine
action would naturally accrue to the UN system of agencies.

Since the signing of the treaty, efforts to alleviate the suffering caused by
landmines have grown tremendously in their scope, sophistication, and effectiveness. Humanitarian mine action has become accepted as the best means to
address the landmine problem, including survey and assessment, marking and
clearing of mines, mine risk education, and quality assurance. There has been
increased transparency, better research, expanded efforts by dedicated field
operators, and the development of new tools, including the Landmine Impact
Survey, the Information Management System for Mine Action, and others, for
the improvement of mine action operations, information management, and
coordination.[4]

But what has been the effect of the treaty on mine clearance? This question
shall be examined in four areas: the international context, the Mine Ban Treaty
process, funding for mine action, and treaty obligations.

The International Context

The mine ban campaign and the treaty have fundamentally changed the context within which mine clearance takes place. The first UN study of mine
clearance globally was written in 1996 and 1997. It noted, "The landmine crisis is not static. Stockpiling and the sowing of new minefields continue to out-
pace the resources which are available to counter the crises. The actual number of new minefields being created annually is not known but given the
widespread use of mine-warfare in contemporary conflicts, there is every danger that proliferation outpaces clearance."[5] Ten years later, this is no longer the
case on a global basis.

The HALO Trust entertainingly interjected at the 2004 First Review Conference of the Mine Ban Treaty that the good news is that landmines don't have
sex—they don't multiply—and therefore systematic mine action will make
headway against the problem.[6] In line with this comment, the ban campaign is
the movement and the treaty is the instrument that neutered landmines. Without them mine action would still be attempting to bail water out of the sea.

The treaty exerts its influence beyond its obligations and its formal adherents in two ways. First, the weapon has been so stigmatized that although the
treaty is, regrettably, not universal, its provisions with few exceptions are *de*

facto universal in that major nations not party to the treaty largely abide by its provisions. Second, although the treaty specifically bans only antipersonnel landmines, the use of antivehicle mines has dropped as well. There are significant exceptions to this phenomenon. Mines are still being laid by the governments of Burma (Myanmar) and Russia (in Chechnya), and by rebels in those locations, Colombia, and a handful of other places. Mine action has made almost no impact on the situation in those countries. Nonetheless, the important progress that has been made since the signing of the treaty in significantly halting the use of this weapon cannot be overstated.

The Mine Ban Treaty Process

In 1999, at the First Meeting of State Parties in Maputo, Mozambique, a final report was approved that established the key role of the treaty in providing the framework for mine action.[7] States Parties agreed in Maputo to create the Intersessional Work Programme, or intersessionals for short: a system of informal meetings to be held between annual Meetings of State Parties. At the intersessionals, Standing Committees would meet to discuss topics, including mine clearance, mine risk education, research and technology, and victim assistance, and to make plans and review progress in these areas.[8] The deliberations and recommendations of these committees would be reported back to the Meetings of State Parties, where any formal action and decision-making would occur.

The process has had several very positive results. It has provided a regular forum where NGOs working on the ground, mine-affected and donor states, and the UN meet regularly to hear reports on progress and problems, discuss best practices, and raise money for local projects. It has encouraged governments to engage in more effective and urgent planning and implementation of the different aspects of mine action. The bilateral meetings, conversations over coffee in the halls, and meals after hours produce fantastic opportunities for doers and donors to interact. It has been in these informal sessions that effective education and exchange has taken place. The intersessionals and annual meetings have also served the political purpose of keeping the momentum of the treaty and the mine eradication effort alive.

On the downside, the notion of the Mine Ban Treaty as the focal point for global mine action left the largest donor, the United States, on the sidelines of the process. Moreover, the intersessional sessions have become increasingly formalized as the years pass. Reporting by states and others has taken on a repetitive quality that registers progress being made, but does not proactively push the envelope in a way one would desire.

Also, while the UN has remained a diligent participant, over time it has developed a parallel structure of consultation and coordination in UN-sponsored meetings that draw together the national directors of mine action centers with UN advisors, NGOs, and donor state representatives. In recent years, this annual meeting has become equally as important an institutional focus for coordination and competence sharing and competence building.

The Mine Ban Treaty process has held together the various players in an amazing and unprecedented coalition of concern, where inherent tensions have been kept below the surface. The civil society advocacy style versus the diplomatic consensus style has been kept under control. The north-south split that plagues many international efforts has never become a public issue.

There is another less recognized potential conflict between those who focus primarily on the necessity of meeting the treaty's obligations (and clearance of all mined areas in particular) and those, especially aid operators, who see mine action in a broader development context of limited resources and hard choices. This potential conflict has been held in check as long as mine action funding was on the increase. But as the first clearance deadlines in 2009 approach amidst signs that funding may be beginning a long-term decline, this "fulfilment of treaty obligations versus development concerns" issue is sure to become ever more important and contentious.

Raising Consciousness and Funds

The role of the Mine Ban Treaty—and the ban movement more generally—in mobilizing funds is, up to a point, a fantastic success. It highlighted the existence of the landmine problem and moved the mine clearance agenda from an esoteric backwater of military science and doctrine to an issue of public concern and responsibility in the context of humanitarian and development assistance in postconflict societies. The work of the ICBL and others brought funding out of the humanitarian war victim assistance closet and created legitimacy to fund clearance and mine risk education.

No comprehensive, confirmed figures are available, but it is estimated that in 1997, USD$139 million was pledged to mine action by national donors. By 2004, the total had increased to $399 million, a nearly threefold increase. From 2003 through 2005, donors provided over $1.1 billion dollars. Some $3 billion has been spent on mine action since 1997.[9] This is an incredible achievement.

However, in 2005 for the first time aggregate global donor funding declined, from $399 million to $376 million. The largest mine action donor, the United States, has announced that it will reduce funding beginning in 2008. Other significant donors are quietly planning for similar reductions. While the best face is put on a deteriorating situation at public meetings, it is clear that the level of donor commitment is beginning to decrease. In addition to decreased funding, some states have downgraded the staffing of their dedicated mine action bureaus. Although there has been increasing funding supplied by mine-affected countries to their own programs, they still remain largely dependent on foreign assistance. Only Croatia's mine action program is mostly funded by its own government.

No one wishes it, but there is a specter that haunts the future of mine action funding. The reality is that donors break down funding into budget lines with corresponding bureaus and divisions to spend the various monies allocated. Mine action has been primarily funded by the crisis, humanitarian and dedicated budget lines, and to a lesser extent, those related to development. Crisis funding is limited, often arbitrarily, to relatively short time frames.

As casualty rates drop, humanitarian funding departments are beginning to look to other sectors. Development funding lines will support mine action only up to a point. Where donor governments have shifted emphasis for mine action to their development departments, it does not appear to be competing well with development issues such as HIV/AIDS, clean drinking water, agricultural credit, and others. Disarmament budget lines for mine action are virtually nonexistent with the exception in some cases of stockpile destruction.

In short, after making solid contributions in the ten years since the Mine Ban Treaty was signed, the crisis and humanitarian budget lines for mine action are growing soft, and the slack is not being taken up by development or disarmament budget lines.

Mine Ban Treaty Obligations

Articles 5 and 6

There are two main articles concerning mine clearance in the Mine Ban Treaty—Articles 5 and 6. Article 5 requires a variety of mine action activities by mine-affected countries, including a time-bound clearance obligation, while Article 6 deals with cooperation and assistance by all States Parties. According to Article 5, each State Party must:

- "make every effort to identify all areas in its jurisdiction or control in which anti-personnel mines are known or suspected to be emplaced,"
- "ensure as soon as possible" that these areas "are perimeter-marked, monitored and protected by fencing or other means, to ensure the effective exclusion of civilians until all anti-personnel mines contained therein have been destroyed," and,

- "destroy or ensure the destruction of all anti-personnel mines in mined areas under its jurisdiction or control, as soon as possible but not later than ten years after the entry into force of this Convention \$for that State Party."
- In the event a State Party cannot meet the deadline, it may ask for an extension of up to ten years. Such requests require detailed explanation for failure to meet the deadline and must be approved by a majority of States Parties voting.

States Parties, contrary to popular opinion, are not required to be mine-free. They are required to make "every effort" to identify all known or suspected mined areas and to clear them of mines. Even the most scrupulous efforts may miss some areas.

Article 6 says that "Each State Party in a position to do so shall provide assistance for mine clearance and related activities . . . for the care and rehabilitation, and social and economic reintegration, of mine victims, and for mine awareness programs . . . [and] for the destruction of stockpiled anti-personnel mines."

Thus, the treaty contains an interesting asymmetry. Mine-affected countries have clear final responsibility for demining, where failure to do so constitutes a treaty violation, while nonaffected states have an undefined and voluntary admonishment to assist if they feel they are "in a position to do so." To date, this nonbinding request to assist has been taken seriously by many States Parties that have provided generous funding focused largely on mine-affected countries that are part of the treaty.

Investigate

The treaty obligates State Parties to identify all areas known or suspected to have landmines. This makes good sense: if you want to solve a problem, one of the first things you need to do is determine its size and nature. But, reasonable people may disagree on the best measure—mines in the ground, square kilometers polluted, number of victims, impacted communities, or other factors. This problem has been understood almost from the very beginning.

Yet after all this time no one can provide a truly reliable estimate of the global size of the landmine problem, even in the largely discredited measure of square kilometers. For an industry that has consumed about \$3 billion and claimed its goal was to solve the problem, this is not an encouraging fact. Of the twenty-nine States Parties with clearance deadlines in 2009 and 2010, only twenty-one even have an estimate of suspected hazard areas, and none have a firm figure for mined areas that require clearance.

The treaty requires States Parties to identify both known and suspected areas. This makes sense because it is the very nature of landmines to create fear far in excess of the actual threat and therefore deny access to the maximum amount of land. If suspicion keeps a farmer from tilling a field, the distinction, in terms of socioeconomic impact, between suspected and real is moot.

The question becomes, how do you reduce suspected areas to known mined areas? This is a critical question because clearance is required by the treaty in known areas. It is also critical because most mine-affected countries have reported suspected hazard areas that are now known to be far larger than the actual minefields that may be imbedded within them.[10]

The International Mine Action Standards (IMAS), produced by the United Nations, indicate that suspected hazard areas may be reduced to smaller mined areas by means of cancellation. According to IMAS, a Cancelled Area is "an area previously recorded as a hazardous area which subsequently is considered, as a result of actions other than clearance, not to represent a risk from mines and ERW."[11] This definition is helpful but does not give guidance on how one actually cancels land.

To date, most mine action activity in countries has been focused, like the treaty itself, on clearance. Yet the time and money needed for cancellation are far less than for clearance. According to one estimate, cancellation of suspected hazard areas costs roughly one cent per square meter while clearing that same area will cost between ninety cents and five dollars per square meter.[12] Some states such as Bosnia and Herzegovina and Croatia are making substantive progress in systematically and transparently reducing their suspected areas to mined areas for clearance, but most countries are fairly vague on the process.

The challenge for most States Parties is to develop intellectually and morally acceptable systems for reducing the suspected areas to known areas. However this process of reduction is undertaken, it will involve judgement and ultimately a calculation of acceptable risk. Such risk calculation is best left to the communities and states that will live with the consequences.

Analysis of aggregated data from ten national landmine impact surveys indicates that less than 10 percent of all suspected hazard areas have a probability of claiming a victim in a two-year period.[13] From the data, these suspected areas can be named and located. The findings need to be field tested but provide hope that serious area reduction can still be accomplished in a timely and cost-effective manner from the data that is now available.

Mark, Fence, Clear

Article 5 requires States Parties to mark or fence mined areas to exclude civilians prior to clearing. This has not been done systematically. Once a suspected area is reduced to a mined area, mine action authorities generally seek to clear it immediately. Marking may be used as an interim step. But fencing is not as critical as envisioned by the treaty.

Article 5 creates specific deadlines for clearing mines from mined areas and several countries have declared themselves to have met the goal, including Bulgaria, Costa Rica, the Czech Republic, Guatemala, Honduras, and Suriname. Far more countries, including some of the most mine-affected, however, have indicated, formally or informally, that they will not reach the goal and can only speculate on how close they actually are. Of the first twenty-nine State Parties facing the 2009 and 2010 deadlines, only thirteen have reported an ability or intent to meet their deadline, and in several cases this commitment is contingent on substantially increased outside funding.[14]

First, it must be recognized that the Article 5 clearance obligation is not as absolute as it may first appear. The key concept is not absolute but judgmental. Affected State Parties are required to "make every effort" to identify their mine problem. How states do that varies considerably. Methods range from Landmine Impact Surveys that inventory impacted communities and identify suspected areas in each community to postconflict desktop surveys using military maps and zones of conflict analysis perhaps augmented by some degree of ground truth. How much effort meets the "make every effort" standard of the treaty? The assumption is that each country will determine this level of effort for itself.

Then the question arises as to what constitutes "destruction of all anti-personnel mines." The International Mine Action Standards suggest that clearance to a depth of 13 centimeters is acceptable. Some countries allow legislated shallower depths; for instance, Cambodia by national regulation clears to 10 centimeters. The treaty wisely sets no standards, which should appropriately be set by the affected nation. While 13 centimeters is arguably a safer standard than 10, on the other hand no one claims that 13 centimeters is without risk. It is largely a number determined by the technical ability of metal detectors and dogs' noses, and by the depth beyond which most landmines will not be triggered by people walking over the surface. At some point a reasoned judgment on risk enters the picture, and the affected State Party must make a decision on standards to define mine clearance.

This should not been seen as a lawyerly attempt to wiggle out of the intent of Article 5. National authorities, as the owners of the problem, should be in the front line of making a series of judgments on how, in good faith, to meet the terms of Article 5. Those who carry the heaviest responsibility should take the lead in outlining operational definitions of how to meet the clearance responsibility. As funding levels begin a long-term decline, the hard choices will have to be made by national authorities.

The Mine Ban Treaty and Mine Action:
Convergence and Divergence

In its disarmament aspects, the Mine Ban Treaty focuses solely on antipersonnel landmines. In the field, operators treat antipersonnel mines, antivehicle mines, and other explosive remnants of war as a common problem. Mine action is committed to a larger task than only eliminating antipersonnel mines. While most operators support the Mine Ban Treaty, few if any, would say that they only work to eliminate antipersonnel mines.

In the early years, when first clearance deadlines of 2009 seemed far away and funding was relatively easy, not much attention was paid to the fact that the treaty language and, particularly, Article 5 converged on a subset of mine action—antipersonnel mines—while the dynamic of mine action diverged from this specific focus to a larger humanitarian crisis of ERW. This divergent tendency is increasing as antipersonnel mine use decreases, and mine action operators find themselves responding to such things as cluster munition strikes in Afghanistan, Iraq, and Lebanon.

It is not a little ironic that, in many ways, the movement that created the treaty and the institutions that carry the treaty forward have supported this divergence. Perhaps most notably, an element of this divergence that is not supported by many key treaty proponents is investigation of risk management approaches to mine action.

This dilemma is captured nicely by a current International Mine Action Standard definition of mine action:

> Mine Action: activities which aim to reduce the social, economic and environmental impact of mines and ERW. Mine action is not just about demining; it is also about people and societies, and how they are affected by landmine and ERW contamination. The objective of mine action is to reduce the risk from landmines and ERW to a level where people can live safely; in which economic, social and health development can occur free from the constraints imposed by landmine and ERW contamination, and in which the victims' needs can be addressed. . . . [15]

The preamble to the treaty clearly puts forth the treaty's human security emphasis on a people-focused approach, as does this definition. But strict adherence to Article 5 could run counter to the second part of the IMAS definition that states the objective of mine action to be to "reduce the risk"—if reducing risk is meant, as most people believe it to be, to stop short of full clearance.

There is no right or wrong to convergence or divergence. They respond to differing needs and have a logic of their own. But as the treaty stays focused on States Parties' responsibilities under the treaty and the mine action community increasingly responds to concerns outside it, the vision at the First Meeting of States Parties in Maputo of the treaty as the organizing focus for mine action becomes less relevant.

A Changing Appreciation of the Threat

While the treaty's requirement to destroy all antipersonnel mines in mined areas may not be as absolute as some believe, it is clearly a very high standard. However, from a humanitarian and development point of view we are learning that at least some mined areas may not be all that dangerous, especially when compared to other threats such as unsafe drinking water, HIV/AIDS, or auto fatalities, and especially when considering the realities of limited funding in the humanitarian and development world.

Implicit in the Article 5 requirement, and a widely shared point of view at the time the treaty was written, was that all mined areas were a clear and present danger to the population. The Article provides for immediate fencing and marking if identified areas cannot be cleared immediately. Yet in practice, almost no fencing takes place and marking is not systematic or felt to be particularly effective in some places. Yet, the absence of fencing or the universal and effective marking has not led to a bloodbath.

This raises the question of how lethal these mined areas really are. Obviously some mined areas are genuine killing fields such as the notorious K5 minefield in Cambodia. But overall evidence would suggest that the average mined area is not a clear and immediate threat to the local population. In part, this may be due to increased local familiarity with a problem whose parameters are not changing over a period of time and/or effective mine risk education.

Another reality in assessing the threat is that while victims have been at the center of the definition of the mine problem from the very beginning, rates of new victims each year are dropping. Landmine impact surveys are showing drops in victim rates both in countries with an active and mature mine action program and those without a mine action program.[16]

It is also interesting to note that villagers are undertaking mine clearance as a village-level risk management activity. More evidence is now being collected on the amount of informal demining by villagers with little or no training and virtually no standard equipment. Two studies in Cambodia indicate the practice is more widespread than previously understood, and the accident rates appear not to be significantly more than rates for formal demining.[17]

The Survey Action Center has studied similar activities in Afghanistan and Angola. Although the evidence of villagers directly clearing mines is less clear than in Cambodia, these studies indicate that villagers are not always waiting for the professionals to arrive and declare some suspected hazard areas free of significant risk. The villagers are doing this on their own. The Landmine Impact Survey indicates that in several countries villagers are simply assessing the risk of working in suspected areas and releasing a significant amount of land for productive use.

Conclusion

As the landmine crisis has abated, the argument that while lives were in imminent danger one could not afford the time or money to invest in long-term planning is no longer valid (if indeed it ever was). The Mine Ban Treaty process could remain a vital forum for encouraging long-term planning and for sharing successes and learning from failures. But a focus on immediate action to reach Article 5 deadlines and standards mitigates against an understanding that countries will have to live with landmines for a long time, and that the best strategy is one that recognizes the long haul and plans appropriately.

National authorities have the capacity to cope with the problem once it has been reduced to a residual problem, and this is possible if the international community and operators act accordingly. The goal should be to move as quickly as possible to a point where national authorities have the information, analysis, and capacity to define the remaining landmine problem and solve it on their own.

In the end, internationally supported mine action will never fully disappear. Bilateral agencies will continue to support international meetings for sharing lessons learned, management training courses, and assistance in refreshing aging equipment inventories. But the bulk of the effort should be locally funded, with the possible exception of victim assistance. This subsector of mine action was present before the ban movement and treaty and will probably survive and carry on as the world churns up new conflicts and creates more war victims. But in the future, thanks to the learning process of the last ten years, victim assistance will move beyond direct medical care for war victims and expand to include assistance in the context of disability rights for all.

The Mine Ban Treaty has catalyzed a movement and made possible an amazing worldwide effort to stigmatize the antipersonnel landmine, reduce its victims to virtually zero, and remove major impediments to development. This alone marks it as a signal achievement in terms of a global response to an ugly weapon of war. The results in terms of total eradication are less clear. While some countries will be free of known mines, the majority will remain with known and uncleared fields well into the future. How this is interpreted and addressed in terms of Article 5 of the treaty is open to speculation. Possibilities include repeated extensions, flexible interpretation of "known" mined areas, and acceptance of nationally defined risk management. Whatever the result, it will not be as neat and clean as the wording of Article 5 appears to be.

The overwhelming requirement is for national authorities to develop transparent systems to reduce their suspected hazard areas to "known" mined areas. Once this is accomplished, an assessment of available national and international resources and varying level of risk will be made in order to determine the best course of action. This may or may not bring a State Party into compliance with Article 5. But the fundamentals for an effective and efficient mine action are unchanged.

Notes

1. Mine action is generally defined as containing five pillars: mine survey, marking and clearing; victim assistance; stockpile destruction; advocacy; and mine risk education. This chapter focuses on survey, marking, and clearing.

2. Protocol V of the Convention on Conventional Weapons defines explosive remnants of war as comprising both unexploded ordnance (UXO) and abandoned explosive ordnance (AXO).

3. This decision was informed by a highly critical outside evaluation in 1991. Colonel B. Florence and Professor James Freedman, "Evaluation of the Mine Clearance Programme in Afghanistan," Report to the Personal Representative of the Secretary-General of the United Nations in Afghanistan, July 1991.

4. See KBL, "Executive Summary," *Landmine Monitor Report 2004* (Washington, DC: Human Rights Watch, 2004), for facts and analysis of developments in mine action in the first five years of the Mine Ban Treaty.

5. Bob Eaton, Norah Niland, and Chris Horwood, *Study Report: The Development of Indigenous Mine Action Capacities* (New York: UN Department of Humanitarian Affairs, 1996), p. 15, para. 26.

6. Statement by Guy Willoughby, HALO Trust, on behalf of the NGO Perspective, "Landmines and Sex," Nairobi, November 30, 2004, http://www.icbl.org/layout/set/print/news/summit_update_2/landmines_and_sex.

7. First Meeting of the States Parties to the Convention on the Prohibition of the Use, Stockpiling, Production, and Transfer of Anti-Personnel Mines and on Their Destruction, "Final Report," Maputo, May 3–7, 1999, APLC/MSP.1/1999/1, May 20, 1999.

8. There were initially five Standing Committees of Experts which subsequently became four Standing Committees, including: (1) Mine Clearance, Mine Risk Education, and Mine Action Technologies; (2) Victim Assistance and Socio-Economic Reintegration; (3) Stockpile Destruction; and, (4) General Status and Operation.

9. ICBL, "Executive Summary," *Landmine Monitor Report 2006* (Ottawa: Mines Action Canada, 2006), p. 64.

10. Bosnia and Herzegovina represents a case in point. As part of the Dayton Peace Agreement of 1995, Bosnia and Herzegovina produced a map of suspected hazard areas that measured over 4,000 square kilometers. This was based on military maps of minefields, desktop analysis of lines of conflict and limited reporting from the ground. In 2003, on the basis of village-by-village investigations throughout the country, the Landmine Impact Survey concluded that the suspected areas were half the size previously reported. Survey Action Center, "Bosnia-Herzegovina Landmine Impact Survey, March 2002–August 2004," http://www.sac-na.org/surveys_bosnia.html.

11. IMAS 04.10, "Glossary of mine action terms, definitions and abbreviations," January 1, 2003, 2nd Edition Incorporating amendment numbers 1, 2 & 3, http://www.mineactionstandards.org/.

12. This is drawn from a calculation in 2006 by the Yemen Mine Action Center and the Survey Action Center as part of the UN Development Programme Completion Initiative.

13. Survey Action Center, "Update #2 Threat Prediction," June 1, 2005.

14. ICBL, "Executive Summary," *Landmine Monitor Report 2006*, p. 34.

15. IMAS 04.10, "Glossary of mine action terms, definitions and abbreviations," section 3.150.

16. For example, the rate drops in Yemen and Bosnia and Herzegovina are about the same, yet Yemen had no mature mine action program in place at the time of the data collection. The same relationship exists for another pair of similar rate drops: Thailand and Afghanistan.

17. Ruth Bottomley, *Crossing the Divide: Landmines, Villagers, and Organizations* (Oslo: International Peace Research Institute/PRIO, 2003), pp. 7–8; Michael L. Fleisher, *Informal Village Demining in Cambodia. An Operational Study* (Brussels: Handicap International Belgium, 2005).

9

Beyond the Rhetoric: The Mine Ban Treaty and Victim Assistance

Sheree Bailey and Tun Channareth

T HE MINE BAN TREATY HAS BEEN DESCRIBED as a "victory for humanity [and] the cause of humanitarian values in the face of cruelty and indifference."[1] Not only is it one of the fastest global multilateral arms control treaties to enter into force, it is also the first in history to make humanitarian provision for the victims of a particular weapon system.[2]

When you are injured in a landmine explosion, it is easy to think that your life is over and that there is no hope for the future. How can you provide for your family? How can you live a normal life? The signing ceremony of the Mine Ban Treaty in December 1997 was watched with great optimism by many mine survivors who had played a key role in making the dream of a treaty a reality. It provided hope that the international community would better understand the situation of people living in mine-affected communities. It gave hope for a better future.

The suffering of mine victims provided a major impetus for efforts to ban antipersonnel landmines. Although the number of new casualties has dropped since the treaty entered into force on March 1, 1999, the International Campaign to Ban Landmines (ICBL) estimates that between fifteen thousand and twenty thousand people, mostly civilians, are still killed or injured in landmine and unexploded ordnance (UXO) incidents every year.[3] The ICBL also estimates that there are between three hundred fifty thousand and four hundred thousand mine/UXO survivors in the world today.[4]

Article 6.3 of the treaty requires that "each State Party in a position to do so shall provide assistance for the care and rehabilitation, and social and economic reintegration, of mine victims. . . . " This obligation is as relevant for the affected State Party with responsibility to care for all its citizens, including mine victims, as it is for the State Party in a position to provide financial or other resources to assist affected States. According to the article, assistance may be provided through a variety of means, including "the United Nations system, international, regional or national organizations or institutions, the International Committee of the Red Cross (ICRC), and national Red Cross and Red Crescent societies and their International Federation, non-governmental organizations, or on a bilateral basis."

Even though the treaty resulted in terms like "mine victims" and "assistance" for victims becoming embedded in international law, these terms were not defined and States Parties were faced with the challenge of understanding exactly what could and should be done. Five years after the treaty entered into force, and on the eve of its First Review Conference, the ICBL continued to report that "in the vast majority of mine-affected countries, neither the national governments nor international donors are doing nearly enough" and the assistance available to address the needs of survivors remained "desperately inadequate."[5]

So what has the Mine Ban Treaty meant to mine survivors around the world? Is it living up to the promise contained in the commitments made by States Parties in the preamble to put an end to the suffering and to do their utmost to provide assistance for the care, rehabilitation, and social and economic reintegration of mine victims? Are the commitments being matched by actions on the ground to make a meaningful difference in the quality of life of mine survivors?

This chapter explores developments and progress in the provision of mine victim assistance since the treaty entered into force to determine whether in fact it is living up to its promise. Progress (or lack thereof) is reviewed through an examination of the activities of governments, and NGOs and international agencies, in particular, through the work of the treaty's Standing Committee on Victim Assistance and Socio-Economic Reintegration, and the ICBL and its member organizations.

Progress is examined from two perspectives: implementation of the treaty at the international level, including the outcomes of the 2004 Review Conference, and implementation and its impact on the lives of mine survivors living in affected communities.

The chapter starts with an overview of the reality of daily life for many mine survivors and concludes with an assessment of the challenges that remain in ensuring that the promise of the treaty is matched by an improvement in the quality of life of mine survivors and their families.

Reality of Life for Landmine Survivors in Affected Communities

There is no doubt that the daily lives of some mine survivors have improved as a direct result of the Mine Ban Treaty. New programs have been implemented, and there is now a greater understanding of both the rights of survivors and the needs that must be addressed. Nevertheless, limited financial and human resources mean that the assistance available continues to fall far short of meeting the needs.

In many affected countries, years of conflict have destroyed hospitals, roads and other infrastructure, and weakened the government. Affected states are often unable to meet the health, education, and economic needs of the general population, let alone provide specialized services needed by mine survivors. Too many people continue to die from their landmine injuries because of a lack of emergency medical care and transportation in remote areas. For some casualties it takes hours or days to reach the nearest equipped medical facility—on donkeys, on bicycles, in wheelbarrows, in the back of a truck, and carried by friends and relatives. Those who survive the explosion may not have access to facilities that would make possible their full recovery.

Landmines not only destroy lives and cause injury but also exacerbate the difficulties of postwar reconstruction and long-term development. Extreme poverty is widespread in the majority of affected communities, and landmine survivors and other people with disabilities are often the poorest and most vulnerable. They can face discrimination and misunderstanding from their families and communities. Even if laws protecting the rights of people with disabilities exist, the government may not be in a position, either politically or economically, to fully implement them.

Hospital services and other costs are often beyond the limited means of mine victims and their families. Families often sell land or other assets such as livestock, or borrow money, frequently at high interest rates, to cover the costs of emergency medical care. If the person killed or injured was the main provider, the family is not only faced with the loss of the food or income that he or she provided, but the added burden of debt. The costs associated with the rehabilitation phase or the fitting of artificial limbs can also be problematic.

Many mine survivors and the families of those killed or injured need support to overcome the psychological trauma of the landmine explosion and to promote their social well-being. However, social reintegration is often hindered by a lack of understanding among the general population of the rights, needs, and capacities of people with disabilities. It is acknowledged that the psychosocial needs of mine victims are not being adequately addressed due to a lack of attention and/or resources.[6]

For many mine survivors their most important issue is the lack of oppor-tunities to earn an income and resume their roles as productive members of their communities and within their families. Obstacles to economic reinte-gration include limited prospects for education and vocational training; lack of access to microcredit schemes to assist with the costs of setting up income generating activities; limited access to transport, footpaths, and buildings; dis-crimination and negative stereotypes in their communities; and economies with few jobs and high unemployment in the general population.

Data collected by Jesuit Service Cambodia as part of its outreach program in 1999 and 2000 revealed that of 1,663 survivors interviewed: 71 percent did not have adequate housing, 7 percent had no house at all, 45 percent had to travel more than five minutes to get water for drinking and washing, 89 per-cent reported food insecurity, 32 percent had no land for housing or cultiva-tion, 28 percent received a government pension, 50 percent had a "job" (in-cluding rice farming), and the children of at least 46 percent did not go to school.

As a result of the survey, mine survivors developed a twelve-point plan to address their needs and priorities: (1) a house that shelters the family from the weather; (2) enough food; (3) access to water for drinking and cleaning; (4) access to school for children and learning opportunities for adults; (5) access to primary health services; (6) access to income generating possibilities for family expenses; (7) no mines left in the housing, farming, and recreational areas of the village; (8) villagers deprived of land due to war and landmines receive title to available mine-free land; (9) access to prosthetics, wheelchairs, hearing aids, counseling services; (10) roads to market, with bridges and water control systems; (11) villagers participate in common projects, social and cul-tural events, and in decisions that affect their lives; and (12) villagers discuss and solve issues affecting them. The plan continues to be relevant for mine survivors in Cambodia, and many other affected countries, as the poor are still poor and daily life is still difficult.

Implementation of the Treaty at the International Level

Prior to entry into force of the treaty, limited attention was given to improv-ing the coordination and delivery of assistance to mine victims at the interna-tional level.[7] One of the first attempts to deal with the problem was the draft-ing of a strategic framework for planning integrated landmine victim assistance programs. Developed in 1999 by Switzerland in the lead-up to the treaty's First Meeting of the States Parties, in cooperation with the ICRC, the World Health Organization (WHO), UNICEF, and the ICBL, the framework was based on seven principles: (1) nondiscrimination of victims; (2) an integrated and comprehensive approach; (3) co-participation of all relevant actors; (4) national ownership and institutional support; (5) transparency and efficiency; (6) sustainable development approach; and (7) the empowerment of victims. Pilot projects were carried out in Afghanistan, Bosnia and Herzegovina, Mozambique, and Nicaragua.[8] Although some progress was made in establishing coordination committees and drafting action plans, it would appear that a lack of political will and/or a lack of international support meant that these plans were not implemented.

While the strategic framework did not produce concrete results, numerous national and international NGOs and international agencies have been active through advocacy as well as with programs to improve the quality of life of mine survivors and other people with disabilities. In 1999, the ICRC, which plays a key role in victim assistance advocacy and activities, launched its Special Appeal for Mine Action to support physical rehabilitation, emergency care, and other mine-related issues. By 2006, that Appeal and the ICRC's Special Fund for the Disabled had spent more than 153 million Swiss francs on victim assistance programs.[9] Additionally 110 ICRC-supported rehabilitation centers in thirty-eight countries have provided services since its physical rehabilitation program started in 1979.[10]

Victim assistance also remains a pillar of mine action under the revised United Nations Inter-Agency Mine Action Strategy for the period 2006 to 2010. Specific actions include ensuring the establishment of mine casualty monitoring systems, supporting efforts to ensure the rights of mine survivors within the context of national programs, facilities for persons with disabilities, and advocating for increased resources and support.[11] Agencies active in victim assistance-related activities since 1999 include the WHO, International Labor Organization, UN Development Programme (UNDP), UNICEF, UN Office for Project Services, the United Nations Mine Action Service (UNMAS), and more recently, the UN Office of the High Commissioner for Human Rights.

One particular issue of concern is the lack of long-term funding commitments that are essential to build sustainable national capacities to address the needs. States Parties have acknowledged "the fundamental importance of the international donor community" supporting victim assistance activities in affected countries.[12] Nevertheless, at an April 2007 meeting of the Standing Committee on Victim Assistance, the cochairs noted that "the potential for progress in some States Parties has been hindered by a lack of financial resources."[13]

While it is difficult to precisely track victim assistance funding, the ICRC has warned that "a creeping disengagement at national and international levels is threatening prospects for progress," adding "that a number of victim assistance projects in affected countries have been forced to scale down their activities due to insufficient funding."[14]

Arguably, the most significant progress in victim assistance at the international level came with the greater understanding of the issues recorded by the First Review Conference of the Mine Ban Treaty and the adoption of the Nairobi Action Plan.

First Review Conference and the Nairobi Action Plan

At the First Review Conference, also known as the Nairobi Summit on a Mine-Free World, the international community was reminded that "[t]he very purpose of the Convention is to put an end to the suffering and casualties caused by antipersonnel mines."[15] The conference provided an opportunity to further raise awareness on the rights and needs of mine victims and to identify the key challenges to be addressed to fulfill the promise to mine survivors that the treaty implied. States Parties adopted a clear understanding of principles to guide their efforts. Four statements were particularly important:

- victim assistance "does not require the development of new fields or disciplines but rather calls for ensuring that existing health care and social service systems, rehabilitation programmes and legislative and policy frameworks are adequate to meet the needs of all citizens—including landmine victims;"
- ". . . the call to assist landmine victims should not lead to victim assistance efforts being undertaken in such a manner as to exclude any person injured or disabled in another manner;"
- "assistance to landmine victims should be viewed as a part of a country's overall public health and social services systems and human rights frameworks;" and,
- ". . . providing adequate assistance to landmine survivors must be seen in a broader context of development and underdevelopment. . . . "[16]

States Parties acknowledged that all states have a responsibility to assist mine survivors. However, twenty-four States Parties indicated that they had significant numbers of mine survivors—hundreds, thousands or tens of thousands— and "the greatest responsibility to act, but also the greatest needs and expectations for assistance" in providing adequate services for their care, rehabilitation and reintegration.[17] These countries are now the subject of "a more focused challenge" for States Parties in the period 2005–2009 leading up to the Second Review Conference.

A key outcome of the First Review Conference was the adoption of the ambitious five-year Nairobi Action Plan. With respect to victim assistance, the plan aims to "enhance the care, rehabilitation and reintegration efforts" through eleven "actions." It commits affected states to do their utmost to establish and enhance healthcare services to respond to the immediate and ongoing medical needs of mine victims, to increase national physical rehabilitation capacities, to develop capacities to meet the psychological and social support needs of mine victims, to actively support the socioeconomic reintegration of mine victims, to ensure that national legal and policy frameworks effectively address the needs and fundamental human rights of mine victims, to develop or enhance national mine victim data collection capacities, and to ensure that in all victim assistance efforts, emphasis is given to age and gender considerations. States Parties committed to provide assistance to affected states for the care, rehabilitation, and reintegration of mine victims. Additionally, all States Parties committed to monitoring and promoting progress in achieving the victim assistance goals and ensuring the effective participation of mine victims in the work of the treaty.[18]

It is important to note that the outcomes of the First Review Conference were the culmination of the efforts of numerous actors in the years since entry into force of the treaty, and before, including the Standing Committee on Victim Assistance and the ICBL and its member organizations.

Standing Committee on Victim Assistance and Socioeconomic Reintegration

The Standing Committee on Victim Assistance and Socio-Economic Reintegration has been integral to advancing understanding and identifying the needs in relation to mine victim assistance among the States Parties. The Standing Committee on Victim Assistance is part of the Intersessional Work Programme established at the First Meeting of the States Parties in May 1999 to advance implementation of the treaty.[19]

Two States Parties serve as cochairs, and another two as corapporteurs, on an annual basis between meetings of the States Parties.[20] Standing Committee on Victim Assistance meetings are conducted in what has been described as a "spirit of practical cooperation, inclusivity and collegiality."[21] Mine survivors, the ICBL, the ICRC, UN agencies, and numerous NGOs have worked closely with States Parties to advance the work of the Standing Committee on Victim Assistance.

One of the Standing Committee on Victim Assistance's first tasks was to clarify terms such as "mine victim" and "victim assistance" and identify key elements of victim assistance that have been fundamental to focused discussions on fulfilling the aims of the treaty. The Standing Committee on Victim Assistance promotes a comprehensive integrated approach to victim assistance that rests on a three-tiered definition of a landmine victim. A "mine victim" includes directly affected individuals, their families, and mine-affected communities, while "victim assistance" is viewed as a wide range of activities that benefit individuals, families, and communities. The priority areas of victim assistance include understanding the extent of the challenge faced, including through data collection; emergency and continuing medical care; physical rehabilitation, including physiotherapy, prosthetics, and assistive devices; psychological support and social reintegration; economic reintegration; and the establishment, enforcement, and implementation of relevant laws and public policies. While accepting the broader definition of "victim assistance," States Parties acknowledged that most attention is being directed toward the individuals directly affected by a landmine explosion, in particular the survivors.[22]

Significant progress was made in October 2001 when Canada hosted a workshop to discuss how to frame future activities by the Standing Committee on Victim Assistance and to identify the key issues to be addressed.[23] As a result of the workshop, UNMAS was invited in 2002 to undertake a consultative process to identify priority areas for future victim assistance discussions within the Standing Committee on Victim Assistance. Five key areas were identified: emergency and continuing medical care; physical rehabilitation/prosthetics; psychological and social support; economic reintegration; and laws, public policies, and national planning.

As a result of this process, in 2003 the Standing Committee on Victim Assistance started to place greater emphasis on obtaining concrete plans of action from affected states for the care and rehabilitation of landmine survivors. States were encouraged to present their plans, progress and priorities for mine victim assistance, and their problems in meeting the needs.

The Nairobi Action Plan provided a framework on which to act during the period 2005 to 2009, but States Parties still lacked a clear appreciation of what should or could be achieved. One thing that was clear, however, was that the ultimate responsibility to improve the quality of life of mine survivors lay with the affected state. While various forms of assistance could be provided, "real and sustainable progress" could not be made without the affected state owning the challenge and the solutions to it.[24]

In 2005, the Standing Committee on Victim Assistance, under the cochairing of Nicaragua and Norway, increased its efforts to ensure concrete progress in meeting the needs of landmine victims before the Second Review Conference in 2009. In early 2005, the cochairs developed a questionnaire, with assistance from the treaty's Implementation Support Unit (ISU), and in consultation with key stakeholders including the ICBL and ICRC, to assist the twenty-four most affected States Parties in developing their plans of action for mine victim assistance.[25]

The questionnaire called for responses to four key questions: What is the situation in 2005 in each of the six main thematic areas of victim assistance? What does the state wish the situation to be (objectives) in each of the six thematic areas by 2009? What are the plans to achieve these objectives in each of the six thematic areas by 2009? What means are available or required to implement these plans? Sent to the twenty-four States Parties in March 2005, the questionnaire was intended to assist them in producing objectives that were specific, measurable, achievable, relevant, and time-bound (SMART) before the Sixth Meeting of the States Parties in November 2005.[26] Two regional workshops were organized by the cochairs for states to share experiences and develop their answers to the questionnaire.[27]

The Zagreb Progress Report, adopted by States Parties at the Sixth Meeting of States Parties, contains a lengthy annex that summarizes the responses made by twenty-two of the twenty-four relevant States.[28] The quality of responses to the questionnaire was mixed, and the Zagreb Progress Report acknowledged that the questionnaire "is not an end-product but rather an initial step in a long-term planning and implementation process."[29]

Since 2005, cochairs have recognized that the best way to assure progress in achieving the aims of the Nairobi Action Plan and to support the establishment of SMART objectives and national plans of action, is to work intensively, on a national basis with as many of the relevant States Parties as possible. To assist the cochairs, in January 2006 a victim assistance specialist was recruited by the ISU to provide process support. The goal of process support is that those States Parties with good objectives would develop and implement good plans; those with vague objectives would develop more concrete objectives; and those that had not engaged, or had engaged very little, would do so. By November 2007, in-country process support had been provided to nineteen of the twenty-four relevant States Parties.[30]

International Campaign to Ban Landmines and Its Member Organizations

A significant and enduring feature of the movement to ban antipersonnel landmines and subsequent efforts to implement the treaty has been the remarkable level of cooperation between the ICBL and the States Parties. The ICBL, through its member organizations[31] and national campaigns, has been able to harness a considerable level of international expertise on the issue of victim assistance based on extensive experience "on the ground" assisting victims of landmines. This experience enabled the ICBL to speak with credibility to influence the thinking of States Parties and advance the issue.

The ICBL Working Group on Victim Assistance, in particular under the leadership of Becky Jordan of Landmine Survivors Network until 2004, played a key role in guiding the thinking of States Parties on victim assistance. Since its inception in 1998, the Working Group on Victim Assistance has had four main goals: (1) to advocate for, monitor, and provide guidance to the international community as to where, what, and how victim assistance is needed; (2) to promote increased coverage, funding, and sustainability of victim assistance programs; (3) to promote improvements in the quality of programs for landmine victims/survivors and other persons with disabilities; and (4) to facilitate the inclusion of landmine survivors in treaty-related processes.

The Working Group on Victim Assistance's close collaboration with States Parties has resulted in aspects of victim assistance that might otherwise have been neglected or avoided becoming part of the Standing Committee on Victim Assistance's general discussions. Collaboration has allowed governments, NGOs, and international organizations to become allies on some issues and to better understand each other's perspectives. As noted by the ICBL, it also "allowed for more perspectives, ideas, strategies, and mutual accountability among the various actors. . . . than would have ever been possible in a more limited forum."[32]

In 2000, the Working Group on Victim Assistance released two position papers—"Victim Assistance: Context, Principles, and Issues" and "Guidelines for the Care and Rehabilitation of Survivors." The ideas contained within the documents formed a strong foundation for language that subsequently appeared in the Final Report of the First Review Conference, and the Working Group on Victim Assistance played a key role in drafting the wording of the victim assistance sections. It has also been instrumental in linking mine victim assistance with broader disability issues and other international human rights frameworks.

Another key strength of the ICBL in pushing the victim assistance agenda is the strong voice given to mine survivors to advocate for their own rights. From the very beginning, mine survivors have played a visible and vocal role in raising awareness of their rights and needs and in pushing governments to do more to address them. By relating their own stories at international gatherings, they humanized the landmine problem. Arguably, without the efforts of survivors, and in particular the efforts of Landmine Survivors Network and other committed NGOs and individuals, it is unlikely that the treaty would have had a victim assistance provision. Three of the five ICBL Ambassadors are mine survivors.[33]

Survivors are also well represented in the Working Group on Victim Assistance with Margaret Orech Arach of Uganda serving as cochair between 2003 and 2006. The "Raising the Voices" program, implemented by Landmine Survivors Network from 2001 to 2004 worked with more than sixty survivors from around the world.[34] The program, supported by the governments of Canada and Norway, aimed to build the capacity of survivors to become advocates for the rights of landmine survivors and other people with disabilities in their communities in the context of implementing the treaty. "Raising the Voices" graduates have gone on to find valuable employment, to join in the work of their national campaigns to ban landmines, to participate in Landmine Monitor research efforts, to develop programs to assist their peers, and to raise the awareness in their communities of both landmine and disability issues. In addition, survivors actively participate in intersessional meetings, annual Meetings of the States Parties, and other key landmine-related meetings, fulfilling a goal of Nairobi Action Plan to "ensure effective integration of mine victims in the work of the Convention."[35]

On the eve of the First Review Conference, Landmine Survivors Network organized a summit in Nairobi to focus attention on victim assistance. It brought together forty-five mine survivors from thirty countries and key government representatives to discuss the rights and needs of survivors and progress in implementation of the treaty. The Survivor Summit Declaration, signed by survivors and government representatives, acknowledged work that has been done but called on all governments to do more to ensure the rights and needs of mine survivors and other persons with disabilities are met, and that survivors are included in decision-making processes.[36]

The ICBL's Landmine Monitor initiative has been instrumental in advancing knowledge of the extent of the challenges faced in assisting the victims of landmines. Arguably, it provides the most comprehensive information available on the number of new landmine casualties globally and on states' efforts to address the needs. Through its research network, which includes mine survivors, the annual *Landmine Monitor* reports have documented problems and progress in implementing the treaty.

Members of the ICBL have also played a role in advancing understanding of the main victim assistance issues and in producing guidelines to assist in the planning and implementation of programs.[37]

And finally, in keeping with the commitment of the Nairobi Action Plan to "monitor and promote progress in the achievement of victim assistance goals,"[38] the Working Group on Victim Assistance through its member organizations, Standing Tall Australia and Handicap International (HI), continues to assist in advancing understanding of victim assistance issues by producing an annual report, *Landmine Victim Assistance in 2006: Overview of the Situation in 24 States Parties.*[39]

Implementation of the Treaty at the National Level

States Parties have acknowledged that victim assistance "is more than just a medical or rehabilitation issue—it is also a human rights issue."[40] However, at the national level, many affected states lack the capacity, resources, and in some cases, the political will to take a rights-based approach to meeting the needs of mine survivors and other people with disabilities. Until the barriers of discrimination and segregation are removed, people with disabilities will continue to be dependent on assistance for their most basic rights, including access to food, shelter, health care, and education.

The ultimate responsibility for addressing the needs of mine survivors lies with the affected states, but it would appear that many affected countries lack the capacity, both in human and financial terms, to adequately meet the needs of their citizens, including mine survivors. The Nairobi Action Plan acknowledges the key role to be played by international and regional organizations, the ICRC and other NGOs, in supporting the victim assistance initiatives of affected states.[41]

In its overview of the first five years of the life of the treaty, *Landmine Monitor Report 2004* concluded that in the majority of affected countries at least one or more aspects of survivor assistance were inadequate. The report stated that while "new programs have been implemented in many mine-affected countries and the survivors that have access to these and other pre-existing services report an improved quality of life . . . significant gaps remain in areas such as geographic coverage, affordability, and quality of available facilities and while more is known about the numbers of mine survivors receiving assistance, the extent to which landmine survivors' needs are not being met is generally still unknown . . . a lack of resources to implement or maintain programs continues to limit activities."[42]

In other efforts to evaluate progress, Handicap International convened a workshop in May 2004 that brought together rehabilitation experts working in affected countries. The workshop concluded that there had been little lasting improvement in medical and surgical care; developing physical rehabilitation programs takes a long time; rehabilitation works best when it is comprehensive, holistic, and multilayered; few physical rehabilitation programs are sustainable as currently constituted; all physical rehabilitation stakeholders must coordinate resources, planning, and training; collaboration and coordination are essential for program sustainability; psychosocial support plays a critical role in successful rehabilitation; capacity building of local personnel is essential for program sustainability; and economic integration is the primary unmet need identified by beneficiaries in every affected country.[43]

A key concern raised by mine survivors and other actors implementing programs in affected countries is the lack of or limited knowledge among key people working on disability issues at the national level of the work done internationally on mine victim assistance. The Nairobi Action Plan sought to address this problem with its call to "ensure an effective contribution in all relevant deliberations by health, rehabilitation and social services professionals and officials inter alia by encouraging States Parties—particularly those with the greatest number of mine victims—and relevant organizations to include such individuals on their delegations."[44] At the Seventh Meeting of States Parties in September 2006, seventeen of the twenty-four relevant states included specialists with experience in disability issues on their delegations.

Another concern is that in some countries the only focus on mine victim assistance appears to come from mine action centers. Mine clearance will end long before the needs of mine survivors disappear so unless a mine action center works in close collaboration with the relevant ministries and other key actors in the disability sector, victim assistance activities will likely not be sustainable.

While the Standing Committee on Victim Assistance questionnaire provided a framework for affected states to begin developing a national response to address the needs of mine survivors, the quality of responses was mixed. Few States Parties responded with SMART objectives, some failed to detail the status of victim assistance activities, and victim assistance objectives did not take broader national plans into consideration. Two of the twenty-four relevant States Parties failed to respond at all. Mine survivors have expressed concerns that the responses made by some States Parties on the current status of victim assistance does not reflect the reality on the ground and urged states to include survivors and other key actors in the disability sector in the process of formulating objectives and developing plans of action.[45]

Nevertheless, some progress is being made in strengthening objectives and developing plans of action as a result of the process support provision. In May 2006, Albania and Tajikistan presented revised national action plans for the period to 2009, including SMARTer objectives, to the Standing Committee on Victim Assistance. The plans were developed in collaboration with all relevant actors in the disability sector, including mine survivors. Afghanistan, as cochair of the Standing Committee on Victim Assistance, led by example and established an interministerial coordination group to oversee the development of a national response to meet the aims of the Nairobi Action Plan. The plan of action was

presented to States Parties at the Seventh Meeting of States Parties in September
2006. In 2007, other States Parties, including Angola, Bosnia and Herzegovina,
Cambodia, El Salvador, Ethiopia, Sudan, Thailand, and Uganda have undertaken specific activities to move forward with the process.

Conclusion

Victim assistance, as part of the broader disability and development context,
is a long-term business. The needs will never disappear. Activities to implement the Mine Ban Treaty have helped raise awareness of the rights and needs
of all persons with disabilities, including mine survivors. In many affected
countries this focus has seen the building of infrastructure and capacities to
address some of the needs of people with physical disabilities, regardless of the
cause. Nevertheless, the assistance available remains inadequate to meet the
needs. Furthermore, many affected countries remain dependent on international organizations and agencies to assist mine survivors and other vulnerable groups. The problems faced in providing adequate assistance are similar in
most affected countries, though to varying degrees.[46]

In April 2007, health, rehabilitation, and social services professionals from
seventeen of the twenty-four relevant States Parties, mine survivors, and disability experts met and reaffirmed some of the key challenges in addressing
the rights and needs of mine survivors and other persons with disabilities, including:

- Services not meeting the needs in terms of both quantity and quality;
- Lack of accessibility to or awareness of services;
- Disability often not seen as a priority by policy makers;
- Lack of political will to effect change;
- Lack of capacity to address disability issues at all levels including within
  the governmental and nongovernmental sectors;
- Poverty and lack of development in affected communities hindering the
  economic reintegration of survivors;
- Lack of donor support;
- Lack of inclusion of persons with disabilities in decision-making processes;
- Victim assistance not given the same priority as other pillars of mine ac-
  tion; and,
- Disability still seen as a charity issue not a human rights issue.

The participants also reaffirmed the importance of the following in the development of plans of action to address these challenges:

- National ownership;
- Building local capacities;
- Sustainability of services;
- A holistic approach to assisting mine survivors and other persons with disabilities;
- Collaboration and cooperation between government ministries and other actors;
- Inclusion of persons with disabilities in decision-making processes; and,
- Taking into account available resources—not being too ambitious about what can be achieved in a limited time frame.[47]

The ultimate responsibility for the care and well-being of its citizens, including mine victims, lies with the affected state which must decide what can and should be done to meet the needs. Therefore, the challenge is to develop a national response and a national action plan, with the goal of improving the quality of life of mine survivors and other persons with disabilities. This challenge could be addressed through the establishment of an intersectoral group, representing all key stakeholders—relevant government ministries, international agencies, nongovernmental organizations, associations of persons with disabilities, and mine survivors themselves—with the responsibility and authority to develop the plan.[48]

In conclusion, mine survivors are often the poorest of the poor in remote communities where people suffer from the obstacles of poverty, including lack of access to health care and rehabilitation services, housing, water, food, and an income. Consequently, an improvement in the daily lives of people with disabilities cannot be separated from the sustainable development of their community as a whole. For people with disabilities to benefit from development activities, this usually means addressing their rights as well as their needs—and raising awareness of these rights within their communities to reduce discrimination and bring about social change.

It is important to remember that mine survivors are not viewed as a problem to be solved. They are individuals with hopes and dreams for the future. They are assets with the capacity to be productive contributors to their communities. The challenge is to provide the environment that will enable mine survivors and other people with disabilities to reach their full potential.

Sustainability is the key to making a real difference in the daily lives of mine survivors. In addition to the provision of adequate levels of long-term funding, assistance should be viewed as part of general development planning on issues such as health, education, and labor for communities as a whole. However, there should also be specific activities and policies implemented at the same time that are targeted at landmine survivors and other people with disabilities to ensure access to appropriate rehabilitation facilities and aids and opportunities for socioeconomic integration. This twin track approach to disability should be an integral component of any victim assistance or development program.

Significant progress has been made at the international level to develop a better understanding of the key issues facing mine survivors. The First Review Conference provided a clear framework for the planning and implementation of victim assistance programs. However, much more needs to be done at the national level to ensure that words on paper are turned into actions on the ground. Just as mine clearance requires probing below the surface to find the mines and UXO, so too must disability and development program planners look deeper to find the most vulnerable living in isolated communities who also have a right to benefit from the work that is being done to implement the Mine Ban Treaty and achieve the aims of the Nairobi Action Plan.

At the opening of the First Review Conference, Song Kosal, ICBL Youth Ambassador and mine survivor from Cambodia, issued a powerful challenge: "Many mines have been cleared, BUT not enough. Many people have got new legs, BUT not enough. Many people have been given wheelchairs and assistance, BUT not enough. Many people disabled by landmines are working hard in their rice fields, repairing machines, sculpting, selling things, learning to use computers and mobile phones. This is GOOD news, BUT we need to do more."[49]

Kosal's words were echoed by the ICRC when it stated that "as this Convention matures we must never lose sight of those who have inspired our efforts: the victims and survivors of landmine incidents. We need to do far more to ensure that the Convention's promises to survivors are fulfilled."[50] Only time will tell if the international community, and affected states themselves, are up to the challenge.

Notes

1. Statement by Cornelio Sommaruga, president of the International Committee of the Red Cross (ICRC), to Treaty Signing Conference and Mine Action Forum, Ottawa, December 3, 1997.

2. The preamble to the treaty expresses the desire of the States Parties "to do their utmost in providing assistance for the care and rehabilitation, including the social and economic reintegration of mine victims." This wish is translated into an obligation in article 6.3: "each State Party in a position to do so shall provide assistance for the care and rehabilitation, and social and economic reintegration, of mine victims. . . . "

3. International Campaign to Ban Landmines (ICBL), *Landmine Monitor Report 2006* (Ottawa: Mines Action Canada, July 2006), p. 44.

Ali Saied Attia, twelve years old, lives with his family in the Egyptian province of Matrouh, which was the scene of much fighting during World War II. He is standing by some unexploded ordnance including landmines that was uncovered by local shepherds. © Mary Wareham, NSP, December 2005.

Representatives of the International Campaign to Ban Landmines. © Brian Liu, ToolboxDC/NSP Films, December 2004.

The Nairobi Summit on a Mine-Free World (The First Review Conference of the 1997 Mine Ban Treaty). © Brian Liu, Tool-boxDC/NSP Films, December 2004.

A Danish Demining Group deminer at work in the center of Kabul, Afghanistan, on Bibi Mahroun hill, named after a famous Afghan playwright. The site contains four water reservoirs as well as a graveyard. © Brian Liu, ToolboxDC/NSP Films, April 2004.

A Mines Advisory Group deminer in northern Iraq marks out the perimeter of a mined area. © Brian Liu, ToolboxDC/NSP Films, March 2004.

A group of deminers employed by Mines Advisory Group in northern Iraq engage in training on a new metal detector. © Brian Liu, ToolboxDC/NSP Films, March 2004.

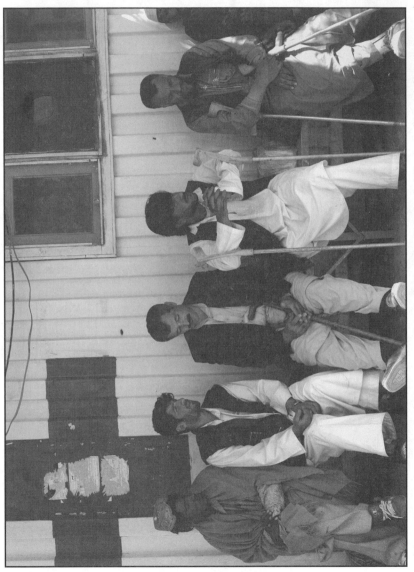

Afghan mine victims and other amputees await treatment at the Kabul rehabilitation clinic of the International Committee of the Red Cross. © Brian Liu, ToolboxDC/NSP Films, April 2004.

ICBL Youth Ambassador Song Kosal (right) and her Cambodian mine survivor colleague Sophally Chim at the Nairobi Summit on a Mine-Free World. © Brian Liu, ToolboxDC/ NSP Films, December 2004.

These metal casings are remnants of POMZ stake mines manufactured in the former Soviet Union. Retrieved from arms caches around Kabul, the mines were melted down for use as the city's manhole covers. © Brian Liu, ToolboxDC/NSP Films, April 2004.

An unexploded BLU-97 cluster munition lies in an unmarked field outside a village near Erbil, Iraq. The weapon was deployed by the United States during the air war of 2003. © Brian Liu, ToolboxDC/NSP Films, March 2004.

4. ICBL, *Landmine Monitor Report 2006*, p. 47.

5. ICBL press release, "Winning the War Against Antipersonnel Mines: Biggest Challenges Still Ahead," November 17, 2004, http://www.icbl.org/news/lm_2004.

6. First Review Conference of the States Parties to the Convention on the Prohibition of the Use, Stockpiling, Production, and Transfer of Anti-Personnel Mines and on Their Destruction, "Final Report: Part II. Review of the Operation of the Status of the Convention on the Prohibition of the Use, Stockpiling, Production, and Transfer of Anti-Personnel Mines and on Their Destruction: 1999-2004," Nairobi, November, 29–December 3, 2004, APLC/CONF/2004/5, February 9, 2005, p. 31, para. 76.

7. Statement by Cornelio Sommaruga, ICRC, to the Treaty Signing Conference and Mine Action Forum, December 3, 1997.

8. See Swiss Agency for Development and Cooperation, "Victim Assistance: A Comprehensive Integrated Approach" presentation by Dr. Flavio Del Ponte, Chief Medical Advisor, Swiss Federal Department of Foreign Affairs, presentation to the Standing Committee on Victim Assistance and Socio-Economic Reintegration, Geneva, May 7, 2001.

9. ICBL, *Landmine Monitor Report 2006*, pp. 87–88; ICBL, *Landmine Monitor Report 2005* (Ottawa: Mines Action Canada, 2005), p. 79; ICBL, "Executive Summary," *Landmine Monitor Report 2004* (Washington, DC: Human Rights Watch, 2004), p. 69.

10. ICRC, "Physical Rehabilitation Programme: Annual Report 2006," Geneva, April 2007, p. 6.

11. "United Nations Inter-Agency Mine Action Strategy: 2006–2010," May 8, 2006, http://www.mineaction.org/downloads/1/UN_IAMAS_online.pdf (accessed August 17, 2007), pp. 9 and 11.

12. "Review of the Operation of the Status of the Convention on the Prohibition of the Use, Stockpiling, Production, and Transfer of Anti-Personnel Mines and on Their Destruction: 1999–2004," p. 32, para. 81.

13. Presentation by the cochairs of the Standing Committee on Victim Assistance and Socio-Economic Reintegration, "Status of Implementation of the Convention in Relation to Victim Assistance," Geneva, April 24, 2007.

14. Statement by Dr. Jacques Forster, vice-president of the ICRC, to the Sixth Meeting of States Parties to the Convention on the Prohibition of the Use, Stockpiling, Production, and Transfer of Anti-Personnel Mines and on their Destruction, Zagreb, November 28, 2005.

15. "Review of the Operation of the Status of the Convention on the Prohibition of the Use, Stockpiling, Production, and Transfer of Anti-Personnel Mines and on Their Destruction: 1999–2004," APLC/CONF/2004/5, p. 11, para. 1.

16. "Review of the Operation," pp. 27–28, para. 65–67.

17. The States Parties are: Afghanistan, Albania, Angola, Bosnia and Herzegovina, Burundi, Cambodia, Chad, Colombia, Croatia, Democratic Republic of the Congo, El Salvador, Eritrea, Ethiopia, Guinea-Bissau, Mozambique, Nicaragua, Peru, Senegal, Serbia, Sudan, Tajikistan, Thailand, Uganda, and Yemen. See "Review of the Operation of the Status of the Convention on the Prohibition of the Use, Stockpiling, Production, and Transfer of Anti-Personnel Mines and on Their Destruction: 1999–2004," p. 33, para. 85. Ethiopia was added to the list of focus countries after ratifying the Mine

Ban Treaty in December 2004. With the separation of Serbia and Montenegro in 2006, Serbia has remained the focus of attention.

18. See First Review Conference of the States Parties to the Convention on the Prohibition of the Use, Stockpiling, Production, and Transfer of Anti-Personnel Mines and on Their Destruction, "Final Report: Part III. Ending the Suffering Caused by Anti-Personnel Mines: Nairobi Action Plan 2005-2009," Nairobi, November 29–December 3, 2004, APLC/CONF/2004/5, February 9, 2005, pp. 99–101, para. 5.

19. The "Standing Committee on Victim Assistance and Socio-Economic Reintegration" was originally called the "Standing Committee of Experts on Victim Assistance, Socio-Economic Reintegration and Mine Awareness." At the Third Meeting of the States Parties in 2001, issues relating to mine awareness/mine risk education were transferred to the Standing Committee that held responsibility for mine clearance.

20. The Standing Committee on Victim Assistance has been cochaired by Austria and Sudan since September 2006. Corapporteurs Cambodia and New Zealand will become the cochairs in November 2007. Other cochairs since 1999 have been Mexico and Switzerland (1999/2000), Japan and Nicaragua (2000/2001), Canada and Honduras (2001/2002), Colombia and France (2002/2003), Australia and Croatia (2003/2004), Nicaragua and Norway (2004/2005), and Afghanistan and Switzerland (2005/2006).

21. Report of the Meeting of the Standing Committee on Victim Assistance, Socio-Economic Reintegration and Mine Awareness, May 7–8, 2001.

22. "Review of the Operation of the Status of the Convention on the Prohibition of the Use, Stockpiling, Production, and Transfer of Anti-Personnel Mines and on Their Destruction: 1999–2004," APLC/CONF/2004/5, pp. 27-28, para. 64, 69.

23. The workshop was attended by representatives of the governments of Canada, Honduras, France, Nicaragua, and Japan, together with representatives of UNMAS, ICBL, Landmine Monitor, and other NGOs.

24. Kerry Brinkert, Manager, Implementation Support Unit, "Making Sense out of the Anti-Personnel Mine Ban Convention's Obligation to Landmine Victims," March 31, 2006, http://www.apminebanconvention.org/fileadmin/pdf/publications/VA_Paper_Brinkert_JMA_31Mar2006.pdf (accessed August 17, 2007).

25. The 1999 Maputo Strategy provided a useful tool in the preparation of the questionnaire.

26. Kerry Brinkert, Manager, Implementation Support Unit, "Efforts to assure that the 24 States Parties to the Convention which have reported significant numbers of landmine survivors develop 2009 victim assistance objectives in time for the 2005 Sixth Meeting of the States Parties: Update to interested stakeholders, 26 September 2005."

27. The workshops were held in the Americas (Managua, Nicaragua, April 26–27, 2005) and in Africa (Nairobi, Kenya, May 31–June 2, 2005). The workshop in the Americas was attended by Colombia, El Salvador, Nicaragua and Peru; and in Africa by Angola, Burundi, DR Congo, Eritrea, Ethiopia, Guinea-Bissau, Mozambique, Senegal, Sudan, and Uganda.

28. Burundi and Chad did not respond to the questionnaire. See Sixth Meeting of States Parties to the Convention on the Prohibition of the Use, Stockpiling, Production, and Transfer of Anti-Personnel Mines and on Their Destruction, "Final Report:

Part II. Achieving the Aims of the Nairobi Action Plan: The Zagreb Progress Report," Zagreb, November 28–December 2, 2005, APLC/MSP.6/2005/5, April 5, 2006 (hereinafter Zagreb Progress Report).

29. Zagreb Progress Report, para. 72.

30. See "The General Status of Victim Assistance in the Context of the Convention and the *Nairobi Action Plan*," presentation by the cochairs to the Standing Committee on Victim Assistance and Socio-Economic Reintegration, Jordan, November 2007, http://www.apminebanconvention.org/.

31. For example Handicap International, Landmine Survivors Network, Medico International, Physicians for Human Rights, POWER, Vietnam Veterans of America Foundation, and World Rehabilitation Fund.

32. ICBL, "Working Group on Victim Assistance," *Landmine Monitor Report 2002* (Washington, DC: Human Rights Watch, 2002), p. 871.

33. The three Ambassadors are Song Kosal, Margaret Arach Orech, and Tun Channareth.

34. The survivors represented Abkhazia, Afghanistan, Albania, Angola, Azerbaijan, Belarus, Bosnia and Herzegovina, Cambodia, Chad, Chechnya, Colombia, Croatia, Ecuador, El Salvador, Eritrea, Ethiopia, Georgia, India, Jordan, Laos, Lebanon, Mozambique, Nepal, Nicaragua, Russia, Rwanda, Senegal, South Africa, Sri Lanka, Sudan, Syria, Thailand, Uganda, Ukraine, and Yemen.

35. "Ending the Suffering Caused by Anti-Personnel Landmines: Nairobi Action Plan 2005-2009," p. 101, para. 5.

36. "Survivor Summit Declaration," Nairobi, November 28, 2004, http://www.icbl .org/news/survivor_summit_declaration/ (accessed August 17, 2007).

37. See the ICBL's Index on Landmines, http://www.icbl.org/index/text/Victim_ Assistance/ (accessed August 17, 2007).

38. "Ending the Suffering Caused by Anti-Personnel Landmines: Nairobi Action Plan 2005-2009," APLC/CONF/2004/5, pp. 100-101, para. 5.

39. *Landmine Victim Assistance in 2006: Overview of the Situation in 24 States Parties*, April 2007, http://www.standingtallaustralia.org/. It should be noted that the ICBL advocates that all states have a responsibility to provide for the well-being of mine survivors and other persons with disabilities in their countries, regardless of whether or not they have ratified or acceded to the treaty.

40. "Review of the Operation of the Status of the Convention on the Prohibition of the Use, Stockpiling, Production, and Transfer of Anti-Personnel Mines and on Their Destruction: 1999–2004," APLC/CONF/2004/5, p. 28, para. 68.

41. "Ending the Suffering Caused by Anti-Personnel Landmines: Nairobi Action Plan 2005–2009," APLC/CONF/2004/5, p. 99, para. 5.

42. ICBL, *Landmine Monitor Report 2004* (Washington, DC: Human Rights Watch, 2004), p. 47.

43. See Handicap International, "Lessons Learned Workshop: A Review of Assistance Programs for War Wounded and other Persons Living in Mine-Affected Countries," Paris, May 25–28, 2004, http://www.handicap-international.org/.

44. "Ending the Suffering Caused by Anti-Personnel Landmines: Nairobi Action Plan 2005–2009," APLC/CONF/2004/5, p. 100, para. 5.

45. Presentation by Jesús Martinez and Omara Khan to the Standing Committee on Victim Assistance and Socio-Economic Reintegration, Geneva, May 9, 2006.

46. See "Review of the Operation of the Status of the Convention on the Prohibition of the Use, Stockpiling, Production, and Transfer of Anti-Personnel Mines and on Their Destruction: 1999–2004," APLC/CONF/2004/5, pp. 29–32, para. 70-78; *Landmine Monitor Report 2005*, pp. 52–53.

47. Standing Committee on Victim Assistance and Socio Economic Reintegration, "Report of the Co-Chairs on Parallel Programme for Victim Assistance Experts," Geneva, 25–26 April 2007, http://www.apminebanconvention.org/.

48. See presentation by Sheree Bailey, Victim Assistance Specialist, Geneva International Centre for Humanitarian Demining, to the Standing Committee on Victim Assistance and Socio-Economic Reintegration, "Developing SMART Objectives and a National Plan of Action—the Role of Inter-ministerial Coordination," Geneva, May 9, 2006, http://www.apminebanconvention.org.

49. Song Kosal, ICBL Youth Ambassador, Opening Ceremony, First Review Conference of the States Parties to the Convention on the Prohibition of the Use, Stockpiling, Production, and Transfer of Anti-Personnel Mines and on Their Destruction, Nairobi, November 27, 2004.

50. Statement by Dr. Jakob Kellenberger, president of the ICRC, to the First Review Conference, Nairobi, December 2, 2004.

10

Outside the Treaty Not the Norm: Nonstate Armed Groups and the Landmine Ban

Yeshua Moser-Puangsuwan

> "I was a rebel commander for 14 years. I laid mines and ordered the laying
> of mines. It was not the international campaign that convinced me, but it
> was what I saw—what mines can do to people, what mines can do to the
> people you want to liberate and what mines can do to the land you want to
> liberate."

Aleu Ayieny Aleu,
former Sudan People's Liberation Army commander,
September 2003

OVER THE PAST DECADE, there has been ever-growing attention to the importance of getting nonstate armed groups (NSAGs) to embrace a ban on antipersonnel mines.[1] As the 1997 Mine Ban Treaty has taken hold, there has been a growing impression that these actors have become a bigger problem with respect to antipersonnel mines than governments. There is both some truth and some fallacy to that impression.

The mine ban movement focused nearly all of its initial efforts on getting *governments* to ban antipersonnel landmines. This was clearly the first strategic step, since governments produced and stockpiled the weapon in massive quantities and were the primary users who scattered them across the face of the planet. It also reflected the reality that only governments could negotiate a legally binding international treaty.

Moreover, almost every rebel movement that possessed and used large quantities of antipersonnel landmines acquired them from a government as part of a bigger package of military support. One such example was the massive number of mines supplied, along with other weapons, to the Khmer Rouge by China via the Thai military during the Cambodian civil war.

The situation has changed dramatically. Use of antipersonnel mines by government forces has declined precipitously, even among those not party to the Mine Ban Treaty—as of mid-2007 only Burma (Myanmar) and Russia were using them regularly. The number of government producers has dropped from more than fifty to no more than thirteen, some of whom have not actively produced any antipersonnel mines in a number of years. Eighty States Parties to the Mine Ban Treaty have destroyed their stockpiles of antipersonnel mines. Trade in the weapon has halted almost completely, with only small-scale illicit trafficking still occurring.

In recent years, nonstate armed groups have consistently used antipersonnel mines in more countries than have government forces. In some countries, notably Colombia and Burma (Myanmar), guerrillas have been using mines in very large numbers and causing significant numbers of civilian casualties. Some armed groups have been manufacturing their own antipersonnel mines or mine-like explosive devices. Notable examples include the Liberation Tigers of Tamil Elam (LTTE) in Sri Lanka, perhaps the most sophisticated rebel military organization in the world, which has produced a variety of antipersonnel mines, and the Revolutionary Armed Forces of Colombia (FARC), which has produced thousands of crude, victim-activated mine-like devices.

What has not been widely recognized, however, is that while the Mine Ban Treaty does not apply directly to nonstate armed groups, the treaty—and the ban movement more generally—have had a big impact on stopping the use of antipersonnel mines by NSAGs, and in changing their policies and practices with respect to mine warfare. This has been the case in large part because of practical realities: with governments having—with few exceptions—stopped use, production, trade, and stockpiling, NSAGs no longer have ready access to antipersonnel mines. But it is also true that the stigmatization of antipersonnel mines by the ban community has spread to many NSAGs and caused them to renounce the weapon as well.

Standard sources and methods by which NSAGs acquired state-manufactured mines in the past have dried up, such as direct sales from authorities with access to state arsenals, capture during military operations against state forces, and lifting mines laid by their adversaries and reusing them. Access by nonstate armed groups to state designed and manufactured mines has, for the most part, ended. Fewer and fewer rebel groups possess and use such mines.

Thus, we are witnessing a situation in which attention to the problem of nonstate armed groups and landmines is increasing, but possession and use of the weapon by NSAGs is actually decreasing. Still, until the conditions that cause armed conflict in the first place are addressed, there will be rebel movements, and the asymmetric relationship of state versus rebel armed forces likely will continue to make the antipersonnel landmine a weapon of choice for some armed groups.

Why Nonstate Armed Groups Use Antipersonnel Mines

"How can a People's Liberation Army use an Anti-People's weapon?"

Eduardo Mariño, Colombian Campaign to Ban Landmines,
December 1998.

Groups that undertake armed opposition to a state do so for a wide variety of political, economic, and social reasons, but one thing they have in common is that the state almost always has access to superior numbers of soldiers (or a population from which it can conscript them), and superior access to arms, both in number and in their quality and lethality.

Guerrilla groups must wage a struggle that maximizes their minimal resources against such a military opponent. As history has demonstrated, it is difficult for rebel movements to forego the opportunity to employ a mechanized soldier who never sleeps, strikes fear in the heart of an adversary, and can be constructed out of locally accessed materials in even the most impoverished conflict environments. When questioned about the rationale for using mines in light of the inevitable civilian casualties, a Burmese insurgent commander responded, "We know how landmines affect our communities, but what should we do? This is war." In a conversation with a different Burmese guerrilla, I asked how many of his mines caused casualties among his own people. He paused before answering and then looked at me and said, "Half kill the enemy." After another pause he continued, "The other half kill our soldiers, our people, and the animals. For us, mine warfare really doesn't make sense." Nonetheless, his organization chose to continue using mines.

The mine ban movement has never accepted the argument that the military utility of the weapon outweighs the humanitarian cost, regardless of the sympathies some may feel for a particular group's struggle. The most persuasive military argument against mine use was one that resulted from a military consultation on antipersonnel mines by the International Committee of the Red Cross (ICRC), which is summarized in a report entitled *Anti-personnel Mines: Friend or Foe.*[2] The ICRC asked a group of serving and retired military officers to examine the use of antipersonnel mines from World War II until the present, and they found that the use of antipersonnel mines never determined the final outcome of any war.

But neither humanitarian nor military arguments have been enough to convince many rebel groups to forego mine use. They either deny casualties caused by their own landmines, cover up the statistics, or label the casualties as victims of the armed struggle (in the sense of being martyrs for the cause).

Early Efforts to Address Nonstate Actors on Landmines

It was clear from the beginning that the mine ban movement would have to approach nonstate armed groups with a sophisticated package that included both persuasion and condemnation, both rewards and penalties, utilizing what little leverage existed over groups who were already acting beyond the law.

An opportunity to provide an important encouragement to nonstate mine users was lost during Mine Ban Treaty negotiations in September 1997 in Oslo. Colombia called for the treaty to specifically regulate the activities of armed opposition groups as well as states.[3] The ICRC proposed treaty text would bind armed opposition groups. With field operations in war zones, it was of immediate benefit to the Red Cross to bind combatants on both sides of a conflict to carry out their humanitarian activities more effectively and safeguard, as much as possible, war-affected populations. The ICRC proposal had the support of the ICBL and a number of governments, but due to opposition by many governments it did not make it into the final treaty text.

Two sections in the Mine Ban Treaty are sometimes associated with NSAGs. Article 9, titled "National Implementation Measures," has been interpreted by some as applying to nonstate armed groups.[4] This article calls for the imposition of penal sanctions to suppress activity prohibited under the treaty and undertaken by persons or on territory under the state's jurisdiction or control. However, for the purpose of engaging NSAGs, Article 9 may be counterproductive as it is based on coercive measures by a state with which they are already in conflict and runs counter to encouraging adherence to the norm for humanitarian reasons. In the preamble, there is a clause stating that the treaty is based on the principles of international humanitarian law, which is addressed not just to states, but to "parties to an armed conflict," which would include nonstate armed groups.[5] This does not, however, constitute application of the treaty itself to NSAGs or provide for any formal adherence capacity.

Even before the Mine Ban Treaty was opened for signature, some campaigners understood the need to focus attention and activity on groups who could not join the international treaty. Campaigners from countries experiencing insurgencies—Colombia and the Philippines—and a country in which the insurgency had recently become the government—South Africa—took the lead.

Attorney Soliman M. Santos, Jr., of the Philippines Campaign to Ban Landmines made a presentation on the role of nonstate actors in a global landmine ban during a panel discussion at the December 1997 signing ceremony of the Mine Ban Treaty.[6] In that presentation he outlined the key areas of concern for the mine ban movement, and these observations framed much of the movement's future approach to the issue:

- Most landmines were planted during civil wars between governments and opposition forces. Since the Mine Ban Treaty only applied to governments, rebel groups may not feel bound by it.
- Involvement of nonstate armed groups would enable the ban to be truly universal.
- If a government in armed conflict knew that an armed rebellion would adhere to a landmine ban, that government might be more likely to join the Mine Ban Treaty.
- Some rebel groups eventually become governments.
- Rebel groups can provide essential knowledge and access relating to mine use for demining programs.

The ICBL decided shortly thereafter to establish a Non-State Actors Working Group (NSAWG) to investigate and develop a methodology for the campaign to engage armed groups in a ban.

Activity to approach and engage armed groups, who by their very existence challenge the legitimacy of some governments, was controversial within the mine ban movement. Some ICBL members were concerned that any attempt to involve armed groups in a landmine ban would endanger the working relationship that the campaign had with particular proban governments. There was also doubt and some skepticism about the ability to achieve tangible results, as well as fears the ICBL could be used to "legitimize" some guerrilla or even terrorist organizations.

There was a more general concern that such activity would alienate states toward the treaty or be used as a pretext for noncooperation with the mine ban. Legal and safety issues about contact with armed groups and a North-South lack of understanding about how some member campaigns went about this engagement made early efforts by ICBL activists and the new working group difficult.

In 2000, the NSA Working Group defined the key elements of an armed group that might make it a candidate for engagement. These included a political program and an antistate agenda. The Working Group subsequently defined its target as "armed groups who operate autonomously from recognized governments. Known as nonstate actors (NSAs), they include rebel groups, irregular armed groups, insurgents, dissident armed forces, guerrillas, liberation movements, and *de facto* territorial governing bodies. In ideology, objectives, strategies, form and level of organization, support-base, legitimacy, and degree of international recognition, NSAs vary greatly."[7]

As an NSA Working Group flyer noted at that time,

> An increasing number of NSAs have acknowledged the need to reconsider their use of landmines. Unilateral statements and bilateral agreements with clear references to mines have been made by nonstate armed groups in Sudan, the Philippines, Somalia, Colombia, Western Sahara, Kosovo/Yugoslavia and Afghanistan, among others. Some of these groups have already publicly committed themselves to a ban on landmine use. Others have indicated their willingness to make a renunciation of mines, contingent on their opponent governments doing the same. Still others appear willing to support mine clearance and victim assistance programs in areas under their control. These promising developments encourage a systematic and concerted approach to engaging NSAs in the landmine ban. NSA adherence to a total ban may, in addition, help pressure their government opponents to accede to the Mine Ban Treaty.[8]

In addition, some well-known armed movements, such as the Irish Republican Army and the Basque ETA were never known to use landmines. The Taliban controlling Afghanistan had placed a ban on landmine use or possession, punishable under Sharia.[9] The Sudan People's Liberation Army/Movement had agreed to cooperate with demining operations through a trilateral program sponsored by the United Nations called Operation Lifeline Sudan.[10]

Understanding the Problem and Responding

While there were, as noted by the ICBL, some promising developments, the global situation for the most part looked chaotic. According to *Landmine Monitor Report 2002*, and additional interviews with its researchers, sixty-six armed groups were using or alleged to be using antipersonnel mines in thirty-four countries.[11] There was a wide disparity of situations among militant movements around the world.

Through consultations held mostly on the margins of the annual Meetings of States Parties to the Mine Ban Treaty, the Non-State Actors Working Group both raised the issue of mine use by nonstate armed groups and lobbied for support for coherent efforts to engage these groups in the landmine ban. The first of these meetings was held in Geneva in 2001 and brought together representatives of governments, UN agencies, ICBL country campaigns, and other NGOs, as well as representatives of six nonstate armed groups. This was followed by a conference held in 2003 prior to the Meeting of States Parties in Bangkok that assessed engagement efforts up to that time and outlined lessons learned in the process. Prior to the First Review Conference of the Mine Ban Treaty in Nairobi in November 2004, another meeting assessed the role of the mine ban as a part of peace processes. The last meeting of this series, held at the time of the Sixth Meeting of States Parties in Zagreb in November 2005, considered the role of NSAs and mine action.[12]

Gradually, three general means of engaging nonstate armed groups have been developed: unilateral agreements, bilateral agreements, and trilateral agreements.

Unilateral Agreements or Statements

One method proposed by Eduardo Mariño, formerly of the Colombian Campaign to Ban Landmines, was a "parallel process" for nonstate armed groups to be able to commit to a ban. He noted in a 1999 proposal that while the Mine Ban Treaty did not have an option similar to Additional Protocol 1 of the Geneva Conventions[13] which would have allowed nonstate armed groups to make a unilateral declaration of adherence, an independent document of adherence to the obligations of the Mine Ban Treaty could be created if a governmental repository could be found. Many ICBL NSA Working Group members collaborated to write a document that would allow armed groups to unilaterally, but more formally, adhere to the mine ban. Entitled the Deed of Commitment, it required renunciation of use, as well as destruction of any arsenal of antipersonnel mines such groups may have, and cooperation with any mine action activities. Most radically, it requested the signatory group to allow for inspection and verification missions.

The Deed of Commitment has since been administered by a nongovernmental organization named Geneva Call, which facilitated the deposit of the Deed with the Canton of Geneva which had agreed to serve as repository.[14] Signatories are invited to sign the document in a publicized ceremony in Geneva in the same splendid and ornate hall in which the Geneva Conventions were signed. This provides the signatory group with a level of prestige it may not have experienced, while also making its unilateral commitment more broadly known and thereby increasing the political cost to the organization should it violate the pledge.

Thanks to early activity by ICBL campaigns, particularly in Asia and Africa, the Deed of Commitment garnered several signatures. The first groups approached were those who were already engaged in mine action activities such as the Sudan People's Liberation Army/Movement and the armed militias in Iraqi Kurdistan, as well as several groups in the Philippines.

By mid-2007, a total of thirty-four groups had signed the Deed of Commitment in nine countries.[15] As with the Mine Ban Treaty, not all groups that have signed the document have used mines. One signatory in Burundi, one in Sudan, and two in the Kurdish Regional Government of Iraq have since become a formal part of governments which are States Parties to the Mine Ban Treaty and bound by its obligations. Two signatories in India, two signatories in the Philippines, and one from Burma claim not to have used antipersonnel mines. Some groups that signed have since become militarily inactive. One group in Turkey, one from the Philippines, and three from Burma were known to be mine users prior to signing the Deed of Commitment. Besides halting mine use, the Deed of Commitment requires that groups which have stocks destroy them and to cooperate in monitoring and providing reports of their actions. As of mid-2007, it does not appear that any group that signed, and was previously known to be a mine user, has completed full destruction of its stockpile.[16]

Some entities have stated that this signing option was not suitable for them due to political reasons and not because they wished to use antipersonnel mines. Especially those who were *de facto* governing bodies, such as in Somaliland, felt that they should be able to accede to the treaty as a state and not make a unilateral commitment as a nonstate entity.

Among those who have over the years issued unilateral declarations on a mine ban apart from the Deed of Commitment are the Guatemalan National Revolutionary Unit (URNG), the Taliban (then *de facto* government) in Afghanistan, the Casamance Movement of Democratic Forces (MFDC) in Senegal, and the Somali Patriotic Movement (SPM).[17]

Bilateral Agreements

Bilateral agreements between governments and nonstate armed groups are much stronger than unilateral ones because if a mine ban element in a bilateral agreement were to be violated, the entire agreement could be in jeopardy.

One such example, negotiated in the Hague in 1998, is the Comprehensive Agreement on Respect for Human Rights and International Humanitarian Law (CARHRIHL) between the government of the Philippines and the National Democratic Front of the Philippines. This agreement does not constitute, while short of a formal cease-fire or peace agreement, but it lays out certain thresholds of violence that must not be breached. The section on "Respect for Human Rights" contains a specific right of the people of the Philippines not to be subjected to the use of landmines. This agreement fully reflects the government of the Philippines' obligations as a State Party to the Mine Ban Treaty, but also, by entering into a comprehensive agreement, extended that obligation to the rebellion. The CARHRIHL is monitored by the parties to the agreement, and also by several civil society actors, including the Philippines Campaign to Ban Landmines.[18]

In June 2003, the ICBL NSA Working Group sent a mission to Nepal to encourage the inclusion of a ban on mine use in the twenty-two-point Code of Conduct put in place in January 2003 to regulate the cease-fire then in effect between the government of Nepal and the Communist Party of Nepal/ Maoist.[19] The 2003 cease-fire later broke down, but a new Code of Conduct accompanied a subsequent cease-fire between the parties in May 2006. That Code contains a specific article prohibiting new mine use, as well as another allowing the parties to request independent verification missions should an allegation of a violation arise.[20] The November 2006 Comprehensive Peace Agreement committed the parties to neither use nor transport mines and to assist each other to mark and clear the landmines and booby traps used during the conflict.[21]

Nonstate armed groups have also joined governmental authorities in bilateral agreements in Sudan.[22]

Trilateral Agreements

In trilateral agreements, a third party may be involved in brokering an agreement between two combatants and may also participate in the implementation of the agreement, its oversight, or in some other defined role. UN entities undertook this role in Western Sahara and Sudan. In Western Sahara, mine warfare left hundreds of thousands of landmines on front lines and in other areas prior to a cease-fire in 1991. Due to the ongoing threat from the mines, in 1999 the UN observer mission brokered a military agreement with Moroccan and Polisario forces to begin some marking, removal, and destruction of antipersonnel landmines and other explosive ordnance. Since that time, more than thirty-seven thousand pieces of explosive ordnance and landmines have been destroyed, and other hazards have been marked.

States Parties to the Mine Ban Treaty have also started to focus on such agreements. The Nairobi Action Plan, developed at the First Review Conference of the Mine Ban Treaty, contains a specific request (Action Point 5) to member governments to promote the mine ban in peace processes. This would include the good offices offered by those states acting as a third party supporter to a specific peace accord. For example, Norway has played that role to encourage agreement between the government of Sri Lanka and the Liberation Tigers of Tamil Elam, including promotion of mine action as an element of trust building between the parties to the agreement. Norway has also financially supported (with other governments) mine removal activities under this joint agreement.

Mine Action as Peace Building

Broadly, mine action includes minefield marking and clearance, assistance to people who have already fallen victim to landmines, education to change behaviors of people living in mine-affected areas to avoid more victims, and destruction of stockpiled mines so as prevent future use and additional victims.

All of these activities have in some specific cases taken place with nonstate armed groups prior to formal cease-fires. Interestingly, this has usually occurred in situations where a trilateral agreement has been brokered. One such example is the case of the Western Sahara described above. Another is Operation Lifeline Sudan (OLS), facilitated by the UN in 1996 despite the lack of a cease-fire between the warring parties. This opened the way for later mine action by establishing an agreed upon framework of humanitarian principles for relief operations.

One of the Sudanese combatants described the effect of joint mine action to me as follows: "The first thing we had done with the other side, besides shoot at them, was to start removing mines. You have to realize that removing mines is a positive activity. In other words, before ceasing fire, we were doing something positive, together. This had an effect on us. We realized if we could do this, we could also cease-fire together. It laid the trust basis for the eventual cease-fire and the Comprehensive Peace Accord. What I would tell other combatants is that even if you can't stop shooting today, you can stop laying mines."[23]

In Sri Lanka, the reopening of the major highway connecting the north of the country was an item of negotiation in the cease-fire. To reopen the road, coordinated demining had to take place with the agreement of the LTTE and the Sri Lankan Army on both sides of the frontline. This was achieved with third party assistance, when the ICRC's independent monitoring facilitated the necessary exchange of information between the two parties in the demining process. Both sides had something to gain if the road was opened, but this would require a new type of activity: cooperating together. This important action was almost derailed when the Asian Development Bank, which was responsible for providing funds for the rebuilding of this highway as a part of its peace support efforts, neglected to set aside funds for mine removal. Humanitarian demining NGOs already operating in the area saved the project by doing the demining themselves once the Sri Lankan Army and LTTE came to agreement on it, even though no one had given them any extra funding to do so. The resulting improvement in the daily life of the people in the area has been enormous and undeniable and simultaneously provided tangible grassroots support for a continuation of efforts for a permanent peace settlement.[24]

Beginning in mid-2006, increased tension and armed conflict has brought a halt, for the time being, to these gains.

Achieving a Truly Universal Ban

Despite the fact that nonstate armed groups cannot formally adhere to the Mine Ban Treaty, governments have addressed the issue within the States Parties' meetings in formal presentations, in consensual documents, and by attending side events organized by nongovernmental organizations. Some States Parties have reported on use by NSAGs, as well as agreements on the ban or mine action involving nonstate armed groups, in their reports on the implementation of various aspects of the treaty. At the 2004 Review Conference, States Parties produced an Action Plan to bring about universal acceptance and compliance with the treaty. That document included four points which were either directly or indirectly related to nonstate armed groups and the mine ban or mine action.[25]

However, it is by joining the Mine Ban Treaty that governments directly affect the actions of nonstate armed groups. The steady increase of the number of governments that have joined the treaty and therefore dismantled their mine-producing facilities and destroyed their stockpiles has limited the supply of the weapon. The fact that most armed movements obtain their arms from state arsenals is revealed by the effectiveness of the Mine Ban Treaty in denying access to the weapon. In a July 2006 meeting, a representative of an armed group from Ethiopia told me, "We don't use landmines because we cannot obtain them. If the government forces were using them, then we would have them."

Antipersonnel landmine use by nonstate armed groups has consistently fallen since 2004. The annual Landmine Monitor report recorded use by nonstate armed groups in sixteen countries in 2004, thirteen countries in 2005, and ten countries in 2006, most of which were in states that had not yet joined the Mine Ban Treaty.[26]

There are also examples of post-Mine Ban Treaty armed rebellions, which previously would have been likely users of landmines but have not been known to deploy them. When a section of the armed forces in Côte d'Ivoire rebelled and seized control of the northern half of the country and renamed themselves as the New Forces, they might have deployed antipersonnel mines along their line of confrontation with loyalist forces controlling the southern part of the country, *if* they had access to them. However, prior to the rebellion, Côte d'Ivoire had already joined the Mine Ban Treaty and had no antipersonnel mines in its arsenal. All of Côte d'Ivoire's neighboring countries had also joined the treaty. Antipersonnel mines were not locally available to the New Forces. Since that time, the UN forces monitoring the line of control between the two factions have stated that they have never come across an antipersonnel mine within the country.

In Nigeria, the Movement for the Emancipation of the Niger River Delta also has not been known to use antipersonnel mines in its activities. Nigeria and all surrounding countries are parties to the Mine Ban Treaty, and the rebels would have to find sources for mines much more distant than those for the other arms used in their rebellion.

By comparison, the Baluchistan Liberation Army in Pakistan began deploying an increasing number of landmines as it escalated armed activities aimed at Pakistani security forces in Baluchistan Province in 2003. Incidents of mine use, and victims from them, have increased since that time. Baluchistan is surrounded by two mine producers—Pakistan and Iran—which have yet to join the treaty.

The goals of a specific nonstate armed group can influence whether it is likely to be a major landmine threat. Nonstate armed groups which are concerned with the control of a specific geographic territory, such as the Liberation Tigers of Tamil Elam who seek to establish a separate Elam state, are more likely to deploy large quantities of antipersonnel mines over a wide geographic area as either a defensive or separation tactic. It is noteworthy that conflicts of this type are dwindling; fewer insurgencies aimed at a separate state are emerging as the era of anticolonial struggles is, hopefully, drawing to a close.

Other armed groups who primarily seek political goals, such as a policy change or a share of power rather than separation, may from time to time deploy a victim-activated device but are unlikely to have large stockpiles of mines, nor seek to acquire them or use them in large numbers.

While there has been a decline in the use of victim-activated explosive devices by armed groups, it appears there has been a reciprocal increase in their use of command-detonated devices, such as time, suicide, radio, or remotely activated improvised explosive bombs. This may be in part due to the success of such tactics in Iraq but likely also reflects sensitivity to use of antipersonnel mines (or mine-like victim-activated devices), as well as lack of availability and even lack of military utility of such mines.

Balanced against the perceived military interests of armed groups in having antipersonnel mines is the stigmatization of the weapon. The humanitarian principles on which the mine ban movement was founded, and the successful spread of the ban throughout the world, have had a moral persuasive effect on some nonstate armed groups—leading to their not using landmines even when having access to them.

Bilateral agreements between governments and warring groups, especially those with a provision for independent monitoring, form the strongest deterrent to use by nonstate armed groups. Unilateral commitments such as Geneva Call's Deed of Commitment may have a persuasive effect on some armed groups, but this remains to be seen. While unilateral statements and pledges are much less credible to the international community, they are, nonetheless, welcome and should be publicized to increase the cost of backtracking.

Promoting mine action activities in conflict zones as a peace-building activity could be more vigorously pursued. There is significant space to apply creative mine action as a forerunner to peace action. It is the unfortunate political history of traditional humanitarian interventions in conflict zones to see the boundaries of their activities constrained to "nonpolitical" ones. Until this is rethought, the application of mine action as a political intervention to foster trust building will be avoided or overlooked. Similarly, mine-free zones, and other conflict interrupting initiatives have never been declared by local, conflict plagued communities in landmine affected areas and should be encouraged and supported. Zones of peace (which by definition should include a ban on use of mines) have been a part of some cease-fire and peace processes, but this remains an area where creative potential could be realized.

Conclusion

In revisiting the observations made by Soliman Santos in 1997, we can see in retrospect that despite the lack of a formal method of adherence to the Mine Ban Treaty, some rebel groups now do feel obliged to abide by, or answer to, the global norm the mine ban movement and the treaty are putting in place. Some governments that have not yet joined the Mine Ban Treaty have nonetheless reached agreements specifying nonuse of mines in cease-fire protocols with armed adversaries, such as in Nepal. Once these peace processes are completed, there will be no obvious impediment for these states to adhere to the Mine Ban Treaty. In some states that have joined the treaty and where conflict has come to an end, rebels have become a part of the solution, where once they were the problem. One such example is in Cambodia, where a former commander of the antigovernment Khmer People's National Liberation Front became the director of the Cambodian Mine Action Center.

Ultimately, the mine ban depends on developing political will, whether in a state or a nonstate armed group. The people's movement to ban landmines has proven to be the key element in the creation of that will. Through consistent and creative political intervention a diminishing number of states and

nonstate armed groups remain outside the global norm, with a corresponding, and self-inflicted, loss of legitimacy.

Notes

1. The International Campaign to Ban Landmines (ICBL) uses two operational
definitions for nonstate armed groups, one for advocacy purposes, applying here, and
another for its Landmine Monitor research into the global impact of the weapon and
efforts to eradicate it. For advocacy purposes the definition is limited to opposition
political organizations carrying out armed rebellion or insurrection, while for research
purposes, the Landmine Monitor includes a broader range of nonstate entities, including criminal gangs and state-supported proxy forces.

2. ICRC, *Anti-personnel Landmines: Friend or Foe? A Study of the Military Use and
Effectiveness of Anti-Personnel Mines* (Geneva: ICRC, 1997, 2004).

3. Stuart Maslen, *Commentaries on Arms Control Treaties, Volume 1, The Convention on the Prohibition of the Use, Stockpiling, Production, and Transfer of Anti-Personnel Mines and on their Destruction* (Oxford: Oxford University Press, 2004), pp. 64,
74–75.

4. Article 9 states: "Each State Party shall take all appropriate legal, administrative
and other measures, including the imposition of penal sanctions, to prevent and suppress any activity prohibited to a State Party under this Convention undertaken by
persons or on territory under its jurisdiction or control."

5. The preamble states, "The States Parties . . . *Basing* themselves on the principle
of international humanitarian law that the right of the parties to an armed conflict to
choose methods or means of warfare is not unlimited, on the principle that prohibits
the employment in armed conflicts of weapons, projectiles and materials and methods of warfare of a nature to cause superfluous injury or unnecessary suffering and on
the principle that a distinction must be made between civilians and combatants, Have
agreed as follows:" (Articles of the Convention).

6. "An Agenda for Mine Action: A Global Ban on Landmines," Ottawa, Canada,
December 2–4, 1997, p. 56. (Informal report by the Department of Foreign Affairs and
International Trade, Government of Canada.)

7. Non-State Actors Working Group of the International Campaign to Ban Landmines brochure, March 2001.

8. Text from the first informational flyer published by the ICBL Non-State Actors
Working Group, http://www.icbl.org/problem/solution/ban/nsa/.

9. From this 1998 declaration by the Taliban until 2001, Landmine Monitor did
not register any use of antipersonnel mines by the Taliban. Since the time of the U.S.
invasion, there have been reports of resumed use.

10. UNICEF negotiated an agreement with the SPLM/A and the government of
Sudan for the provision of humanitarian relief to war affected populations. This
process, the first of its kind, led to a set of humanitarian principles agreed between the
SPLM/A and UNICEF. While these did not include a landmine ban, they led eventually to a demining program and a unilateral statement against mine use by the

SPLM/A, prior to the formal cease-fire with the government of Sudan. For further information, see Kristian Berg Harpviken and Rebecca Roberts (eds.), *Preparing the Ground for Peace: Mine Action in Support of Peacebuilding* (Oslo: PRIO, 2004).

11. "Landmine Monitor Fact Sheet 2002: Non-State Actors and the Ban on AntiPersonnel Landmines," prepared by Nonviolence International, February 2003.

12. For more information on these meetings, please see the full conference reports, http://www.icbl.org. The 2003, 2004, and 2005 meetings were jointly organized by the ICBL NSA Working Group and the Swiss NGO Geneva Call.

13. Additional Protocol 1, Article 96 (3) reads: The authority representing a people engaged against a High Contracting Party in an armed conflict of the type referred to in Article 1, paragraph 4, may undertake to apply the Conventions and this Protocol in relation to that conflict by means of a unilateral declaration addressed to the depositary. Such declaration shall, upon its receipt by the depositary, have in relation to that conflict the following effects: (a) The Conventions and this Protocol are brought into force for the said authority as a Party to the conflict with immediate effect; (b) The said authority assumes the same rights and obligations as those which have been assumed by a High Contracting Party to the Conventions and this Protocol; and (c) The Conventions and this Protocol are equally binding upon all Parties to the conflict.

14. Geneva Call is a Swiss NGO, and ICBL members are no longer a part of its governing body.

15. The number of signatories listed in Geneva Call's Annual Report 2006 and those on its website in 2007 do not match. Their website has decreased the number of signatories in Somalia, which was explained to the author by a member of Geneva Call as former signatories becoming defunct; however, there does not appear to be any explanation of the change in the status of organizations that cease to be an armed threat or become a part of a government.

16. This is based on the author's review of available literature by Geneva Call. For a comprehensive review of the achievements and shortcomings of the Deed of Commitment process, see Soliman M. Santos Jr., "A Critical Reflection on the Geneva Call Instrument and Approach in Engaging Armed Groups on Humanitarian Norms: A Southern Perspective," October 31, 2003, paper prepared for Curbing Human Rights Violations by Armed Groups conference by the Armed Groups Project, http://www.armedgroups.org.

17. Soliman M. Santos Jr., "The Ottawa Treaty and Non-State Actors," Manila, 1999.

18. The full text can be found on the website of the National Democratic Front of the Philippines, available at: http://www.philippinerevolution.net/cgi-bin/ndf/ptoks.pl?id=carhrihl;fn=19980316;la=eng/.

19. The Code did not specifically refer to landmines, but two lawyers on the mission offered the opinion that seven of the existing twenty-two points implied the use of mines as banned. The Code included a provision for monitoring of the agreement.

20. ICBL update, "Nepal: No New Use of Landmines under New Code of Conduct Offers a Glimmer of Hope," May 30, 2006, http://www.icbl.org/news/nepal_code_of_conduct/.

21. Comprehensive Peace Agreement held between Government of Nepal and Communist Party of Nepal (Maoist), 21 November 2006, points 5.1.1(h); 5.1.2 and 5.1.4.

22. Humanitarian Cease Fire Agreement on the Conflict in Darfur, N'Djamena, 2004, between factions of the Sudan Liberation Movement/Army and the Justice and Equality Movement and the Government of Sudan.

23. This remark was made in 2004 during a discussion facilitated by the author between a member of the Sudan People's Liberation Army, which had halted mine use, and a member of the Karen National Union in Burma who was still involved in using antipersonnel landmines.

24. Harpviken and Roberts (eds.), *Mine Action in Support of Peacebuilding.*

25. Points 7, 46, and 64 of the Nairobi Action Plan directly mention nonstate actors. Point 7 requests governments to support mine action in areas under the control of an NSAG, as does point 46. Point 64 calls for coercive elements of Article 9 of the treaty to be applied when an NSAG uses mines within a state, which is a party to the treaty. Point 5 (promoting the mine ban in peace processes) is also relevant. First Review Conference of the States Parties to the Convention on the Prohibition of the Use, Stockpiling, Production, and Transfer of Anti-Personnel Mines and on Their Destruction, "Final Report: Part III. Ending the Suffering Caused by Anti-Personnel Mines: The Nairobi Action Plan, 2005-2009," Nairobi, November 29–December 3, 2004, APLC/CONF/2004/5, February 9, 2005.

26. Landmine Monitor reported NSAG use of antipersonnel mines or antipersonnel mine-like IEDs in 2006 in three States Parties (Burundi, Colombia, and Guinea-Bissau) and in seven non-States Parties (Burma, India, Iraq, Nepal, Pakistan, Russia/Chechnya, and Somalia); in 2005 in five States Parties (Burundi, Colombia, Philippines, Turkey, and Uganda) and in eight non-States Parties (Burma, Georgia, India, Iraq, Nepal, Pakistan, Somalia, and Russia, including in Chechnya, Dagestan, and North Ossetia); in 2004 in eight States Parties (Bolivia, Burundi, Colombia, Democratic Republic of Congo, Peru, Philippines, Turkey, and Uganda) and in eight non-States Parties (Bhutan, Burma, Georgia, India, Iraq, Nepal, Russia, including Chechnya and North Ossetia, and Somalia).

II

BEYOND LANDMINES

11

Citizen Diplomacy and the Ottawa Process: A Lasting Model?

Jody Williams and Stephen D. Goose

WHEN SIX NONGOVERNMENTAL ORGANIZATIONS came together in October 1992 to form an International Campaign to Ban Landmines, every government that we met with at that time—without exception—viewed the young campaign as a quixotic effort doomed to failure.[1] Most people around the world—except of course those in countries contaminated by landmines—were completely unaware of the humanitarian problems caused by this weapon. Yet within the short span of five years, conventional wisdom about humanitarian law and arms control negotiations was turned on its head as the 1997 Mine Ban Treaty was born. For the first time in history, a weapon widely used for many decades was banned.

The process that evolved in those years and brought about the treaty—commonly referred to as the Ottawa Process—gave the promise of a new dimension in diplomacy, of "citizen diplomacy," and generated hope for its wider applicability.

In awarding the 1997 Nobel Peace Prize to the International Campaign to Ban Landmines (ICBL) and its coordinator, Jody Williams, the Nobel Committee highlighted the ICBL's role in both the process and the treaty, stating that the campaign had been able to "express and mediate a broad range of popular commitment in an unprecedented way. With the governments of several small and medium-sized countries taking the issue up . . . this work has grown into a convincing example of an effective policy for peace." It concluded, "As a

This chapter benefited significantly from the early input of Dr. David Atwood, Executive Director, Quaker UN Office (QUNO), Geneva.

model for similar processes in the future, it could prove to be of decisive importance to the international effort for disarmament and peace."

There clearly was reason for such hope. The mine ban movement demonstrated that it is possible for nongovernmental organizations (NGOs) to put
an issue—even one with international security implications—on the international agenda, provoke urgent actions by governments and others, and serve
as the driving force behind change. It showed that civil society can wield great
power in the post-Cold War world. Moreover, the mine ban movement
demonstrated the power of partnerships by achieving rapid success internationally through common and coordinated action by NGOs, like-minded governments, and other key actors such as UN agencies and the International
Committee of the Red Cross (ICRC). It showed that that change is most likely
to be effected through concerted action. The mine ban movement also
demonstrated that it is possible for small and medium size countries, acting
in concert with civil society, to provide global leadership and achieve major
diplomatic results, even in the face of opposition from bigger powers. It
showed that it is possible to work outside of traditional diplomatic forums,
practices, and methods and still achieve success multilaterally.

And indeed, the new diplomatic model was inspiring people of all stripes
around the world to explore new possibilities of multilateral responses to
global issues. But at the same time, there were immediate, negative responses
to the approach by some governments—and even some people outside of
government—in an effort to confine it to a "one-off" success, one that worked
only for the "special case" of antipersonnel landmines.[2] For many states, citizen diplomacy was simply unacceptable. Involving civil society actors in treaty
negotiations added too many unpredictable and uncontrollable elements to
diplomatic processes forged over centuries.[3]

Apart from those who actively wished to see the model fail, there were—
and still are—some observers who believed that it would not be possible to
replicate the mine ban experience because it was not so much a model as an
example of "all the stars aligning properly." This view holds that the Ottawa
Process only succeeded because of the confluence of a variety of factors, such
as the particular timing (in terms of world affairs); the skill and audacity of a
handful of key government officials and representatives of nongovernmental
and international organizations; the reality of the limited military utility of
antipersonnel mines and the limited economic stake involved; and the fact the
campaign only had to focus on a single weapon and had the advantages of an
easy to grasp message with highly emotional content.

This chapter looks at how the model has stood up in the ten years since the
Mine Ban Treaty was signed by 122 nations in two triumphant days at the end
of 1997. What have its strengths and weaknesses been? What lessons from and

aspects of the model have been applied by NGOs in their work on other issues? Has the Ottawa Process model proven to be of "decisive importance" as hoped by the Nobel Committee—or of any meaningful importance at all? Is there a future for such a model of campaigning and diplomacy, particularly in the post-9/11 world?

We will look first at lessons learned from the campaigning side of the model, and then at the diplomatic side, before considering the applicability of the model to other issues.

The Campaigning Model[4]

The NGOs of the International Campaign to Ban Landmines have correctly been seen as the engine behind the Ottawa Process that resulted in the Mine Ban Treaty. The work of the members of the ICBL in the movement to ban antipersonnel mines has been held up by many as a quintessential example of global citizen diplomacy.

It is somewhat odd to consider lessons from the ICBL since it continues to develop and flourish and is by no means "past history." But with the ICBL's track record of fifteen years and ten years into the life of the Mine Ban Treaty, there is much to consider and much to be learned.

Following are the key campaigning lessons that we identify, which also can be seen to constitute key elements of the model: organizing skills; a flexible coalition structure; strong leadership and committed workers; action plans and deadlines, with outcome-oriented conferences; communication skills; follow-up and follow-through; expertise and documentation; clear and simple articulation of goals and messages; use of multiple fora to promote the message; a focus on the human cost; inclusivity and diversity, yet speaking with one voice; and, finally, recognition that international context and timing matter.

Know how to organize. A positive mythology often invoked about NGOs is that they are selfless and tireless and that they inherently "know how to campaign." Nothing could be further from the truth, particularly with regard to the latter. The reality is that the typical members of many NGO coalitions, including research and advocacy organizations and even grassroots organizations, usually do not have skills and experience in large-scale organizing. There is often little understanding of coalition-building and how to work successfully in coalition. Campaigners may have in-depth understanding of their issue, but if they can't work together effectively that expertise may prove of little value. Without a firm grasp of these fundamentals, it can be extremely difficult to campaign successfully.[5]

Maintain a flexible structure. We are convinced that the ICBL's informal and loose structure has been one of its major strengths.[6] The lack of centralization was a conscious decision. Each NGO has to find a way to participate in making the campaign work. This helps to ensure that the ICBL belongs to all of its members and that these members have to be active in the process to achieve the campaign's goals. There is no bureaucratic structure that either dictates to members how they should contribute to the campaign or does the work for them. ICBL members have met regularly to strategize and plan joint actions, but each NGO and national campaign has been free to carry out whatever aspects of the work best fit its individual mandate, political culture, and circumstances.

Need for leadership and committed workers. Successful coalitions will naturally be large and diverse, but experience shows that most operate on the extensive work of a committed and dedicated few, supported by the many. Most organizations cannot devote full-time staff to coalition efforts, but it is essential that there be a core of people working full time. With diverse coalitions, strong and effective leadership provided by a handful of organizations and individuals is essential. The leadership of the ICBL has been and continues to be those who choose to step up to the plate and follow up their words of commitment with concrete and consistent action that advances the goals of the ICBL. (This applies equally to governments as it does NGOs.)

Always have an action plan and deadlines, with outcome-oriented meetings. The Ottawa Process can be characterized as an ongoing series of international, regional, and national conferences and meetings, both NGO and diplomatic. While it is easy, and perhaps usually correct, to criticize costly get-togethers, in the case of the mine ban movement, face-to-face contact is carefully planned with concrete objectives in mind, with the intention of one meeting building on another, and most importantly, with an action plan emerging in which various actors took responsibility for specific tasks to move the ban forward. Deadlines are essential to spurring action: negotiate the treaty by December 1997, get the forty ratifications needed for entry into force within one year, accede by the Second Meeting of States Parties, and so on.

ICBL meetings also usually include campaign capacity-building workshops and training sessions. Unlike some NGO participation at some international conferences, the ICBL has not brought individual campaigners to multilateral meetings simply for the sake of numbers. It has worked hard and strategically, putting campaigners to work at meetings—for example, asking more experienced NGOs to accompany new campaigners to lobby delegates as training or asking other NGOs to take assignments speaking with the press—so they do not aimlessly wander the halls and develop a sense of detachment from the campaign of which they are a part.

Communication, communication, and more communication. Clear and consistent communication is an irreplaceable element of success. Information is power, and it is absolutely key that information is shared throughout a coalition. In the early days of the campaign, individual members gained strength by being able to speak with authority about what was happening everywhere to eliminate the problem. Sharing the successes and failures of the work empowered all organizations and lessened the possibility of isolation of any one. Because of strong communication, the ICBL often has known of developments before governments, which made the ICBL a focal point of information for governments and NGOs alike.

From the beginning, ICBL leaders recognized that in order to hold NGOs of such diverse interests together, the organizations would have to feel an immediate and important part of developing the work of the campaign. In the early years of the ICBL, this was achieved by extensive use of the fax and regular mailings to campaign members of documents and informational updates. The ICBL relied on fax and telephone communication for much of its almost daily communications until 1996. Since then, electronic mail has permitted the ICBL to carry out its priority of frequent and timely internal communication to a greater degree than ever before. The importance of electronic mail to the success of the campaign has been often noted and often overstated. Certainly the ease and speed of communication as a result of technological developments have had a great impact on the ability of civil society from diverse cultures to dialogue and formulate global political strategies, but email and the Internet alone have not "moved the movement."

As important—and many might contend more so—as fax, phone, e-mail, and the Internet have been to link together the huge coalition, networking has also been effective through travel and the building of personal relationships, both within the campaign and between campaigners and various government representatives. Regular landmine-related meetings and conferences have helped to build and maintain a sense of a "ban community."

Follow-up and follow-through. It has been remarked that although there are plenty of good treaties, conventions, and international laws in existence, the problem is implementation. The same is true of coalition work. There are always plenty of good ideas about what needs to be done. The difficulty is implementing those ideas. Follow-up and follow-through are what make the difference. Holding individuals and NGOs accountable for commitments made has worked in the ICBL, and when commitments have been broken, other campaigners have quickly stepped in to fill the void. A large measure of the trust that governments have for the ICBL has been the result of its consistency in following up and following through on its words with actions.

Provide expertise and documentation. The founding members of the ICBL were NGOs engaged in clearing mines, putting prosthetics on victims, and documenting the impact of mines on civilians. NGOs carried out a concerted research agenda and published informational materials extensively and distributed them widely to governments as well as the public. They provided comprehensive materials on the impact of landmines around the world, on global mine production, trade, stocks and use, as well as sophisticated legal analysis, all of which were powerful tools for advocacy. Since the treaty entered into force in 1999, the ICBL has further expanded this role through its Landmine Monitor initiative, the first time that NGOs have come together in a sustained, systematic, and coordinated fashion to monitor and report on the implementation of an international disarmament or humanitarian law treaty (see chapter 4).

Articulate goals and messages clearly and simply. The importance of clear, concise, and consistent articulation of goals and messages is hard to overstate. This is true not only with respect to the overarching goals of a campaign, coalition, or movement, but also for each phase, conference, or event. While it is necessary to demonstrate expertise and an understanding of complexities and subtleties, for campaigning purposes simple and direct is always better.

Focus on the human cost. Much of the success of the ICBL has been due to keeping the international focus on the human beings who have suffered because of landmines—the humanitarian aspects of the issue, not the arms control or security aspects. This has been crucial not only in influencing public opinion, but also in influencing governments. One example has been ICBL efforts to encourage government officials dealing with development and aid issues to take the lead, or at least be part of diplomatic delegations, rather than those dealing with military or disarmament issues.

Use as many forums as possible to promote the message. Though it seems obvious, few take advantage of the many opportunities available internationally to get an issue on the agenda and language in final statements and declarations and resolutions to support their cause. It can take considerable effort to do this, first to identify the forum and then to do the necessary advocacy to bear fruit; but with every success, new audiences are reached.

Be inclusive, be diverse, yet speak with one voice. The ICBL has always ascribed to the big tent theory. To join, it was only necessary for an NGO to inform the coordinator that it shared and endorsed the campaign's call for a total ban on antipersonnel mines, as well as increased resources for mine clearance and victim assistance programs. No dues, no requirements, no restrictions. The big tent had built-in diversity almost from the start because so many different countries, as well as so many different fields, sectors, and interest groups were affected by mines. The ICBL has sought to reflect this diversity in various campaign bodies, such as its Advisory Board, which includes representatives from mine-affected states, organizations involved in mine clearance and victim assistance programs, as well as human rights, humanitarian aid, and religious organizations. There have been occasional tensions in the campaign about the need for greater diversity and/or more structured diversity within the leadership. But, the general principle has been, and remains, that leadership positions should only go to those willing and able to bear the burden of the work, and not just be names on letterheads.

Beyond the sheer numbers of NGOs and individuals involved in the ban movement, there have been other benefits when one can speak as a coalition on behalf of many. Often, even when pursuing similar objectives as NGOs, governments have traditionally been reluctant to deal with NGOs as partners or to permit their meaningful participation in diplomatic meetings, in no small part because of the fear of being overwhelmed by numbers and diverse views. In that respect, the ability of the ICBL to serve as a banner for nearly every NGO working on the issue, and to speak authoritatively with one voice, has served the movement very well. The campaign has been able to have a seat at the table, with virtually the same status as states during the Ottawa Process diplomatic meetings and since. It would not have been possible to achieve this status with a larger number of NGOs each working independently, and perhaps in competition, advocating for their particular vision of what was needed.

Recognize that international context and timing do matter. The changing global situation in the late 1980s and early 1990s was a critical factor in the development of the movement to ban landmines. With the end of the Cold War, governments and NGOs began to look at war and peace issues differently, and many governments were no longer as constrained in their possible responses to issues of global humanitarian and security concern. Many NGOs were looking for new issues in which to become engaged. Increased attention was being devoted to conventional, as opposed to nuclear, weapons at the same time that the impact of antipersonnel landmines was reaching a crescendo, due to widespread and increasing use from the mid-1960s forward. In the global political context the ban movement emerged and achieved dramatic success. Earlier efforts to ban the weapon in the late 1970s only resulted in the weak Landmine Protocol of the Convention on Conventional Weapons.

The Diplomatic Model

NGO campaigning has been an important part of the success of the mine ban movement, but many other factors have contributed. Perhaps the most notable feature of the "new diplomacy" has been the partnership formed between key governments and civil society to achieve common humanitarian aims. Other vital elements have been meaningful and consistent NGO involvement; leadership by smaller and mid-sized states; and a willingness to operate outside the UN system when necessary, including rejection of consensus rules. These elements have been sustained since the signing of the treaty in what might be called the Mine Ban Treaty Process, building on the Ottawa Process.

Without the close cooperation of NGOs (primarily through the ICBL), governments, the ICRC, and UN agencies, there is little question that the Mine Ban Treaty would not have come into existence in 1997, and it would not have been so effectively universalized and implemented in the past decade. The mine ban movement certainly was not the first where civil society lobbied for change and governments responded positively.[7] But it has likely been unique in the level of closeness, openness, and cooperation of the partnership and the degree to which it has been sustained over so many years.

Historically, NGOs and governments have often seen each other as adversaries, not colleagues—and in many cases rightly so. And at first many in the NGO mine ban community worried that governments were going to "hijack" the issue in order to undermine a ban. But a relationship of trust among the relatively small "core group" of governments (most notably Canada, Norway, Austria, and South Africa) and ICBL leadership quickly developed and has been maintained and expanded over the years.[8]

The willingness of certain governments and individuals in those governments to engage in nontraditional diplomacy and to take risks (to say nothing of their dedication, energy, and talent) has been crucial to the success of the Mine Ban Treaty Process. It has been especially noteworthy that small and mid-size states have provided such leadership in the face of opposition from bigger states.

The partnership has continued to flourish during the past ten years, devoted to universalizing and implementing the Mine Ban Treaty, and has not diminished into simple lip service to the word. Even the fact that some of the annual Meetings of States Parties are held in Geneva under the auspices of the UN has not led to a return to "diplomacy as usual" —though there are some concerns that things are increasingly moving in that direction.

The partnership and the special status accorded the ICBL has continued to be in virtually every aspect of the working of the Mine Ban Treaty as is evident from other chapters in this book. The ICBL's role in the Intersessional Work Programme, the Contact Groups (especially on universalization), and even the formal annual Meetings of States Parties, is not duplicated in any other diplomatic forum. "Open and inclusive" is the mantra for the Mine Ban Treaty, with informality (by diplomatic standards) the norm.

The ICBL's Landmine Monitor initiative is a prime example of its pioneering work in civil society involvement in the development of international law, with its establishment of a unique role for the ICBL and its members in the ongoing monitoring of implementation of and compliance with the treaty (see chapter 4).

Not all campaigners have been comfortable, however, with such close collaboration with governments. Some believe that it is more reflective of NGO co-optation by governments than partnership and are wary of the relationship. Others have been outspokenly critical of the cooperation, considering it a "sellout." They hold a belief that the proper role of NGOs is always that of opposition and as opposition; they must always be searching for the "worm in the apple" rather than cooperate in ways that make governments "look good."

At the same time, not all governments share the same degree of enthusiasm for the partnership either, and the relative informality of treaty-related meetings has caught more than one diplomat off guard.[9] And despite the long-standing partnership and the joint efforts to advance treaty compliance through "cooperation" rather than coercion, at times there have been serious strains in the partnership when NGOs have differed with governments in interpretation of some of the treaty's obligations—in particular those related to its arms control aspects. Because of those differences of interpretation, the ICBL has continued to press governments to develop common positions on those issues and that continued lobbying has not always been welcome (see chapter 7).

So at times, what has been the great strength of the mine ban movement—the civil society-government partnership—has almost paradoxically been problematic. When the partners cannot or will not recognize and accept differing rights and responsibilities of each other, it can be quite difficult to navigate those waters and maintain the cooperative nature of the process that has resulted in such continued momentum in the work to eliminate landmines.

Is the Model Applicable to Other Issues?

A number of governments showed great vision and leadership in recognizing that "normal" diplomacy was not adequate to tackle the mine problem and dared to think outside the box. They recognized that in the post-Cold War world things could and should be done differently. Yet, even as some governments were anxious to apply the landmine model to other issues, others were trying to make sure that the process was understood to be "unique to the landmine issue" and not precedent setting in multilateral diplomacy—particularly in arms control or other security related issues.

Apart from the desire of some to see the model fail, it seems apparent that the mine ban coalition and the process it generated are not necessarily universally applicable. There are many factors that influence how civil society organizes to bring about change and how governments respond.

In the past ten years, there have been campaigning and coalition efforts that demonstrate both the applicability and nonapplicability of the landmine campaign experience. Among those that most closely resemble the ICBL and Ottawa Process model are the efforts on the International Criminal Court, child soldiers, cluster munitions (see chapter 13), and the Disability Rights Convention (see chapter 14). Those that have not taken much from the model include small arms and light weapons, blood diamonds, global poverty, and "human security." We will look more closely at one example from each category.

The International Criminal Court

The successful negotiation of the Rome Statute in July 1998 creating the International Criminal Court (ICC) came quickly on the heels of the Mine Ban Treaty success. Various aspects of that effort recall the work of the landmine ban movement, with governments and NGOs pressing for the creation of an international criminal court—a goal harkening back to the Nuremburg Trials after World War II.

As with landmines, a coalition of NGOs came together to lobby for a court, and "like-minded" governments came together to press for a diplomatic meeting on the subject. When it was decided in the latter part of 1997 that a diplomatic conference would be held in Rome in mid-1998, both governmental and NGO activities took on increased urgency and NGOs pressed the governments to agree to fundamental elements of the court.

As Don Hubert succinctly describes in comparing the ICC work with that of the landmine movement, there were many similarities.[10] The expertise offered by NGOs was first rate, especially on substantive legal issues related to an international criminal court. The NGO Coalition produced newsletters daily, as had the ICBL in the Oslo negotiations. NGOs were given observer status, and individual NGO representatives were on a number of government delegations. Although the Rome Conference was a UN negotiating session, rules of procedure were somewhat like those used in Oslo for the Mine Ban Treaty—issues could be decided by a two-thirds majority vote and were not held hostage to consensus. As with the Mine Ban Treaty and ICBL, the NGO Coalition for the ICC undertook a ratification campaign to help ensure that the Rome Statute became international law as quickly as possible, and it continues to work to ensure the Court is functioning effectively.

In one notable difference, the United States exhibited fevered opposition to the ICC and aggressively sought to undermine it. It did not sign the Mine Ban Treaty, but rarely openly attacked it, and, with some exceptions, did not make serious efforts to dissuade other countries from joining.

Some have argued that it was not simply the success of the Ottawa Process that raised the hackles of powerful nations used to calling the shots, but the one-two punch of the Mine Ban Treaty followed so closely by the success of the Rome conference.

Small Arms and Light Weapons

As governments and NGOs began to organize themselves to take more serious action on small arms and light weapons (SALW), the ICBL and the Ottawa Process were on the minds of many of them but on both sides with more negative than positive lessons learned. While the many problems related to the proliferation of small arms and light weapons have been documented for years, it was not until 1998 that NGOs came together to form a new network, the International Action Network on Small Arms (IANSA). The NGOs in the network wanted to try to enhance cooperation and communication as they pressed governments to take action to deal with the problem.

When IANSA was being formed, some among its leadership felt the ICBL as a model was overly centralized and dominated by NGOs from the North. IANSA instead focused its work on the regional level with regional coordinators. The leadership body was deemed the Facilitation Committee, rather than a steering or coordination committee. There was no central focal point to develop common messages and there were no global spokespeople. As one participant in the work put it, this structure led to "paralyzation" with little coordination, and no one to make decisions. The network appeared consumed with form and structure, rather than substance. Matters improved after 2001, when IANSA built a secretariat based in London, but some actively involved still describe the network as a whole as very inefficient.[11]

While NGOs were not exactly clear on what shape their work on small arms and light weapons should take, many governments were clear that they wanted any work on the issue to be carried out under the auspices of the UN. Although there was cooperative work between NGOs and governments in the lead up to a 2001 conference on the "Illicit Trade in Small Arms and Light Weapons in All its Aspects," that conference was carried out within the UN; consensus ruled and NGOs were largely kept outside of the deliberations—as the ICBL had been during the early days of the Convention on Conventional Weapons (CCW) Review Process through 1996.

The outcome of the 2001 conference was a Programme of Action to take steps to deal with SALW and which would lead to another conference in 2006. Although cooperative work between NGOs and governments increased in those five years, and NGO representatives were included on some government delegations at the 2006 Conference, IANSA and other NGOs acting on their own behalf were still not permitted meaningful participation in that meeting. As one SALW campaigner wrote, "It is a frequent refrain amongst small arms diplomats and government officials that 'we' must keep the global process on small arms control within the UN. This constant referencing of the specter of the Ottawa Process and the success of people-centered campaigning in the late 90's has certainly had a negative influence on the imagination of government officials."[12]

While perhaps little of the ICBL/Ottawa Process model can be clearly seen here, some informal work between governments and NGOs toward implementation of the Programme of Action in the lead-up to the 2006 Conference has been useful. Particularly notable have been the efforts of the Geneva Forum—a partnership of the Quaker UN Office, the UN Institute for Disarmament Research, and the Program for Strategic and International Security Studies of the Graduate Institute of International Studies—in bringing together governments and others working on SALW in a Geneva Process, focusing on implementation of the Programme of Action. Other NGOs have formed partnerships to track and report on government action on small arms through "Biting the Bullet," while the Control Arms initiative has focused international attention on the need to establish an Arms Trade Treaty.[13]

Growing civil society pressure helped bring about the encouraging adoption of a UN General Assembly resolution in December 2006 in support of an Arms Trade Treaty, with 153 governments voting in favor.[14] The resolution requested the UN Secretary-General "to seek the views of Member States on creating a legally binding instrument and to establish a group of governmental experts, commencing in 2008, to examine the feasibility, scope and draft parameters of such an instrument."[15] As work unfolds around the Arms Trade Treaty, it remains to be seen how governments and NGOs will interact in the process, but it clearly will not be on a fast track.

The Convention on Conventional Weapons

Developments in the Convention on Conventional Weapons forum also provide an interesting gauge of the impact of the mine ban movement model. The failure of the CCW to deal adequately with antipersonnel mines during deliberations from 1993–1996 as part of its first Review Conference led to Canada's call for an outside process aimed at a ban on the weapon. Those were extremely frustrating years for NGOs on the diplomatic front as they were blocked from participation in all sessions except the rare plenary meetings.

In the wake of the Mine Ban Treaty experience, the situation in the CCW, in many respects, changed significantly, and for the better. At the Second and Third Review Conferences in 2001 and 2006, respectively, and in the working meetings in between and since (carried out under the banner of Groups of Governmental Experts), NGOs have rarely been excluded from participation. They have not only made statements during plenary meetings but have had the opportunity to intervene and respond on a regular basis during deliberations, and more notably have been asked to give presentations on a wide range of subjects.

Most importantly, during the development of what became CCW Protocol V on explosive remnants of war from 2001 to 2003, there was extensive consultation and cooperation—though largely behind the scenes—among NGOs, the ICRC, and some key governments, especially the Netherlands, which took the lead on the protocol. Without the backdrop of the mine ban experience and the relationships and working methods formed during that process, it is unlikely that Protocol V would have come into being.

Without question, the CCW has evolved in a positive way as a result of the Ottawa Process. It is interesting to note that this has not occurred in the other quintessential security forum based in Geneva, the Conference on Disarmament (CD). And it is likely not a coincidence that the CD has not been able to accomplish anything over the past decade, struggling even to agree on an agenda or work program.

But, as discouraging as it is to acknowledge, things have not changed in a fundamental way in the CCW. This is true even though only fifteen of the CCW's 102 members are not party to the Mine Ban Treaty. While mostly the same people are in the room, the atmosphere and the way of doing business stand in stark contrast to Mine Ban Treaty meetings.[16] This is due in large part to the fact that decisions—such as they are—are made by consensus among governments, ensuring minimal change, implemented at a snail's pace, if at all. This undermined the potential of the protocol on explosive remnants of war, which in the end was watered down to the point that it contains few binding obligations and is more of a voluntary regime. The notion of a joint sense of commitment to humanitarian aims seems inevitably to lose out in the CCW to narrowly defined assertions of national security interests.

The reality of the fundamentally unchanged nature of the CCW is what led Norway to propose pursuit of a new treaty outside of the CCW banning cluster munitions that cause unacceptable harm to civilians after the Third Review Conference in November 2006 rejected a proposal backed by two dozen states to begin CCW negotiations on cluster munitions. This was the Ottawa Process model taking full flight, with a new treaty process rising out of the failure of the CCW, focused on protection of civilians, uniting like-minded governments with NGOs once again on a fast-track solution to a pressing humanitarian problem. Yet even here, some Mine Ban Treaty States Parties have been hesitant to embrace fully the Oslo Process and are advocating efforts to continue to deal with the issue in the CCW (see chapter 13).[17]

Conclusion: Enduring Partnerships Take Constant Work

The ICBL and the Ottawa Process have clearly had a significant impact apart from the landmine issue in terms of inspiring and serving as a model for other endeavors to use if they choose, as has been the case with the new legal regimes on the International Criminal Court, child soldiers, explosive remnants of war, disability rights, and, soon, cluster munitions. That is an extremely impressive résumé of impact for a decade.

But other initiatives have not reflected the landmine model, perhaps most notably the work on small arms and light weapons. Some traditional diplomatic forums have been affected by and changed somewhat as a result of the mine ban experience, including the CCW, but the reality is likely that none have been fundamentally altered. Diplomatic "business as usual" is still the norm.

What does the future hold? The Ottawa Process happened in a post-Cold War, but pre-9/11 world, where both civil society and governments felt there was room for new multilateral efforts and perhaps even new ways to consider "security." But after the terrorist attacks of 9/11 and the "war on terror" and all that has come with it, creative thinking about security and multilateralism has a much more perilous future.

It is not in the least bit surprising that many—perhaps even most—governments would want to return to the known, controllable, and comfortable world of traditional negotiations, closed to civil society, particularly in relation to arms control, disarmament, and security issues. It is fair to say that some have worked to ensure that the Ottawa Process was an anomaly and not a precedent.

What is surprising is that, in some instances, even prominent pro-Ottawa Process states seem reluctant to apply the model to other issues. Some glaring examples have been the lack of NGO-government cooperation in the "human security" endeavor (see chapter 16) and the desire of so many states to cling to the CCW to deal with cluster munitions, despite the Oslo Process launched in 2007.

Key nations of the mine ban movement, emboldened by the success of the Ottawa Process, launched the Human Security Network at a meeting of foreign ministers held in Oslo on May 21, 1999. And although there is much debate on the merits of a "human security framework," the initiative has not gained significant traction and momentum in large part because it has been almost entirely government-driven with minimal inclusion of civil society. Given that the founders of the Network are the same governments that worked side by side with NGOs—and continue to do so to this day—to ensure the success of the Mine Ban Treaty, it is difficult not to wonder about their broader commitment to inclusion of civil society in dealing with global issues.

But civil society and NGOs have to some extent been their own worst enemies. Too often it appears that NGOs themselves have not changed the way they work. Instead of insisting that the ground rules have shifted, for example, it seems when they hear "No you cannot participate," it is accepted as defeat, rather than seeing it as a challenge to be overcome. It should not be a question of "if" NGOs are included but "how." As some observers have pointed out, just being inside a conference room during discussions and negotiations does not necessarily mean real "access" to the desired outcome.[18]

Not as many NGOs as one might expect have sought out the ICBL to discuss lessons learned—both positive and negative—from the work to ban landmines. On the other hand, the ICBL has done little to proactively share those lessons. This is not to say that there is or even should be a "cookie cutter approach" to dealing with various issues. Not all methods work in all circumstances. But in order to make decisions about strategies and tactics, civil society should learn from efforts that have come before—both those that have succeeded and those that have failed.

The world has benefited from the partnership between government and civil society that resulted in the Mine Ban Treaty. In this globalized world, transnational civil society has a role to play in finding solutions to our common problems. But it will be up to civil society to ensure that the Ottawa Process model does endure. If the partnership is to grow and develop and be applied to resolve many issues in the world, it will be up to civil society to press harder and more consistently, based on a clear understanding of what works and what does not.

One helpful step, perhaps at the initiative of the ICBL given its pioneering role, would be to bring NGOs and different coalitions and campaigns together in various configurations to share what they have learned and to identify what still needs to be learned to ensure that the voice of civil society is heard on issues that affect our individual and collective human security. Such discussions would benefit at an early stage from input from "like-minded" government allies who share the vision of new frameworks of security, developed and put into practice through a partnership of governments, civil society and NGOs, and international organizations.

Notes

1. The six NGOs were Handicap International (France), Medico International (Germany), Mines Advisory Group (UK), Physicians for Human Rights (USA), the Vietnam Veterans of America Foundation (USA), and the host of the meeting in New York, Human Rights Watch (USA). One of the more memorable dismissals of the campaign came from then Minister of Foreign Affairs of Australia, Gareth Evans, who in 1995 described the call for a ban on landmines as "hopelessly utopian." Questions without Notice, Australian Senate, June 1, 1995.

2. Some outside of government questioned the appropriateness and legitimacy of unelected and possibly nonrepresentational NGOs playing a major role in state decisions and actions.

3. As used by the Centre for Civil Society of the London School of Economics, "Civil society refers to the arena of uncoerced collective action around shared interests, purposes and values. In theory, its institutional forms are distinct from those of the state, family and market, though in practice, the boundaries between state, civil society, family and market are often complex, blurred and negotiated. Civil society commonly embraces a diversity of spaces, actors and institutional forms, varying in their degree of formality, autonomy and power. Civil societies are often populated by organisations such as registered charities, development non-governmental organisations, community groups, women's organisations, faith-based organisations, professional associations, trade unions, self-help groups, social movements, business associations, coalitions and advocacy groups." See Centre for Civil Society of the London School of Economics, "What Is Civil Society?" http://www.lse.ac.uk/collections/CCS/what_is_civil_society.htm (Last updated: March 1, 2004).

4. This section draws on earlier writing by the authors, including Jody Williams, "Politics Unusual: A Different Model of International Cooperation," *Harvard International Review*, vol. 22, issue 3, fall 2000; Stephen Goose and Jody Williams, "The Campaign to Ban Antipersonnel Landmines: Potential Lessons," in Richard Matthew, Bryan McDonald, and Kenneth Rutherford (eds.), *Landmines and Human Security: International Politics and War's Hidden Legacy* (Albany: State University of New York Press, June 2004), pp. 239–50.

5. The ICBL has produced educational materials and carried out workshops on how to organize national campaigns, prepare for major conferences, interact with the media, and other aspects of international campaigning work. In addition to advancing the work to ban landmines, these skills can be used by campaigners in many ways and in other work for social change (see chapter 3).

6. Indeed, the ICBL was not even a legally registered entity until after it received the Nobel Peace Prize at the end of 1997. There has never been a secretariat or central office

of the ICBL, and until 1998, no "ICBL" employees or joint ICBL budget. Various NGOs in essence seconded (and provided funding for) individuals to work on the campaign.

7. For a fascinating example, see Adam Hoschild, *Bury the Chains: Prophets and Rebels in the Fight to Free an Empire's Slaves* (New York: Houghton Mifflin, 2005).

8. Given the success of the Ottawa Process and the Mine Ban Treaty, few now recognize or acknowledge the risks involved to both sides as we ventured into that partnership and worked to ensure the success of the "rogue" negotiating process of the Mine Ban Treaty. There were many times when we were not at all certain of the outcome and felt we were working with "smoke and mirrors," convinced that the fragile process could collapse at any moment. Had the process fallen apart, it no doubt would have had a chilling effect on any future civil society–government partnerships and dampened any governmental "thinking outside the box" in trying to find new solutions to global problems.

9. One example that still causes amusement in the retelling is when a new diplomat replaced his predecessor and apparently had not been fully briefed about the informal nature of meetings. The cochair of a session had given the floor to Steve Goose, calling him by his first name only, who then spoke about the ICBL position on some aspect of the treaty. Subsequent speakers kept on referring to "Steve," and finally the new diplomat was called upon and in quite apparent frustration started his remarks with "And who IS this *Steve?*" Many in the room could not stifle their laughter—which likely added to the diplomat's discomfort.

10. Don Hubert, "The Landmine Ban: A Case Study in Humanitarian Advocacy," Thomas J. Watson, Jr. Institute for International Studies, Occasional Paper #42, 2000, pp. 41–44.

11. NGOs that are part of both the ICBL and IANSA have often complained to the authors about the inability of IANSA to fully engage its members and make them feel like important, contributing stakeholders.

12. E-mail from Felicity Hill, antinuclear activist, in response to questions from the authors and after discussion with SALW activist Cate Buchannan, August 9, 2006.

13. For a comprehensive discussion of these various mechanisms, see David Atwood, "NGOs and Multilateral Disarmament Diplomacy: Limits and Possibilities," in John Borrie and Vanessa Martin Randin (eds.), *Thinking Outside the Box in Multilateral Disarmament and Arms Control Negotiations* (Geneva: UNIDIR, 2006).

14. Twenty-four nations abstained from the vote, and the United States was the only country to vote against the resolution. For more information, see IANSA website at: http://www.iansa.org/un/2006/GAvote.htm; also Irwin Arieff, "UN Seeks New Treaty Restricting Global Arms Sales," *Reuters*, December 6, 2006, http://www .alertnet.org/thenews/newsdesk/N06439629.htm/. See also "Arms Trade Treaty: A Nobel Peace Laureates' Initiative," http://www.armstradetreaty.com/.

15. UN Department of Public Information, Media Release, "Arms Trade Treaty, 'Nuclear-Weapon-Free World,' Outer Space Arms Race Among Issues, as General Assembly adopts 54 First Committee Texts," December 6, 2006, http://www.un.org/ News/Press/docs/2006/ga10547.doc.htm/.

16. For an interesting analysis, see Rosy Cave, "Disarmament as Humanitarian Action? Comparing Negotiations on Anti-Personnel Mines and Explosive Remnants of

War," in John Borrie and Vanessa Martin Randin (eds.), *Disarmament as Humanitarian Action: From Perspective to Practice* (Geneva: UNIDIR, 2006).

17. Among others, this includes Belgium, which has already banned cluster munitions, France, Germany, Italy, the Netherlands, the United Kingdom, and even Canada.

18. See Atwood, "NGOs and Multilateral Disarmament Diplomacy: Limits and Possibilities," *Thinking Outside the Box in Multilateral Disarmament and Arms Control Negotiations*, pp. 37–39.

12

Unacceptable Behavior:
How Norms Are Established

Peter Herby and Kathleen Lawand

PUBLIC ABHORRENCE OF THE WIDESPREAD DEATH, mutilation, and suffering caused to civilians by antipersonnel mines led governments to ban these weapons in 1997 through the Mine Ban Treaty. This marked the first time that states had agreed to completely prohibit a weapon that was already in widespread use around the world, owing to its appalling human cost. The agreement was adopted in record time for a multilateral treaty—less than one year from the launch of the negotiation process in October 1996 by then Foreign Minister of Canada Lloyd Axworthy. The speed with which the treaty was concluded has been attributed to the unique negotiation process—commonly referred to as the Ottawa Process—conducted in a spirit of equal partnership between like-minded governments, nongovernmental organizations (NGOs), and international organizations.[1]

Yet this tells only part of the story behind the ban on antipersonnel mines. How is it that a weapon once considered indispensable had become unacceptable? The groundwork for the adoption of the Mine Ban Treaty was laid when antipersonnel mines had become abhorrent to the citizenry of a critical mass of governments. Each of these governments responded to the change in what their societies deemed unacceptable by unilaterally renouncing the use of these weapons. These changes in societal perception were informed by the public campaigns and statements of the International

The views expressed in this chapter are those of the authors and do not necessarily reflect the position of the International Committee of the Red Cross (ICRC). The research assistance of Pierre-Olivier Marcoux is gratefully acknowledged.

Campaign to Ban Landmines (ICBL) and the International Committee of the Red Cross (ICRC) as voices of "public conscience."[2] Senior military experts from around the world also played a role in convincing their governments to agree to ban antipersonnel mines, with the argument that the limited military utility of the weapon is far outweighed by its high human cost.[3]

Today, the international norm banning antipersonnel mines embodied in the Mine Ban Treaty legally binds the 155 states that have joined the agreement. Moreover, most of the forty states that are not party to the treaty are in practice respecting its prohibitions on their transfer, production, and use. This can be attributed to the stigmatization of these weapons in the eyes of the public. In the increasingly rare cases where some of these states have used antipersonnel mines, reaction has been swift and vigorous, spearheaded by the ICBL. Yet despite the adherence of more than three-quarters of the world's states to the Mine Ban Treaty and the fact that the great majority of states not party to the treaty are respecting most of its prohibitions, the antipersonnel mine ban norm is not considered by legal experts to be a rule of "customary" international law binding on all states; in other words it is not yet universal.

The first part of this chapter examines the norm-making process and attempts to draw insights into how new rules are made. The term "norm" is taken in a sociological sense to mean a rule that is socially enforced, be it through law (including international treaties) or through social opprobrium. It is argued that the formation of a "social norm" banning antipersonnel mines preceded the establishment of the "legal norm" by legislation and treaty, and that this process is relevant to other weapons fields. The second part of this chapter explains why it is that antipersonnel mines are deemed unacceptable by the public and most governments, yet the norm banning them is not yet universally binding law. It examines the behavior of states outside of the Mine Ban Treaty and shows that most of them are in fact respecting its key prohibitions due to the pressure exerted by the "social norm" or the stigmatization of the weapon. The chapter concludes by looking at social norms that may be emerging in relation to other weapons of concern that are not specifically regulated by international law.

The authors' approach to these questions is not so much based on scientific analysis as it is drawn from their experience gained in work for the prohibition of antipersonnel landmines over more than a decade and their involvement in recent efforts to identify current customary international humanitarian law relevant to arms. As such, it stands to be refined by other more scholarly works, past or future.

The Norm-Making Process around Antipersonnel Mines

When the global movement to ban antipersonnel mines emerged in the early 1990s, most analysts were of the view that achieving a prohibition would not be feasible. The weapons were being produced by some fifty countries at a rate of millions of units per year. They were part of the arsenals of the armed forces of most states, totaling approximately two hundred million stockpiled mines. And they were in widespread use in conflicts around the world, being inexpensive and easily available.[4] With the adoption of the Mine Ban Treaty, the skeptics were confounded.

The norm-making process around antipersonnel mines is instructive for a number of reasons. First, the norm has proved powerful beyond all expectations, having an impact beyond the 155 (and counting) States Parties to the Mine Ban Treaty, as shown later in this chapter. Secondly, it was created primarily by engagement of the "public conscience" through civil society action. And thirdly, the norm is being enforced through a unique combination of state and civil society monitoring. Whether this process is relevant to efforts in relation to other problematic weapons will depend on the extent to which the human cost of such weapons resonates within the public.

What Are Norms and Why Do People Make Them?

As "law" is almost universally considered the domain of experts, it is easy to forget that it is above all a construction of societies—and therefore of people. It is intended to serve the purposes of the society within which it is constructed (unless it is simply imposed from outside or above). The "society" may be a local community, a national state, or the still vaguely defined "international community" made up of states and a range of other actors. The impulse to make law may be to protect life, human rights, or property; to provide for predictability; to provide a means of regulating disputes; to prevent unacceptable behavior; or to facilitate the running of governmental structures. The content of specific laws will be largely determined by what limits specific societies deem to be necessary and acceptable and by the relationships of power within those societies.

In the campaign against antipersonnel landmines, the most relevant of the purposes mentioned above are the protection of life and human rights and the prevention of unacceptable behavior (for example, the intentional or inadvertent killing and maiming of innocents as a result of military operations). Previous efforts to protect civilians, in the form of military doctrine and the relatively ambiguous rules on antipersonnel mines found in the original version of Protocol II to the Convention on Conventional Weapons (CCW), had been unsuccessful.[5] In the early 1990s antipersonnel mines were killing or injuring an estimated twenty-four thousand people per year, mostly civilians, while causing some of the most horrific injuries ever treated by war surgeons.[6] The strongest argument of the ICBL and of the ICRC in support of a ban was moral and social: that the level of suffering caused by the weapon was "beyond the pale" and unjustified by any military consideration. Indeed a central turning point in the ICRC's efforts was a decision in 1995 to "stigmatize" antipersonnel mines as a weapon of war through public communications and advertising to this end—much more of a social than legal process.

The experience of the ban campaign suggests that it is essential for future efforts in the humanitarian field to consciously focus on societal perceptions, also labeled the "public conscience." Whether the objective is to highlight the need for new norms or to change the existing ones, progress is unlikely until there is an overriding perception, shared by significant elements of public opinion and eventually by policymakers, of the unsustainability of the status quo and therefore of the need for new regulation. A narrow focus on the need for legal norms in the absence of work to affect public perception is more likely to lead simply to political debate than to the desired results. Indeed, the story of the antipersonnel mine ban norm clearly illustrates that "the norms that are the most successful are those that have arisen from the bottom up."[7]

The Role of Societal Change in Norm-Making

With the passage of time since the adoption of the Mine Ban Treaty in 1997, those seeking insights from the mine ban movement often develop the perception that its success was based upon convincing large numbers of countries that there should be a legally binding international ban on these weapons. At some point, it is assumed, a large group of countries decided it was time to negotiate such a treaty. The process therefore was primarily international and political. While such steps did occur, they only tell part of the story of a process which was much more national and social in nature.

The most telling historical fact highlighting the processes going on at other levels is that before the Canadian Foreign Minister invited states to join Canada in a process aimed at the adoption of a treaty banning antipersonnel mines in October 1996, thirty states had already unilaterally renounced or suspended the future use of these weapons.[8] The window of opportunity for normative development at the international level was created by sociopolitical developments in these countries where the option of continued use of antipersonnel mines by their own armed forces had become unsustainable. These national decisions had, in turn, been forced by the social process of stigmatization of antipersonnel mines, in part as a result of widespread media attention to their human costs. This, in turn, was driven by the work of NGOs, development and aid agencies, and National Red Cross and Red Crescent Societies.

It could be argued that for many other legal developments, from the prohibition of slavery to bans on smoking in public places, changes in societal norms of what is acceptable have preceded changes in the law.[9] The adoption of legal norms may codify the change in social norms that has already occurred. But without the evolution of the social norm, adoption of the legal norm would be unlikely.

Are Legal Rules Respected Purely Out of Fear of Being Caught and Punished or Because of the Expected Societal or Cultural Responses to Unacceptable Behavior?

The question of why people obey legal rules is as relevant to international law as to the laws of a given society. In most societies, respect for legal norms depends more on their internalization as part of a social process—you want to be someone who "doesn't break the law"—than on the fear of detection and punishment. As discussed in the second part of this chapter, this social process also operates between states at the international level, where enforcement mechanisms are weak or nonexistent.

In the campaign against antipersonnel mines a crucial turning point in the internalization of the norm came as individuals (whether ordinary citizens, military officers, or policymakers) came to the conclusion that the high human costs of the weapon outweighed whatever military benefits it might provide. Once this conclusion was reached by an adequate proportion of those with influence within a given society, the renunciation of the weapon became not only a possibility but a moral duty. It was upon this basis that many states renounced their own use of antipersonnel mines long before an international prohibition was within sight.

How Long Can Legal Rules Remain Relevant after Their Societal or Cultural Basis Erodes?

A number of rules of international law have become obsolete or their content altered by state practice over decades. One such example in the weapons field is the St. Petersburg Declaration of 1868, which prohibited the use of any "projectiles" less than 400 grams containing explosives. Over the following century, state practice moved in the direction of using precisely such bullets for antimateriel purposes while generally prohibiting their antipersonnel use.

A recent study of customary international humanitarian law has concluded that only the intentional antipersonnel use of such exploding bullets remains prohibited.[10]

In the ten years since its adoption, the prohibition of antipersonnel mines has been upheld and extended by the continued mobilization of individuals and organizations through the ICBL, including the ICBL's monitoring of state practice with its annual Landmine Monitor reports, and the continued engagement of the International Red Cross and Red Crescent Movement. This has been reinforced by the efforts of many committed officials within government and military circles. The maintenance of such "societal" pressure for respect of the antipersonnel mine ban norm is essential to its strength and integrity in the future and to achieve its universalization.

In the absence of continued "societal" pressure, erosion of the norm prohibiting antipersonnel mines could come from two fronts. Although virtually all of the major military powers still remaining outside the norm say they support its objectives and may eventually join, the absence of continued pressure to actually adhere to the Mine Ban Treaty could relegate it to the status of an optional approach rather than the primary international regime covering antipersonnel mines. In the absence of universal or at least near universal adherence to the antipersonnel mine ban norm, even current State Parties may be tempted to opt for a less ambitious approach if they find themselves facing difficult conflict situations and/or new internal dynamics.

The norms contained in the Mine Ban Treaty could also be altered over time by inconsistent practice by States Parties. Since the treaty entered into force in 1999, examples have arisen of inconsistent interpretation and application of the Article 1 prohibition to "assist" in carrying out a banned activity (for example, whether a State Party is in violation of the treaty if it allows the transit through its territory of antipersonnel mines belonging to a state not party), the Article 2 definition of "antipersonnel mines" (in relation to so-called anti-vehicle mines with fuses so sensitive that they function as antipersonnel mines), and the acceptable quantity of mines retained for training purposes pursuant to Article 3.

While such inconsistencies in practice to date have been tolerated by States Parties and none have been widespread enough to threaten the integrity of the regime itself, they highlight the need for monitoring and dialogue to prevent just that. Of even more importance will be the manner in which states interpret their obligation to "clear all mined areas." If this central obligation is taken to require anything less than the clearance of all areas in which mines are feared or known to be present, the central prohibition of the "use" of antipersonnel mines could be threatened.

The Antipersonnel Mine Ban Norm as a
Universal Norm-in-Waiting?

The "antipersonnel mine ban norm" refers essentially to the prohibitions to use, develop, produce, acquire, stockpile, retain, or transfer antipersonnel mines. The states that are party to the Mine Ban Treaty are legally required to respect these specific prohibitions by paragraph 1 of Article 1 of the treaty. But what is the effect of the norm outside of the Mine Ban Treaty? Has it become "universal?" In other words is it "customary" international law binding on all countries of the world, including those that are not parties to the treaty? How has the stigmatization of the weapon by public conscience and by three-quarters of states affected the behavior of states that remain outside of the treaty? If their behavior is significantly influenced, does it really matter that they are not parties to the treaty?

Is the Antipersonnel Mine Ban Norm a Rule of Customary
International Law Binding All States?

International law has two main sources: treaties, which create legal obligations only for the states that are party to them and unwritten "customary international law," which binds all states.

Customary international law is basically defined as "general practice of states accepted as law."[11] As such, its rules tend to represent the lowest common denominator of what states uniformly consider as law. The formation of a rule of customary international law requires the presence of two elements: (1) state practice and (2) a *belief* by states "that such practice is required, prohibited or allowed, depending on the nature of the rule, as a matter of law."[12] International lawyers refer to the latter criterion by the Latin maxim *opinio juris*, meaning a "belief in the legally permissible or obligatory nature of the conduct in question."[13] The "conduct" in question can be an act or an omission. Thus, the rules embodied in the Mine Ban Treaty would only be considered "customary" if the states that are not party to the treaty not only follow them in practice, but also if they *believe* that they are required to do so as a matter of law. One must therefore look at the behavior (practice) and views (beliefs/opinions) of the forty states that are not party to the treaty to determine whether the prohibition of antipersonnel mines is a universal customary norm, binding all states.

State practice can be either physical—for example, the use or nonuse of antipersonnel mines or verbal—for example, provisions in military manuals and instructions to armed forces regarding the use or nonuse of antipersonnel mines. Verbal practice is indicative of the state's beliefs as to the existence of a rule. Whether a rule of customary international law exists depends on the "density" of state practice. In particular, practice must be virtually uniform. In other words different states must not be engaged in substantially different conduct. Practice must also be both "extensive and representative."[14]

The *belief* of a state that it is required to carry out the practice as a matter of law is often difficult to distinguish from the *practice* itself. However, in the case of a rule that requires *abstention* from certain conduct, such as the prohibition to use antipersonnel mines, it must be shown that the state's omission to perform a certain act, for example its practice of *not* using antipersonnel mines, is driven by a belief that the act is prohibited. In other words, a state that stockpiles antipersonnel mines but does not use them cannot be presumed to believe that it is bound by the prohibition to use these weapons. In this regard, it is instructive that the International Court of Justice, in its 1996 landmark case on the legality of nuclear weapons, was unable to find a customary law norm prohibiting the use of these weapons, although no state had used them in over forty years.[15]

So does the behavior and beliefs of states not party to the Mine Ban Treaty add up to a rule of customary law prohibiting antipersonnel mines? After a decade of extensive research and widespread consultation with experts, a study published in 2005 by the ICRC on customary international humanitarian law concluded that "it cannot be said at this stage that the use of antipersonnel landmines is prohibited under customary international law."[16] It grounded this conclusion on the practice of several states not party, including China, Finland, India, South Korea, Pakistan, Russia, and the United States, which continue to reserve the right to use antipersonnel mines, and most of which stockpile large quantities of these weapons. The study also pointed to the continued use in recent conflicts of antipersonnel mines by a small number of states, as reported by *Landmine Monitor*.

The ICRC study nonetheless found a number of rules of customary international law restricting the use of landmines—both antipersonnel and antivehicle mines—for the purpose of protecting civilians from their effects. In particular, it found that states were bound to exercise certain precautions when using landmines and it identified three specific rules in this regard: (1) when landmines are used, particular care must be taken to minimize their indiscriminate effects; (2) a party to the conflict using landmines must record their placement, as far as possible; and (3) at the end of active hostilities, a party to the conflict which has used landmines must remove or otherwise render them harmless to civilians, or facilitate their removal.[17] These rules barely match the basic provisions of the original 1980 Protocol II on mines, booby-traps, and other devices of the CCW, again indicating that customary international law tends to represent the lowest common denominator of norms that states consider themselves legally bound to abide by.

Is the Antipersonnel Mine Ban Norm an Emerging Rule of Customary International Law?

Although the ICRC study could not find a customary norm prohibiting antipersonnel mines, it observed that states not party to the Mine Ban Treaty that are not in favor of immediately banning these weapons have nonetheless "agreed that they need to work towards the eventual elimination of antipersonnel landmines." It concluded that current verbal practice of states "*appears to indicate that an obligation to eliminate antipersonnel mines is emerging.*"[18] It pointed in particular to several international declarations and resolutions, including the Final Declaration adopted by consensus by the States Parties to the CCW at the Second Review Conference in 2001 in which they "solemnly declare[d] . . . their conviction that all States should strive towards the goal of the eventual elimination of antipersonnel mines globally."[19] This declaration is particularly significant because it was endorsed by all major military powers that remain outside the Mine Ban Treaty and that continue to stockpile antipersonnel mines and reserve the right to use them.[20]

Another important indication of a "soft" commitment of states not party to eventually join the treaty is the agreement of states at the 28th International Conference of the Red Cross and Red Crescent in 2003 to pursue the goal of the "*eventual global elimination of anti-personnel mines.*"[21] Virtually all States Parties to the 1949 Geneva Conventions—in other words, all countries of the world including states not party to the Mine Ban Treaty—were represented at the Conference and endorsed this goal.[22]

In addition, nearly every year a growing number of states not party to the Mine Ban Treaty vote in favor of the annual UN General Assembly resolution on the treaty's universalization and implementation. The preamble of the resolution emphasizes "the desirability of attracting all states to the Convention." Its first operative paragraph invites nonsignatory states to accede "without delay," and the second urges signatory states to ratify "without delay." Out of 161 states voting in favor of the 2006 UNGA resolution,[23] twenty were states not party to the treaty.[24] Seventeen states not party cast votes of abstention on the resolution, and none voted against. In their statements explaining their vote, some of the abstaining states made clear that the use of antipersonnel mines still formed part of their defense strategies and that they could not *yet* support a complete ban on the weapon.

These multilateral declarations and resolutions would point to an understanding by all states that antipersonnel mines are destined to be totally eliminated at some point in the future. However, the national policies and practices of states not party to the Mine Ban Treaty paint a more mixed picture of their intentions. In terms of production, *Landmine Monitor Report 2006* identified thirteen states not party to the Mine Ban Treaty that in 2006 were either actively producing antipersonnel mines or reserved the right to do so.[25] As for use, while most states not party have not laid new antipersonnel mines for many years, and many have emphasized in their official statements that they are not using them, *Landmine Monitor Report 2006* found that the armed forces of a small number of states continued to lay new mines.[26]

National policies and practices are most clear-cut with regard to the trade in antipersonnel mines. Indeed, their transfer between states has virtually ended. Thirteen states not party, including the major military powers that remain outside of the Mine Ban Treaty, have had moratoria in place prohibiting the trade in antipersonnel mines, for most since the mid-to-late 1990s.[27] According to *Landmine Monitor Report 2006*, "For the past decade, global trade in antipersonnel mines has consisted solely of a low-level of illicit and unacknowledged transfers."[28]

It is also significant that a number of states not party have professed agreement with the treaty's goals and have gone so far as to file transparency reports pursuant to Article 7 of the treaty on a voluntary basis. These include states not party that have in the recent past used and are affected by antipersonnel mines, such as Morocco and Sri Lanka. In recent years, China, which is believed to stockpile vast quantities of the weapon, has stated that it agrees with the treaty's objectives and is considering filing an Article 7 report on a voluntary basis.[29]

Although the ban on trade, production, and use of antipersonnel mines has been largely been respected in practice by states not party to the Mine Ban Treaty, most of them are stockpiling antipersonnel mines, some in vast quantities. Even states not party that have professed agreement with the treaty's objectives maintain that for now their stockpiles are needed for national defense purposes. It can therefore be said that although most states not party are respecting the ban norm's prohibition of "active" acts such as using, producing, and trading, they are not abiding by the prohibition of "passive" acts such as stockpiling.

Thus, from a strictly legal standpoint, the practice of states not party to the Mine Ban Treaty taken together is insufficient to conclude that these states consider themselves bound by a norm of customary law comprehensively prohibiting antipersonnel mines. However, much of their behavior and statements give rise to an expectation that they will eventually, at some undetermined point in the future, fully adhere to the antipersonnel mine ban norm. At best, it can be said to be a "universal-norm-in-waiting."

Does It Matter That There Is No Universally Binding Rule Banning Antipersonnel Mines?

Why are so many states abiding by the antipersonnel mine ban norm although they are not legally required to do so? Have antipersonnel mines been so stigmatized globally that even states not party to the Mine Ban Treaty are reluctant to engage in activities prohibited by the treaty? If so, does it matter that the norm is not universally binding law?

States not party to the Mine Ban Treaty face two forms of pressure not to transgress the antipersonnel mine ban norm. The first is the fact that a large majority of countries have foresworn antipersonnel mines forever by joining the Mine Ban Treaty. This makes it impractical for states not party to engage in activities prohibited by the treaty due to the ever-shrinking pool of countries among which the weapons can be lawfully traded or used in joint military operations. But this alone does not satisfactorily explain why many states not party are not engaging in certain activities banned by the treaty, often as a matter of national policy.

Over and above practical considerations, there are good political reasons for them to refrain from carrying out acts that are illegal for over three-quarters of their peers, reasons which stem from the general propensity of states to seek to reduce as much as possible areas of friction in their international relations. What motivates states not party to "comply" with the antipersonnel mine ban norm, or at least parts of it, would be the same reason that drives states party to the Mine Ban Treaty (and to any other treaty for that matter) to comply with their obligations: the need to be seen and accepted as members in good standing of the international community.[30]

This could very well explain the lengths to which, as previously mentioned, some states not party have gone to demonstrate their interest in the treaty, for instance by proclaiming their agreement with its objectives in their official statements and policies, participating as observers in Meetings of the States Parties, and voluntarily providing Article 7 transparency reports. Just as social pressures lead individuals to internalize inhibitions against breaking social norms, states also appear to be inhibited from going against widely accepted norms and standards in their international relations. In this regard, the antipersonnel mine ban norm is rendered all the more influential on states not party by the fact that the Mine Ban Treaty enjoys an exceptional level of compliance by its States Parties, demonstrating that the treaty norm is exceptionally strong.

Yet peer pressure alone cannot fully explain what motivates certain states not party to publicly profess their agreement with the Mine Ban Treaty's objectives and passively observe some or all elements of the norm. In doing so, they are also responding to the relentless pressure exerted by civil society, led by the ICBL. States not party to the Mine Ban Treaty that would wish to preserve their good name internationally would not risk being "named and shamed" by actively engaging in acts prohibited by the treaty. Those few states not party to the Mine Ban Treaty that purport to be insensitive to such pressures and that do carry out acts banned by the norm are met with vigorous international, as well as national, reaction. While such reaction is driven by civil society, it is often complemented by the intervention of other stakeholders in the mine ban norm, including through the "quiet diplomacy" of the ICRC and the United Nations, and of course of Mine Ban Treaty States Parties who regularly criticize new antipersonnel mine use and call on states not party to join the treaty.

To give but one example, the announcement by Pakistan at the end of 2006 that it planned to lay antipersonnel mines along its border with Afghanistan to prevent illegal transborder movements met with strong international opposition, notably from the ICBL, which urged Pakistan "to avoid joining the ever-dwindling 'club of shame,'"[31] but also from other key actors such as Canada, Afghanistan, and the United Nations.[32] In later statements on this issue, Pakistan emphasized that fencing and other means of border control were being explored and that if the mine-laying were carried out it would be as a last resort and very limited. The breadth of international condemnation of Pakistan's original plan undoubtedly played a role in its shift.

In contrast, a few states not party to the Mine Ban Treaty appear to be unresponsive to being "named and shamed" for using or producing antipersonnel mines. The two states not party that have continuously used antipersonnel mines over the last decade—Russia and Burma (Myanmar)—have not been moved to cease use despite relentless criticism by the ICBL. But notwithstanding their behavior, even these two states have expressed their support for the objective of the eventual global elimination of antipersonnel mines.[33]

In the case of the United States, the Clinton administration had set the goal of joining the Mine Ban Treaty by 2006 after identifying suitable alternatives. In February 2004, the Bush administration reversed this policy by stating it would only eliminate "persistent" antipersonnel mines that do not contain self-destruct features. It stated, "The United States will not join the Ottawa Process [Mine Ban Treaty] because its terms would have required us to give up a needed military capability."[34] Yet, the United States has not used antipersonnel mines since 1991, exported them since 1992, or produced them since 1997.

However, recent developments highlight a divergence in the positions of the executive and the legislative branches of the U.S. government over the possible resumption of the production of landmines, even if "non-persistent." When the U.S. Defense Department indicated in 2005 it planned to produce the so-called

Spider system with an option to make the munitions in the system function like antipersonnel mines, Congress required the Pentagon to conduct a review of the system and report back on its possible indiscriminate effects before going ahead with production.[35] In August 2006, in a further move by legislators to prevent new production, bipartisan legislation was proposed in Congress to prohibit the U.S. military from procuring landmines or other weapons that are "victim-activated" owing to their indiscriminate effects.[36]

These examples show that the stigma attached to use, production, and trade in antipersonnel mines is such that most, if not all, states not party to the Mine Ban Treaty are reluctant to engage in these activities to avoid being singled out. In other words, the mine ban norm is influencing the behavior of countries that have not formally adhered to it by becoming party to the Mine Ban Treaty. Since most states are respecting the ban on use, production, and trade of antipersonnel mines, does it matter that that there is no universally binding law prohibiting antipersonnel mines?

The extent to which the weapon has been stigmatized by public conscience, to the point of influencing the behavior of states not party to the treaty, is evidence of the strength of the antipersonnel mine ban norm. Still, the fact that a number of states not party continue to use or produce antipersonnel mines and that most continue to stockpile them means that the norm remains under constant threat of erosion. Until it becomes universally binding law, it will require constant vigilance by its stakeholders, namely by states party to the treaty, the ICBL, the ICRC, the UN, and other actors.

In the meantime, it is unlikely that a customary international law rule comprehensively banning antipersonnel mines will emerge any time soon. Based on the above-mentioned practice of states not party to the Mine Ban Treaty, if a customary law rule does emerge, it is likely to cover only certain parts of the ban, such as the prohibition to trade antipersonnel mines. In any case, as explained earlier, customary law is difficult to identify, and it typically embodies the lowest common denominator of what all states collectively recognize as legally binding. In the end, the goal of the global elimination of antipersonnel mines will not be attained in the absence of a legally binding commitment of virtually all states to rid themselves completely of these weapons. The most effective way to attain this goal is through the adherence of all states to the Mine Ban Treaty, and this is where future efforts should be focused.

Conclusion: Lessons in Norm Creation for Other Weapons?

Can the norm-making process that led to the comprehensive ban on antipersonnel mines in the Mine Ban Treaty be applied in other weapons fields? As was the case for antipersonnel mines a decade ago, certain weapons which are not prohibited or regulated per se by international law nonetheless provoke strong public concern, voiced in the media, parliaments, and other public spheres. Notable examples include the antipersonnel use of white phosphorous, the use of other incendiary weapons such as napalm, and cluster munitions.[37] Although the use of nuclear weapons is not prohibited per se by international law, there is arguably a strong taboo against their use upheld by "public conscience," such that it is difficult to imagine that a nuclear weapon could be used today without eliciting widespread condemnation.

The steady mobilization against cluster munitions today resembles in many ways that of antipersonnel mines a decade ago. Their indiscriminate effects on civilians, in particular when they fail to detonate, have been especially visible in conflicts during the last decade, including in Eritrea and Ethiopia in 1998, Kosovo in 1999, Afghanistan in 2001, Iraq in 2003, and Lebanon in 2006. Cluster munitions are becoming unacceptable weapons in the eyes of the public. Today, use of cluster munitions typically elicits widespread attention from the media, which usually characterizes these weapons as "controversial," highlighting the continued threat posed to civilians by unexploded cluster submunitions long after hostilities have ceased. Civil society, most visibly through the Cluster Munition Coalition, has mobilized and been instrumental in informing public perceptions. In response a number of governments and parliaments have adopted, or are considering the adoption of, legislation and policies unilaterally renouncing or suspending the use of some or all cluster munitions.[38]

As was the case for antipersonnel mines a decade ago, the stage is set for action at the international level. In February 2007, Norway convened like-minded states to a meeting to negotiate a new instrument dealing with the humanitarian problems posed by cluster munitions. Forty-seven states endorsed the Final Declaration of the Oslo Conference, in which they committed themselves to conclude by 2008 a legally binding international instrument that will comprehensively prohibit cluster munitions that cause unacceptable harm to civilians. In addition, States Parties to the Convention on Conventional Weapons, which includes all major military powers, will address the cluster munitions issue in 2007, ensuring the engagement of nearly all cluster munition producers and users in one or both of these two processes. Although the legal norms that may emerge from this mobilization are not yet clear, what is evident is that a norm-building process is underway. As with antipersonnel mines, it is already influencing the behavior of states, legislators, and weapons designers, and the driving force is the "public conscience."

In the past decade, antipersonnel mines have been prohibited, a protocol assigning responsibility for clearing explosive remnants of war has been adopted and is in force,[39] and a large proportion of existing cluster munitions may soon be slated for elimination due to their severe long-term effects on civilians. The common thread in these developments is that today there is an expectation that civilians should not face the same fate from other munitions as they have from antipersonnel mines. Indeed, it could be argued that the unique movement which created the Mine Ban Treaty norm is on the way to establishing an even more fundamental norm of "public conscience" that is not weapon-specific. Simply stated, this norm is that civilians must not be victimized, after the fighting stops and long after wars have ended, by weapons that have ceased to serve any military purpose.

Notes

1. For a detailed history and analysis of the negotiation process, see Don Hubert, *The Landmine Ban: A Case Study in Humanitarian Advocacy* (Providence: Thomas J. Watson Institute for International Studies, 2000).

2. Paragraph eight of the Mine Ban Treaty preamble stresses "the role of public conscience in furthering the principles of humanity as evidenced by the call for a total ban of anti-personnel mines and recognizing the efforts to that end undertaken by the International Red Cross and Red Crescent Movement, the International Campaign to Ban Landmines and numerous other non-governmental organizations around the world."

3. See *Anti-Personnel Landmines: Friend or Foe? A Study of the Military Use and Effectiveness of Anti-Personnel Mines* (Geneva: ICRC, 1996). This study was carried out by senior military experts at the request of the ICRC. Its conclusions and its 2004 update have been endorsed by over eighty senior military from some thirty countries.

4. Alex Vines, "The Crisis of Anti-Personnel Mines," in Maxwell A. Cameron, Robert J. Lawson, and Brian W. Tomlin (eds.), *To Walk Without Fear: The Global Movement to Ban Landmines* (Toronto: Oxford University Press, 1998), pp. 118–135.

5. In the mid-1990s, under pressure to effectively deal with the epidemic of death and injury caused by antipersonnel mines, states first attempted to address the problem in the context of the CCW. At the time, Protocol II to the CCW was the only multilateral treaty imposing some restrictions on the use of landmines. At the conclusion of the CCW Review Conference in May 1996, the States Parties adopted Amended Protocol II, which imposed stricter restrictions on the use of antipersonnel mines. However, these were complex and difficult to apply and fell far short of the complete ban on these weapons sought by many governments, the ICRC, the ICBL, and UN agencies. It was this inability of the CCW to respond commensurately to the urgency of the humanitarian crisis caused by antipersonnel mines that brought about the Ottawa negotiation process, which led to the adoption of the Mine Ban Treaty in September 1997.

6. ICRC, *The Worldwide Epidemic of Landmine Injuries: The ICRC's Health-Oriented Approach* (Geneva: ICRC, 1995).

7. "Interview with Terence Taylor," *International Review of the Red Cross*, vol. 88, no. 859, September 2005, p. 422.

8. As of September 18, 1997, according to information compiled by the ICRC, twenty-four states had permanently renounced or prohibited, and six states had suspended, the use of antipersonnel mines. In addition, 117 states had stated publicly that they would support a global ban on antipersonnel mines. See "Report of the Secretary-General on the work of the Organization," United Nations, September 3, 1997, A/52/1, p. 14, para. 93.

9. For an overview of how civil society changed public conscience in the United Kingdom to ban the slave trade, see Adam Hochschild, *Bury the Chains: Prophets and Rebels in the Fight to Free an Empire's Slaves* (New York: Houghton Mifflin, 2005).

10. Jean-Marie Henckaerts and Louise Doswald-Beck (eds.), *Customary International Humanitarian Law*, vol. I (Cambridge: Cambridge University Press, 2005), rule 78, pp. 272–274.

11. Statute of the International Court of Justice, Article 38(1)(b).

12. Jean-Marie Henckaerts, "Study on Customary International Humanitarian Law: A Contribution to the Understanding and Respect for the Rule of Law in Armed Conflict," *International Review of the Red Cross*, vol. 87, no. 857, March 2005, p. 178.

13. Maurice H. Mendelson, "The Formation of Customary International Law," 272 *Recueil des cours* (1998), p. 269.

14. As determined by the International Court of Justice in *North Sea Continental Shelf cases*, Judgment, February 20, 1969, *ICJ Reports 1969*, p. 43, §74, quoted in Henckaerts, "Study on Customary International Humanitarian Law," *International Review of the Red Cross*, p. 180.

15. *Advisory Opinion on the Legality of the Threat or Use of Nuclear Weapons*, July 8, 1996, *ICJ Reports 1996*, p. 226.

16. Henckaerts and Doswald-Beck (eds.), *Customary International Humanitarian Law*, p. 282.

17. Henckaerts and Doswald-Beck, *Customary International Humanitarian Law*, rules 81, 82, and 83, pp. 280–286.

18. Henckaerts and Doswald-Beck, *Customary International Humanitarian Law*, p. 283.

19. Second Review Conference of the States Parties to the CCW, Final Declaration, Geneva, December 11–21, 2001, CCW/Conf.II/2, p. 11, para. 12. The Final Declaration of the 2006 Third Review Conference of the CCW was silent on this point.

20. The Final Declaration of the CCW Second Review Conference was adopted by consensus of all CCW States Parties, including China, India, Pakistan, Russia, South Korea, and the United States.

21. See ICRC, "Declaration, Agenda for Humanitarian Action Agenda," 28th International Conference of the Red Cross and Red Crescent, December 2–6, 2003, Final Goal 2.1 and Action 2.1.2, p. 16.

22. The International Conference of the Red Cross and Red Crescent meets every four years and comprises all states party to the Geneva Conventions of 1949 (194

states) and all components of the International Red Cross and Red Crescent Movement, namely the ICRC as well as the over 180 national Red Cross and Red Crescent Societies and their International Federation.

23. UN General Assembly Resolution 61/84, December 6, 2006.

24. In addition to three signatory states (Indonesia, Marshall Islands, and Poland), these included countries where antipersonnel mines have been used and that are mine-affected (Armenia, Azerbaijan, Georgia, Iraq, Morocco, and Sri Lanka), countries that are known to stockpile antipersonnel mines (China, Finland, Mongolia, and Singapore), and countries that have expressed interest in the treaty (Bahrain, Kuwait, Micronesia, Oman, Palau, Tonga, and United Arab Emirates). Indonesia ratified the treaty on February 20, 2007. Kuwait acceded to the treaty on July 30, 2007, and Iraq acceded to the treaty on August 15, 2007. In September 2004, Finland announced that it would join the Mine Ban Treaty by 2012, six years later than its previously stated goal and would destroy its stockpiled antipersonnel mines by 2016. ICBL, *Landmine Monitor Report 2006* (Ottawa: Mines Action Canada, 2006), p. 886. Three other countries were absent from the vote but have supported the resolution in the past: Nepal, Somalia, and Tuvalu.

25. These producer countries are Burma (Myanmar), China, Cuba, India, Iran, North Korea, South Korea, Nepal, Pakistan, Russia, Singapore, the United States, and Vietnam. ICBL, *Landmine Monitor Report 2006* (Ottawa: Mines Action Canada, 2006), p. 10.

26. *Landmine Monitor Report 2006*, p. 7, reports that "since May 2005, three governments are confirmed to have used antipersonnel mines: Burma (Myanmar), Nepal and Russia. These same governments, as well as Georgia, were identified as using antipersonnel mines in the previous Landmine Monitor reporting period." With respect to Nepal, the November 2006 peace agreement between the government of Nepal and Maoist rebels commits both sides to cease use of landmines and to disarm these and other weapons. Although today armed nonstate actors account for most instances of use of antipersonnel mines, their practice is not directly relevant to the establishment of a norm of international law binding states. *Landmine Monitor Report 2006*, pp. 8–9.

27. The states, and the year in which they first put in place a moratorium on the export of antipersonnel mines according to written instruments or as reported in their official statements, are China (1996), Egypt (2004), Finland (1997), Georgia (1996), India (1996), Iran (1997), Israel (1994), Kazakhstan (1997), Pakistan (1999), Poland (1995), Russia (1994), Singapore (1998), South Korea (1997), and the United States (1992). See ICBL, *Landmine Monitor Report 2006* reports for each of these countries.

28. ICBL, *Landmine Monitor Report 2006*, p. 11.

29. ICBL, *Landmine Monitor Report 2006*, pp. 868–869.

30. This is fundamentally what would motivate states to comply with their multilateral treaty obligations rather than fear of punishment. See Abram Chayes and Antonia Handler Chayes, "A Theory of Compliance," in *The New Sovereignty: Compliance with International Regulatory Agreements* (Cambridge: Harvard University Press, 1995), pp. 22–27.

31. ICBL press release, "ICBL Urges Pakistan to Drop Plan to Lay Landmines on Afghan Border," January 12, 2007, http://www.icbl.org/news/pakistan_minelaying_plans.

32. "Landmines Not Answer to Border Problem, MacKay Tells Pakistan," *CBC News*, January 9, 2007, http://www.cbc.ca/world/story/2007/01/09/mackay-pakistan .html; "Pakistan Pushes Border Fence Plan," *BBC News*, January 4, 2007, http://news .bbc.co.uk/1/hi/world/south_asia/6229833.stm; Press Briefing by Chris Alexander, Deputy SRSG in Afghanistan, *UN News Centre*, January 8, 2007, http://www.un.org/ apps/news/infocusnews.asp?NewsID=1131&sID=1.

33. Notably through their endorsement of the 2003 International Conference of the Red Cross and Red Crescent resolution. To this effect, see ICRC, "Declaration, Agenda for Humanitarian Action Agenda," 28th International Conference of the Red Cross and Red Crescent.

34. U.S. Department of State, Bureau of Political-Military Affairs, "Fact Sheet: New United States Policy on Landmines: Reducing Humanitarian Risk and Saving Lives of United States Soldiers," February 27, 2004.

35. ICBL press release, "Congress Delays New Landmine Production: Requires Pentagon to Review Indiscriminate Effects of New Weapons Before Production," February 13, 2006, http://www.icbl.org/news/us_spider.

36. The Victim-Activated Landmine Abolition Act, as the bill is called, was being considered by legislators as of mid-2007. ICBL press release, "Senators Seek to Block First U.S. Landmine Production in Nine Years," August 1, 2006, http://www.icbl.org/ news/usa_spider.

37. See for example, "Israel Admits It Used Phosphorous Weapons," *The Guardian*, October 23, 2006; "Incendiary Weapons: The Big White Lie," *The Independent*, November 18, 2005.

38. In 2006, Belgium adopted legislation banning cluster munitions, while Austria, Hungary, and Norway have each adopted a moratorium on the use, production, and transfer of cluster munitions. Germany announced in June 2006 that it will not procure any new cluster munitions and will examine whether its existing cluster munitions can be entirely replaced by alternative munitions. Argentina, Canada, Denmark, Germany, Norway, and Switzerland have stated that they will not procure, and in some cases will not use, cluster munitions that have a hazardous dud rate of greater than 1 percent and will not use those without the capacity to self-destruct or self-neutralize. Draft legislation or resolutions to prohibit or restrict cluster munitions have been introduced in the parliaments of Australia, Austria, Denmark, France, Germany, Italy, Luxembourg, Netherlands, Sweden, Switzerland, the United Kingdom, and the United States. See Human Rights Watch, "A Dirty Dozen Cluster Munitions," February 2007.

39. Protocol V on Explosive Remnants of War of the Convention on Conventional Weapons was adopted in 2003 and entered into force in 2006.

13

Cluster Munitions in the Crosshairs: In Pursuit of a Prohibition

Stephen D. Goose

C AN THE PHOENIX RISE from the ashes—again? Can lightning strike twice? Can the Oslo Process on cluster munitions replicate the Ottawa Process on antipersonnel mines? Can cluster munitions, which almost inevitably leave behind large numbers of "duds" that function like landmines, be comprehensively banned like antipersonnel mines?

These are questions that many people, including veterans of the mine ban movement, have been asking—and attempting to answer—with ever increasing intensity. No other international issue has been so closely linked to, or so closely resembled, the landmine campaign.

In 1996, in the wake of the failure of the Convention on Conventional Weapons (CCW) to deal adequately with antipersonnel mines, Canada challenged the world to conclude a ban treaty in one year's time. This author and others have said that the Ottawa Process and consequent 1997 Mine Ban Treaty were like a phoenix rising from the ashes of the CCW.

Now, in the wake of the failure of the CCW to address cluster munitions in 2006, Norway is spearheading a process aimed at a ban treaty by the end of 2008. Once again, civil society has managed to thrust a crucial humanitarian issue to the top of the international security and disarmament agenda. Once again, nongovernmental organizations (NGOs) are working in close partnership with key government allies, the International Committee of the Red Cross (ICRC), and United Nation (UN) agencies to respond urgently to a humanitarian imperative. Once again, nontraditional diplomacy is bearing fruit.

Yet there are also some important differences, both between the two types of weapons and between the two efforts to achieve a prohibition. While it can be difficult to write about such a fast-moving issue, this chapter charts international efforts to deal with cluster munitions. After considering why this weapon warrants attention, this chapter looks at past efforts, including the failed attempts to tackle cluster munitions through the CCW from 2001–2006. It then considers the Oslo Process formally launched in February 2007 to secure a new treaty "prohibiting cluster munitions that cause unacceptable harm to civilians" by the end of 2008. The chapter looks at national steps and the positions taken by various key governments (both supporters and detractors), as well as the role of NGOs and other actors, including the ICRC and UN agencies. It concludes with an assessment of the challenges to and prospects for a new treaty.

A Pernicious Weapon

As was the case with antipersonnel mines, cluster munitions have been singled out for prohibition because they are clearly not "just another weapon." Cluster munitions have a long and consistent history of causing excessive and persistent harm to civilian populations. In a May 2007 statement in support of the Oslo Process, Jody Williams on behalf of the Nobel Women's Initiative called cluster munitions a "pernicious weapon of ill-repute" that has "become synonymous with civilian casualties."[1]

Most people think of cluster "bombs" dropped from aircraft, but other common cluster munitions include artillery shells and ground rocket systems. The bombs, shells, and rockets typically contain dozens or hundreds of submunitions (or bomblets) that are released in the air and strewn across a wide area or "footprint." The submunitions usually are designed to explode on contact, though many fail to do so and remain dangerous to the unsuspecting touch.

The very nature of the weapon makes it objectionable, not just its potential to be misused by military forces. While there are many different types of cluster munitions, most, if not all, are highly inaccurate weapons that indiscriminately blanket a broad area, often the size of a football field or more. Most, if not all, are very unreliable weapons that fail to function properly, resulting in landmine-like contamination.

There is a common misperception that cluster munitions are sophisticated weapons. In fact, almost none of the vast existing stockpiles of cluster munitions are "advanced" from a humanitarian point of view. Very few of the "containers" (the bombs, shells, or rockets) are guided in any way, even fewer of the submunitions have any guidance mechanisms, and none of the containers and submunitions are precision-guided. Only a tiny percentage of submunitions employ technology in an attempt to make them more reliable, such as self-destructing devices, and experience has shown that even those with such devices fail all too often.

Thus, cluster munitions pose double danger to civilians, both during attacks because of their indiscriminate wide area effect (making it impossible to target precisely military objectives) and long after because of the landmine-like effect of a multitude of duds. And like landmines, the impact of cluster munitions goes beyond needless civilian casualties, as cluster contamination can have far-reaching socioeconomic ramifications, hindering postconflict reconstruction and development.

While all weapons have a failure rate, cluster munitions are more dangerous because of the large numbers of submunitions they release and because certain design characteristics determined by cost and size considerations increase the likelihood of submunition failure. Manufacturers and militaries have indicated that failure rates for submunitions under test conditions often range between 5 and 20 percent. Actual failure rates in combat conditions have been higher. As a result, cluster munition strikes predictably leave behind great quantities of unexploded submunition duds. This unexploded ordnance can be highly unstable and can explode at the slightest touch, becoming *de facto* landmines that kill or injure civilians returning to the area after an attack.

Antipersonnel mines are *inherently* indiscriminate because they are designed to be victim-activated, without distinguishing whether their victim is civilian or military. The landmine campaign has argued that this makes any use of antipersonnel mines a violation of international humanitarian law (IHL), also know as the law of armed conflict. Cluster munitions, on the other hand, are designed to explode on impact and as such are not inherently indiscriminate but clearly prone to indiscriminate use because of their wide area effect. Moreover, the predictably numerous hazardous duds left by cluster strikes are indiscriminate in effect.

While it is possible to use cluster munitions without violating international humanitarian law, in every conflict where there is significant documentation and the evidence is clear, the weapon has been used in violation of IHL. Experience has shown that in conflicts where cluster munitions are used, they usually are used in or near populated areas and in very large numbers. Often older and highly unreliable models are used, sometimes alongside newer models. Indiscriminate and/or disproportionate use—where the negative effect on civilians exceeds the military benefit—is the standard, not the exception.

Various countries protest that their forces use or intend to use cluster munitions responsibly, but this does not stand up to the scrutiny of past use by a wide range of nations, none of whom used the weapon responsibly, including

Israel, Russia, the United Kingdom, and the United States. Cluster munitions caused more civilian casualties than any other weapon system during both the NATO bombing campaign in Kosovo in 1999 and the invasion of Iraq in 2003.

While the number of conflicts in which cluster munitions have been used to date is still relatively limited, the danger of the problem growing exponentially is great. At least fourteen states and a small number of nonstate armed groups have used cluster munitions in at least twenty-six countries and five other areas.[2] According to Human Rights Watch, thirty-four countries have produced over 210 different types of cluster munitions, and at least thirteen countries have transferred over fifty different types of cluster munitions to at least sixty other countries, as well as nonstate armed groups.[3]

Most worrisome, at least seventy-six countries stockpile cluster munitions, and the number of submunitions in existing arsenals is staggering, likely in the billions.[4] The United States alone has an estimated one billion submunitions. If even a small percentage of existing stocks are used in the future, there will be a global humanitarian crisis that far exceeds that posed by antipersonnel mines ten years ago.

Slow-Building Opposition to a Growing Problem

Cluster munitions were first used by the Germans and Soviets in World War II, but the beginning of the cluster munition problem is usually traced to massive use of the weapon by the United States in Southeast Asia in the 1960s and 1970s. The ICRC estimated that in Laos alone, nine to twenty-seven million unexploded submunitions still remained three decades later, and some eleven thousand people had been killed or injured, of which more than 30 percent were children.[5] Largely in response to the disastrous effects of cluster munitions in Southeast Asia during the Vietnam War, a small number of countries proposed a prohibition on the weapon during the preparatory work to establish the Convention on Conventional Weapons in the late 1970s, but the notion received little serious consideration from other governments or NGOs.

Instead, the 1970s and 1980s witnessed a huge expansion in the procurement of cluster munitions, particularly in NATO and Warsaw Pact nations. Indeed, most cluster munitions in arsenals today were conceived as Cold War weapons, intended for use against massive formations of armor and personnel. The most extensive use of cluster munitions since the Vietnam War occurred in the Gulf War of 1991.[6] The United States and its allies dropped sixty-one thousand cluster bombs containing some twenty million submunitions, as well as an unknown but possibly similar number of ground-delivered submunitions.[7]

The Gulf War prompted the first in-depth research on and meaningful op-position to cluster munitions in the NGO community.[8] Some of the awareness and opposition was also linked to the growing movement to ban antiperson-nel mines, as many groups made the connection between the two weapons and issues. Yet from the outset, the International Campaign to Ban Landmines (ICBL) decided to focus on antipersonnel mines, rather than taking on the re-lated issues of antivehicle mines and cluster munitions as well.[9] Neither the ICBL, the ICRC, nor any government ever proposed the inclusion of cluster munitions in what became the 1997 Mine Ban Treaty. The treaty did, however, bring greater attention to the cluster issue and significantly spurred efforts to address their impact, as the subsequent expansion of clearance, risk educa-tion, and victim assistance programs benefited communities affected by all types of unexploded ordnance, not just by mines.

Cluster munitions were pushed back into the public's eye during the NATO bombing campaign in Kosovo and Serbia in 1999. The United States, the United Kingdom, and the Netherlands dropped 1,765 cluster munitions with about 295,000 submunitions, killing 90 to 150 civilians and injuring many more. The civilian casualties incurred as a result of the so-called humanitar-ian intervention drew extensive media coverage and prompted public outrage. Human Rights Watch provided detailed research on the cluster strikes and be-came the first NGO to call for a global moratorium on the use of all cluster munitions, a call soon picked up by many others in the humanitarian com-munity.[10]

Though largely unnoticed by most of the world, cluster munitions were used in numerous conflicts in the 1990s besides the Gulf War and Kosovo. These included Albania, Angola, Bosnia and Herzegovina, Chechnya, Croatia, Democratic Republic of Congo, the Ethiopia-Eritrea border war, Nagorno-Karabakh, Sierra Leone, Sudan, and Tajikistan.

Outrage over the use of cluster munitions in Kosovo died away all too quickly, but a small number of NGOs and the ICRC attempted to keep the issue alive and sought to force governments to pay attention through the only diplomatic, disarmament, or humanitarian forum readily available: the Con-vention on Conventional Weapons. The CCW was entering into preparations for its Second Review Conference, to be held in 2001.

The NGOs—most notably Human Rights Watch and Landmine Action UK, as well as Handicap International and Mines Action Canada—began pressing governments to put cluster munitions on the agenda for the Review Conference, with an eye to developing a new protocol specific to cluster mu-nitions. The ICRC launched a major initiative on "explosive remnants of war" (ERW), which in large part was aimed at spurring action on cluster munitions in the CCW and elsewhere.[11]

The United States' use of cluster munitions in Afghanistan in its post-9/11 campaign against the Taliban brought the issue back into the headlines. From October 2001 into 2002, the United States dropped some 248,000 submunitions. Human Rights Watch again conducted an investigative mission and found that the U.S. Air Force had largely heeded the criticism from Kosovo and made a deliberate effort to minimize use of cluster munitions in populated areas, but that dozens of avoidable civilian casualties still occurred during strikes, and more than 120 in the first year after.[12]

At the Second CCW Review Conference held in November and December 2001, few states responded directly to the NGO call to begin work on cluster munitions, except in the negative. However, a number saw the ICRC's approach of addressing cluster munitions as part of the larger problem of ERW as an attractive option, and CCW States Parties agreed to a "discussion mandate" to talk about cluster munitions at future CCW meetings, without any commitment to pursue a new protocol.

The Netherlands in particular showed leadership in promoting the ERW issue and made clear that it viewed it as a first step toward dealing with the humanitarian problems of cluster munitions. Over the next two years, two Dutch diplomats, Ambassador Chris Sanders and Alex Verbeek, pushed forward to develop a new protocol without ever receiving a formal mandate for negotiations. Sanders and Verbeek did their best to import positive aspects of their experience working in the Mine Ban Treaty process. Unlike past CCW meetings, NGOs were welcomed into the room, allowed to make speeches and interventions, and even asked to make presentations during the sessions. Even more important, NGOs and the ICRC engaged extensively with the Netherlands and other key progressive governments (including Austria, Canada, Norway, and Sweden) on the margins and in a series of very informal retreats hosted by the Dutch at which draft protocol language was developed, and strategies and tactics discussed.

Reality from the ground again dramatically intruded on the international diplomatic efforts, as United States and United Kingdom forces fired some two million submunitions during the March–April 2003 invasion of Iraq. While the U.S. Air Force to an even greater degree than in Afghanistan avoided use in populated areas, the U.S. Army had not learned this lesson and cascaded cluster munitions, mostly rocket and artillery systems, into Baghdad and many other urban environments. A Human Rights Watch field investigation concluded that cluster munitions had caused hundreds of civilian casualties during the invasion, more than any other weapon (other than small arms fire).[13]

Just after the invasion, in April 2003, Pax Christi Ireland and the Irish government hosted an important conference on ERW and development. At the end of the meeting, NGOs gathered separately and decided that the time had come to form a new NGO coalition to carry out more effective work on cluster munitions. As this author noted during the meeting, it had become very evident that NGOs were mostly operating in emergency response mode on cluster munitions, sounding alarm bells whenever they were used in major conflicts, but that biannual outrage would not suffice. The time had come—with Kosovo, Afghanistan, Iraq, and CCW deliberations having raised the stakes and the possibilities—to establish expanded, sustained, proactive, and coordinated NGO work on cluster munitions.

A group of about ten organizations volunteered to work together on the practical and substantive issues related to a formal launch of an NGO campaign on clusters and ERW.[14] The Cluster Munition Coalition (CMC) was subsequently launched in the Hague, with the Dutch Foreign Minister present, on November 13, 2003.

CCW States Parties agreed to the new Protocol V on explosive remnants of war on November 28, 2003.[15] This was a notable achievement in some respects. Getting anything agreed in the CCW's consensus rules is an accomplishment, and ERW succeeded when work on antivehicle mines and other matters floundered. The new protocol further reinforced the principle that protection of civilians must be a paramount consideration during and after warfare and that states must take at least some responsibility for the detritus of war that they leave behind. The protocol makes a state responsible for clearance of all ERW (including submunition duds) in territory under its control; the user of weapons that become ERW is to provide assistance for clearance of that ERW on territory not under its control.

But the protocol engendered little enthusiasm from the NGO community, even among those like Human Rights Watch that had put a good deal of effort into it.[16] The instrument had been put through the CCW grinder, and too little emerged on the other side. It only deals with "post-conflict remedial measures" and does not address issues related to time of use. The protocol only applies to future conflicts and thus has no effect on the existing ERW problem around the globe. It is replete with so many qualifiers that virtually all key provisions are essentially voluntary in nature, and not compulsory.

As the negotiations on ERW progressed, a number of countries stressed the need to tackle more directly the issue of submunitions. In June 2003, Switzerland called for the establishment of a mandate as soon as possible to negotiate a new protocol on submunitions. Supportive countries included Austria, Belgium, Canada, Denmark, France, Ireland, Mexico, the Netherlands, New Zealand, Norway, and Sweden. Those opposed to further work on submunitions included China, Pakistan, Russia, and the United States. In the end, governments agreed only to discuss possible technical improvements for submunitions and whether or not existing international humanitarian law is sufficient to address issues related to submunitions.[17]

Throughout 2004 and 2005, NGOs and the ICRC continued to press for meaningful work on cluster munitions in the CCW. Expectations were by no means high, but they recognized that the CCW provided an opportunity to keep the issue on governments' agendas and to educate them about the dangers of the weapon. They also pressed states to take action at the national level.

This was a period where the slow pace of opposition to cluster munitions picked up speed, and there was steady progress. It was a period of bringing governments along step-by-step, first getting them to acknowledge that cluster munitions posed special humanitarian problems, and then convincing them to take some actions to begin to address the problems.[18] Virtually no government was willing to consider a prohibition, but more and more were embracing the notion that inaccurate and unreliable cluster munitions were not acceptable.

2006: The CCW Fails,
but the Battle Against Cluster Munitions Thrives

Pressures and activities intensified greatly during 2006, as governments prepared to hold the Third CCW Review Conference in November. The CMC early on stressed that the time had come for the CCW to act on cluster munitions or to admit failure. If States Parties could not agree to a negotiating mandate on cluster munitions at the Review Conference, then it was time to consider action outside of the CCW. NGOs began meeting quietly and informally with sympathetic governments to prepare for this eventuality.

Surprising almost everyone, Belgium became the first country to comprehensively ban cluster munitions in February 2006. Norway declared a moratorium on use in June 2006.

Israel's massive and horrifying use of cluster munitions in Lebanon in July and August 2006 provided a major impetus to the already growing momentum, perhaps even a decisive push. According to the UN, Israel fired some four million submunitions into Lebanon leaving behind as many as one million duds.[19] Unexploded munitions blanketed many urban areas, and civilian casualties mounted rapidly as people who had fled returned to their homes and fields. The media coverage and the moral outcry from around the globe were unprecedented.

At a CCW preparatory meeting held in September 2006, Sweden and Austria took the lead in introducing for consideration at the Review Conference a draft mandate to begin negotiations on cluster munitions. But, as proved to be more important, Norway's foreign minister announced in October 2006: "The case of Lebanon clearly demonstrates that there is a real need to strengthen humanitarian law in this area. In the Government's view, the human suffering caused by the use of cluster munitions is unacceptable. This is why Norway will take the lead—together with other like-minded countries and international humanitarian actors—to put in place an international prohibition against cluster munitions."[20] This was the first public indication that any government was considering going outside the CCW.

The momentum against cluster munitions increased greatly in the lead-up to and during the Third CCW Review Conference held in Geneva from November 7–17, 2006. On the opening day of the conference, UN Secretary-General Kofi Annan issued a statement calling for a "freeze" on the use of cluster munitions in populated areas and the destruction of "inaccurate and unreliable" cluster munitions.[21] The ICRC called on states not only "to immediately end the use of inaccurate and unreliable cluster munitions" but also to destroy their stocks of such weapons.[22]

By the end of the Review Conference, nearly thirty states had expressed support for a proposal to begin negotiations in the CCW on a "legally-binding instrument that addresses the humanitarian concerns posed by cluster munitions."[23] However, the proposal was rejected by a number of other states, including China, Russia, the United Kingdom, and the United States in favor of a weak mandate to continue discussions on explosive remnants of war, with a focus on cluster munitions.

The anticluster munition states issued a declaration on the final day of the Review Conference calling for an agreement that would prohibit the use of cluster munitions "within concentrations of civilians," prohibit the use of cluster munitions that "pose serious humanitarian hazards because they are for example unreliable and/or inaccurate," and require destruction of stockpiles of such cluster munitions.[24] Norway then announced it would start an independent process outside the CCW to negotiate a treaty banning cluster munitions that cause unacceptable humanitarian harm and invited governments to join. The large NGO contingent in the room broke into sustained applause.

The Oslo Process

Norway's announcement meant an immediate shift into high gear as like-minded governments began extensive consultations to rapidly develop the treaty, and NGOs started to undertake full-blown campaigning in support of the initiative. Reinforcing the troops was a first order of business. Norway set about identifying a core group of governments willing to invest heavily in the new process by providing the leadership and resources necessary to carry out an initiative outside of traditional forums and without UN staff to take of administrative and bureaucratic matters. The initial group included Norway, Austria, Ireland, Mexico, New Zealand, and Sweden. Later, Sweden dropped out (largely due to a backsliding in domestic policy), and Peru joined.

On the NGO front, a significant development came with the decision in December 2006 by the International Campaign to Ban Landmines to expand its work to include cluster munitions—the first time since its inception that it would actively engage on any issue other than antipersonnel mines. The ICBL brought with it an experienced and vast network of national campaigns and campaigners, ready and excited to take on cluster munitions.

Understanding that the first meeting in this bold and unconventional initiative could easily make or break it, the core group of governments worked closely with NGOs, the ICRC, and select UN representatives to strategize about the nature and desired outcomes of the meeting, to develop the agenda, to draft the Oslo declaration which became the underpinning for the entire process, and to ensure sufficient and appropriate participation by states and others. Discussion also began on the shape and approach of a future treaty.

In keeping with the urgency demanded by the issue, Norway scheduled the meeting to take place as soon as possible, on February 22–23, 2007. Every country that had publicly stated its support for a future treaty on cluster munitions was invited, with a carefully worded invitation indicating that participants should be prepared to work toward a treaty rapidly. But the meeting was open to all states; those not explicitly invited could ask to attend, as long as they shared the objectives of the other participants.

The Oslo Conference on Cluster Munitions was a roaring success. The conference was characterized by a palpable sense of excitement as the participants realized they were present at the beginning of a potentially historic undertaking that could have a major humanitarian impact. Austria announced its moratorium on cluster munitions at the beginning of the meeting, setting the right tone.

A total of forty-six of the forty-nine participating states endorsed the final conference statement to conclude a treaty banning cluster munitions by 2008.[25] The Oslo Declaration committed states to create a legally binding international instrument to "prohibit the use, production, transfer and stockpiling of cluster munitions that cause unacceptable harm to civilians" and include provisions on clearance, victim assistance, risk education, and stockpile destruction.[26] The comprehensive and integrated humanitarian approach, mirroring the Mine Ban Treaty, was seen as a vital corollary to the disarmament prohibitions.

There was a good measure of drama and uncertainty over the course of the conference as no one was sure on the final day how many of the governments present would endorse the Oslo Declaration and how many would bail out; some were clearly getting last-minute instructions. The NGOs feared that a dozen or more nations would decline to endorse the declaration (including Canada, Denmark, France, Germany, Italy, South Africa, and the United Kingdom). Only Japan, Poland, and Romania declined to support the Oslo Declaration, however. Among the most surprising endorsers were Egypt and Finland, two countries that have not joined the Mine Ban Treaty.

A road map to develop and negotiate the treaty was outlined, with an ambitious series of meetings in core group countries (Peru, Austria, New Zealand, and Ireland). Norway's Foreign Minister Jonas Ghar Støre explained that the "strict timeline to conclude our work by 2008" was "ambitious but necessary to respond to the urgency of this humanitarian problem."[27]

More than one hundred NGO representatives participated in the Oslo Conference. NGOs were given high visibility speaking slots and intervened on the same basis as states. This has been the case with subsequent Oslo Process meetings as well. The Cluster Munition Coalition hosted a civil society forum on the day prior to the Oslo Conference, a practice it continued at subsequent meetings.

At the first follow-up meeting held in Lima, Peru, on May 23–25, 2007, an additional twenty-eight states joined the process, including many from Africa, as well as Laos, the country most affected by unexploded submunitions.[28] The core group of governments distributed a draft treaty text prior to the meeting—a text that had been developed in consultation with NGOs as well as other governments. It closely resembled the Mine Ban Treaty.

While specific treaty language was not discussed in Lima, the sixty-eight states present reached broad agreement on the framework of a future treaty and its essential elements. In addition to the prohibition on use, production, and trade, the treaty will include requirements and deadlines for stockpile destruction and clearance of contaminated areas, as well as an obligation to provide victim assistance. On the negative side, some states proposed exempting large categories of submunitions from the ban, such as those that have self-destruct mechanisms or a specific reliability rate.[29] Many of the same states insisted that discussions on cluster munitions in the CCW should take precedence over the Oslo Process. At the Peru meeting, Hungary announced a moratorium on cluster munitions.

A regional Latin America Conference on Cluster Munitions, held in Costa Rica on September 4–5, 2007, further added to the momentum of the Oslo Process as four more countries pledged their support for the process (El Salvador, Honduras, Nicaragua, and Uruguay), bringing the total to eighty. Eighteen Latin American governments participated in the San Jose meeting, and

Brazil was the only one that did not express its support for the Oslo Process. Cuba was the only invitee that declined to participate.

Just prior to the meeting, Argentina officially informed the Cluster Munition Coalition that it had destroyed all of its stockpiles of cluster munitions and that it no longer produced the weapons. During the meeting, Chile stated that it had halted production and that it had no intention of doing so in the future. Nearly all of the Latin American governments endorsed a proposal from Peru and Costa Rica to create a regional Cluster Munition Free Zone. Many of the governments stressed that a so-called technical solution to the cluster munition problem, through self-destruct devices or required reliability rates, was not feasible.

Another major Oslo Process meeting took place on October 3–4, 2007, in Serbia: the Belgrade Conference of States Affected by Cluster Munitions. More than twenty countries that have suffered from the effects of cluster munitions attended. The conference was aimed at getting more affected states to join the Oslo Process, and just as importantly, to get those that are part of the process to play more of a leadership role and take significant ownership of the issue, ensuring that the new treaty is responsive to their needs. Belgium will host a European regional meeting in Brussels on October 30, 2007, focused on the topics of stockpile destruction and victim assistance.

The remaining major international meetings in the Oslo Process will take place in Vienna, Austria, from December 5–7, 2007, where discussion of specific treaty text will take place; in Wellington, New Zealand, from February 18–22, 2008, where it is hoped that agreement can be reached on a treaty text that will serve as a basis for formal negotiations; and in Dublin, Ireland, from May–30, 2008, where it is planned that negotiations will be concluded. A signing ceremony would be held in Oslo later in the year, following intense efforts to get the maximum number of countries possible on board.

There have been many other events and activities at the national and regional levels to promote the Oslo Process, many of which were "piggybacked" onto plans related to mines, ERW, or other topics. While space precludes a comprehensive listing, in 2007 the CMC, ICBL and their members took action on clusters in such far-flung places as Argentina, Azerbaijan, Cambodia, Tajikistan, and Yemen. National campaigners have been active in dozens of countries, raising public and government awareness, working with parliamentarians, and engaging in media activities. Norway's large and high profile events in September 2007 surrounding the 10th anniversary of the conclusion of the Mine Ban Treaty negotiations had a major focus on cluster munitions as the next crucial humanitarian imperative.

The ICRC held an "Expert Meeting on the Humanitarian, Military, Technical and Legal Challenges of Cluster Munitions," in Montreux, Switzerland, on

April 18–20, 2007. Thirty-two governments were represented, more than half of which were part of the Oslo Process, as well as a small number of NGOs and UN agencies. The ICRC has also hosted or cosponsored a number of other meetings that have dealt at least in part with cluster munitions and explosive remnants of war.

Though some countries have said they are reluctant to embrace the Oslo Process because it is "outside the UN," in fact, the United Nations, and especially the UN Development Programme (UNDP), has played an important role in the Oslo Process. The Oslo Process is outside the CCW, but not the UN. The UNDP has provided invaluable assistance for many of the Oslo Process meetings and has taken the lead in developing the UN's position and actions on cluster munitions. UNIDIR has from the beginning given its expert advice. UNICEF has also been engaged. When the treaty comes into existence, it is envisioned that the UN Secretary-General will be the depositary.

In September 2007, the United Nations announced an important development in its position on cluster munitions. Whereas previously the UN had spoken of a freeze on use in populated areas and had plainly straddled the fence between the Oslo Process and the CCW, the new position is clearly fully consistent with and supportive of the Oslo Process, even incorporating key language from the Oslo Declaration. In it the UN calls on member states to address immediately the horrendous humanitarian, human rights, and development effects of cluster munitions by concluding a legally binding instrument of international humanitarian law that prohibits cluster munitions that cause unacceptable harm to civilians, requires the destruction of stockpiled munitions, and provides for clearance, risk education and other risk mitigation activities, victim assistance, assistance and cooperation, and compliance and transparency measures. Until such a treaty is adopted, the UN calls on member states to "take domestic measures to immediately freeze the use and transfer of all cluster munitions."[30]

In another important development, the Organization for Security and Cooperation in Europe (OSCE) Parliamentary Assembly adopted a resolution on July 9, 2007, that calls on OSCE states to adopt legislation banning cluster munitions "that gravely affect civilian populations," and urges them to "stimulate a global campaign and a process that could lead to an international ban on cluster bombs."

National Steps

States are also pursuing domestic measures to address cluster munitions. Austria, Hungary, and Norway have all declared moratoria on use of the weapon.

Belgium became the first country to adopt a comprehensive ban on cluster munitions in February 2006. Switzerland also announced in May that federal law would be amended with a prohibition on cluster munitions that cause unacceptable harm to civilians, and pending entry into force of the prohibition, Switzerland would observe a moratorium on such weapons; however, it is unclear what weapons are covered by the moratorium. Bosnia and Herzegovina announced in May that it will no longer produce cluster munitions and intends to adopt a moratorium on use in the near future. On May 31, 2007, the Danish Parliament adopted a resolution encouraging the government to consider a national moratorium on all types of cluster munitions before the end of November 2007.

In September 2007, at the Costa Rica cluster munitions conference, Argentina declared that it does not produce cluster munitions and had already destroyed its stockpile.[31] At the same time, Chile announced that it would no longer produce cluster munitions. Canada is in the process of destroying all of its stockpiled cluster munitions.

In August 2006, Germany announced that it would not procure any new cluster munitions, would cease using the two types of cluster munitions in its arsenal with dud rates higher than 1 percent, and would examine whether its existing cluster munitions could be replaced entirely by an alternative weapon. The German Parliament passed a resolution effecting these changes on September 28, 2006. Several weeks later, on October 12, 2006, the Parliament of Luxembourg adopted a motion calling on the government to join international initiatives to ban cluster munitions and to elaborate a law banning cluster munitions.

In addition to Denmark, Germany, and Luxembourg, there are or have been parliamentary initiatives to restrict or prohibit cluster munitions in Australia, Austria, Denmark, France, Italy, the Netherlands, Sweden, Switzerland, the United Kingdom, and the United States.

Many countries have in recent years decided to remove from service and/or destroy cluster munitions with high failure rates, and some have called for a prohibition on use in populated areas. Argentina, Denmark, Germany, Norway, Switzerland, and the United States, among others, have announced they will not procure cluster munitions in the future with a failure rate greater than 1 percent; Poland and South Africa have said they will establish minimum reliability rates. Countries that have also decided to remove from service and/or destroy cluster munitions with high failure rates include Australia (Rockeye), Belgium (BL-755), Czech Republic (RBK), Denmark (Rockeye), France (BLG-66), Germany (BL-755, DM-602, DM-612), the Netherlands (BL-755, M26 MLRS, M483A1), Norway (Rockeye), Portugal (BL-755), Switzerland (BL-755), and the United Kingdom (M483 DPICM).

Challenges on the Path Ahead

By September 2007, there was considerable optimism and confidence among key Oslo Process governments and NGOs that a new cluster munition treaty would be achieved. The overriding question appeared to be not so much whether there would be a treaty, but how good it would be, and how many countries would agree to it.

The author shares the optimism, but it is evident that the path ahead will not be smooth or easy. Many challenges must be overcome. Some relate to the content of the treaty itself, while others relate to the process and the ability of the key players to make it successful.

The great unknown at the time of this writing is the fate of cluster munitions in the Convention on Conventional Weapons. While certain CCW states had scuttled the proposal in November 2006 to begin negotiations on clusters inside the CCW, the success of the Oslo Process brought a rapid reassessment of that strategy. The CCW meeting in June 2007 was recast from one that would devote a couple of hours at most to cluster munitions to one that spent nearly the entire week on the subject. At the meeting the United States in particular went from insisting that there was no need even to continue discussions on cluster munitions to stating that it was prepared to negotiate a new legally binding instrument—but only in the CCW.[32] This sudden shift looked not so much like an attempt to deal with cluster munitions but an attempt to handle the runaway Oslo Process. Germany formally submitted the text of a new protocol (first distributed at the ICRC meeting in Montreux), but this received little attention; it was too weak for committed Oslo Process states but too strong for key CCW states. In the end, nothing more was agreed than to consider the possibility of an unspecified future mandate on clusters at the next meeting in November 2007.

It remains to be seen what will occur at the November 2007 CCW meeting, but a number of states have been working on language for a negotiating mandate and on language for a new protocol. Should CCW states agree to begin negotiations on cluster munitions, the impact on the Oslo Process is uncertain. More than a few countries would likely state that they are concentrating their efforts on the CCW, secure in the knowledge that if a CCW protocol is agreed to—a very big if, given the past history of years of talks producing no results—it would be much less far-reaching than an Oslo Process treaty and likely to take effect at a much later date.

Many countries have latched on to the notion that efforts to deal with clusters in the CCW and in the Oslo Process are "complementary," with the Oslo track for states willing to move far and fast and the CCW for those who are less ambitious. In truth, this makes little sense. Instead of setting a standard against cluster munitions that all should feel compelled to obey, the dual negotiations would signal that states should merely do whatever is comfortable and least demanding for them. Fundamentally, the Oslo Process is aimed at a prohibition on cluster munitions that cause unacceptable harm to civilians, while the CCW track is for those nations that want to continue to use cluster munitions that have already been proven to cause unacceptable harm, such as those used by Israel in Lebanon in 2006 and by the United States in Iraq in 2003. These are not complementary approaches, they are contrary approaches. The CCW track will only legitimize cluster munitions, not stigmatize them.[33]

Some argue that the CCW must be provided with every possible chance to deal with the cluster munition issue before "defaulting" to the Oslo Process. The thinking hinges on the notion that the CCW has "all the stakeholders" involved and that "major powers" and the big users, producers, and stockpilers of cluster munitions are only willing to engage in the CCW context. Besides the fact that the CCW has already had years to take action on cluster munitions, the convention has only about half of the world's nations as States Parties, is notably lacking in participation from developing countries, and does not have many of the countries affected by cluster munitions. The Oslo Process already has about half of the producers and stockpilers of cluster munitions, and more are likely to join in the coming months.

Despite the concerns about states that are not yet on board the Oslo Process, the Mine Ban Treaty experience shows that many states are likely to join in only very late and that some of those states then become the most active and ardent supporters. The landmine experience also has shown that a good, strong treaty will have a powerful effect even on those that do not sign on right away. It will set a new standard of behavior that nearly every government will adhere to. By 2007, just two governments were using antipersonnel mines, even though forty are not party to the 1997 Mine Ban Treaty. A similar effect is likely for cluster munitions as the weapon will be stigmatized to such an extent that governments will be increasingly reluctant to use it. Once a treaty is in place, very few will want to endure the international condemnation that will accompany any use of cluster munitions anywhere in the world.

The importance of this standard-setting phenomenon is also relevant to the content of the treaty itself. Some Oslo Process participants have already been talking about the "trade-off" between a strong treaty and the need to bring as many countries on board as possible ("universalization"), or talking about the need to "balance" these two elements. The lesson to take from the Ottawa Process on antipersonnel mines ten years ago is that the integrity of the treaty matters most. If the bar is set low to appeal to certain nations, they will only drag the bar down to a lower level, if they deign to join at all. If the bar is set high, most nations will, over time, rise up to that level and embrace it, as the international community more broadly does so. If there are governments that will not accept the humanitarian standard that most others are aspiring to with the treaty, they should not be part of the process.

The most challenging aspect of the development and negotiation of the treaty text will almost certainly be the definition. What cluster munitions will be captured by the definition, and will certain cluster munitions be exempt? The agreed premise of the Oslo Process is a prohibition on cluster munitions that cause unacceptable harm to civilians, but what constitutes "unacceptable harm?"

There will almost certainly be some noncontroversial "exceptions" to the prohibition on cluster munitions, such as those with nonexplosive or inert submunitions; smoke, flare, and illuminating submunitions; nuclear warheads; incendiary submunitions; and landmines (with the latter two covered under existing international instruments).

The most contentious proposals will be those calling for a broad exception for cluster munitions with submunitions that have self-destruct mechanisms, and/or for an exception for cluster munitions with submunitions that meet a certain reliability standard (the figure of 99 percent has been mentioned by some). More than a dozen countries have indicated they might support one or both of these measures, including France, Germany, and the United Kingdom.[34]

The draft treaty text circulated by the core group of governments prior to the Lima meeting does not contain exceptions for self-destruct mechanisms or reliability standards. A number of other states have spoken out against such "technical fix" approaches, especially the affected countries and those from the developing "South." The Cluster Munition Coalition has said that these are "red line" issues for it and that it could not support a treaty with such broad exceptions. The CMC and others have pointed out that there is strong evidence—including from Israeli use in Lebanon in 2006 of submunitions considered among the most advanced in the world—that self-destruct mechanisms simply do not work as advertised far too often and that there is no real relationship between reliability rates achieved in test conditions and those encountered in the field.

The most notable exception that is included in the draft treaty text is one for Sensor Fuzed Weapons (SFW). While there are several different types, these typically contain a small number of submunitions, each with an infrared guidance system directing the submunition to an armored vehicle. It is argued that these will not present the same dangers to civilians as most existing cluster munitions because they are capable of more accurate targeting and are more reliable; in theory they will not have an indiscriminate wide area effect and will not leave behind large numbers of hazardous duds.

The CMC has said that the mindset from the start should be that all cluster munitions cause unacceptable harm to civilians and that all cluster munitions are inaccurate and unreliable. The burden of proof should then be on governments and militaries to demonstrate that there is such a thing as a cluster munition that will not cause unacceptable harm, and that is sufficiently accurate and reliable. If governments want exceptions, they should make the humanitarian case and prove that such weapons do not have the same indiscriminate and long-lasting effects as other cluster munitions. It would not make sense to start with exceptions for weapons about which there is little hard information. Sensor fuzed weapons, for example, have only been used once, during the invasion of Iraq in 2003, and there is no publicly available data about their performance—there is no truth from the ground.

Some states have suggested other possible provisions for the future treaty that, in the view of the CMC, would prove unacceptably damaging. These include a transition period before key prohibitions take effect and a provision to address "interoperability" concerns. Both notions fly against the humanitarian case that underlies the effort to conclude a treaty on cluster munitions. How could states ban cluster munitions because of their unacceptable impact on civilians but then agree to allow ongoing use for a number of years (ten has been suggested) while militaries acquire new weapons to replace them? And agree that, while the humanitarian imperative demands your own military forces give up cluster munitions, it is not objectionable for your ally's forces to continue using them in your joint military operations?

Another, though different kind of, challenge is to improve upon the articles in the Mine Ban Treaty that deal with victim assistance, clearance, risk education, transparency, and compliance. The many years of experience in implementing the Mine Ban Treaty have yielded lessons in these areas that should be transferred to a new cluster munition treaty.

Finally, there is the challenge of ensuring that the partnership of key governments, NGOs (mainly through the Cluster Munition Coalition), the ICRC, and UN agencies is as strong as possible in trying to lead the way outside of traditional diplomatic channels to a new treaty-prohibiting cluster munitions. Within the core group of governments, Norway has had to bear a disproportionate burden, and there is a need for others to contribute (in a variety of ways) at a higher level. There is also a need to expand the core group for greater geographic diversity and representation from affected states. The CMC is a smaller and less experienced coalition than the ICBL at a similar stage in the treaty process, and there is especially a need for greatly expanded campaigning at the national level around the world. The ICRC has not thrown its full weight behind the Oslo Process in the way it did the Ottawa Process.

Support from the UN needs to come from the highest levels and not be deferential to the CCW.

Conclusion

There may be few steps that governments can take that will offer greater protection to civilians in future armed conflicts than to prohibit the use, production, trade, and stockpiling of cluster munitions. No conventional weapon is in greater need of stronger national and international laws. Urgent action is necessary to bring under control the immediate danger that cluster munitions pose to civilians during attacks, the long-term danger they pose after conflict, and the potential future dangers of widespread proliferation.

The Oslo Process offers a rare opportunity to effect a major change that will have a tremendous humanitarian impact, literally saving thousands of lives for generations to come, while also reinforcing the power that civil society and governments can have working together on a common goal.

Notes

1. Statement by the Nobel Women's Initiative to the Lima Conference on Cluster Munitions, May 23, 2007. The Nobel Women's Initiative, founded in 2006, is a common effort by six Nobel Peace Laureates (Jody Williams, Shirin Ebadi, Wangari Maathai, Rigoberta Menchu Tum, Betty Williams, and Mairead Corrigan Maguire) to support women working around the world for peace and women's human rights.

2. The fourteen users are Eritrea, Ethiopia, France, Israel, Morocco, the Netherlands, Nigeria, Russia (USSR), Saudi Arabia, Sudan, Tajikistan, the United Kingdom, the United States, and FR Yugoslavia. The twenty-six affected countries are Afghanistan, Albania, Angola, Bosnia and Herzegovina, Cambodia, Chad, Croatia, DR Congo, Ethiopia, Eritrea, Iraq, Israel, Kuwait, Laos, Lebanon, Montenegro, Saudi Arabia, Serbia, Sierra Leone, Sudan, Syria, Tajikistan, Russia (USSR), Uganda, the United Kingdom, and Vietnam. The five affected areas are Chechnya, Falkland Islands, Kosovo, Nagorno-Karabakh, and Western Sahara.

3. Human Rights Watch (HRW), "Updated Human Rights Watch Cluster Munition Information Chart," June 2007, http://hrw.org/arms/pdfs/munitionChart061507.pdf; HRW, "Human Rights Watch Cluster Munition Information Chart," March 2006, http://hrw.org/arms/pdfs/munitionChart.pdf.

4. Algeria, Angola, Austria, Azerbaijan, Bahrain, Belarus, Bosnia and Herzegovina, Brazil, Bulgaria, Chile, China, Croatia, Cuba, Czech Republic, Denmark, Egypt, Eritrea, Ethiopia, Finland, France, Georgia, Germany, Greece, Guinea, Guinea Bissau, Honduras, Hungary, India, Indonesia, Iran, Iraq, Israel, Italy, Japan, Jordan, Kazakhstan,

Montenegro, North Korea, South Korea, Kuwait, Libya, Moldova, Mongolia, Morocco, the Netherlands, Nigeria, Norway, Oman, Pakistan, Peru, Poland, Portugal, Romania, Russia, Saudi Arabia, Serbia, Singapore, Slovakia, South Africa, Spain, Sri Lanka, Sudan, Sweden, Switzerland, Syria, Thailand, Turkey, Turkmenistan, Uganda, Ukraine, United Arab Emirates, the United Kingdom, the United States, Uzbekistan, Yemen, and Zimbabwe.

5. ICRC, "Explosive Remnants of War: The Lethal Legacy of Modern Armed Conflict," June 2003, p. 6.

6. The Soviet Union used huge numbers of cluster munitions as well as mines in Afghanistan from 1979–1989. Other instances of use in the 1970s and 1980s include by Israel in Syria in 1973 and in Lebanon in 1978 and 1982, by Morocco in the Western Sahara (dates unknown), by the United Kingdom in the Falkland Islands in 1982, and by France and Libya in Chad in 1986–1987.

7. See HRW, "U.S. Cluster Bombs for Turkey?" December 1994, pp. 15–19. A decade later, submunition duds had killed 1,600 civilians and injured more than 2,500 in Iraq and Kuwait, and thousands of duds were still being cleared each year, despite one of the most extensive and expensive clearance operations in history after the conflict.

8. The pioneer in this work was William Arkin of the United States, often publishing in his capacity as consultant to Human Rights Watch.

9. ICBL leadership discussed this explicitly at a number of meetings. The ICBL encouraged its member organizations to work on antivehicle mines and cluster munitions but decided against making them part of the broader campaign's call or plan of action.

10. Human Rights Watch called for a halt to use of cluster munitions by allied forces during the Kosovo conflict and later that year formally called for a global moratorium. See HRW, "Ticking Time Bombs: NATO's Use of Cluster Munitions in Yugoslavia," May 1999; "Cluster Bombs: Memorandum for CCW Delegates," December 16, 1999; and "Civilian Deaths in the NATO Air Campaign," February 2000.

11. Explosive remnants of war include cluster munition duds and all other types of explosive ordnance (such as bombs, rockets, mortars, grenades, and ammunition) that have been used in an armed conflict but failed to explode as intended, thereby posing ongoing dangers. ERW also includes abandoned explosive ordnance that has been left behind or dumped by a party to an armed conflict.

12. HRW, "Fatally Flawed: Cluster Bombs and Their Use by the United States in Afghanistan," December 2002.

13. HRW, *Off Target: The Conduct of the War and Civilian Casualties in Iraq* (New York: Human Rights Watch, November 2003).

14. Much of this work was done via e-mail, leading up to a September 2003 meeting in Geneva during which a number of key decisions were made by the volunteer, interim Steering Committee, including the name of NGO alliance (Cluster Munition Coalition), its call to action, initial work plan, and the date and place of the formal launch. The name was suggested by Human Rights Watch, and the call was a variation on HRW's own call for a global moratorium on use, production, and trade of all cluster munitions until the humanitarian problems were successfully addressed.

15. After the necessary twenty ratifications, the protocol entered into force on November 12, 2006. As of September 2007, thirty-four states had ratified but not China, Russia, the United Kingdom, or the United States.

16. HRW Press Release, "New International Law on Explosive Remnants of War," November 28, 2003, http://hrw.org/english/docs/2003/11/28/global13294_txt.htm

17. In the compromise language, States Parties agree: "To continue to consider the implementation of existing principles of international humanitarian law and to further study, on an open-ended basis and initially with particular emphasis on meetings of military and technical experts, possible preventative measures aimed at improving the design of certain types of munitions, including submunitions, with a view to minimizing the humanitarian risk of these munitions becoming ERW. Exchange of information, assistance and cooperation would be part of this work."

18. While calling for an immediate moratorium on use of all cluster munitions, Human Rights Watch and others proposed a variety of positive interim steps that could be taken, including a ban on use in or near populated areas, a ban on use of "worst offenders" (cluster munitions known to have high failure rates, to produce large numbers of duds, or to be very inaccurate), and measures to improve reliability and accuracy.

19. UN Department of Public Information, "Press Conference by Emergency Relief Coordinator," August 30, 2006, http://www.un.org/News/briefings/docs/2006/060830_Egeland.doc.htm

20. Norwegian Ministry of Foreign Affairs, Minister of Foreign Affairs Reply to Olav Akselsen's (Labour Party) question regarding the war in Lebanon and the use of cluster munitions, Written question No. 61 (2006-2007), October 24, 2006 [Translation from the Norwegian], http://www.odin.dep.no/ud/english/news/speeches/minister_a/032171-090682/dok-bu.html (accessed October 25, 2006).

21. UN Secretary General, Message to the Third Review Conference of the CCW, Geneva, November 7, 2006.

22. ICRC, Statement of Dr. Philip Spoerri to the Third Review Conference of the CCW, Geneva, November 7, 2006.

23. "Proposal for a Mandate to Negotiate a Legally-Binding Instrument that Addresses the Humanitarian Concerns Posed by Cluster Munitions," presented by Austria, Holy See, Ireland, Mexico, New Zealand, and Sweden, CCW/CONF.III/WP.1, October 6, 2006. The proposal was also formally supported by Argentina, Bosnia and Herzegovina, Chile, Costa Rica, Czech Republic, Denmark, Germany, Guatemala, Hungary, Italy, Liechtenstein, Lithuania, Luxembourg, Malta, Peru, Portugal, Serbia, Slovakia, Slovenia, and Switzerland.

24. "Declaration on Cluster Munitions," presented by Austria, Belgium, Bosnia and Herzegovina, Costa Rica, Croatia, Czech Republic, Denmark, Germany, Holy See, Hungary, Ireland, Liechtenstein, Lithuania, Luxembourg, Malta, Mexico, New Zealand, Norway, Peru, Portugal, Serbia, Slovakia, Slovenia, Sweden, and Switzerland, November 17, 2006.

25. Afghanistan, Angola, Argentina, Austria, Belgium, Bosnia and Herzegovina, Canada, Chile, Colombia, Costa Rica, Croatia, Czech Republic, Denmark, Egypt, Finland, France, Germany, Guatemala, Holy See, Hungary, Iceland, Indonesia, Ireland,

Italy, Jordan, Latvia, Lebanon, Liechtenstein, Lithuania, Luxembourg, Malta, Mexico, Mozambique, the Netherlands, New Zealand, Norway, Peru, Portugal, Serbia, Slovakia, Slovenia, South Africa, Spain, Sweden, Switzerland, and the United Kingdom. Subsequently, Cambodia became the forty-seventh country to endorse the Oslo Declaration. Oslo Conference on Cluster Munitions, "Declaration," February 22–23, 2007, http://www.regjeringen.no/upload/UD/Vedlegg/Oslo%20Declaration%20(final)%20 23%20February%202007.pdf (accessed March 2, 2007).

26. This is the full text: "Declaration of the Oslo Conference on Cluster Munitions, 22–23 February 2007. A group of States, United Nations Organisations, the International Committee of the Red Cross, the Cluster Munitions Coalition and other humanitarian organisations met in Oslo on 22–23 February 2007 to discuss how to effectively address the humanitarian problems caused by cluster munitions. Recognising the grave consequences caused by the use of cluster munitions and the need for immediate action, states commit themselves to: 1. Conclude by 2008 a legally binding international instrument that will: (i) prohibit the use, production, transfer and stockpiling of cluster munitions that cause unacceptable harm to civilians, and (ii) establish a framework for cooperation and assistance that ensures adequate provision of care and rehabilitation to survivors and their communities, clearance of contaminated areas, risk education and destruction of stockpiles of prohibited cluster munitions. 2. Consider taking steps at the national level to address these problems. 3. Continue to address the humanitarian challenges posed by cluster munitions within the framework of international humanitarian law and in all relevant fora. 4. Meet again to continue their work, including in Lima in May/June and Vienna in November/December 2007, and in Dublin in early 2008, and welcome the announcement of Belgium to organise a regional meeting." Oslo Conference on Cluster Munitions, "Declaration," February 22–23, 2007, http://www.regjeringen.no/upload/UD/Vedlegg/Oslo%20Declaration%20(final)%2023%20February%202007.pdf (accessed March 2, 2007).

27. Norwegian Ministry of Foreign Affairs press release, "Cluster Munitions to Be Banned by 2008," February 23, 2007, http://www.regjeringen.no/en/ministries/ud/Press-Contacts/News/2007/Cluster-munitions-to-be-banned-by-2008.html?id=454942 (accessed March 2, 2007).

28. The list of African countries new to the process included Burundi, Ghana, Guinea-Bissau, Lesotho, Liberia, Mauritania, Senegal, Tanzania, Uganda, and Zambia.

29. States in favor of such exemptions included Australia, Denmark, Finland, France, Germany, Japan, Poland, and the United Kingdom.

30. Geneva Forum and UNIDIR, Disarmament Insight, http://disarmamentinsight.blogspot.com/2007/09/thinking-outside-bomb-road-from-oslo.html.

31. An Argentine company developed and undertook low-level prototype production of self-destructing artillery cluster munitions, but the government decided against procuring the weapons. It destroyed a variety of imported cluster bombs from four countries.

32. "U.S. Reverses Position and Is Now Willing to Negotiate a Cluster Bomb Treaty," *Associated Press* (Geneva), June 19, 2007, http://www.iht.com/articles/2007/06/19/news/bombs.php.

33. The effect of CCW Amended Protocol II on landmines is instructive. While the Ottawa Process led to a comprehensive ban on antipersonnel mines now embraced by 155 nations, the 1996 protocol has resulted in increased production of mines by countries like India, Pakistan, Russia, and China—mines that meet the requirements of the protocol, but which the rest of the world has prohibited.

34. Others include Australia, Canada, Denmark, Finland, Italy, Japan, the Netherlands, Slovakia, Sweden, and Switzerland.

14

Nothing About Us Without Us: Securing the Disability Rights Convention

Jerry White and Kirsten Young

" *NOTHING ABOUT US WITHOUT US!*" is the rallying cry of landmine survivors and people with disabilities around the world. Inclusion and participation are fundamental principles for people who have been historically denied their voice, their dignity, and their basic human rights for millennia.

Today, people with disabilities comprise over 10 percent of the world's population. Eighty percent—about four hundred million—live in developing countries.[1] Most live in poverty and deplorable conditions, with little or no protection under national antidiscrimination laws.[2] Survivors of landmine explosions are a very small subset of the hundreds of millions of people with disabilities in the world today. But landmine survivors have played a very important leadership role to advance human rights and social empowerment not only in the movement to ban landmines but also in recent negotiations for an international Disability Rights Convention.

Without the strong leadership and participation of landmine survivors in the International Campaign to Ban Landmines (ICBL), there would be no treaty obligation for governments to "do their utmost for the care, rehabilitation and social and economic integration of mine victims." Landmine survivors refused to stand on the sidelines in the 1990s during negotiations for the Mine Ban Treaty. They lobbied hard and successfully for humanitarian mine action to address the urgent needs of mine-injured populations. In the end, the efforts paid off. Mine action would include "victim assistance" as one of its four core pillars.

The fact there has never been a United Nations (UN) treaty to ensure fair treatment for people with disabilities is a huge gap in international human rights law. Nearly half the planet is fundamentally affected by disability.[3] There are international human rights laws to protect the rights of women, children, migrant workers, and minorities, but for too long disability has remained an invisible issue, not "worthy" of the world's attention until disability rights organizations banded together for change.

In recent years, survivors have applied lessons learned from their participation in the Nobel Prize-winning ICBL to leadership in negotiations for the United Nations Convention on the Rights of Persons with Disabilities.

Inspired by the experience of the ICBL, diverse groups came together at the UN in 2002 to draft the first major human rights treaty since the end of the Cold War. The new convention creates a comprehensive international framework to address the dearth of protections and fair treatment that people with disabilities have endured in the workplace, schools, health care, government, recreation, family, and community life.

This chapter examines why the international disability rights movement has achieved success so quickly, from the beginning of the negotiation process in 2002 through the homestretch of treaty negotiations finalized in August 2006. In this process, the treaty evolved from a lofty ideal with minimal support from mainstream human rights groups, humanitarian organizations, and donor government agencies to a comprehensive human rights treaty drafted with participation of over 130 governments and 90 nongovernmental organizations. After being negotiated, the treaty was formally adopted by the 61st UN General Assembly on December 13, 2006. It was opened for signature on March 30, 2007, receiving the most number of signatures of any UN treaty in a single day. It is anticipated the pace of the process will continue and the twenty required ratifications will make the Disability Rights Convention international law in 2008.[4]

This chapter will also answer some fundamental questions: Why did survivors and other people with disabilities deem it necessary to have a convention specifically elaborating their rights? How did having persons with disabilities help to lead the process affect outcomes? And how did survivors and civil society affect decision-making on both process and substance? Finally, we will consider the question of whether the disability rights movement has in fact raised the bar with respect to increased participation and inclusion of civil society in future UN negotiations and multilateral diplomacy. Increasingly, the principles of inclusion, participation, and social empowerment are viewed by civil society as prerequisites for legitimacy as states seek to negotiate and enact international standards, laws, and policies. "Nothing about us without us" is about ensuring the voice and consultation of those people most affected by the laws and policies under discussion.

The Call for a Disability Rights Convention

For people with disabilities, the barriers to cultural, economic, political, and social participation are daunting, to say the least. Underserved populations in vulnerable circumstances are in particular need of a strong framework of international law to ensure equal rights and remedy for discrimination. Regardless of complaints about state noncompliance with international laws and policy, such a framework is crucial and sets a standard for all to follow.

Treaties matter. Take, for example, the international landmine ban. In the early 1990s, governments and militaries strongly resisted calls for a global ban on antipersonnel mines. After years of battling with UN strictures, civil society organizations and key governments took a risk in 1996 when then Canadian Foreign Minister Lloyd Axworthy invited governments to negotiate the Mine Ban Treaty *outside* the UN. The need for action was so pressing, civil society banded together in partnership with Canada and other key governments, such as Norway and Austria, to accomplish the goal of drafting an effective treaty. According to Axworthy, the success was not a unique event: "The landmine campaign was a harbinger of the new multilateralism; new alliances among states, new partnerships with non-state actors, and new approaches to international governance."[5]

In similar fashion, persons with disabilities, their representative organizations, and allied NGOs had grown impatient with the promises of governments to improve disability laws and policies. The rights of persons with disabilities have been on the UN agenda for decades. However, unlike other groups (such as racial or ethnic minorities, women, and children), people with disabilities had never succeeded in securing an international treaty specifically addressing their rights.

Until recently, disability was not even considered a human rights issue, but rather a social welfare, charity, or medical concern. While some governments and societies have adopted a social inclusion and rights-based approach to disability issues, many more rely on charity models of assistance or a narrow medical model that focuses on finding medical "solutions" to limitations caused by a disability. But one might ask how medicine can address employment discrimination and physical barriers to social and civic participation? Medical and welfare approaches ignore the need to address the vast array of limitations created and imposed by discrimination, exclusion, and ignorance. If a person with a disability cannot own property or go to school or get into a government building, is that something a charity or a doctor can fix? Obviously not.

Mainstream human rights organizations have largely not addressed disability-related issues, such as policy development or monitoring violations. Kenneth Roth, Executive Director of Human Rights Watch, acknowledged in 2003 that "an embrace of this broad sector of humanity has barely begun. Remedying this failure is a major challenge facing the movement."[6] This challenge not only lies with the human rights community, but also the disability community. In their important work, *A Study on the Current Use and Future Potential of the UN Human Rights Instruments in the Context of Disability*, Theresia Degener and Gerard Quinn concluded that most disability organizations did not have the capacity or resources to access and effectively advocate within the existing international human rights mechanisms.[7] They were also not able to benefit from opportunities to contribute to monitoring, reporting, and other activities of human rights institutions that complement and enhance domestic advocacy.

For these and other reasons, disability issues for decades remained largely invisible on the international rights agenda. Disability remained a question of "social protection," and there were only sporadic and ineffective efforts to draw attention to disability rights as human rights.[8]

False Starts for Disability Rights

The United Nations declared 1981 the "International Year of Disabled Persons." The most important outcome of that declaration was the *World Programme of Action Concerning Disabled Persons*, adopted by the UN General Assembly in 1982, which proclaimed 1983–1992 as the UN Decade of Disabled Persons to provide a time frame during which governments and organizations could implement the activities recommended.

In 1987, halfway through the work of the decade, a Global Meeting of Experts to Review the Implementation of the World Programme of Action concerning Disabled Persons at the Mid-Point of the United Nations Decade of Disabled Persons was held in Stockholm.[9] The meeting recommended that the UN General Assembly convene a special conference to draft an international convention on the elimination of all forms of discrimination against persons with disabilities, to be adopted at the end of the Decade of Disabled Persons in 1992. In response, Italy submitted a draft treaty outline to the UN General Assembly.[10]

In October 1987, the 42nd Session of the UN General Assembly discussed the desirability of an international treaty but did not agree to proceed. At its

44th Session, Sweden raised the issue again, but delegates balked, citing the existing human rights guarantees as sufficient to protect the rights of persons with disabilities.[11]

In 1993, as a compromise for not developing a treaty, the *UN Standard Rules on the Equalization of Opportunities for Persons with Disabilities* ("UN Standard Rules") were adopted. While an important statement of guiding principles, no government is under any legal obligation to follow them, and they were not effective in placing disability on the international agenda, nor in framing disability as a rights issue.

After a lull, in 2000, Ireland raised the issue at the UN Commission on Human Rights by sponsoring a resolution on human rights and disability that included language explicitly supporting a treaty process. The resolution was not agreed.[12] In August–September 2001 during the World Conference Against Racism, Racial Discrimination, Xenophobia and Related Tolerance, Mexico proposed an initiative to develop a convention for people with disabilities.[13] At the 56th Session of the UN General Assembly in 2001, Mexican President Vicente Fox submitted a proposal to establish a special committee to draft a convention to promote and protect the rights and dignity of persons with disabilities. In December 2001, the General Assembly finally adopted a resolution establishing an Ad Hoc Committee "to consider proposals for a comprehensive and integral international convention to promote and protect the rights and dignities, based on a holistic approach in the work done in the fields of social development, human rights and nondiscrimination."[14]

Just as the landmine issue needed to be reframed as a humanitarian rather than strictly security issue in the 1990s, disability needed to be reframed from an issue of health and social welfare to one of poverty eradication and human rights. These issues are inextricably linked, so the convention process appropriately connected human rights and social development (defined by the UN as poverty reduction, social inclusion, and employment generation). Landmine survivors and disability groups welcomed placing treaty negotiations within the larger picture of Secretary-General Kofi Annan's goals for the UN: mainstreaming human rights into development and mainstreaming development into peace.[15] Finally, disability rights were coming out of the shadows, no longer to be seen as "special rights" and taking their rightful place at a larger table of priority global issues.

The Benefits of Inclusion

Landmine survivors and disability groups viewed the establishment of the Ad Hoc Committee as a critical turning point in their advocacy for a convention, but there were no guarantee this process would result in a convention.[16] In its first two-week meeting in July and August 2002,[17] three main issues emerged: how the Committee's work should be organized; how the treaty drafting process should progress; and how NGOs should be involved.[18] The main point coming out of the session highlighted the "shift in focus from care, social welfare and medical support to an emphasis on the human rights framework necessary to pursue the goals of full participation of persons with disabilities in economic, social and political life, and development on the basis of equality."[19] The primary official outcome was simply an agreement to continue discussions on whether there was, in fact, a real need for a convention.

At first, there were few official delegates and NGOs in the meeting room. But, awareness of the need for change grew, particularly with the increasing participation of people with disabilities. There was a fascinating development in the first week of talks. The original room assigned to this low-profile meeting on disability was not accessible to people with disabilities. Sign language interpreters were unable to interpret without people crossing in front them and interrupting the flow of communication, nor could the room accommodate wheelchairs in the NGO section.[20] A new room had to be found to ensure everyone could participate. Even then, over time as more wheelchair users became members of delegations, space still had to be carved out for them to access their country delegation seats. This resulted in the removal of UN-issued chairs and the relocation of government delegates to nontraditional areas. Suddenly, the principle of inclusion was creating quite a stir, turning UN protocol upside down, and demonstrating the extent to which the UN itself was inaccessible and imposed daunting barriers to participation.

Regarding participation, the European Union stated it was of paramount importance for "the most full and most active participation of all interested NGOs" asserting that "this is both important and necessary."[21] Countries from Latin America and the Caribbean, particularly Mexico, argued that the knowledge and experience of persons of disabilities were required and urged the Committee to "show the greatest possible openness in its deliberations."[22] Uganda also called for NGO participation in the drafting process, noting that "no stakeholder should be left out of this process."[23] While the United States acknowledged that disabled persons organizations "have a particular and unique expertise to offer all governments," it also stressed that NGO participation was "an exception to the rule" rather than a precedent-setting development for future debates in the General Assembly.[24]

The small number of NGOs present, including Landmine Survivors Network, successfully persuaded the Committee to welcome their expertise and perspectives.[25] Specifically, there was agreement for NGOs to have speaking rights and be allowed to submit written material. (In the case of the Mine Ban Treaty negotiations, there was more limited participation of NGOs during formal meetings, though the ICBL and ICRC maintained speaking opportunities throughout.) During negotiations for the disability rights convention, NGO partnerships with governments were even more pronounced in some cases, and, in a key development, NGOs were able to make formal proposals.

Many of the participating disability rights advocates already knew each other through previous collaboration to develop the UN Standard Rules, as well as through a strong European-based lobby. Landmine Survivors Network (LSN), a relative newcomer to the disability rights scene, had to build credentials and credibility over time,[26] first by sharing important lessons learned from our work in the ICBL and then by producing several useful advocacy tools such as the *Disability Negotiations Bulletin* to promote the participatory dialogue essential to the development of an effective convention.[27] The EU and other governments also validated LSN participation with their appreciation for "one of the more creative means of communication of the Ad Hoc Committee, namely the Daily Negotiations Bulletin," noting that "none of us has at any point been in doubt of the engagement of the entire group of NGOs in this meeting and in the future process."[28]

Other tools that Landmine Survivors Network developed to strengthen civil society advocates' negotiating capacity included basic guides on how to navigate the UN system.[29] Concerned that meetings would not be officially recorded, LSN hired and trained a team of rapporteurs with disabilities. The team produced Daily Summaries that were translated and distributed worldwide so people from all corners of the globe could keep up to date and participate in the process real time.[30] During this formative stage, LSN was able to mobilize significant resources to train colleagues and leaders from disability groups around the world.[31]

Effective NGO coordination took time to develop. An important and historic step forward was the formation of the International Disability Caucus (IDC) and its Steering Committee at the second session of the Ad Hoc Committee.[32] The role of the Steering Committee was to prepare proposals for decisions to be taken by the wider Caucus, as well as implementing those decisions. The IDC emerged as the definitive coalition coordinating efforts to draft and lobby for a comprehensive Disability Rights Convention, much the same way the ICBL became the lead coalition to promote the development and implementation of the Mine Ban Treaty in the 1990s. From its inception, members of the IDC lobbied for maximum participation of people with disabilities and their representative organizations. "Nothing about us without us" remained the rallying cry.

Momentum Builds When the
Call for the Convention Is Answered

The second Ad Hoc Committee meeting took place in June 2003 and was attended by over one hundred government delegates, a number of UN agencies, and over two hundred legal experts, disability specialists, and representatives from forty-two NGOs and academic institutions.[33] This time NGOs were more prepared, and they came armed to fight for a treaty. Bringing people with disabilities front and center gave the process additional moral and political weight. It would be very difficult for any government representative to say, "We do fine on disability law," when there was a person in a wheelchair at the table who could not physically access school or government buildings back home.

It had been clear from the first meeting that the NGO side lacked a "campaign" approach. They met regularly, but there was little in the way of joint advocacy material and real coordination, and most organizations put forth their own positions. The only display area was dimly lit and uninviting, and the slim volume of materials available did not relate to treaty advocacy but presented somewhat dated and generic material on disability. To change this approach, a number of things happened. Landmine Survivors Network partnered with Disabled Peoples International to prepare premeeting workshops to equip disability advocates from developing countries for the upcoming negotiations and to help them assume leadership roles in advocating nationally, regionally, and internationally for the convention. These intensive trainings were followed by opportunities for participants to apply what they had learned during the two-week negotiation sessions.

Landmine Survivors Network introduced campaigning, communications, and advocacy skills garnered from years of work in the mine ban negotiation process to boost the impact of NGO participation in the new Disability Rights Convention process. It came armed with T-shirts, posters, and stickers in different languages and launched a simple campaign slogan and call to action: "*Convention YES!*"[34] When Kofi Annan addressed the Ad Hoc Committee for the first time, he picked up one of the pens and expressed his sentiments reinforcing "Convention Yes!"[35] Until that moment, the Secretary-General's office had encouraged deliberations, but Annan had not expressed unreserved and clear support for the Convention itself. Another message was "Disability Rights, a Missing Piece of the Human Rights Puzzle." Landmine Survivors Network held lunchtime briefings and breakout sessions to raise awareness on particular issues being negotiated and included NGOs, governments, and UN agencies. As with international landmine meetings, official receptions after hours became a standard feature providing government delegates and civil society the opportunity to mingle and compare notes.[36]

Based on the UN resolution, NGOs were also able to make interventions, which led to a dramatic increase in submissions.[37] In sum, it started to feel like a treaty negotiation. Within the first few days of the meeting, agreement quickly emerged that a convention should be developed, and the main issue then became *how*. The stakes suddenly changed, and organizations began competing with each other to determine who would be the key actors of influence. This too was reminiscent of the landmine movement. Once it was decided that a treaty would be drafted, individual groups were determined to press hard on their particular priorities.

Survivors and People with Disabilities Are Central Part of Negotiations

At its first session, the Ad Hoc Committee agreed to a list of rules and requirements for NGOs' participation. Subject to time, NGOs could make oral and written statements, although the written statements would not be considered official. The rules also called on NGOs to follow UN standards, stating, "If time is limited, a spokesperson may be selected on a balanced and transparent basis, considering equitable geographical representation, and the diversity of NGOs." The International Disability Caucus made significant efforts to ensure that the latter was implemented in practice.

Landmine survivors and other leading disability rights advocates were determined to leverage *all* opportunities to participate. Similar to the Mine Ban Treaty process, there have been clear allies with regard to NGO participation in the Disability Rights Convention process. In terms of civil society, the main actor was the IDC. The key to its success was its diversity of actors, including the voice of LSN and its experience from landmine ban campaigning. The ICBL had benefited from building a large coalition of endorsing organizations, including human rights, humanitarian, religious, and veteran groups. The more the merrier, proving how cross-cutting the landmine issue was and how all social sector organizations could rally in a common cause to address the injustice of landmine proliferation disproportionately injuring civilian populations.

The Disability Caucus Finds a United Voice

Over time, the International Disability Caucus was able to formulate a coherent vision, mission, and value statement for inside and outside stakeholders:[38]

- *Our Vision*: A world free of barriers of all kinds, a world where each person's voice is heard and respected, and their rights honored.

- *Who We Are*: The International Disability Caucus is the representative voice of persons with disabilities in the process to establish a convention to protect and promote the rights of persons with disabilities. It is composed of more than seventy worldwide, regional, and national Disabled People's Organizations (and allied NGOs) who have decided to work together and coordinate their efforts. The IDC includes all the different disability groups and has organizations from all regions of the world. It is open and inclusive to all Disabled People's Organizations (DPOs) as well as other organizations which recognize and accept the leadership role of DPOs.
- *What We Stand For*: The IDC was established by the disability organizations during the first Ad Hoc Committee meeting in order to ensure that the views of people with disabilities would be taken into account in all stages of the negotiation process of the convention.
- *What We Want to Achieve*: Our shared objective is to obtain a convention, which protects and promotes the human rights of all people with disabilities, regardless of the type of disability and the part of the world where we live. We aim at a convention, which is based on the principles of full participation, respect for human diversity, self-determination, nondiscrimination, and equality between women and men.

The IDC worked through consensus, collaboration, and communication. An electronic Listserve was created early in the process to help the Caucus "get on the same page" regarding substantive input on the text, as well as to agree on priorities and process. The IDC also met daily, with rotating chairs, during the Ad Hoc Committee sessions and created, as needed, task forces to address substantive issues.[39]

Similar to the landmine movement, leadership was needed from governments for the Disability Rights Convention, not just civil society. Without key governments the process would have been stalemated. After the second meeting, many more governments became highly engaged. Mexico and Ecuador were certainly leaders. South Africa was close behind, and Jordan led Middle East efforts. The EU was a strong but mixed force; particularly active members included Ireland, Germany, Sweden, and the United Kingdom.

The fast-growing inclusion of persons with disabilities on government delegations had a significant impact on the content and direction of negotiations. Participants included government employees who were disabled[40] to NGO members sitting on government delegations in advisory capacity.[41] For the most part, they participated as full members of the delegation, including making official substantive interventions.[42]

During the Mine Ban Treaty negotiations, some delegations had an NGO member sitting in an advisory capacity, but no landmine survivors were represented on official delegations at the time. Only as the work on its implementation has evolved, has there been a call for governments to "[e]nsure effective integration of mine victims in the work of the Convention, *inter alia*, by encouraging States Parties and organizations to include victims on their delegations."[43]

For the Disability Rights Convention, a turning point for leadership came during the second meeting of the Ad Hoc Committee when governments broke into informal sessions closed to NGOs. Because of NGO-government relationships, NGOs were able to obtain information about what was being discussed, including the two proposals for a drafting mechanism for the convention: (1) an independent expert group (supported by the EU) and (2) a working group (supported by Mexico and some developing countries). The working group approach ultimately prevailed, and then the most controversial issue became its composition. During this period, LSN and other members of the IDC were adamant: "Our participation and our rights cannot be decided behind closed doors. The legitimacy of a human rights treaty on disability depends on the participation of disabled people themselves. Any procedure which fails on this account will not be recognized as legitimate."[44]

Government support for an active NGO role in the negotiating process was ambiguous and mixed. On the one hand, NGO expertise was highly valued and deemed essential, but, on the other hand, some argued the NGO role should be "advisory in character."[45] Equal status for civil society representatives in a treaty-drafting group could portend something new for the UN— not necessarily a development welcomed by governments.[46] It was advised, for example, the draft working group should consist only of states, "assisted" by NGOs and experts. Finally, in the "spirit of flexibility," twelve nongovernmental seats were agreed to, but a delicate distinction was still made with the working group "comprising" twenty-seven member states and "including" twelve NGOs.[47] No matter how you parse the words, this represented an historic breakthrough for civil society inclusion and participation in the formulation and negotiation of international law at the United Nations.

The Working Group was established to prepare and present a draft text as the basis for negotiation at the third meeting of the Ad Hoc Committee in May–June 2004.[48] The official civil society dimension was a first in UN history and formal recognition of the "Nothing About Us Without Us" principle. During the sessions, both in the formal meeting room and in the many working groups set up, civil society participated on an equal basis with governments. The first comprehensive legal analysis of the convention was produced and disseminated by LSN and was used extensively by NGOs and cited favorably by government delegates on several occasions. Protecting their turf, governments still emphasized that "the working group was not a drafting committee, nor did it undertake negotiations, which is the right and prerogative of the Ad Hoc Committee."[49]

Too Many Voices, Too Little Time

The first discussion of the Working Draft text was a free-for-all, characterized by unruly discussion and resulting in an unwieldy compilation of proposals (over 160 pages). Neither states nor NGOs were exempt from this behavior, with over forty countries and twelve NGOs speaking at will. The article on equality and nondiscrimination alone had forty-two proposed amendments. If negotiations were to continue at this pace, and with only two meetings per year, it would take five years to complete a preliminary draft, let alone negotiate a final draft text for UN adoption.

The equal role that NGOs had played in the Working Group was appreciated and acknowledged, but the chair, Ambassador Luis Gallegos of Ecuador, said at the outset there would be a future "distinction between the input of member states and that of NGOs."[50] This meant only the amendments and proposals made by State delegations would be projected on the meeting room screen, and NGOs could only speak after the list of states had been exhausted.

The International Disability Caucus was only just learning to work as a coalition. Members tended to make broad policy statements rather than much-needed textual suggestions. The chair was not clear how to select among IDC members or prioritize their interventions. It became increasingly clear that the IDC would have to learn to discipline its voice and better coordinate communication or risk becoming irrelevant or balkanized by special interest groups.[51]

This emerging dynamic of special interests had the positive effect of getting the IDC to work even harder to reach agreement on common positions. It established thematic working groups to divide and conquer the drafting of coalition position papers and lobbying strategies. This discipline also led to more coordinated work to prepare for subsequent Ad Hoc Committee meetings. It was clear the Caucus needed to start speaking with a unified voice and to leverage diverse government lobbying contacts.

Drawing from experience and connections in the mine ban campaign, Landmine Survivors Network began to lobby for the participation of more diverse players—those who had not previously been exposed to disability rights advocacy but whose presence and voice would add clout to the movement. Landmine Survivors Network wanted more people to know about the historic negotiations taking place in the basement of the UN, so it reached out to the media, which knew very little of the process and then targeted mainstream human rights and humanitarian organizations, such as Amnesty International, Handicap International, Human Rights Watch, and Save the Children, among others. After all, the slogan "Nothing About Us Without Us" was not meant to be exclusive for people with disabilities. It was about inclusion and rights for all, increasing representation and voice for those who could be affected significantly by these negotiations.

Landmine Survivors Network worked closely with the UN Mine Action Service to send letters to Mine Action Centers and Mine Ban Treaty States Parties, encouraging their engagement in the Disability Rights Convention process. Survivors reminded the landmine Victim Assistance community that improved disability laws and policies would in fact strengthen the implementation of Article 6 of the Mine Ban Treaty, which called on states to provide care, rehabilitation, and socioeconomic integration for mine victims worldwide. Landmine Survivors Network emphasized how the convention would:

- Promote human rights knowledge and advocacy skills for landmine survivors (and service providers) in the areas of medical care, physical rehabilitation, socioeconomic reintegration, and psychological support;
- Encourage survivors to participate actively in the disability rights advocacy locally, regionally, and in future monitoring and evaluation mechanisms of the convention; and
- Increase public awareness and mobilize resources to address issues related to disability and survivor recovery in mine-affected countries.

With each UN Disability Rights Convention meeting, there was renewed excitement and support for NGO participation. New Zealand stated that "a founding principle of this Convention is that NGOs should work in partnership to implement this Convention. It would be ironic and inconsistent if the Convention itself excluded NGOs." This was enthusiastically supported by a range of countries, such as Israel, Mexico, Thailand, and Yemen. Canada eventually said it would refuse to facilitate a meeting if NGOs were excluded. The interventions continued on this point with governments trying to "out" which regional group or countries were in fact opposed to growing NGO participation.[52]

By the fourth round of meetings in 2004, it was clear NGOs, such as Landmine Survivors Network and other IDC members could participate openly in formal plenary sessions, but the Committee had not yet adopted a position on NGO participation during "informal" sessions. Some Asian and African countries were opposed to NGOs even observing, let alone participating. Eventually, governments agreed that NGOs could observe informal public sessions but could only speak during formal sessions.[53] The Chair always formally closed the government speaker list in "informal public session" before immediately reopening the public session in order to let civil society speak. Eventually, the IDC called on the Committee to "include us in the whole process."[54]

To help expedite the sometimes mind-numbing treaty text negotiations, the coordinator, Ambassador Don MacKay of New Zealand, started to engage directly and proactively with delegations. He would not just accept a delegate's statement but would ask what specific changes were proposed and why, or how to resolve any outstanding issues or discrepancies in the text. He also made a practice of calling on "experts" as necessary, which allowed NGOs to take the floor even during "informal" sessions to provide expert opinion on particular issues, such as whether sign language was a language or simply a means of communication. At the Seventh Ad Hoc Committee Meeting, civil society proposed an amended version of the Chair's Text. At the Eighth Ad Hoc Committee Meeting, the Convention on the Rights of Persons with Disabilities was adopted by over one hundred UN member states. This document contains text that is mostly drawn from the members of the International Disability Caucus.

Conclusion

Traditionally, nongovernmental organizations have played a shadow role, behind the scenes, in multilateral negotiations for both arms control and human rights conventions. Since the end of the Cold War, however, there has been a trend toward openness and partnership, exemplified by the landmine ban and disability rights movements. Participation and inclusion are emerging as legal obligations, not just principled guidelines. Emerging efforts, such as the Cluster Munition Coalition and the Responsibility to Protect initiative are calling on survivor groups such as LSN to share lessons learned and offer guidance on survivor participation. When it comes to human rights, the Disability Rights Convention undoubtedly sets an important precedent and legal obligation to ensure stakeholder inclusion and participation.

Governments and civil society chose to jump-start negotiations for the 1997 Mine Ban Treaty by taking the process outside the auspices of the United Nations, following the failure of the Convention on Conventional Weapons to address the issue adequately.[55] It took only one year (1996–997) to develop, negotiate, and conclude the Mine Ban Treaty, with 122 states signing on immediately.

Years later, governments sought to expedite negotiations for a UN Disability Rights Convention by inviting NGOs to participate in negotiations inside the UN. This process has taken about four years (2002–2006), with ongoing collaboration and input from global stakeholders. Both the landmine and disability processes benefited enormously from the expertise and participation of civil society and the lived experience of stakeholders. Both treaty processes broke with tradition to birth innovative, comprehensive, and cross-disciplinary frameworks for dealing with their issues.

One can ask, however, whether the disability rights movement has raised expectations in terms of civil society inclusion and participation in multilateral negotiations and diplomacy. We argue that it has. But what are the lessons learned? What impact might be expected from increased government-civil society collaboration in the future? The answer might depend on the extent to which both sides—government agencies and NGOs—take seriously their respective rights and responsibilities in the matter. On the rights side, it is about inclusion and participation. On the responsibility side, the focus should be on the need for strong collaboration and coordination.

Rights: Participation and Inclusion

In the disability rights movement, there are a number of large membership organizations with built-in constituencies to mobilize support for the convention goals. This grassroots presence globally was enormously helpful to build public awareness and political credibility and clout. Governments knew from experience they would hear directly from disability organizations back home in their capitals.

Nevertheless, the level of participation and inclusion of persons with disabilities in the negotiation process was designated primarily by UN resolutions. Each resolution was careful to state it would not serve as a precedent for future negotiations or UN meetings. That said, once a practice has been implemented, particularly when it has been successful, certain expectations are created, and it becomes rather difficult to backpedal. How does one say to a new lobby group, "Sorry, you are not really as important as the previous group, so you will have to be satisfied with fewer participation rights"?

Responsibility: Collaboration and Coordination

As the IDC increased in influence, we were also called upon by the chair, and by the UN member states, to use our participation power effectively and responsibly. This was important to maintain credibility, to increase impact, and to show less-than-enthusiastic governments that NGO inclusion was clearly *not* a waste of resources and time. Rather civil society contributions are cost-effective and vital opportunities to benefit from community expertise and lived experiences.

It is interesting to observe the impact this level of civil society coordination is having in other contexts. During one of the last Bureau meetings held for the UN Commission on Human Rights, members talked to NGOs about how the transition from the Commission to the new Human Rights Council would transpire. Many NGOs were concerned they would not get the right to speak before the Commission had its final session. In response, one Bureau member recommended that the NGOs consider the approach of the IDC, which had proved to be highly effective in its coordination by speaking with one voice on most issues.

This was significant as it indicated IDC leadership on the NGO process by assuming responsibility for coordination and collaboration. It was also important to raise the issue of disability within the human rights discussion. Perhaps even more interesting was the NGO response. One representative dismissed the IDC's coordination as it was only dealing with the "handicap" issue and did not represent diversity of human interest. This is factually wrong as the governments and NGOs participating in this process have found out in the most challenging way. It also shows how much learning still needs to be done, not just in terms of understanding disability as a rights issue but on NGO responsibility to coordinate, coalesce, and collaborate. Coalition work, and what it requires to be successful, will often be in tension with individual organizational power and identity. This is not necessarily about territory, per se, but rather about accountability to an organization's governing board, as well as to its members and donors.

As highlighted above, the Convention negotiations generated unprecedented government-civil society collaboration and spawned a large global network of nongovernmental organizations committed to the universalization of disability rights as human rights. The challenge remains, however, for these diverse groups to work together in common cause to fulfill the promise of the Convention. This promise, of course, is not meant exclusively for 650 million people with disabilities, but for more than six billion people on the planet, most of whom will experience some form of disability at some point in their lives. "Nothing About Us Without Us" remains a principles slogan heralding the importance of inclusion and participation. But in closing, one might also chant "No Success Without the Rest" to indicate the importance of mainstreaming disability rights globally.

Notes

1. Amartya Sen and James D. Wolfensohn, "Helping Disabled People Out of the Shadows," *The Korea Times*, December 21, 2004, http://search.hankooki.com/times/times_view.php?path=hankooki3/times/lpage/opinion/200412/kt2004122118564454330.htm.

2. People with disabilities make up an estimated 15 to 20 percent of people living in poverty in developing countries. In some communities, people with disabilities are regarded as the most disadvantaged by others in the community, and it is frequently observed that in low-income countries, the disabled poor are among the poorest of the poor. Ann Elwan, *Poverty and Disability: A Review of the Literature*, Social Protection Discussion Paper No. 9932 (Washington, DC: The World Bank, 1999), pp. 15–16.

3. The first disability-related website to publicize this was www.halftheplanet.com. The entire global population of six billion people will be affected by disability at one point given illness and aging. If one considers 650 million people living long-term with disability, largely in developing countries with an average family of six people, then nearly half the planet is indeed struggling with issues of disability.

4. Jamaica deposited its ratification on March 30, 2007, becoming the first country to ratify the convention. On March 30, 2007, eighty-one states and the European Community signed the convention and forty-four states signed the convention's optional protocol. The optional protocol provides for an individual complaint mechanism as well as country inquiries. By August 16, 2007, a total of 102 states had signed the convention, 57 had signed the optional protocol, and 4 had ratified. For update of ratifications, see http://www.un.org/esa/socdev/enable/.

5. Lloyd Axworthy, "Towards a New Multilateralism," in Maxwell Cameroon, Robert J. Lawson, and Brian W. Tomlin (eds.), *To Walk Without Fear: The Global Movement to Ban Landmines* (Toronto: Oxford University Press, 1998), p. 448.

6. Landmine Survivors Network, "Strategy Tactics, Empowerment, and Practice," June 2003, p. 2.

7. Gerard Quinn and Theresia Degener (eds.), *The Current Use and Future Potential of the UN Human Rights Instruments in the Context of Disability* (Geneva: Office of the United Nations High Commissioner on Human Rights, 2002), p. 167.

8. Theresia Degener and Gerard Quinn, "A Survey of International, Comparative and Regional Disability Law Reform," presented at *From Principles to Practice, an International Disability Law and Policy Symposium, October 22–25, 2000* organized by Disability Rights, Education and Defense Fund (DREDF), http://www.dredf.org/international/degener_quinn.html.

9. UN General Assembly Resolution 42/58, November 30, 1987, www.un.org/Depts/dhl/res/resa42.htm.

10. UN General Assembly, "Summary Record of the 16th Meeting," 42nd Session, October 19, 1987, A/C.3/42/SR.16.

11. UN General Assembly, "Summary Record of the 16th Meeting," 44th Session, October 24, 1989, A/C.3/44/SR.16.

12. The draft proposal read: "30. Considers that the next logical step forward in advancing the effective enjoyment of the rights of persons with disabilities requires that the Commission for Social Development should, as a matter or urgency, examine the desirability of an international convention on the rights of people with disabilities, and the form and content of such an instrument, and solicit input and proposals from interested parties, including particularly the panel of experts [set up to assist the UN Rapporteur under the UN Standard Rules]."

13. World Conference Against Racism, Racial Discrimination, Xenophobia and Related Intolerance, "Chapter I: Resolutions adopted by the Conference," Durban, August 31–September 8, 2001, p. 67, para. 180: "Invites the United Nations General Assembly to consider elaborating an integral and comprehensive international convention to protect and promote the rights and dignity of disabled people, including, especially, provisions that address the discriminatory practices and treatment affecting them."

14. UN General Assembly Resolution 56/168, December 19, 2001.

15. UN Secretary-General, "In Larger Freedom: Towards Development, Security and Human Rights For All," Report of the Secretary-General, A/59/2005, March 21, 2005.

16. In UN General Assembly Resolution 56/168 establishing the Ad Hoc Committee, the General Assembly invited, inter alia, nongovernmental organizations (NGOs) with an interest in the matter to make contributions to the work entrusted to the Committee, based on the practice of the United Nations. Participation by NGOs in the work of the Committee is regulated by UN General Assembly Resolution 56/510, July 23, 2002.

17. UN General Assembly, Report of the Ad Hoc Committee on a Comprehensive and Integral International Convention on Protection and Promotion of the Rights and Dignity of Persons with Disabilities, A/57/357, August 22, 2002.

18. Some substantive issues relating to the text of the treaty were also raised, but time did not permit in-depth discussion. There was no negotiating text although the European Union and China produced position papers. See UN Department of Economic and Social Affairs, secretariat for the Disability Rights Convention negotiations, http://www.un.org/esa/socdev/enable/rights/ahc1documents.htm. Mexico submitted a draft that was largely ignored at the time because some governments feared Mexico was trying to dominate the process. Its initial draft was presented at a conference in Mexico City, Mexico, held June 11–14, 2002, but was challenged on the grounds of the process not being sufficiently consultative.

19. United Nations Press Release, "Ad Hoc Committee on Convention on Rights of Persons with Disabilities Begins First-Ever Meeting," HR/4618, July 29, 2002, http://www.un.org/News/Press/docs/2002/hr4618.doc.htm.

20. More energy supplies had to be installed as Braille screen reader programs use more energy than a laptop can accommodate in a three-hour period (the length of the negotiation sessions). In addition, as many colleagues do not have access to this level of technology, the UN received an NGO donation of a Braille printer. This helped facilitate negotiations as all actors had access to written material.

21. Landmine Survivors Network, "Disability Negotiations Daily Summary," vol. 1, no. 1, July 29, 2002.

22. Landmine Survivors Network, "Disability Negotiations Daily Summary," vol. 1, no. 1, July 29, 2002.

23. Landmine Survivors Network, "Disability Negotiations Daily Summary," vol. 1, no. 2, July 30, 2002.

24. Landmine Survivors Network, "Disability Negotiations Daily Summary," vol. 1, no. 2, July 30, 2002.

25. In the report of its first session, the Ad Hoc Committee set modalities for participation of accredited NGOs in its open meetings, deciding that representatives from accredited NGOs could participate in the work of the Committee by attending any public meetings of the Committee. Report of the Ad Hoc Committee on a Comprehensive and Integral International Convention on Protection and Promotion of the Rights and Dignity of Persons with Disabilities, A/57/357, August 22, 2002.

26. Newcomers were subsequently invited to a briefing in the first week of each session, and a "Guide for Newcomers to the Process" was produced, with a lot of material drawn from the "Rough Guide," which was produced in 2002 and 2003. The "Rough Guide" was developed to orient disability advocates who would be participating in the Convention negotiations. Both Spanish and Arabic translations were made available. See Landmine Survivors Network, http://www.landminesurvivors.org/what_rights_roughguide.php.

27. These were of great value. Delegates would approach NGO representatives to lobby to have their government well represented in the Bulletin. The importance was not just at the UN, but also at the national level. For example, New Zealand's Disability Office publication "Disability Issues" reported that they had received the NGO Badge of Honor for good interventions. This Badge of Honor appeared on the first page of each Bulletin edition. This effective "naming and shaming" technique was similar to what the ICBL had used effectively with its *CCW News* and "Good, Bad, Ugly" lists that exposed government positions and practices with respect to the total ban on antipersonnel mines. Landmine Survivors Network, http://www.rightsforall.org/library.php.

28. Landmine Survivors Network, "Disability Negotiations Daily Summary," vol. 1, no. 10, August 9, 2002.

29. Campaign Development Group, "Navigating the Ad Hoc Committee: A 'Rough' Guide to NGO Participation in the Development of a Treaty on the Rights of People with Disabilities" (Washington, DC: LSN, July 2002). The Campaign Development Group was a U.S.-based group that was formed to initiate awareness about the Convention negotiations and engage U.S.-based disability groups. For the second Ad Hoc Committee meeting, LSN produced a generic revised "Rough Guide." In order to enhance access for the South, it produced five regional editions, which provided coverage of regional human rights mechanisms and regional organizations working on disability and human rights issues.

30. Landmine Survivors Network, http://www.rightsforall.org/updates2004.php. This service was later taken over by Disabled Peoples' International, Handicap International, International Service for Human Rights, and Rehabilitation International. No daily summaries were produced for the final negotiation sessions in August 2006.

31. STEP Training: Strategy, Tactics, Empowerment and Practice, An education program in high impact human rights advocacy and global networking for the development of an International Convention on the Rights of People with Disabilities, June 12–27, 2003, United Nations Headquarters, New York. The STEP Training, was administered and delivered through a joint partnership between DPI and LSN.

32. At that time called the International Disability Convention Caucus, the Steering Committee was composed of the then seven members of the International Disability

Alliance (IDA): World Blind Union, Rehabilitation International, World Federation of the Deaf, Disabled Peoples International, World Federation of the Deaf Blind, Inclusion International, and the World Network of Users and Survivors of Psychiatry, six regions represented through different organizations (Africa, Arab region, Asia-Pacific, North America, Latin America and Caribbean, and Europe), LSN, Center for International Rehabilitation (CIR), and a seat through which national and other disability organizations were represented. The IDA was formed in the late 1990s and represents disability specific groups. Current IDA members are World Blind Union, Rehabilitation International, World Federation of the Deaf, Disabled Peoples International, World Federation of the Deaf Blind, Inclusion International, the World Federation of the Hard of Hearing, and the World Network of Users and Survivors of Psychiatry. While the Steering Committee had been formed, it was not until much later in the negotiations that the IDC spoke with a single voice.

33. UN General Assembly, Report of the Ad Hoc Committee on a Comprehensive and Integral International Convention on the Protection and Promotion of the Rights and Dignity of Persons with Disabilities, A/58/111, July 3, 2003. Following the recommendations made by the Ad Hoc Committee at its first session, the General Assembly, by Resolution 57/229 of December 18, 2002, decided that the "Ad Hoc Committee should hold . . . at least one meeting in 2003 of a duration of ten days."

34. Landmine Survivors Network's "Convention YES!" became a slogan used by a number of organizations. DPI's newsletter had a specific section and e-mail dedicated to this <convention_yes@dpi.org>, and the Center for International Rehabilitation launched a Convention YES! website to continue the call for action.

35. Secretary-General Kofi Annan made a brief statement welcoming all participants to the UN and applauded the "important work" taking place since the General Assembly passed the resolution establishing the Ad Hoc Committee. He said it was time to "give it meaning" and emphasized his support for the Convention. Notes by author, UN, New York, June 19, 2003.

36. One of LSN's events, the Grammy Award-winning Blind Boys from Alabama performed in concert with Lou Reed and other musicians in the UN General Assembly Hall, creating excitement and building public awareness for the emergent draft convention.

37. All NGOs, regardless of their consultative status with ECOSOC, could send contributions to the Secretariat, in accordance with UN General Assembly Resolution 57/229, para. 7. There was not a time limit to send these contributions, which were also posted during the session. NGO submissions were distributed in the meeting room only if copies had been made available to the Secretariat (in other words, the Secretariat was not in a position of bearing the photocopying costs). All submissions were posted on the DESA website.

38. International Disability Caucus Value Statement, "Nothing About Us Without Us," January 19, 2006. "The IDC undertakes intensive consultation (both before and during the Ad Hoc Committee meetings) amongst its members and their global and regional networks in order to arrive at common positions on all issues. Decisions are made by consensus and when an issue is exclusive to a specific group of people with disabilities, the organization that represents that group plays a determining role in

defining the IDC position. It is important to ensure that all organizations are part of the discussion so all views can be taken into account. Once a decision on a position is made, all IDC members are expected to be publicly supportive of this position. Diverging positions of IDC members should be discussed within IDC, but not in front of Government delegates. Once the IDC has a common position, this is used as the basis for our advocacy work, by: Drafting proposals as well as information sheets which are distributed to all Government delegates; Presenting the position by IDC representatives during the Plenary sessions and smaller working group meetings or through bilateral meetings with Government delegates. IDC members need to familiarize themselves with the key arguments before approaching Government delegates; Presenting the position at IDC briefing sessions or other side events organized by IDC or IDC members; Using it in contacts with Governments before the Ad Hoc Committee meetings; and Promote the Convention and IDC text and policy in our home countries and encourage feedback."

39. By comparison, the ICBL had a strong coordination mechanism. From the outset, there was a campaign coordinator, Jody Williams, hired by the Vietnam Veterans of America Foundation to bring NGOs together in support of a ban on antipersonnel mines. The ICBL's first conference was held in May 1993, when six sponsoring organizations formed the ICBL Steering Committee. Affiliated national campaigns also had coordinators or chairs. The ICBL developed disciplined lobbying and reporting routines, including regular morning and evening briefings during landmine meetings worldwide.

40. For example, Canada.

41. For example, Bosnia and Herzegovina.

42. At various times, persons with disabilities have been on delegations for the following countries: Argentina, Australia, Bosnia and Herzegovina, Brazil, Canada, Chile, Costa Rica, Croatia, El Salvador, Ethiopia, EU (various members, including Ireland, Italy, Finland, Sweden, and the United Kingdom) Israel, Jordan, Kenya, South Korea, Lebanon, Mexico, Namibia, New Zealand, Norway, Qatar, Serbia and Montenegro, South Africa, Thailand, Uganda, and Yemen.

43. First Review Conference of the States Parties to the Convention on the Prohibition of the Use, Stockpiling, Production, and Transfer of Anti-Personnel Mines and on Their Destruction, "Final Reports: Part III. Ending the suffering caused by antipersonnel mines: Nairobi Action Plan 2005–2009," Nairobi, November 29–December 3, 2004, APLC/CONF/2004/5, February 9, 2005.

44. Landmine Survivors Network, "Disability Negotiations Daily Summary," vol. 2, no. 7, June 24, 2003.

45. Landmine Survivors Network, "Disability Negotiations Daily Summary," vol. 2, no. 8, June 25, 2003.

46. For example, Iran cautioned the "invention of something new within the framework of the UN" and questioned if a working group composed of NGOs and states side-by-side had ever been seen before. Iran also had difficulty with giving NGOs the same status as member states especially if the working group "entailed negotiation" but reiterated that the working group should benefit from the "assistance and expertise" of NGOs. LSN, "Disability Negotiations Daily Summary," vol. 2, no. 8,

June 25, 2003. Malaysia and Indonesia were also concerned about creating precedent but agreed to NGO inclusion.

47. Report of the Ad Hoc Committee on a Comprehensive and Integral International Convention on the Protection and Promotion of the Rights and Dignity of Persons with Disabilities, A/58/111, July 3, 2003, p. 7. "The Working Group shall comprise twenty-seven governmental representatives designated by the regional groups (Asia 7, Africa 7, Latin America and Caribbean 5, Western Europe and Other 5, Eastern Europe 3). The Working Group shall also include twelve representatives of nongovernmental organizations (NGOs), especially organizations of persons with disabilities, accredited to the Ad Hoc Committee, to be selected by those organizations, taking into account the diversity of disabilities and of NGOs, ensuring adequate representation of NGOs from developing countries and from all regions. It will also include a representative from national human rights institutions accredited to the International Coordinating Committee." The NGOs ultimately selected were considered to be the most representative. There were the seven IDA organizations, and five NGOs representing the five regional groups.

48. Landmine Survivors Network played a key role in drafting, proposing, and negotiating treaty text. LSN-Jordan Director Adnan Al Aboudi was one of twelve NGO representatives selected for the Draft Working Group.

49. Landmine Survivors Network, "Disability Negotiations Daily Summary," vol. 4, no. 1, May 24, 2004.

50. Landmine Survivors Network, "Disability Negotiations Daily Summary," vol. 4, no. 1, May 24, 2004.

51. An unexpected dynamic was the arrival of "pro-life" actors who legitimately used the disability negotiations, just as they would any forums, to promote their policies on reproductive rights. They sought to ensure the treaty did not go into "uncharted and controversial directions" by mentioning any sexual relationship outside the context of marriage.

52. South Africa conceded that the African regional group felt, as per UN rules, that if there is no consensus on NGO participation, then only government delegations should participate.

53. Report of the Ad Hoc Committee on a Comprehensive and Integral International Convention on the Protection and Promotion of the Rights and Dignity of Persons with Disabilities on its fourth session, Annex III, A/59/360, September 14, 2004, p. 8. Annex III sets modalities for the participation of accredited NGOs and National Human Rights Institutions in its informal consultations closed meetings during the fourth and fifth session.

54. Landmine Survivors Network, "Disability Negotiations Daily Summary," vol. 5, no. 2, August 24, 2004.

55. Although negotiated outside the traditional UN framework, various UN agencies and the Secretary-General were supportive of and involved in the process, and the Secretary-General is the depository of the treaty.

15

Tackling Disarmament Challenges

John Borrie

A̲ₗₜₕₒᵤ𝓰ₕ LTHOUGH THE SPECTER OF INTERNATIONAL TERRORISM has become preeminent since the 9/11 attacks in 2001, disarmament and arms control
themes also run through some of the major issues of our time. For example,
Iraq was invaded in March 2003 on the grounds that it possessed and was hid-
ing weapons of mass destruction (it was not—at least not by then). In early
March 2006, U.S. President George W. Bush announced a deal with India on
nuclear cooperation, in effect overturning India's international pariah status
for spurning the obligations of the Nuclear Non-Proliferation Treaty (NPT)
in favor of a nuclear arsenal. President Bush has subsequently been sharply
criticized for the harm done to multilateral norms and to U.S. leadership in
containing the spread of nuclear weapons, even by members of his own Republican Party. Later, in October of that year, North Korea detonated a nuclear
device, becoming a *de facto* nuclear power.

Another story dominating news headlines throws this alleged double standard into stark relief: the continuing showdown between Iran and the United
States and the latter's supporters in the International Atomic Energy Agency
(IAEA) and United Nations Security Council over Teheran's nuclear activities. Iran maintains that its enrichment of uranium is intended solely for civil

John Borrie leads a project entitled "Disarmament as Humanitarian Action: Making Multilateral Negotiations Work" at the United Nations Institute for Disarmament Research (UNIDIR) in Geneva. The
views expressed in this paper are the sole responsibility of the author and do not necessarily reflect the
views or opinions of the United Nations, UNIDIR, its staff members, or sponsors. Even so, the author
wishes to thank Vanessa Martin Randin, Aurélia Merçay, and Eoghan Murphy for their comments and
support.

purposes and is within its rights. Iran's critics accuse it of cheating on its nuclear nonproliferation obligations.

Meanwhile, other weapons of mass destruction are at work far from the television cameras and newspaper headlines. Small arms, landmines, cluster munitions, and explosive remnants of war (ERW) claim many thousands of lives each year.[1] Their pernicious effects tend to be worst in the poorest and least developed countries of the world and affect the most vulnerable people. Beyond those they kill or maim, the "indirect" effects of these weapons exacerbate other problems by, for instance, impeding access to clean water, adequate food, medical services, and schools. Greater civilian misery and mortality due to malnourishment, disease, and insecurity are often the result.[2]

To people living in these communities, diplomatic deliberations about nuclear, chemical, or biological weapons must seem rather esoteric. The conceptual gulf can also be hard to bridge from the diplomatic side since international security-related processes are often highly politicized and very technical. Many in the diplomatic elite have had little or no practical experience of the personal consequences of living in insecurity. Those involved in such processes may overlook the reality that failure to disarm has real human costs. They may also be uncertain about how to devise effective responses to disarmament challenges within existing political and procedural constraints.

Disarmament itself has also become a rather loaded term, carrying different connotations depending on who is using it and why. Certainly it is a concept currently out of vogue among the major military powers. This is reflected by their lack of progress on disarmament and arms control measures at the multilateral level in recent years.[3] Despite pressing imperatives, the Conference on Disarmament (CD) in Geneva dedicated to these tasks remains in deadlock after almost a decade—unable even to agree on a Work Program.[4] In May 2005, the five-year review meeting of the NPT failed to achieve anything substantial despite serious challenges to the global nuclear nonproliferation regime.[5] Meanwhile, international efforts to curb the illicit trade in small arms and light weapons remain highly constrained.[6] And after a promising start on tackling the post-conflict effects of ERW, states working in the context of the Convention on Conventional Weapons (CCW) appear to have run out of steam in their efforts to deal with the deadly effects of antivehicle mines and cluster munitions on civilians, prompting the emergence of an international Oslo Process to address the humanitarian impacts of the latter.[7]

Where limited progress in the disarmament and arms control domain has been achieved over the last decade, humanitarian approaches tend to have accompanied it. One element of these approaches is increased emphasis on the individual and the community as referent points for "human security" alongside traditional national security perspectives.[8] Another common element is the involvement of practitioners from the field.[9] The process that led to the 1997 Mine Ban Treaty, in which field-based medical people and deminers played prominent roles, is perhaps the most striking example of the positive difference these perspectives can make although it is by no means the only one.[10]

Alongside these elements, the input and pressure of international organizations, academic and policy researchers, as well as nongovernmental organizations (NGOs) and their networks also usefully supplement the work of governments by proposing alternatives to the orthodox ways of framing and responding to global problems of human insecurity.[11] Current international preoccupations, for instance with terrorism, risk obscuring the importance of maintaining and developing durable multilateral norms and institutions to enhance collective security over the longer term.

This chapter describes multilateral disarmament efforts with a view to explaining the challenges ahead. Terms such as multilateralism, disarmament, and arms control are briefly explained, as well as the main features of how governments conduct disarmament. Current disarmament and arms control efforts are reviewed but found not to be particularly effective (although there are interesting exceptions like the Mine Ban Treaty). While there are no simple answers, the chapter also considers how current efforts can be reframed to better tackle disarmament.

The State of the Art

Multilateralism, as academics use the term, generally means a commitment to maximum participation in dialogue among political, social, economic, and cultural forces to resolve conflicts and design institutional processes.[12] That is rather a mouthful. In practice it is also a concept that is more aspirational than actual because the building block of the contemporary international system is the nation-state, and this imposes constraints on participation. National governments have always made the rules and although varying by issue area, the level of access or influence they are prepared to afford others in multilateral work has usually been guarded.

Recognition of the roles that actors outside of governments may play has traditionally been rather limited in international security. For example, NGOs and even international organizations like the IAEA are not permitted to participate directly in the work of the CD. Access to international meetings on curbing the illicit trafficking in small arms is very limited.[13] Ostensibly this reluctance to allow these actors significant roles is because matters of security are the sovereign prerogative of national governments alone. And, national governments—at least in democratic countries—are accountable to their electorates and so can claim legitimacy that NGOs and others cannot.[14] Historically, it is because transnational civil society initiatives and international organizations appeared later than states and so often remain marginalized as a result.

Disarmament and Humanitarian Action: An Intrinsic Link

Disarmament is "the traditional term for the elimination, as well as the limitation or reduction (through negotiation of an international agreement) of the means by which nations wage war."[15] It shares roots with international humanitarian law (IHL or the "laws of war"). Although taboos have existed on certain weapons or types of behavior in war for many centuries, more explicit IHL prohibitions began to emerge toward the end of the nineteenth century. The 1868 St. Petersburg Declaration banning explosive "dum dum" bullets was followed later by the 1899 and 1907 Hague Conferences—convened at the initiative of Russia, which was lagging in the European arms race and could not afford to keep up with its rivals because of economic weakness. This illustrates that humanitarian objectives have never been divorced from pragmatic considerations.

It was during this period that the modern humanitarian movement also began to emerge, including the establishment of the Red Cross Movement in 1863, which later divided into the International Committee of the Red Cross (ICRC) and national societies, as well as the appearance of many other humanitarian entities in the late nineteenth and twentieth centuries. As an international organization, the ICRC plays an active role in multilateral processes related to IHL to this day although its efforts—for instance in promoting efforts to prevent poison and deliberate spreading of disease—have been resisted by some states who argue the ICRC has strayed too far on to disarmament turf.[16]

During the past century, the dangers to civilians from new types of weaponry have increased greatly. Technologically, civilian populations are potentially more vulnerable today than ever. Underlining this vulnerability, the noted arms control expert Jozef Goldblat observed:

> All laws of war suffer from one common weakness: the rules of conduct established for belligerents in time of peace may not resist the pressure of military expedience generated in the course of hostilities, and the attempts to "humanise" war may sometimes prove futile. The danger that the weapons prohibited may, under circumstances, be resorted to—as has occurred on several occasions—will

not disappear as long as these weapons remain in the arsenals of States. Hence the intrinsic link between the development of the humanitarian laws of war and progress in the field of disarmament.[17]

The Cold War

The struggles of World War II profoundly altered the international landscape and, along with it, the nature of multilateral efforts. Decolonization was beginning. A bipolar world was emerging with the United States and the Soviet Union preeminent. The new United Nations was founded with the promise of maintaining international peace and security, of securing justice and human rights and of promoting, in the words of its Charter, "social progress and better standards of life in larger freedom," something that proved to be impossible in this new polarized environment.[18]

Instead of disarmament, the initial decades of the Cold War saw military escalation. Members of the new North Atlantic Treaty Organization (NATO) and their Warsaw Pact adversaries developed their conventional capabilities for an expected eventual war in Europe alongside nuclear arsenals and chemical and biological weapons programs. Fears grew about the "missile gap" and nuclear strategic doctrines, like Mutually Assured Destruction, were put into effect. Prospects for disarmament seemed bleak.

Nevertheless, due to widespread fears among its members about nuclear war, the UN soon became involved in arms control through its General Assembly, the UN Security Council, a Disarmament Commission (established in 1952 and today wholly deliberative) and various studies and reports over the decades.[19] The General Assembly also set up a disarmament committee in 1959, initially with ten member countries including France, the United Kingdom, the United States, and the Soviet Union, which was only then becoming regarded as having military parity with the Western powers. Over time this negotiating body expanded and went through various name changes until by the middle of the 1980s, it had become known as the Conference on Disarmament, which today has sixty-five member countries.

Arms control is not the same thing as disarmament although the two terms are often used interchangeably. Arms control came into vogue in the 1950s to refer to international agreements intended to limit the arms race between the United States and the Soviet Union. From the 1960s, nonproliferation also became a commonly used term and falls within the umbrella concept of arms control. A more recent term, probably coined in the United States, is that of counterproliferation, or "military efforts to combat proliferation, including the application of military power to protect forces and interests, intelligence collection, and analysis."[20] Counterproliferation became an official pillar of the Bush administration's national security strategy from 2002.[21] It was an important justification for the United States' invasion of Iraq in March 2003 on the grounds that Iraq possessed weapons of mass destruction.

While there is not space to recount the history of arms control or nonproliferation agreements during the Cold War, a few prominent examples stand out:

- The 1968 Nuclear Non-Proliferation Treaty is still regarded as the multilateral cornerstone of international efforts to curb and roll back the spread of nuclear weapons. The treaty creates two classes of state— nuclear weapon states (China, France, Soviet Union, the United Kingdom, and the United States)—and nonnuclear weapon states (everyone else). The basic deal enshrined in the NPT is that the nonnuclear weapon states commit themselves not to develop nuclear weapons in exchange for the right to peaceful nuclear technologies under IAEA safeguards. Nuclear weapon states are supposed to disarm eventually. Nonnuclear weapon states tend to stress the disarmament and technology transfer aspects of the treaty, while nuclear weapon states attach priority to the NPT's nonproliferation obligations. Israel, India, and Pakistan have never joined the treaty and in 2003, North Korea became the first NPT member to invoke the treaty's withdrawal clause.[22]
- The 1972 Bacteriological (Biological) and Toxin Weapons Convention (BTWC) completely bans biological weapons. The BTWC lacks a verification regime to ensure compliance, and instances of cheating include a huge Soviet biological warfare program until the end of the Cold War.[23] Subsequent negotiations on a regime to ensure compliance with the BTWC collapsed in 2001, prompted by American rejection of a draft protocol.[24] Another challenge for the BTWC and the Chemical Weapons Convention (mentioned below) is in responding to new technologies: some countries are trying to develop so-called non-lethal or less-lethal weapons like those used in the 2002 Moscow theater siege that would undermine the spirit and purpose of these treaties.[25]
- The 1980 Convention on Conventional Weapons was negotiated after some countries raised concerns about the use of napalm and cluster bombs during the Vietnam War. To date cluster munitions have still not been specifically addressed, but as a framework treaty the CCW formed the basis for negotiation of useful protocols to restrict various weapon systems including incendiary weapons and blinding lasers. In 2003, agreement was reached on a protocol containing modest measures to reduce the humanitarian impact of ERW after conflicts have ended.[26] This fol-

lowed the CCW's earlier failure to ban antipersonnel mines in 1996, resulting in the Ottawa Process outside of the CCW that led to the Mine Ban Treaty in 1997.[27]

- The 1990 Treaty on Conventional Armed Forces in Europe (CFE) was negotiated within the Organization for Security and Cooperation in Europe (OSCE). This treaty followed a long period of discussions usually referred to in the West as the Mutual and Balanced Force Reduction talks (MBFR), which began in Vienna in 1973. Although these talks ultimately failed to make much progress, they paved the way for the CFE talks from March 1989 that rapidly forged an agreement to achieve major reductions in the levels of NATO and Warsaw Pact conventional military forces stationed in Europe.[28]

This list of examples is obviously selective. For example, it does not feature agreements like the 1963 Partial Nuclear Test Ban Treaty or the 1967 Outer Space Treaty. Nor are the nuclear Strategic Arms Limitation Talks (SALT) agreements or the 1972 Anti-Ballistic Missile (ABM) Treaty covered, which were ostensibly bilateral arrangements between the United States and the Soviet Union—although they did benefit from trust building in multilateral forums like the UN, the MBFR talks, and the CD.[29]

Stalling Efforts

With the end of the Cold War in the early 1990s, there was widespread optimism that a more benign international security environment would improve prospects for disarmament. For the first time there was a glimmer of hope that nuclear arsenals would shrink and perhaps even be totally eliminated. In addition to the CFE Treaty already mentioned, the 1993 Chemical Weapons Convention (CWC) and then the 1996 Comprehensive Nuclear Test-Ban Treaty (CTBT) were negotiated in the CD during this period. The CFE, however, later needed work to fit with changing post-Cold War realities and has faced problems in its implementation.[30] In July 2007, Russia announced that it intended to suspend its involvement in the CFE.[31] With the benefit of hindsight, the CWC's rapid completion (after many years of moribund talks in the CD) was because the United States decided to throw its weight behind the project after the first Gulf War in 1991, in which Saddam Hussein had threatened to use chemical weapons. The CTBT's negotiations were pressured and difficult. Crucially, a decision was made in its final phases to include an entry-into-force formula that depended on a list of "key countries"—a provision that has prevented the treaty from entering into force a decade later.

By the turn of the twenty-first century, multilateral disarmament and arms control progress had slowed practically to a standstill. The CD has not worked since completion of the CTBT because it cannot even agree on its annual Work Program. Derived from an outdated Decalogue of issues agreed to in 1978, the Decalogue itself only persists because countries cannot agree on how to replace it.[32] BTWC protocol negotiations failed in 2001. The NPT— originally a treaty of only a twenty-five-year duration—was indefinitely extended in 1995, and in 2000 "13 steps" on nuclear disarmament were agreed upon.[33] Despite modest bilateral initiatives like the Moscow Treaty in May 2002 between the United States and Russia, the nuclear weapon states have done little to implement these steps and there have been some steps backward like the Bush administration's withdrawal from the ABM Treaty.[34] Moreover, even though there are challenges looming over the nuclear nonproliferation regime, States Parties to the NPT were unable to agree on anything at the review meeting in New York in May 2005, which ended in disarray.[35]

History shows that multilateral forums have not been very effective in building or strengthening new disarmament and arms control norms except in brief bursts, such as in the 1990s. For most of the Cold War, like today, the CD and UN disarmament bodies were able to do little. It is tempting to blame the major powers—and lately the United States in particular—for this failure. Critics have observed that U.S. leadership has often been crucial to the success of these efforts, but that "unilateralism" has become a byword since the Bush administration came to power. They charge that his approach has hurt the prospects of traditional disarmament forums like the CD, and treaty processes like the BTWC. In many respects, it certainly has not helped.[36] But such criticism fails to address valid concerns about the effectiveness of multilateral disarmament processes, even as Washington promotes *other* forms of collective international action like the Proliferation Security Initiative, claiming that such actions are activities, not processes.[37]

Key to tackling current and future disarmament challenges more effectively will be greater recognition that difficulties in multilateral work are not simply due to political problems. Collective perceptions, and the structures of international security politics, also create obstacles to progress for which no single country or person is responsible. This chapter will now consider these factors, alongside questions of perceived national interest, with a view to better disarmament responses.

Let Them Eat Cake

At the heart of all of the tough disarmament negotiations, and all the troubled efforts to reform multilateral processes like the UN or the CD, is a basic problem—and it is about cake. No matter how carefully a parent divides a cake between two children, one kid (or both!) feels slighted with a smaller piece. In other words, the cake problem is a conflict of interests. The solution, of course, is to trust self-interest to ensure fair division: let one child divide the cake and then let the other have first choice. "Both children want the same thing—as much of the cake as possible. The ultimate division of the cake depends both on how one child cuts the cake and which piece the other child chooses. It is important that each child anticipates what the other will do."[38] Rational self-interest indicates that the cutter will try to split the cake as evenly as possible since the chooser will take the bigger of two nearly identical pieces.

This story about cake is not only familiar to every parent, it also illustrates what game theorists refer to as a form of simple two-person decision-making under conditions of uncertainty called the "minimax principle." The cake-cutting exercise highlights a basic question for both the cutter and the chooser: what is the other going to try to do? This is a problem each actor in the much more complex multilateral system faces all the time—uncertainty about the intentions of others and, in addition, about what will happen in the future as they repeatedly interact. ("Actor" here refers not only to countries but can also refer to individuals.) International relations are essentially the problem of cooperation played out among states with different levels of interest, power, and resources and—crucially—differing perceptions of what is in their self-interest. These states can be expected to try to maximize their interests (that is, get the biggest piece of cake they can) *if* they know what is good for them.

In the cake-cutting exercise, the rules have been imposed from outside, and the cutting is zero-sum in the sense that gains for either the cutter or chooser occur at the expense of the other. But in multilateral processes, which are intended to be non-zero sum (that is, everyone should, in theory, get some benefit if they play by the rules), there are many more than two kids. Extra kids results in greater uncertainty. Moreover, the children themselves are responsible for developing and enforcing the rules rather than a hovering parent. What happens if one big, strong kid decides to hell with it—she will help herself to as much cake as she likes? Is it worth other kids getting into a fight with her over the cake? Depending on whether one perceives the cake-cutting exercise to be a one-off encounter or whether it will be repeated with the same kids in the future may affect the answer. Also pertinent is how strong one considers oneself to be. Is it worth living by the rules if you also think you can do better by flouting them when you can? Another difference is that the minimax principle has a clear optimum solution. In complex multilateral negotiations, it can be very difficult to assess what that solution might be.

The cake-cutting story is relevant to how we think about tackling disarmament challenges more effectively because it shows that making decisions based on perceptions of self-interest—whether over dividing a cake or reforming multilateral disarmament processes—is always entangled with the structures (the rules) within which these decisions are made. As such, both context and perceptions of utility are malleable to the effects of the other: "not only can actors in world politics pursue different strategies within an established context of interaction, they may also seek to alter that context through building institutions embodying particular principles, norms, rules, or procedures for the conduct of international relations."[39] Or, for that matter, we may see those actors block progress and ignore or even try to break down an institution when it is considered prejudicial to their self-interest if they are in a position to do so. American abrogation of the ABM Treaty and rejection of BTWC protocol negotiations are two examples in recent years.

In contrast, a favorite chestnut of diplomats is to talk about "lack of political will" to explain why multilateral disarmament and arms control processes fail to achieve results. Political will is fine as shorthand for specific underlying difficulties in a given situation. But in explanatory terms, blaming political will is about as useful as citing "bad karma." Both automatically assume the influence of intentional agency and ignore the influence of structure on our perceptions. Also, political will is often used to explain difficulties *across* different processes without acknowledging that similar-looking obstacles may actually be very different in nature. Correlation is not causality. Blaming all multilateral difficulties on lack (or the wrong kind) of political will fails to help distinguish between problems that are *intentionally* caused and those that are coincidental or *unintended consequences* of previous actions.

This is an important point because multilateralism is sometimes described in mechanistic terms. Diplomats in Geneva, NGOs, and political scientists often talk about "the disarmament machinery"—of a range of institutions that, by inference, function when requested and as intended. Sometimes metaphors are mixed together, and we are told that political will is like fuel powering this machinery. The truth is that multilateral processes *are not* machines in any designed sense. As is clear from the description of how multilateral diplomacy evolved in the first part of this chapter, no engineer took a clean sheet of paper and concocted a rules-based multilateral system from first principles (like the parent imposing the rules in the cake-cutting story). Instead, multilateral disarmament structures such as treaties, institutions, and the collective tendencies of diplomats toward their work—their "community of practice"—are largely inherited.[40] These structures are continually affirmed or progressively modified by the everyday operation of precedent, itself implicitly seen by multilateral practitioners as a way to minimize uncertainty and manage troublesome change.

All of this makes it possible to see how the evolution of multilateral disarmament diplomacy has had unintended consequences for its continued effectiveness. Decision-making at the multilateral level is now too often considered by negotiators in light of its disruptive effects on process rather than matching effective means to ends. Examples include:

- *Tyranny of consensus:* this appears in multilateral disarmament and arms control processes like the CD, the BTWC, and NPT review processes. By exploiting procedural tactics, an obstructive few can—and often do—prevent cooperation that would yield security benefit to all. The problem is that if there is obvious need to negotiate a strong new treaty—say, a ban on cluster munitions for humanitarian reasons—logically, those who use the weapons would likely object to such an agreement and block consensus, which they often do. It is therefore worth noting that unlike disarmament and arms control, making decisions by consensus is not the norm in IHL processes.

- *Outdated and restrictive regional group systems:* rather than facilitate information exchange and likeminded cooperation, these sometimes act as caucuses in which more powerful states can prevent it by slapping others into line. Today's UN regional groups—and those in the CD—of East, West, and South (Non-Aligned) date from Cold War days and bear little resemblance to current realities. For instance, on nuclear issues the divide tends to be between the nuclear weapon possessing states and nonnuclear weapon states rather than East versus West, or North versus South. Moreover, in the CD's Program of Work, the regional group coordination system actually allows those disinclined to cooperate to hide behind others.[41]

- *Command-and-control mentality:* as we have seen, multilateral diplomacy today is based on a state-centered system in which interactions between states determine security pay-offs, for instance on whether to outlaw explosive bullets or reduce numbers of intermediate range nuclear missiles. A convenient fiction maintained is that governments are unitary entities and multilateral negotiators are the tip of the spear of their national bureaucracies political decision-making establishments. Not only is this a poor reflection of how decisions are often made at the domestic level, "top-down" models of problem-solving are becoming less effective in both disarmament and IHL. Problems of interconnection, such as individual perceptions of insecurity driving illicit gun possession or diffusion of technologies that could be turned to hostile use (as seen with the Tokyo nerve gas attacks in 1995 and anthrax-in-the-mail attacks in the United States in 2001), are emerging as key challenges. Individual behavior and social interactions increasingly matter in understanding and addressing security problems.[42] Self-interested behavior related to the use of armed violence will not simply disappear with a wave of the treaty-maker's wand, as those living under the gun in Brazil's *favelas* or South Africa's townships know only too well.

- *Dead precedents*: multilateral institutions can benefit states, for instance, by helping them cope with uncertainty and swap information as well as to reduce the costs of cooperating with each other (a bit like sharing the costs of running the clubhouse). However, because it is hard for states with competing or conflicting interests to sustain cooperation, decision-making processes can become backward looking and try to cope with new problems based on established responses to previous challenges. They do this on grounds that the more similar the next response is to something already agreed upon, the easier it will be to understand its implications and agree on something again. Such a sense of conservatism inhibits innovative ways to effectively tackle new challenges.

What Can Be Done?

There seems to be agreement, even among multilateral disarmament diplomats, that their activities are not as effective as they should be—although states certainly do not agree on remedies. Any genuine attempt at reform will face the reality that reshaping institutions like the CD or the UN is likely to fail unless perceptions of self-interest like the relative values of "ends" (security goals) and "means" (process and procedure) are also reshaped. Principles, procedures, and rules are necessary—they are what distinguish multilateral approaches to problem-solving from anarchic competition and a dog-eat-dog world. But in many disarmament contexts, such as the CD, procedural considerations have become too dominant and stymie progress.

Changing perceptions of self-interest is therefore key because it is naïve to expect governments (any more than individuals) to cooperate altruistically on a sustained basis—to do, in effect, what is not in their best interest. What is also at issue is that governments alone cannot solve many contemporary transborder security challenges. These challenges require sustained cooperation between states in order to be tackled successfully, and with other kinds of actors, including from civil society.

How can perceptions of self-interest be reshaped? One way is to view *disarmament as humanitarian action*. Understanding perceptions of insecurity from the perspective of individuals and their communities can enhance national security viewpoints. In turn, this may allow the reframing of security problems characterized more by their interconnections, like small arms proliferation or the diffusion of new technologies that could be turned to hostile misuse. Such recognition would suggest new ways to understand and influence issues, which legal bans or other "'top-down" regulatory approaches by governments sometimes fail to do. Moreover, including field-based and other civil society perspectives would broaden the diversity of multilateral disarmament policymaking, still dominated by people (still predominantly middle-aged men of a certain economic and cultural standing) who often seem insulated from the human costs of the use of weapons in question.

In other words, key to tackling future disarmament challenges at the multilateral level will be an evolved sense of "enlightened self-interest." An important component of that will be a broader and keener understanding of how the dynamic process of cooperation evolves and that consensus is a possible goal, rather than the prerequisite it is currently often perceived to be. It is no accident that every successful disarmament activity in the multilateral domain in recent years has resulted from the work of like-minded states, often working informally without assuming multilateral consensus. The evolution of European support for the Ottawa Process in the mid-1990s, for instance, reflected this process well: "a few leading states, a number of followers, and a handful of hold-outs."[43] As seen in the Ottawa Process, individual representatives of governments are vital to the trust building that enables this kind of cooperation to be sustained, grow, and become more formal in time.

Conclusion: Shake It Up, Baby

This chapter has ranged freely throughout multilateral disarmament and arms control and has not focused particularly on the Mine Ban Treaty. Instead it has been about trying to connect the dots to see how the challenges of reducing human insecurity in real terms can be better met by multilateral disarmament activities. It is clear that blind faith in multilateral *institutions* is misplaced and that governments, despite their promises, do not have all of the answers. If they did, they would be much more successful than they currently are in disarmament. But this should not be cause for fatalism. Sustainable cooperation does not spring from altruism. It eventually delivers benefit, or it breaks down. These benefits must be the ultimate goal for multilateral efforts, a point on which anxious governments sometimes lose their way in focusing too narrowly or solely on national security. That is why the capacity and willingness to reframe issues of insecurity in alternative terms, like viewing disarmament as humanitarian action, is important.

Reframing disarmament as humanitarian action is by no means an "all singing, all dancing" solution to overcoming obstacles in multilateral diplomacy.

But it can help governments develop a clear sense of what it is they want from disarmament processes—which is sometimes lacking—and prepare them to be more flexible and innovative to achieve it. If they are not working in good faith or see no need to change the way they perceive their national and individual self-interests, no amount of reform is going to make current disarmament forums more successful.

Even so, this does not mean progress in multilateral disarmament is impossible. Humanitarian and "human security" approaches have already had positive impacts in dealing with the humanitarian consequences of antipersonnel mines, ERW, and to a modest degree, to broaden thinking in the UN process on tackling illicit trade in small arms. Such approaches have also spurred the Oslo Process to ban cluster munitions launched in Norway in February 2007. They teach us that disarmament efforts should be guided by concrete objectives rather than the constraints of process, which in any case are ultimately malleable if there is sufficient commitment to those objectives. This is why field-based and other civil society perspectives are important—they add fresh thinking and additional momentum to a multilateral community in sore need of it.

One vital challenge for transnational civil society is to figure out how "human security" and other perspectives can effectively influence areas of disarmament where access is more jealously guarded by states, like in the nuclear arena. Successes like the Ottawa Process aside, civil society actors have a long way to go in this regard.[44] Future success will require moving beyond mobilizing public reaction to current humanitarian crises in order to pressure governments (as the ICBL, ICRC, and others did successfully in the 1990s for the international antipersonnel mine ban) and toward building a strong public interest in *preventive* measures. Challenges in this category include commencing fissile material cut-off negotiations, convincing holdout states to accede to the CTBT, and moving ahead on transparent and verifiable nuclear disarmament measures before nuclear weapons are used, with their awful potential for humanitarian catastrophe.

Other challenges include building an effective "web of prevention" that encompasses life science professionals—and not simply legislating over them—in order to prevent hostile misuse of biotechnology, a field that also holds much therapeutic promise. In the conventional arms arena there are, of course, the massive problems of human insecurity amplified by large numbers of illicitly held small arms. Other urgent priorities with both disarmament and humanitarian dimensions include dealing with effects on civilians of antivehicle mines, cluster munitions, and—overarching the latter—reviewing the use of high-explosive force in populated areas in general.

Problems of human insecurity, augmented by the availability of weapons, are nearer our doorsteps in an interconnected world than we often imagine. Yet in the face of these challenges, some of the multilateral methods used to deal with them predate the modern world and are starting to resemble the Emperor's new clothes. It is not just that these orthodox modes of response have failed to deal effectively with preventing or curbing the human costs of an exchange of nuclear intercontinental ballistic missiles (despite post-Cold War complacency), international terrorism, the militarization of space, and other challenges. They can also constrain the perceptions of those we entrust to try to reduce our insecurity through collective activities like multilateral disarmament and arms control. If disarmament challenges are to be tackled effectively, then these perceptions must change. They will only change if we—whether we regard ourselves as citizens, consumers, negotiators, advocates, or potential perpetrators, and victims of armed violence—take an interest and are prepared to speak truth to power to ensure this happens. Despite potential costs in the shorter term, it is in our individual and collective interest to do so.

Notes

1. ERW are explosive munitions that have failed to function as intended or which have been abandoned. Mines are not included as ERW. Numerous reports and other pieces of research exist about the humanitarian costs of these weapons. For instance, the ICBL's *Landmine Monitor* monitors and promotes implementation of the 1997 Mine Ban Treaty, through comprehensive annual global reports (http://www.icbl.org). Many reports on the humanitarian impact of ERW are available online, for instance from the International Committee of the Red Cross (http://www.icrc.org), Human Rights Watch (http://www.hrw.org), and Landmine Action (http://www.landmine action.org).

2. See Human Security Centre, "Part IV: Counting the Indirect Costs of War," *Human Security Report 2005* (Oxford: Oxford University Press, 2005), pp. 123–143, http://www.humansecurityreport.info.

3. Disarmament was entirely omitted from U.S. *National Strategy to Combat Weapons of Mass Destruction.* See *National Strategy to Combat Weapons of Mass Destruction,* December 2002, http://www.whitehouse.gov/news/releases/2002/12/WMDStrategy.pdf.

4. Statements and documents of the Conference on Disarmament are available at: http://www.unog.ch/disarmament.

5. These challenges include the nuclear activities of Iran and North Korea and the rolling back by the five "official" nuclear weapon states (China, France, Russia, the United Kingdom, and the United States) of political commitments toward nuclear disarmament they made five years before and on which they have largely failed to deliver.

6. See UNIDIR, "Taking Action on Small Arms," *Disarmament Forum*, no. 1, 2006, http://www.unidir.org.

7. See John Borrie, "The Road from Oslo: Emerging International Efforts on Cluster Munitions," *Disarmament Diplomacy*, Autumn 2007, http://www.acronym.org.uk.

8. See "What Is Human Security?" *Security Dialogue*, vol. 35, no. 3, September 2004, pp. 345–372.

9. John Borrie, "Rethinking Multilateral Negotiations: Disarmament as Humanitarian Action" in John Borrie and Vanessa Martin Randin (eds.), *Alternative Approaches in Multilateral Decision Making: Disarmament as Humanitarian Action* (Geneva: United Nations Institute for Disarmament Research, 2005), pp. 7–37.

10. Don Hubert, *The Landmine Ban: A Case Study in Humanitarian Advocacy*, Occasional Paper no. 42, (Providence: Thomas J. Watson Institute for International Studies, 2000).

11. Borrie and Randin (eds.), *Alternative Approaches in Multilateral Decision Making*.

12. Robert Cox, *Program on Multilateralism and the United Nations System 1990–1995* (Tokyo: United Nations University, April 1991), p. 4.

13. International organizations may (in principle) be invited to speak in the Conference on Disarmament. Although proposals have been put forward to invite representatives of the IAEA to address the CD, for instance, this has never been agreed upon.

14. Professor Gerald Steinberg raised these points in a debate in Geneva to commemorate UNIDIR's 25th anniversary. See http://www.unidir.org/html/en/25th_anniversary.html.

15. Robert J. Mathews and Timothy L. H. McCormack, "The Influence of Humanitarian Principles in the Negotiation of Arms Control Treaties," *International Review of the Red Cross*, vol. 81, no. 834, June 1999, pp. 331–352.

16. For more information about the ICRC's public appeal on biotechnology, weapons, and humanity, see http://www.scienceforhumanity.org.

17. Jozef Goldblat, *Agreements for Arms Control—A Critical Survey* (Stockholm: International Peace Research Institute, 1982), p. 89.

18. Charter of the United Nations, Preamble, signed on June 26, 1945, http://www.un.org/aboutun/charter/.

19. A useful source of current information about all of these bodies is http://www.reachingcriticalwill.org.

20. This definition is quoted from the global partnership glossary of the Canadian Department of Foreign Affairs and Trade at: http://www.dfait-maeci.gc.ca/foreign_policy/global_partnership/glossary-en.asp.

21. United States, *National Strategy to Combat Weapons of Mass Destruction*. Counterproliferation was outlined as one of the three main pillars of this strategy along with nonproliferation and consequence management of incidents in which these types of weapon are used. Disarmament was omitted.

22. For more information and analysis about the NPT, see http://www.acronym.org.uk/npt/index.html.

23. Ken Alibek and Stephen Handelman, *Biohazard* (New York: Random House, 1999).

24. See Jez Littlewood, *The Biological Weapon Convention: A Failed Revolution* (Aldershot, UK: Ashgate, 2003).

25. Robin M. Coupland, "Incapacitating Chemical Weapons: A Year after the Moscow Theatre Siege," *The Lancet*, vol. 362, no. 9393, October 25, 2003, p. 1346.

26. This is known as Protocol V on Explosive Remnants of War.

27. Technically the CCW is an international humanitarian law treaty, but arms controllers based in Geneva service it. For more analysis of the CCW's efforts, see Rosy Cave, "Disarmament as Humanitarian Action? Comparing Negotiations on Anti-Personnel Mines and Explosive Remnants of War," in John Borrie and Vanessa Martin Randin (eds.), *Disarmament as Humanitarian Action: From Perspective to Practice* (Geneva: UNIDIR, 2006), pp. 51–78.

28. See Goldblat, *Agreements for Arms Control*, pp. 220–233.

29. See April Carter, *Success and Failure in Arms Control Negotiations* (New York: Stockholm International Peace Research Institute, 1989).

30. For example, in the Caucasus. See International Crisis Group, "Nagorno-Karabakh: A Plan for Peace," Europe Report no. 167, October 11, 2005, http://www .crisisgroup.org/library/documents/europe/caucasus/167_nagorno_karabakh_a_plan _for_peace.pdf.

31. "Cutting Arms Cuts: Russia Threatens Treaties in Europe," *Economist*, July 19, 2007.

32. See John Borrie and Vanessa Martin Randin, *Alternative Approaches in Multilateral Decision Making*, pp. 87–88.

33. 2000 Review Conference of the Parties to the Treaty on the Non-Proliferation of Nuclear Weapons, "Final Document of the 2000 Review Conference of the Parties to the Treaty of the Non-Proliferation of Nuclear Weapons Consists of Four Parts in Three Volumes," New York, April 24–May 19, 2000, NPT/CONF.2000/28.

34. The seventh of the thirteen "steps" agreed upon in 2000 called for the "early entry into force and full implementation of START II and the conclusion of START III as soon as possible while preserving and strengthening the ABM Treaty as a cornerstone of strategic stability and as a basis for further reductions of strategic offensive weapons, in accordance with its provisions."

35. Rebecca Johnson, "Politics and Protection: Why the 2005 NPT Review Conference Failed," *Disarmament Diplomacy*, no. 80, Autumn 2005, http://www.acronym .org.uk.

36. For another view, see Jeffrey A. Larsen, "National Security and Neo-Arms Control in the Bush Administration," *Disarmament Diplomacy*, no. 80, Autumn 2005, http://www.acronym.org.uk.

37. Statement by United States Under-Secretary of State, John Bolton, "Stopping the Spread of Weapons of Mass Destruction in the Asian-Pacific Region: The Role of the Proliferation Security Initiative," Tokyo American Center, Japan, October 27, 2004.

38. William Poundstone, *Prisoner's Dilemma: John von Neumann, Game Theory, and the Puzzle of the Bomb* (New York: Anchor Books, 1992), p. 43.

39. Robert Axelrod and Robert O. Keohane, "Achieving Cooperation Under Anarchy: Strategies and Institutions," *World Politics*, vol. 38, no. 1, October 1985, p. 228.

40. Community of practice in the sense it is used here means a group of people who, over a period of time, share in some set of social practices geared toward some common purpose.

41. See John Borrie, "Cooperation and Defection in the Conference on Disarmament," *Disarmament Diplomacy*, no. 81, Spring 2006, http://www.acronym.org.uk/dd/dd82/82jb.htm.

42. See Aurélia Merçay and John Borrie, "A Physics of Diplomacy? The Dynamics of Complex Social Phenomena and Their Implications for Multilateral Negotiations," *Thinking Outside the Box in Multilateral Disarmament and Arms Control Negotiations* (Geneva: UNIDIR, 2006), pp. 129–164.

43. David Long and Laird Hindle, "Europe and the Ottawa Process: An Overview," in Maxwell A. Cameron, Robert J. Lawson and Brian W. Tomlin (eds.), *To Walk Without Fear: the Global Movement to Ban Landmines* (Toronto: Oxford University Press, 1998), p. 249.

44. David C. Atwood, "NGOs and Disarmament: Views From the Coal Face," *Disarmament Forum*, no. 1, 2002, pp. 5–14.

16

New Approaches in a Changing World: The Human Security Agenda

Jody Williams

> *We need to fashion a new concept of human security that is reflected in the*
> *lives of our people, not the weapons of our country.*

Mahbub ul Haq[1]

THE BERLIN WALL FELL, and we thought the world might be transformed. Throughout the 1990s, there was renewed enthusiasm for multilateralism. Transnational civil society and other actors were playing more significant roles in addressing issues in a rapidly globalizing world. These factors and more helped spark discussions that in a world no longer bipolar perhaps it was time to think about security in new ways. Maybe the more than four hundred-year-old state-centered concept of security no longer adequately met the challenges posed by an inescapably interconnected planet.

The optimism of the time was underscored by some bold new multilateral initiatives tackling arms control and international humanitarian law, as well as unexpected success in traditional arms control negotiations.[2] Nongovernmental organizations (NGOs) worked closely with governments—often the smaller and mid-sized countries—to bring about these changes.

The movement to ban antipersonnel landmines, powered by the International Campaign to Ban Landmines (ICBL), is often held up as the quintessential success story of those efforts. The Ottawa Process—a unique, stand-alone negotiating process conducted outside the UN—resulted in the Mine Ban

---

The serious critique of an earlier draft of this chapter by Dr. David Atwood, Executive Director, QUNO, has made this a much stronger chapter, for which I am sincerely grateful.

Treaty, which for the first time in history eliminated a conventional weapon widely used for almost a century. The successful model of government-civil society partnership that evolved in bringing the treaty about and endures to this day offers a concrete example of how the global community can work together to resolve common problems.[3]

A little over six months after 122 nations signed the Mine Ban Treaty in Ottawa on December 3–4, 1997, similarly like-minded governments—again supported by a coalition of NGOs—negotiated the Rome Statutes in July 1998 to create the International Criminal Court (ICC). The establishment of such a court had been a goal fought for ever since the Nuremberg Trials addressed war crimes and crimes against humanity committed by Nazi Germany.

Neither the Mine Ban Treaty nor the ICC efforts had the support of the United States, Russia, or China, and, in the case of the latter, the United States not only actively opposed the ICC but since its creation has also worked consistently to undermine it. Despite the opposition, these unexpected successes, along with other somewhat similar efforts such as ongoing work to stop the proliferation of small arms and light weapons, encouraged international institutions and states to explore more vigorously new security frameworks to meet the challenges of a rapidly changing world.

A few years earlier, the UN Development Programme (UNDP) had introduced a new concept of human security, which "equates security with people rather than territories, with development rather than arms."[4] The theme was further elaborated at the UN under then Secretary-General Kofi Annan.

Canada was also important in developing the idea, with some differences of emphasis to UNDP's framework. The concept was championed by then Foreign Minister Lloyd Axworthy, who was fundamental to the launch of the Ottawa Process.[5] By 1999, Canada, Norway, and other governments that had been at the core of the landmine ban effort were among those who initiated the Human Security Network.[6]

Human security "idealists" have been attacked and dismissed by national security "realists" as wooly-headed utopians, particularly in the post-9/11 global political environment and the war on terror. The dreams of utopians, of course, are fantasies that could never work in the real world. But is a human security framework a starry-eyed dream? Are human security and national security diametrically opposed and mutually exclusive concepts?

In many ways, at least on the surface, the human security concept seems thus far to have been largely reduced to political rhetoric and academic analysis rather than an agenda for action. If those who began developing it in the 1990s believe it to be important—if not critical—to a more secure world, how can its proponents move human security beyond rhetoric and analysis and begin to demonstrate how its complex view of security can be applied? What roles should governments, international institutions, and NGOs play in advancing human security?

(Re)Defining Security in the Globalized World

Since the mid-1600s, security has been understood to be the security of sovereign nation-states, maintained primarily through military power.[7] Nations cling to this framework even though it is unavoidably clear the global landscape has changed and seems to be changing more rapidly almost daily. Like it or not, there is not much that is not interconnected in today's world, and there are many more factors that influence relations among states and state security. Some of these are outside of state control, and many are transnational in character.

In the global economy, for example, corporations and even some individuals amass fortunes that can dwarf the budget of a nation—or an entire region of the world. Decisions they make often have a huge impact on the world, and yet their accountability is unclear. As the global marketplace continues to evolve, the relationship between states and transnational corporations is less and less clear. For many, it is these financial questions that define "globalization," yet the phenomenon is not only about economics. In addition to global business, international and regional institutions as well as NGOs and civil society all have an impact on today's world.

We are faced not only with war, terrorism, and armed violence around the world, but also with (to name but a few): weapons proliferation, including weapons of mass destruction; global organized crime, including the trafficking of human beings, particularly women and children; perhaps irreversible destruction of our environment and the threats posed by global warming; widespread, pervasive poverty; and new and deadly diseases. With global telecommunications, 24-hour "news," and increased and faster travel, we live in an international marketplace of ideas and interactions that can unpredictably influence how problems evolve as well as possible responses to them.

In such an environment, does the security of the state really provide for the security of the individual citizen? Is it realistic for anyone to believe that the state can or should try to isolate its population by focusing the concerns of citizens on "domestic issues," while asserting control over "foreign policy" and "security?" The lines between domestic and international issues and policies have become too blurred, and often the domestic impact of foreign policy decisions has become too glaring for citizens to ignore.

One horrific example is the September 11, 2001, terrorist attacks on the United States. Those attacks had roots in decades of U.S. foreign policy decisions toward the Middle East, decisions viewed as unfair by people in the region and that have fueled intense dislike and distrust of the country. It is fair to say that the overwhelming majority of U.S. citizens had virtually no understanding of those policies and therefore no tools to understand the "why" of those attacks.

In light of such complexities, old concepts of state-based security do not offer long-term answers to today's transnational threats and challenges. Yet the resistance by national security proponents to meaningful analysis and discussion of what will bring us security—collectively and individually—is extremely strong and pervasive. Despite the resistance, such discussions are ongoing, among governments, UN agencies, NGOs, academics, and others. But they must be much broader and deeper, and most importantly, they *must* be coupled with *collective action* to change the global mindset about what really constitutes security.

What Is "Human Security"?

Since the 1990s, many inside and outside of government have begun to look at today's world through the lens of human security. Two of its key early proponents were the United Nations Development Programme, primarily in its 1994 *Human Development Report*, and the government of Canada.[8] The pioneering work of UNDP offered a very broad understanding of human security that should offer people "freedom from want" and "freedom from fear."[9] These freedoms would not be the result of weapons and war but through "sustainable human development."

Canadian thinking was also developing around that time and was very much fueled by its leadership in the landmine movement. Canada's evolving position was articulated on various occasions by its foreign minister at that time, Lloyd Axworthy. In an address to the UN General Assembly in September 1996, Axworthy outlined key elements of Canadian thinking stating, "[I]n the aftermath of the Cold War, we have re-examined and redefined the dimensions of international security to embrace the concept of sustainable human security. There has been a recognition that human rights and fundamental freedoms, the right to live in dignity, with adequate food, shelter, health and education services, and under the rule of law and good governance, are as important to global peace as disarmament measures. We are now realizing that security cannot be limited to the state's domain, but must incorporate civil society."[10] Not insignificantly, that address came during the fortieth anniversary of UN Peacekeeping, which Canada played a significant role in helping to develop. Canada considers peacekeeping and peace building to be key elements in advancing a human security agenda.[11]

Building upon that thinking, and growing out of discussions between Canada and Norway expressly as a result of their collaboration in creating the Mine Ban Treaty, a small group of "like-minded" countries launched the "Human Security Network" at a ministerial meeting in Norway on May 20, 1999. Its goal is to address international problems through a human security perspective that promotes peace and development and aims to prevent and/or solve conflict situations.

Ministers of the member countries have continued to meet annually for on-going dialogue about human security as its members work to identify issues that benefit from collective action.[12] The group does not dismiss traditional state security but sees it as coequal with people-centered security and considers military force a secondary tool. While it shares much of the thinking of the UNDP, it takes a narrower approach and concentrates on protecting people from various forms of political violence.[13]

In 2000, expanding upon the seminal work of the UNDP, during the Millennium Summit the UN launched an independent Commission on Human Security.[14] In its two-year life, the Commission studied conflict and development and issued its final report, *Human Security Now,* on May 1, 2003.[15] The recommendations of the Commission were to be carried out by an Advisory Board on Human Security, established as a result of the Commission's work.[16] Further, in May 2004, the UN established a Human Security Unit in the UNDP to "integrate human security in all UN activities."[17]

The Commission argued that human security is advanced, first, through protection—which is primarily a state-based responsibility to protect people from critical and pervasive threats. Other institutions, civil society and non-governmental actors, and the private sector also play key roles in that protection. Second, human security is also enhanced by developing the capabilities of individuals and communities to make informed choices and to act on their own behalf.[18] Protection and empowerment mean not only protecting people from threats, but also "creating political, social, environmental, economic, military and cultural systems that, when combined, give people the building blocks for survival, livelihood and dignity."[19]

These actors, as well as many others, have contributed to developing concepts of security that are not primarily concerned with security of the nation-state but instead with that of people inside and outside the confines of national boundaries. Terrorism, crime, and war are all examples of violence that destabilize the security of people. But their security is also affected by deprivation—whether it is the result of poverty, environmental pollution, disease, malnutrition, illiteracy, or all of them combined.

While human security proponents might have somewhat varying definitions of the concept, most would likely agree that human security encompasses commitments to human rights and humanitarian law, good governance, and access for the peoples of the world to economic opportunity, education, and health care.[20]

Human Security, the 2005 UN World Summit, and the Responsibility to Protect

In terms of taking the security of the individual as key, regardless of national boundary, the concept of the responsibility to protect (sometimes called R2P) could be seen as a significant development. Responsibility to protect grew out of concerns about humanitarian intervention—both action and nonaction by the international community—in the face of atrocities.[21] Several reports outline developments in thinking about responsibility to protect.

In 2000, Secretary-General Kofi Annan challenged UN member states to develop principles and processes for humanitarian intervention, and the first response was Canada's establishment of an independent International Commission on Intervention and State Sovereignty that year. Its 2001 report, presented to the UN, is "about the so-called 'right of humanitarian intervention': the question of when, if ever, it is appropriate for states to take coercive—and in particular military—action, against another state for the purpose of protecting people at risk in that other state."[22] Its purpose was to contribute to the development of international consensus on the issue.

Subsequently, the UN launched a high-level panel in 2003 to look at the wide range of threats to security and recommend how the UN could be reformed to maximize its effectiveness. Its 2004 report, "A More Secure World: Our Shared Responsibility," endorsed the concept of collective responsibility to protect people from mass atrocities and called upon the General Assembly and Security Council to adopt guidelines governing the use of force in such situations.[23] The issues presented in those two reports were to be deliberated at the 2005 UN World Summit.

In the lead-up to that September Summit, in March 2005 the Secretary-General issued "In Larger Freedom: Towards Development, Security and Human Rights for All," which described essentially a human security framework "in a world of interconnected threats and opportunities." The report states: "Events since the Millennium Declaration demand that consensus be revitalized on key challenges and priorities and converted into collective action. The guiding light in doing so must be the needs and hopes of people everywhere. The world must advance the causes of security, development and human rights together, otherwise none will succeed. Humanity will not enjoy security without development, it will not enjoy development without security, and it will not enjoy either without respect for human rights."[24]

Addressing the General Assembly in March 2005, Annan told the assembled states that in the report "I urge all states to agree to strengthen the rule of law, human rights and democracy in concrete ways. In particular, I ask them to embrace the principle of the 'Responsibility to Protect,' as a basis for collective action against genocide, ethnic cleansing and crimes against humanity—recognising that this responsibility lies first and foremost with each individual state, but also that, if national authorities are unable or unwilling to protect their citizens, the responsibility then shifts to the international community; and that, in the last resort, the United Nations Security Council may take enforcement action according to the Charter."[25] By the time states met for their World Summit in September 2005, much of the dramatic reform that the Secretary-General called for had been watered down, but the principle of the responsibility to protect passed by consensus.[26]

Criticisms of the Framework

It does not take much imagination to consider how national security "realists" view human security. For them, it is a wishy-washy effort by "lesser powers"—read irrelevant—who do not have the military might or the "spine" to deal with real security issues. "Real" security is based upon "sovereign" states maximizing their individual power inevitably at a cost to the rest. In this view and traditionally, only states have the requisite insider knowledge and the expertise to appropriately determine what best protects the security of its citizens. Therefore realists argue that foreign policy and national security is generally far too complex for the average citizen to understand let alone have a voice in.

Critics of human security also tend to take the position that either you are for human security or you are for national security, and they see no possible coexistence or complementarity. For some—particularly U.S. neoconservatives—discussion of the concept is not an attempt at an objective assessment of what really would make the world as a whole more secure, but is an attack on American values and state sovereignty.

As one article states: "This is a dramatic and fundamental distortion of the right to be secure. The effort to 'broaden our view of what is meant by peace and security' obscures and runs counter to the long-standing right of nation-states to secure their own territories and populations from external threats—a principle upon which international legal traditions and treaty organizations such as the UN are based. The human security agenda has the potential to undermine not only the nation-state model on which the UN was founded, but also the principles of sovereignty, accountability, and national security that the United States holds as fundamental."[27]

The framework is also criticized as being too vague and a catchall attempt to try to resolve all problems facing humanity rather than confine itself narrowly—therefore effectively, of course—to real security issues. How could such a far-reaching, or perhaps overreaching, concept possibly replace the centuries-old system of nation-states interacting through a delicate balance of a global chess match of power?

Others argue that it simply cannot work, that its rhetoric is not matched with "concrete policy that makes a difference to the safety of people whose security is threatened."[28] This criticism takes a narrow view of the concept and focuses on the difficulties of ensuring the security of people being attacked by their own governments in internal conflict. Certainly the principle of responsibility to protect rings hollow, for example, in Darfur which has been described as the largest scale humanitarian disaster in the world today.

Almost two years after the UN embraced the principle, the war crimes, crimes against humanity, and ethnic cleansing carried out by the Sudanese government in Darfur continue unabated. Despite tremendous and growing public pressure for concrete action, there has been no coherent collective action to alleviate the suffering. Empty threats have only emboldened the government and increased its sense of impunity.

For many, this begs the question: what does human security really mean in the face of such atrocity? At the same time, humanitarian intervention is a hotly debated issue in and of itself. While an important element of a fully functioning human security paradigm, humanitarian intervention should not be the centerpiece of a human security approach to global security.[29]

Human Security Applied—Progress to Date

Providing for human security is a global challenge that requires a global response. As one proponent has written, "[H]uman security is truly a useful new construct only if it explains how to connect and gain synergy from (among other things) simultaneous economic development, growing respect for human rights, increasing public sector capacity, and accountability and maturation of civil societies."[30] Or as Kofi Annan said, "The world must advance the causes of security, development and human rights together, otherwise none will succeed."[31]

Clearly the world is nowhere near such a simultaneous, coordinated response. However, positive results have been made in specific issue areas which arguably do contribute to a growing concrete understanding of how a human security paradigm, if embraced, could result in reaching the goal of a world where people can live at least largely free from fear and free from want. Many of these examples are issues that the Human Security Network lists as being of key interest to its members: "The Network's current efforts to achieve greater human security include issues such as the universalization of the Ottawa Convention on Anti-personnel Landmines, the establishment of the International Criminal Court, the protection of children in armed conflict, the control of small arms and light weapons, the fight against trans-national organized crime, human development and human security, human rights education, the struggle against HIV/AIDS, addressing implementation gaps of international humanitarian and human rights law, and conflict prevention."[32]

The success of the Ottawa Process and the continuing progress in implementing the Mine Ban Treaty in the ten years since it was created are examples of contributions to human security. Another is Protocol V to the Convention on Conventional Weapons (CCW), which addresses the problem of explosive remnants of war (ERW). Like the Mine Ban Treaty this is a people-centered protocol. Both seek to deal with the effects of conventional weapons that threaten the daily lives of people in countries around the world. These are not international laws that are centered on state security.

Another example still in progress is the Oslo Process on cluster munitions, launched in February 2007, which mirrors the work of the Ottawa Process. It is a stand-alone negotiating process, resulting from the failure of the CCW to deal with cluster munitions, just as happened with the landmine issue. Its goal is to achieve a treaty to deal with cluster munitions in 2008 (see chapter 13).

There have also been important and ongoing efforts to curb the proliferation of small arms and light weapons—an issue of greater complexity than banning landmines or even dealing with ERW and cluster munitions—with a resolution passed by the UN General Assembly calling for an Arms Trade Treaty. The resolution "calls for the establishment of a group of experts to look at the feasibility, scope and parameters of the treaty, which must report back to the first committee by the fall of 2008."[33]

Outside of arms control, two other recent international treaties are also important to a human security agenda. The establishment of the International Criminal Court (ICC) through the Rome Statutes negotiated in July 1998 is nothing if not "people-centered." In essence, it provides the possibility of legal recourse when a state does not exercise its responsibility to protect its citizens from genocide, war crimes, crimes against humanity, and ethnic cleansing. The ICC and the responsibility to protect principle do not do away with state sovereignty but begin to pierce what has until now been accepted as virtually untouchable.[34] The second is a treaty contributing to the body of human rights law—the UN Convention on the Rights of Persons with Disabilities concluded in August 2006 (see chapter 14).

Some of these treaties have been negotiated within the UN, but others have not—the Ottawa and Oslo Processes being cases in point. Although much work has been done on human security in some UN agencies, the formal mechanisms of the body are sometimes slow to reflect it. But concrete contributions to people-centered security in UN-related work include mine action and development work; small arms work in disarmament, demobilization, and reintegration of former combatants; work on child soldiers and the impact of armed conflict on children; and the evolution of the work foreseen for the UN Peacebuilding Commission. Broad concepts of "human security" serve as a basis for their work.[35]

A final example, which can help to move the understanding of human security beyond academic debate, is the work of the Human Security Report Project which issued a major report on human security in 2005: *Human Security: War and Peace in the 21st Century*.[36] While not all agree with some of its conclusions, particularly concerning the numbers of armed conflicts, it attempts analysis of human security based on real data. A follow-up report was released in December 2006, the *Human Security Brief 2006*. Such work is an important step, as empirical data is fundamental to sound policy formulation.[37]

Where Do We Go From Here?

If the human security agenda is a viable approach to global security in a world in rather desperate need of new visions for the future, why has it not had more traction? An examination of the launch and subsequent work of the Human Security Network, as well as the human security efforts of the UN, provides some issues to consider regarding the relatively limited success so far. Action and inaction on the part of NGOs are also important factors.

The Role of Governments and International Institutions

When governments met in Oslo to launch the Human Security Network in May 1999, NGO involvement was minimal at best. Invitations to attend the meeting in Oslo were late in coming, and NGOs were only invited to sit in on a few hours of the daylong meeting. It is not clear at all how much, if any, meaningful discussion was held between governments and civil society as the idea of the Network was being developed.

With the same governments leading the Ottawa Process and the Human Security Network, such as Canada and Norway, it is curious that there was so little discussion about human security with the NGOs that have been instrumental in the ban movement. While the process of banning landmines helped fuel thinking on human security, human security was not explicitly part of discussions before or during the Ottawa Process itself—either between governments and NGOs or among NGOs themselves.

The Human Security Network describes building a broad coalition of governments, international institutions, NGOs, and wider civil society to promote and advance the framework. If that is taking place, it is a stealth operation. Many of the activities that the Network cites as part of its work seem completely independent of the Network itself. For example, it cites the Nairobi Review Conference of the Mine Ban Treaty in December 2004, which was focused entirely on treaty implementation.[38] Yet, since all the significant actors involved in the ban movement were in Nairobi for that Review Conference, it could have been an opportune moment for human security discussions between governments and NGOs.

The Network appears to seek NGO involvement in events related to specific issues that it deems to be components of a human security agenda. However, there does not seem to be any mechanism for ongoing discussion and action between governments and NGOs to address the human security framework writ large. If advancing the framework must be through broad and integrated responses to global problems, this fragmenting of issues and answers to them does not serve the human security agenda well, nor does an ad hoc approach to working with NGOs and civil society.

The situation appears much the same in the work on human security at the UN. Neither its Commission on Human Security nor the subsequent Advisory Board on Human Security have NGO involvement or even informal mechanisms for ongoing dialogue with them regarding this "people-centered" framework.

It is extremely difficult to see how a new agenda for security can be effectively advanced against the traditional national security framework when it seems to be essentially a "top down" effort and not one built on an effective and broad government-civil society partnership.

The Role of NGOs and Civil Society

This top-down disconnect has had a longer-term impact on NGOs, who have put too little effort into understanding human security or how it relates to their own work or what an important alternative framework it could be to a "national security only" concept of global security. Neither NGOs nor civil society in general have done much to connect the dots on human security.

While it would be safe to argue that many NGOs dealing with the myriad problems confronting societies today have little faith in the national security framework as an effective means to enhance global security, NGOs have been strangely absent from discussion of alternatives. While not particularly warmly embraced by governments or international institutions working on human security, NGOs themselves have not really taken a serious look at it either.

Precious few NGOs who do embrace a human security agenda bring it up overtly in their own work. This conceptual fragmentation does little to unite civil society behind alternative approaches to national security. To call for global security is one thing, to offer suggestions as to how to make that happen is another. For NGOs and civil society to have even the possibility of advancing a human security alternative, there must be much more clarity about the framework as "a response to the needs of civil society throughout the world" and how the issues they work on fit into that framework.

Wherever appropriate and whenever possible, NGOs should situate their work as part of a larger human security agenda, especially when reaching out to the general public. Thus for example, NGOs must embrace and promote the view that work for human rights enhances human security and that efforts to advance sustainable development enhance human security. Every time there is success in limiting the flow of weapons of war, or regulating or banning weapons outright, human security is enhanced. Involving women meaningfully in all aspects of conflict prevention and peace building (and decision-making in general) enhances human security. Addressing poverty through debt reduction, fair trade, and better aid—coupled with promoting good governance and tackling corruption—is enhancing human security.

Too often NGOs lose—or worse yet do not even see—opportunities to make those connections. The delinking of issues undercuts the building of collective efforts to promote a broader understanding and acceptance of a human security agenda as the framework to prevent violent conflict and strengthen global security. Unfortunately, instances of delinking of issues abound. One glaring example is the case of the 2005 campaign to "Make Poverty History," especially given its high profile.

The major target of that effort was the call for the G-8 nations to do more to reduce poverty, including debt forgiveness. Many argued that to tackle effectively pervasive poverty required more than debt forgiveness, and they called upon the campaign to broaden understanding of other elements contributing to and creating poverty.[39] For example, five of the G-8 nations are responsible for at least 80 percent of weapons trade in the world and those weapons fuel conflict, which in turn disrupts sustainable development and contributes to poverty. Calling upon those countries to increase aid with one hand, while not calling upon them to stop offering weapons with the other can only undercut attempts to promote sustainable development and prevent violent conflict in the poorest nations of the world.

The poverty campaign also ignored promotion of good governance in the developing countries it was targeting. Despite pleas from activists in some of those countries to include calls for government reform in connection with poverty alleviation, their input into how best to respond to their problems was brushed aside. Willfully ignoring these obvious contradictions to make outreach "easier" or more "palatable" to some lessens the ability to effectively campaign and lobby over the long-term to create a new agenda for a more secure world.

Another example is the work to limit the proliferation of small arms and light weapons, which has for the most part not contextualized the efforts as part of a broader human security framework. Even many NGO members of the International Campaign to Ban Landmines, much lauded as the engine that resulted in the new model of partnership with governments and that also helped crystallize government thinking about human security, have missed opportunities both to reinforce that model and to advance the human security agenda. This is explained by their focus on maintaining their *own* momentum to reach the goal of a world free of landmines. But to be able to advance the human security framework as a viable multifaceted approach to security, NGOs must recognize that human security is indeed an overarching framework and they must recognize their own place in it.

Conclusion

Our interconnected world is changing fast, but thinking about approaches to security in that world is not keeping pace. Despite the fact that today many actors *can* and *do* have an impact on how problems and conflicts both evolve and are responded to, the prevailing view of security is still the state-based national security model. Even though environmental destruction threatens us all, even though HIV/AIDS does not respect national borders, even though terrorism takes many forms in many places around the world, people still look to individual states to deal with these and other problems.

Transnational problems need transnational solutions. Governments, NGOs, and international institutions alike must change their thinking, their rhetoric and their approaches to the problems of the world in order to develop a security framework that works in today's global environment. To live in a secure world, a new partnership for human security must be forged that can meaningfully address the gross political, social, and economic inequalities that are the roots of conflict. The search for solutions must be broadly inclusive and based on effective multilateralism, dialogue, and conflict resolution. That is a huge challenge in a world increasingly dominated by the few, who give the perception of not caring much for the needs of the many.

Efforts to challenge accepted thinking about how to address violence or the myriad challenges to human security must not be brushed aside as "weak responses" to security threats in the globalized world. Part of the challenge is demystifying thinking about violence. Violence must not be dismissed with the commonly heard explanation that it is simply "human nature" to be violent. At any level, the decision to resort to violence is a choice. Governments and civil society must work together to advance human security as a viable alternative to militarism and violence and war.

If those advocating for the human security framework—governments and civil society alike—really believe that violence is a choice, they must set an agenda that promotes the making of nonviolent choices to resolve conflicts and that promotes integrated, comprehensive action to resolve the root causes of those conflicts. Change will not happen overnight, but that should not be an excuse to not seek change. It is possible to reverse the slide toward further ideologically driven division and increased violence.

To move the world away from a national security only view of global security, then, there must be consistent and integrated work to change the collective mindset about what constitutes global security. In considering the success, for example, of the movement to ban landmines, a fundamental element of its effective campaigning was setting the terms of the debate. It appears that neither governments nor NGOs have come anywhere close to setting the terms of debate about effective global security—either independently or collectively. If governments and NGOs do not work together toward this end, freedom from want and freedom from fear will remain very elusive goals.

Civil society, NGOs, and governments alike have roles to play in developing new strategies and policies to ensure our collective security. But just as in the landmine ban movement or in the creation of the International Criminal Court, those actors must accept the challenges of working together to seek new ways to address threats to our common security. Fragmented, disconnected responses to the various problems and challenges will not strengthen a human security framework. Giving lip service to the involvement of civil society and NGOs in finding solutions to the problems will not strengthen or advance a human security agenda. Efforts to resolve conflict as well as social and economic inequalities must be integrated and unified, and all relevant actors must be part of the solutions. Only through a broad, new partnership will it be possible to debunk the collective myth that enhancing global security through a human security framework is a fuzzy dream of utopian idealists.

Notes

1. Mahbub ul Haq was a consulting economist considered key to developing the concept of human security in the UN Development Programme. See Mahbub ul Haq, "New Imperatives of Human Security," Rajiv Gandhi Institute for Contemporary Studies Paper no. 17 (New Delhi: Rajiv Ghandi Foundation, 1994).

2. Almost unnoticed was work carried out by the International Committee of the Red Cross and Human Rights Watch during the review of the 1980 Convention on Conventional Weapons, which resulted in 1995 in a new protocol banning blinding laser weapons—before they ever made it to production. That success in a traditional UN arms control forum was overshadowed by the landmine issue.

3. One of the best books written on the ban movement and the Ottawa Process is *To Walk Without Fear*, an edited volume with chapters contributed by various actors involved in the Process. One of the editors, Bob Lawson, a Canadian diplomat, played a key role in the evolution of the Ottawa Process. Maxwell Cameroon, Robert J. Lawson, and Brian W. Tomlin (eds.), *To Walk Without Fear: The Global Movement to Ban Landmines* (Toronto: Oxford University Press, 1998). See also Don Hubert, *The Landmine Ban: A Case Study in Humanitarian Advocacy*, Thomas J. Watson Jr. Institute for International Studies, Brown University, Occasional Paper #42, 2000.

4. UNDP, *Human Development Report 1994* (New York: Oxford University Press, 1994), http://hdr.undp.org/reports/global/1994/en/.

5. For an excellent analysis of UNDP and Canadian views on human security, see Kanti Bajpai, "Human Security: Concept and Measurement," Kroc Institute Occasional Paper #19:OP:1, Notre Dame University, August 2000, http://kroc.nd.edu/ocpapers/op_19_1.PDF. See also Dr. Dan Henk, "Human Security: Relevance and Implications," *PARAMETERS*, US Army War College Quarterly, summer 2005, http://www.carlisle.army.mil/usawc/Parameters/05summer/henk.htm.

6. See Human Security Network, http://www.humansecuritynetwork.org/network-e.php/.

7. This Westphalian model of state sovereignty can be traced back to the 1648 Peace of Westphalia in which major European powers, except for England, accepted the principle of territorial integrity. Proponents perceive that global stability—what might be called peace—is maintained through a balance of power among nations, and it is the state that decides how to best protect its citizens, though some would argue that what is really being protected is the state itself and those who control it.

8. Thinking about human security did not spring out of the ether but is related to ongoing work since the 1960s that challenged accepted ideas about development and security. See Kanti Bajpai, "Human Security: Concept and Measurement," Kroc Institute, pp. 4–7.

9. UNDP, *Human Development Report 1994*, p. 3.

10. Notes for an Address by the Honourable Lloyd Axworthy, Minister of Foreign Affairs, to the 51st General Assembly of the United Nations, New York, New York, September 24, 1996, http://w01.international.gc.ca/minpub/PublicationContentOnly.asp?publication_id=377017&Language=E&MODE=CONTENTONLY&Local=False/.

11. For more on the particulars of Canada's view of human security, see Canada's Human Security website, http://www.humansecurity.gc.ca/.

12. Countries that are part of the Network include Austria, Canada, Chile, Costa Rica, Greece, Ireland, Japan, Jordan, Mali, the Netherlands, Norway, Slovenia, Sweden, Switzerland, and Thailand. South Africa is an observer. See Human Security Network, http://www.humansecuritynetwork.org/nctwork-e.php/.

13. See Christian Ruge, "Mitigating the Effects of Armed Violence through Disarmament: The Human Costs," in John Borrie and Vanessa Martin Randin (eds.), *Disarmament as Humanitarian Action: From Perspective to Practice* (Geneva: United Nations Institute for Disarmament Research, 2006).

14. Commission on Human Security, http://www.humansecurity-chs.org/.

15. The complete report is available online at: http://www.humansecurity-chs.org/finalreport/index.html/.

16. For information on the Advisory Board, see: http://ochaonline.un.org/webpage.asp?MenuID=9671&Page=1494/.

17. The Unit is in the UN Office for the Coordination of Humanitarian Affairs (OCHA), see its webpage at: http://ochaonline.un.org/webpage.asp?MenuID=10472&Page=1516/.

18. OCHA "Human Security" webpage, at http://ochaonline.un.org/webpage.asp?MenuID=9671&Page=1494.

19. OCHA "Human Security" webpage, at http://ochaonline.un.org/webpage.asp?MenuID=9671&Page=1494.

20. For comparisons of various definitions see, for example, The Global Development Research Center website at http://www.gdrc.org/. In "Human Security: Relevance and Implications," Dr. Henk states that South Africa's expression of human security, developed after the end of Apartheid, is the clearest anywhere: "In the new South Africa national security is no longer viewed a predominantly military and police problem. It has broadened to incorporate political, economic, social, and environmental matters. At the heart of this new approach is a paramount concern with the *security of people.* Security is an all-encompassing condition in which *individual citizens* live in freedom, peace, and safety; participate fully in the process of governance; enjoy the protection of fundamental rights; have access to resources and the basic necessities of life; and inhabit an environment which is not detrimental to their health and well-being."

21. Nonaction in the cases of Rwanda (1994) and Srebrenica (1995) horrified the world; unilateral action by NATO in Kosovo in 1999 was controversial.

22. The Responsibility to Protect website of the Human Security Policy Division, Foreign Affairs Canada, http://www.iciss.ca/menu-en.asp/.

23. The report is available at http://www.un.org/secureworld/.

24. UN Secretary-General, "In Larger Freedom: Towards Development, Security and Human Rights For All," Report of the Secretary-General, A/59/2005, March 21, 2005.

25. The Secretary-General, Statement to the General Assembly, March 21, 2005, http://www.un.org/largerfreedom/sg-statement.html/.

26. UN Department of Public Information, "Fact Sheet, 2005 World Summit, High-Level Plenary Meeting, September 14–16, 2005," September 2005, http://www.un.org/summit2005/presskit/fact_sheet.pdf/.

27. James Jay Carafano and Janet A. Smith, "The Muddled Notion of 'Human Security' at the U.N.: A Guide for US Policymakers," The Heritage Foundation, Backgrounder #1966, September 1, 2006, http://www.heritage.org/Research/Worldwide-Freedom/bg1966.cfm/.

28. T.S. Hataley and Kim Richard Nossal, "The Limits of the Human Security Agenda: The Case of Canada's Response to the Timor Crisis," *Global Change, Peace & Security,* vol. 16, no. 1, February 2004.

29. For examples of the debate on "humanitarian intervention," see Ken Roth, "War in Iraq: Not a Humanitarian Intervention," *World Report 2004* (New York: Human Rights Watch, 2004), http://hrw.org/wr2k4/3.htm/; David Rieff, "Humanitarian Intervention," in Roy Gutman and David Rieff (eds.), *Crimes of War* (New York: W. W. Norton, 1999), http://www.crimesofwar.org/thebook/humanitarian-intervention.html; "Humanitarian Intervention and Assistance," Listing compiled by Terry Kiss, Bibliographer, Air University Library, Maxwell Air Force Base, http://www.au.af.mil/au/aul/bibs/human.htm/.

30. Henk, "Human Security: Relevance and Implications," *PARAMETERS*, pp. 97–98.

31. UN Secretary-General, Executive Summary, "In Larger Freedom."

32. The Human Security Network, October 20, 2006, http://www.humansecurity network.org/network-e.php.

33. For a text of the Resolution, see http://www.iansa.org/un/documents/Arms TradeTreatyL55.pdf/. See also, Haider Rizvi, "UN Passes Arms Trade Treaty Over US Opposition," *InterPress Service,* October 27, 2006, http://www.commondreams.org/headlines06/1027-01.htm/.

34. The first indictments by the ICC were made on February 27, 2007, against two individuals for war crimes and crimes against humanity in the case of Darfur; see website of the International Criminal Court, http://www.icc-cpi.int/cases/Darfur/c0205.html/.

35. E-mail from David Atwood, Executive Director, QUNO, November 12, 2006.

36. The report is available at: http://www.humansecurityreport.info/. The Human Security Report Project was located at the Human Security Centre, Liu Institute for Global Issues, University of British Columbia from February 2002 to May 2007. It subsequently moved to the School for International Studies, Simon Fraser University, Vancouver.

37. For discussion of the relevance of data to human security issues, see Ruge, "Mitigating the Effects of Armed Violence," UNIDIR, pp. 28–42.

38. Human Security Network, http://www.humansecuritynetwork.org/events-e.php/.

39. "Make Poverty History" was a broad coalition made up of NGOs but also coalitions of NGOs. Some did have broader messages in their particular work on the campaign effort, but the main public message—perhaps as best exemplified by the "Live 8 Concerts" that were part of the effort—was quite limited.

Appendix:
1997 Mine Ban Treaty and Its Status

Convention on the Prohibition of the Use, Stockpiling, Production and
Transfer of Anti-Personnel Mines and on Their Destruction

Preamble

The States Parties,

Determined to put an end to the suffering and casualties caused by anti-personnel mines, that kill or maim hundreds of people every week, mostly innocent and defenceless civilians and especially children, obstruct economic development and reconstruction, inhibit the repatriation of refugees and internally displaced persons, and have other severe consequences for years after emplacement,

Believing it necessary to do their utmost to contribute in an efficient and coordinated manner to face the challenge of removing anti-personnel mines placed throughout the world, and to assure their destruction,

Wishing to do their utmost in providing assistance for the care and rehabilitation, including the social and economic reintegration of mine victims,

Recognizing that a total ban of anti-personnel mines would also be an important confidence-building measure,

Welcoming the adoption of the Protocol on Prohibitions or Restrictions on the Use of Mines, Booby-Traps and Other Devices, as amended on 3 May 1996, annexed to the Convention on Prohibitions or Restrictions on the Use of Certain Conventional Weapons Which May Be Deemed to Be Excessively Injurious or to Have Indiscriminate Effects, and calling for the early ratification of this Protocol by all States which have not yet done so,

Welcoming also United Nations General Assembly Resolution 51/45 S of 10 December 1996 urging all States to pursue vigorously an effective, legally-binding international agreement to ban the use, stockpiling, production and transfer of anti-personnel landmines,

Welcoming furthermore the measures taken over the past years, both unilaterally and multilaterally, aiming at prohibiting, restricting or suspending the use, stockpiling, production and transfer of anti-personnel mines,

Stressing the role of public conscience in furthering the principles of humanity as evidenced by the call for a total ban of anti-personnel mines and recognizing the efforts to that end undertaken by the International Red Cross and Red Crescent Movement, the International Campaign to Ban Landmines and numerous other non-governmental organizations around the world,

Recalling the Ottawa Declaration of 5 October 1996 and the Brussels Declaration of 27 June 1997 urging the international community to negotiate an international and legally binding agreement prohibiting the use, stockpiling, production and transfer of anti-personnel mines,

Emphasizing the desirability of attracting the adherence of all States to this Convention, and determined to work strenuously towards the promotion of its universalization in all relevant fora including, inter alia, the United Nations, the Conference on Disarmament, regional organizations, and groupings, and review conferences of the Convention on Prohibitions or Restrictions on the Use of Certain Conventional Weapons Which May Be Deemed to Be Excessively Injurious or to Have Indiscriminate Effects,

Basing themselves on the principle of international humanitarian law that the right of the parties to an armed conflict to choose methods or means of warfare is not unlimited, on the principle that prohibits the employment in armed conflicts of weapons, projectiles and materials and methods of warfare of a nature to cause superfluous injury or unnecessary suffering and on the principle that a distinction must be made between civilians and combatants,

Have agreed as follows:

Article 1

General obligations

1. Each State Party undertakes never under any circumstances:
   a. To use anti-personnel mines;
   b. To develop, produce, otherwise acquire, stockpile, retain or transfer to anyone, directly or indirectly, anti-personnel mines;
   c. To assist, encourage or induce, in any way, anyone to engage in any activity prohibited to a State Party under this Convention.
2. Each State Party undertakes to destroy or ensure the destruction of all anti-personnel mines in accordance with the provisions of this Convention.

Article 2

Definitions

1. "Anti-personnel mine" means a mine designed to be exploded by the presence, proximity or contact of a person and that will incapacitate, injure or kill one or more persons. Mines designed to be detonated by the presence, proximity or contact of a vehicle as opposed to a person, that are equipped with anti-handling devices, are not considered anti-personnel mines as a result of being so equipped.
2. "Mine" means a munition designed to be placed under, on or near the ground or other surface area and to be exploded by the presence, proximity or contact of a person or a vehicle.
3. "Anti-handling device" means a device intended to protect a mine and which is part of, linked to, attached to or placed under the mine and which activates when an attempt is made to tamper with or otherwise intentionally disturb the mine.
4. "Transfer" involves, in addition to the physical movement of anti-personnel mines into or from national territory, the transfer of title to and control over the mines, but does not involve the transfer of territory containing emplaced anti-personnel mines.
5. "Mined area" means an area which is dangerous due to the presence or suspected presence of mines.

Article 3

Exceptions

1. Notwithstanding the general obligations under Article 1, the retention or transfer of a number of anti-personnel mines for the development of and training in mine detection, mine clearance, or mine destruction techniques is permitted. The amount of such mines shall not exceed the minimum number absolutely necessary for the above-mentioned purposes.
2. The transfer of anti-personnel mines for the purpose of destruction is permitted.

Article 4

Destruction of stockpiled anti-personnel mines
Except as provided for in Article 3, each State Party undertakes to destroy or ensure the destruction of all stockpiled anti-personnel mines it owns or possesses, or that are under its jurisdiction or control, as soon as possible but not later than four years after the entry into force of this Convention for that State Party.

Article 5

Destruction of anti-personnel mines in mined areas

1. Each State Party undertakes to destroy or ensure the destruction of all anti-personnel mines in mined areas under its jurisdiction or control, as soon as possible but not later than ten years after the entry into force of this Convention for that State Party.
2. Each State Party shall make every effort to identify all areas under its jurisdiction or control in which anti-personnel mines are known or suspected to be emplaced and shall ensure as soon as possible that all anti-personnel mines in mined areas under its jurisdiction or control are perimeter-marked, monitored and protected by fencing or other means, to ensure the effective exclusion of civilians, until all anti-personnel mines contained therein have been destroyed. The marking shall at least be to the standards set out in the Protocol on Prohibitions or Restrictions on the Use of Mines, Booby-Traps and Other Devices, as amended

on 3 May 1996, annexed to the Convention on Prohibitions or Restrictions on the Use of Certain Conventional Weapons Which May Be Deemed to Be Excessively Injurious or to Have Indiscriminate Effects.

3. If a State Party believes that it will be unable to destroy or ensure the destruction of all anti-personnel mines referred to in paragraph 1 within that time period, it may submit a request to a Meeting of the States Parties or a Review Conference for an extension of the deadline for completing the destruction of such anti-personnel mines, for a period of up to ten years.

4. Each request shall contain:
   a. The duration of the proposed extension;
   b. A detailed explanation of the reasons for the proposed extension, including:
      i. The preparation and status of work conducted under national demining programs;
      ii. The financial and technical means available to the State Party for the destruction of all the anti-personnel mines; and
      iii. Circumstances which impede the ability of the State Party to destroy all the anti-personnel mines in mined areas;
   c. The humanitarian, social, economic and environmental implications of the extension; and
   d. Any other information relevant to the request for the proposed extension.

5. The Meeting of the States Parties or the Review Conference shall, taking into consideration the factors contained in paragraph 4, assess the request and decide by a majority of votes of States Parties present and voting whether to grant the request for an extension period.

6. Such an extension may be renewed upon the submission of a new request in accordance with paragraphs 3, 4 and 5 of this Article. In requesting a further extension period a State Party shall submit relevant additional information on what has been undertaken in the previous extension period pursuant to this Article.

Article 6

International cooperation and assistance

1. In fulfilling its obligations under this Convention each State Party has the right to seek and receive assistance, where feasible, from other States Parties to the extent possible.

2. Each State Party undertakes to facilitate and shall have the right to participate in the fullest possible exchange of equipment, material and scientific and technological information concerning the implementation of this Convention. The States Parties shall not impose undue restrictions on the provision of mine clearance equipment and related technological information for humanitarian purposes.

3. Each State Party in a position to do so shall provide assistance for the care and rehabilitation, and social and economic reintegration, of mine victims and for mine awareness programs. Such assistance may be provided, inter alia, through the United Nations system, international, regional or national organizations or institutions, the International Committee of the Red Cross, national Red Cross and Red Crescent societies and their International Federation, non-governmental organizations, or on a bilateral basis.

4. Each State Party in a position to do so shall provide assistance for mine clearance and related activities. Such assistance may be provided, inter alia, through the United Nations system, international or regional organizations or institutions, non-governmental organizations or institutions, or on a bilateral basis, or by contributing to the United Nations Voluntary Trust Fund for Assistance in Mine Clearance, or other regional funds that deal with demining.

5. Each State Party in a position to do so shall provide assistance for the destruction of stockpiled anti-personnel mines.

6. Each State Party undertakes to provide information to the database on mine clearance established within the United Nations system, especially information concerning various means and technologies of mine clearance, and lists of experts, expert agencies or national points of contact on mine clearance.

7. States Parties may request the United Nations, regional organizations, other States Parties or other competent intergovernmental or non-governmental fora to assist its authorities in the elaboration of a national demining program to determine, inter alia:
   a. The extent and scope of the anti-personnel mine problem;
   b. The financial, technological and human resources that are required for the implementation of the program;
   c. The estimated number of years necessary to destroy all anti-personnel mines in mined areas under the jurisdiction or control of the concerned State Party;
   d. Mine awareness activities to reduce the incidence of mine-related injuries or deaths;
   e. Assistance to mine victims;

f. The relationship between the Government of the concerned State Party and the relevant governmental, inter-governmental or non-governmental entities that will work in the implementation of the program.

8. Each State Party giving and receiving assistance under the provisions of this Article shall cooperate with a view to ensuring the full and prompt implementation of agreed assistance programs.

Article 7

Transparency measures

1. Each State Party shall report to the Secretary-General of the United Nations as soon as practicable, and in any event not later than 180 days after the entry into force of this Convention for that State Party on:
   a. The national implementation measures referred to in Article 9;
   b. The total of all stockpiled anti-personnel mines owned or possessed by it, or under its jurisdiction or control, to include a breakdown of the type, quantity and, if possible, lot numbers of each type of anti-personnel mine stockpiled;
   c. To the extent possible, the location of all mined areas that contain, or are suspected to contain, anti-personnel mines under its jurisdiction or control, to include as much detail as possible regarding the type and quantity of each type of anti-personnel mine in each mined area and when they were emplaced;
   d. The types, quantities and, if possible, lot numbers of all anti-personnel mines retained or transferred for the development of and training in mine detection, mine clearance or mine destruction techniques, or transferred for the purpose of destruction, as well as the institutions authorized by a State Party to retain or transfer anti-personnel mines, in accordance with Article 3;
   e. The status of programs for the conversion or de-commissioning of anti-personnel mine production facilities;
   f. The status of programs for the destruction of anti-personnel mines in accordance with Articles 4 and 5, including details of the methods which will be used in destruction, the location of all destruction sites and the applicable safety and environmental standards to be observed;
   g. The types and quantities of all anti-personnel mines destroyed after the entry into force of this Convention for that State Party, to include

a breakdown of the quantity of each type of anti-personnel mine destroyed, in accordance with Articles 4 and 5, respectively, along with, if possible, the lot numbers of each type of anti-personnel mine in the case of destruction in accordance with Article 4;

h. The technical characteristics of each type of anti-personnel mine produced, to the extent known, and those currently owned or possessed by a State Party, giving, where reasonably possible, such categories of information as may facilitate identification and clearance of anti-personnel mines; at a minimum, this information shall include the dimensions, fusing, explosive content, metallic content, colour photographs and other information which may facilitate mine clearance; and

i. The measures taken to provide an immediate and effective warning to the population in relation to all areas identified under paragraph 2 of Article 5.

2. The information provided in accordance with this Article shall be updated by the States Parties annually, covering the last calendar year, and reported to the Secretary-General of the United Nations not later than 30 April of each year.

3. The Secretary-General of the United Nations shall transmit all such reports received to the States Parties.

Article 8

Facilitation and clarification of compliance

1. The States Parties agree to consult and cooperate with each other regarding the implementation of the provisions of this Convention, and to work together in a spirit of cooperation to facilitate compliance by States Parties with their obligations under this Convention.

2. If one or more States Parties wish to clarify and seek to resolve questions relating to compliance with the provisions of this Convention by another State Party, it may submit, through the Secretary-General of the United Nations, a Request for Clarification of that matter to that State Party. Such a request shall be accompanied by all appropriate information. Each State Party shall refrain from unfounded Requests for Clarification, care being taken to avoid abuse. A State Party that receives a Request for Clarification shall provide, through the Secretary-General of the United Nations, within 28 days to the requesting State Party all information which would assist in clarifying this matter.

3. If the requesting State Party does not receive a response through the Secretary-General of the United Nations within that time period, or deems the response to the Request for Clarification to be unsatisfactory, it may submit the matter through the Secretary-General of the United Nations to the next Meeting of the States Parties. The Secretary-General of the United Nations shall transmit the submission, accompanied by all appropriate information pertaining to the Request for Clarification, to all States Parties. All such information shall be presented to the requested State Party which shall have the right to respond.

4. Pending the convening of any meeting of the States Parties, any of the States Parties concerned may request the Secretary-General of the United Nations to exercise his or her good offices to facilitate the clarification requested.

5. The requesting State Party may propose through the Secretary-General of the United Nations the convening of a Special Meeting of the States Parties to consider the matter. The Secretary-General of the United Nations shall thereupon communicate this proposal and all information submitted by the States Parties concerned, to all States Parties with a request that they indicate whether they favour a Special Meeting of the States Parties, for the purpose of considering the matter. In the event that within 14 days from the date of such communication, at least one-third of the States Parties favours such a Special Meeting, the Secretary-General of the United Nations shall convene this Special Meeting of the States Parties within a further 14 days. A quorum for this Meeting shall consist of a majority of States Parties.

6. The Meeting of the States Parties or the Special Meeting of the States Parties, as the case may be, shall first determine whether to consider the matter further, taking into account all information submitted by the States Parties concerned. The Meeting of the States Parties or the Special Meeting of the States Parties shall make every effort to reach a decision by consensus. If despite all efforts to that end no agreement has been reached, it shall take this decision by a majority of States Parties present and voting.

7. All States Parties shall cooperate fully with the Meeting of the States Parties or the Special Meeting of the States Parties in the fulfilment of its review of the matter, including any fact-finding missions that are authorized in accordance with paragraph 8.

8. If further clarification is required, the Meeting of the States Parties or the Special Meeting of the States Parties shall authorize a fact-finding mission and decide on its mandate by a majority of States Parties present and voting. At any time the requested State Party may invite a fact-finding

mission to its territory. Such a mission shall take place without a decision by a Meeting of the States Parties or a Special Meeting of the States Parties to authorize such a mission. The mission, consisting of up to 9 experts, designated and approved in accordance with paragraphs 9 and 10, may collect additional information on the spot or in other places directly related to the alleged compliance issue under the jurisdiction or control of the requested State Party.

9. The Secretary-General of the United Nations shall prepare and update a list of the names, nationalities and other relevant data of qualified experts provided by States Parties and communicate it to all States Parties. Any expert included on this list shall be regarded as designated for all fact-finding missions unless a State Party declares its non-acceptance in writing. In the event of non-acceptance, the expert shall not participate in fact-finding missions on the territory or any other place under the jurisdiction or control of the objecting State Party, if the non-acceptance was declared prior to the appointment of the expert to such missions.

10. Upon receiving a request from the Meeting of the States Parties or a Special Meeting of the States Parties, the Secretary-General of the United Nations shall, after consultations with the requested State Party, appoint the members of the mission, including its leader. Nationals of States Parties requesting the fact-finding mission or directly affected by it shall not be appointed to the mission. The members of the fact-finding mission shall enjoy privileges and immunities under Article VI of the Convention on the Privileges and Immunities of the United Nations, adopted on 13 February 1946.

11. Upon at least 72 hours notice, the members of the fact-finding mission shall arrive in the territory of the requested State Party at the earliest opportunity. The requested State Party shall take the necessary administrative measures to receive, transport and accommodate the mission, and shall be responsible for ensuring the security of the mission to the maximum extent possible while they are on territory under its control.

12. Without prejudice to the sovereignty of the requested State Party, the fact-finding mission may bring into the territory of the requested State Party the necessary equipment which shall be used exclusively for gathering information on the alleged compliance issue. Prior to its arrival, the mission will advise the requested State Party of the equipment that it intends to utilize in the course of its fact-finding mission.

13. The requested State Party shall make all efforts to ensure that the fact-finding mission is given the opportunity to speak with all relevant persons who may be able to provide information related to the alleged compliance issue.

14. The requested State Party shall grant access for the fact-finding mission to all areas and installations under its control where facts relevant to the compliance issue could be expected to be collected. This shall be subject to any arrangements that the requested State Party considers necessary for:

    a. The protection of sensitive equipment, information and areas;
    b. The protection of any constitutional obligations the requested State Party may have with regard to proprietary rights, searches and seizures, or other constitutional rights; or
    c. The physical protection and safety of the members of the fact-finding mission.

    In the event that the requested State Party makes such arrangements, it shall make every reasonable effort to demonstrate through alternative means its compliance with this Convention.

15. The fact-finding mission may remain in the territory of the State Party concerned for no more than 14 days, and at any particular site no more than 7 days, unless otherwise agreed.

16. All information provided in confidence and not related to the subject matter of the fact-finding mission shall be treated on a confidential basis.

17. The fact-finding mission shall report, through the Secretary-General of the United Nations, to the Meeting of the States Parties or the Special Meeting of the States Parties the results of its findings.

18. The Meeting of the States Parties or the Special Meeting of the States Parties shall consider all relevant information, including the report submitted by the fact-finding mission, and may request the requested State Party to take measures to address the compliance issue within a specified period of time. The requested State Party shall report on all measures taken in response to this request.

19. The Meeting of the States Parties or the Special Meeting of the States Parties may suggest to the States Parties concerned ways and means to further clarify or resolve the matter under consideration, including the initiation of appropriate procedures in conformity with international law. In circumstances where the issue at hand is determined to be due to circumstances beyond the control of the requested State Party, the Meeting of the States Parties or the Special Meeting of the States Parties may recommend appropriate measures, including the use of cooperative measures referred to in Article 6.

20. The Meeting of the States Parties or the Special Meeting of the States Parties shall make every effort to reach its decisions referred to in paragraphs 18 and 19 by consensus, otherwise by a two-thirds majority of States Parties present and voting.

Article 9

National implementation measures
Each State Party shall take all appropriate legal, administrative and other measures, including the imposition of penal sanctions, to prevent and suppress any activity prohibited to a State Party under this Convention undertaken by persons or on territory under its jurisdiction or control.

Article 10

Settlement of disputes

1. The States Parties shall consult and cooperate with each other to settle any dispute that may arise with regard to the application or the interpretation of this Convention. Each State Party may bring any such dispute before the Meeting of the States Parties.
2. The Meeting of the States Parties may contribute to the settlement of the dispute by whatever means it deems appropriate, including offering its good offices, calling upon the States parties to a dispute to start the settlement procedure of their choice and recommending a time-limit for any agreed procedure.
3. This Article is without prejudice to the provisions of this Convention on facilitation and clarification of compliance.

Article 11

Meetings of the States Parties

1. The States Parties shall meet regularly in order to consider any matter with regard to the application or implementation of this Convention, including:
   a. The operation and status of this Convention;
   b. Matters arising from the reports submitted under the provisions of this Convention;
   c. International cooperation and assistance in accordance with Article 6;
   d. The development of technologies to clear anti-personnel mines;
   e. Submissions of States Parties under Article 8; and

f. Decisions relating to submissions of States Parties as provided for in Article 5.

2. The First Meeting of the States Parties shall be convened by the Secretary-General of the United Nations within one year after the entry into force of this Convention. The subsequent meetings shall be convened by the Secretary-General of the United Nations annually until the first Review Conference.

3. Under the conditions set out in Article 8, the Secretary-General of the United Nations shall convene a Special Meeting of the States Parties.

4. States not parties to this Convention, as well as the United Nations, other relevant international organizations or institutions, regional organizations, the International Committee of the Red Cross and relevant non-governmental organizations may be invited to attend these meetings as observers in accordance with the agreed Rules of Procedure.

Article 12

Review Conferences

1. A Review Conference shall be convened by the Secretary-General of the United Nations five years after the entry into force of this Convention. Further Review Conferences shall be convened by the Secretary-General of the United Nations if so requested by one or more States Parties, provided that the interval between Review Conferences shall in no case be less than five years. All States Parties to this Convention shall be invited to each Review Conference.

2. The purpose of the Review Conference shall be:
   a. To review the operation and status of this Convention;
   a. To consider the need for and the interval between further Meetings of the States Parties referred to in paragraph 2 of Article 11;
   a. To take decisions on submissions of States Parties as provided for in Article 5; and
   a. To adopt, if necessary, in its final report conclusions related to the implementation of this Convention.

3. States not parties to this Convention, as well as the United Nations, other relevant international organizations or institutions, regional organizations, the International Committee of the Red Cross and relevant non-governmental organizations may be invited to attend each Review Conference as observers in accordance with the agreed Rules of Procedure.

Article 13

Amendments

1. At any time after the entry into force of this Convention any State Party may propose amendments to this Convention. Any proposal for an amendment shall be communicated to the Depositary, who shall circulate it to all States Parties and shall seek their views on whether an Amendment Conference should be convened to consider the proposal. If a majority of the States Parties notify the Depositary no later than 30 days after its circulation that they support further consideration of the proposal, the Depositary shall convene an Amendment Conference to which all States Parties shall be invited.
2. States not parties to this Convention, as well as the United Nations, other relevant international organizations or institutions, regional organizations, the International Committee of the Red Cross and relevant non-governmental organizations may be invited to attend each Amendment Conference as observers in accordance with the agreed Rules of Procedure.
3. The Amendment Conference shall be held immediately following a Meeting of the States Parties or a Review Conference unless a majority of the States Parties request that it be held earlier.
4. Any amendment to this Convention shall be adopted by a majority of two-thirds of the States Parties present and voting at the Amendment Conference. The Depositary shall communicate any amendment so adopted to the States Parties.
5. An amendment to this Convention shall enter into force for all States Parties to this Convention which have accepted it, upon the deposit with the Depositary of instruments of acceptance by a majority of States Parties. Thereafter it shall enter into force for any remaining State Party on the date of deposit of its instrument of acceptance.

Article 14

Costs

1. The costs of the Meetings of the States Parties, the Special Meetings of the States Parties, the Review Conferences and the Amendment Conferences shall be borne by the States Parties and States not parties to this

Convention participating therein, in accordance with the United Nations scale of assessment adjusted appropriately.

2. The costs incurred by the Secretary-General of the United Nations under Articles 7 and 8 and the costs of any fact-finding mission shall be borne by the States Parties in accordance with the United Nations scale of assessment adjusted appropriately.

Article 15

Signature
This Convention, done at Oslo, Norway, on 18 September 1997, shall be open for signature at Ottawa, Canada, by all States from 3 December 1997 until 4 December 1997, and at the United Nations Headquarters in New York from 5 December 1997 until its entry into force.

Article 16

Ratification, acceptance, approval or accession

1. This Convention is subject to ratification, acceptance or approval of the Signatories.
2. It shall be open for accession by any State which has not signed the Convention.
3. The instruments of ratification, acceptance, approval or accession shall be deposited with the Depositary.

Article 17

Entry into force

1. This Convention shall enter into force on the first day of the sixth month after the month in which the 40th instrument of ratification, acceptance, approval or accession has been deposited.
2. For any State which deposits its instrument of ratification, acceptance, approval or accession after the date of the deposit of the 40th instrument of ratification, acceptance, approval or accession, this Convention shall enter into force on the first day of the sixth month after the date on which that State has deposited its instrument of ratification, acceptance, approval or accession.

Article 18

Provisional application
Any State may at the time of its ratification, acceptance, approval or accession, declare that it will apply provisionally paragraph 1 of Article 1 of this Convention pending its entry into force.

Article 19

Reservations
The Articles of this Convention shall not be subject to reservations.

Article 20

Duration and withdrawal

1. This Convention shall be of unlimited duration.
2. Each State Party shall, in exercising its national sovereignty, have the right to withdraw from this Convention. It shall give notice of such withdrawal to all other States Parties, to the Depositary and to the United Nations Security Council. Such instrument of withdrawal shall include a full explanation of the reasons motivating this withdrawal.
3. Such withdrawal shall only take effect six months after the receipt of the instrument of withdrawal by the Depositary. If, however, on the expiry of that six-month period, the withdrawing State Party is engaged in an armed conflict, the withdrawal shall not take effect before the end of the armed conflict.
4. The withdrawal of a State Party from this Convention shall not in any way affect the duty of States to continue fulfilling the obligations assumed under any relevant rules of international law.

Article 21

Depositary
The Secretary-General of the United Nations is hereby designated as the Depositary of this Convention.

Article 22

Authentic texts

The original of this Convention, of which the Arabic, Chinese, English, French, Russian and Spanish texts are equally authentic, shall be deposited with the Secretary-General of the United Nations.

States Parties to the Mine Ban Treaty (as of Semptember 2007)

Afghanistan	Central African	Ghana
Albania	Republic	Greece
Algeria	Chad	Grenada
Andorra	Chile	Guatemala
Angola	Colombia	Guinea
Antigua and Barbuda	Comoros	Guinea-Bissau
Argentina	Congo (Brazzaville)	Guyana
Australia	Congo, Democratic	Haiti
Austria	Rep.	Holy See
Bahamas	Cook Islands	Honduras
Bangladesh	Costa Rica	Hungary
Barbados	Côte d'Ivoire	Iceland
Belarus	Croatia	Indonesia
Belgium	Cyprus	Iraq
Belize	Czech Republic	Ireland
Benin	Denmark	Italy
Bhutan	Djibouti	Jamaica
Bolivia	Dominica	Japan
Bosnia and	Dominican Republic	Jordan
Herzegovina	Ecuador	Kenya
Botswana	El Salvador	Kiribati
Brazil	Equatorial Guinea	Kuwait
Brunei Darussalem	Eritrea	Latvia
Bulgaria	Estonia	Lesotho
Burkina Faso	Ethiopia	Liberia
Burundi	Fiji	Liechtenstein
Cambodia	France	Lithuania
Cameroon	Gabon	Luxembourg
Canada	Gambia	Macedonia FYR
Cape Verde	Germany	Madagascar

Malawi
Malaysia
Maldives
Mali
Malta
Mauritania
Mauritius
Mexico
Moldova
Monaco
Montenegro
Mozambique
Namibia
Nauru
Netherlands
New Zealand
Nicaragua
Niger
Nigeria
Niue
Norway
Panama
Papua New Guinea

Paraguay
Peru
Philippines
Portugal
Qatar
Romania
Rwanda
Saint Kitts and Nevis
Saint Lucia
Saint Vincent and the
   Grenadines
Samoa
San Marino
São Tomé e Principe
Senegal
Serbia
Seychelles
Sierra Leone
Slovak Republic
Slovenia
Solomon Islands
South Africa
Spain

Sudan
Suriname
Swaziland
Sweden
Switzerland
Tajikistan
Tanzania
Thailand
Timor-Leste
Togo
Trinidad and Tobago
Tunisia
Turkey
Turkmenistan
Uganda
Ukraine
United Kingdom
Uruguay
Vanuatu
Venezuela
Yemen
Zambia
Zimbabwe

Non-States Party (as of September 2007)

Armenia
Azerbaijan
Bahrain
Burma
China
Cuba
Egypt
Finland
Georgia
India
Iran
Israel
Kazakhstan
Kyrgyzstan

Lao PDR
Lebanon
Libya
Marshall Islands
Micronesia
Mongolia
Morocco
Nepal
North Korea
Oman
Pakistan
Palau
Poland
Russian Federation

Saudi Arabia
Singapore
Somalia
South Korea
Sri Lanka
Syria
Tonga
Tuvalu
United Arab Emirates
United States
Uzbekistan
Vietnam

Index

Afghanistan, 20, 21, 29n7, 34, 42, 54–55, 73, 115, 122, 128, 137–38, 147, 155, 168, 170, 210, 212, 222–23

Africa, ix–x, 69, 75–77, 80, 110, 169, 227, 253, 262n52; African Union, 71, 76; North Africa, 44, 51, 76; Organization of African Unity, 34; South Africa, ix–x, 3, 34, 88–91, 94–95, 109, 166, 188, 227, 230, 250, 262n52, 274, 292n20; West Africa, 54

Albania, 34, 155, 221

Angola, 20, 54, 113, 116, 119, 138, 156, 221

antihandling device, 57–58, 118–19

antipersonnel (land)mine: assistance, 10, 57, 106, 118–19, 204; casualties, 4, 22, 102, 148, 199, 202, 213n5; definition, 10, 58, 118–19, 204, 211, 219; deployment, 13n2, 20, 113, 173–74; emplacement, 9, 112, 113, 122, 133; military utility, 18, 19, 29, 81, 165, 182; norm, 11, 18–19, 59, 69, 105, 120, 200–209, 211; production, 5, 19, 55, 59, 60, 66n37, 77, 121, 164, 208, 210–11; retention 9, 106, 115–17; self-destruction, 210; stockpile, 5,

13n2, 19–20, 33, 58, 70, 73–74, 78, 81, 85n15, 87, 97, 104n25, 105, 114, 119–20, 124n10, 125n27, 206–8, 215n24; stockpile destruction, 18, 19, 29n6, 58, 114–16, 121, 164, 169, 215n24; transfer, 5, 9–10, 19, 55, 60, 77, 113–14, 118–19, 121–22, 204, 208, 215n27; use, 5, 10, 13n2, 13n8, 14n8, 19–21, 30n10, 54–55, 58–60, 73, 77–79, 108–9, 111–13, 118–19, 121–22, 124n17, 125n26, 137, 139, 163–65, 168, 170, 173–74, 176n9, 178n23, 178n26, 187, 199–211, 214n8, 215n24, 215n26, 219, 232. *See also* ban

antitank mine. *See* antivehicle mine

antivehicle mine, 10, 39, 42, 118–19, 131, 137, 206, 221, 223, 236n9, 264, 276

Arach-Orech, Margaret, 153, 161n33

Argentina, 94, 228, 230

Armenia, 34, 44, 59, 75, 77, 121

arms control, x, 2, 12, 24, 50, 63, 106–8, 143, 181, 186, 189, 194, 254, 263–68, 270, 272–73, 275, 277, 281, 289; arms embargo, 29n5, 114, 122; Arms Trade Treaty, 192, 197n14, 289, 297n33;

About the Authors

The Editors

Stephen D. Goose is executive director of the Arms Division of Human Rights Watch. He has been Human Rights Watch's point person on landmines since 1993. Goose has been the International Campaign to Ban Landmines' (ICBL) head of delegation since 1998 and served as the editor-in-chief of the ICBL's Landmine Monitor annual report from 1999 to 2004. Previously he was a Congressional staffer and a researcher at the Center for Defense Information.

Mary Wareham is advocacy director at Oxfam New Zealand. From 1998 to 2006, she worked for the Arms Division of Human Rights Watch, coordinating the ICBL's Landmine Monitor initiative. In 1996–1997, she coordinated the US Campaign to Ban Landmines.

Jody Williams is a Nobel Peace laureate and founder of the Nobel Women's Initiative. Since 2003 she has been a distinguished visiting professor at the University of Houston, where in 2007 she became the first holder of the Cele and Sam Keeper Endowed Professorship in Peace and Social Justice at the university's Graduate College of Social Work. Williams was the founding coordinator of the ICBL, and she has served as an ICBL ambassador since 1998. From 1984 to 1992, she developed and directed humanitarian relief projects on behalf of Medical Aid for El Salvador and the Nicaragua-Honduras Education Project.

The Contributors

Sheree Bailey has advised States Parties on victim assistance issues as part of the Mine Ban Treaty's Implementation Support Unit since 2006. She served as the ICBL's Landmine Monitor victim assistance research coordinator from 2000 to 2005. Bailey is also a founding director of Standing Tall Australia (STAIRRSS), a nonprofit that aims to directly support survivors in mine-affected communities.

Elizabeth Bernstein is director of the Nobel Women's Initiative, a network of six women Nobel Peace Laureates. She served as coordinator of the ICBL from 1998 to 2004 and was appointed as an ICBL ambassador in 2006. Bernstein lived in Thailand and Cambodia from 1986–1996, where she worked with local advocacy organizations on various peace, justice, and policy issues.

John Borrie leads the United Nations Institute for Disarmament Research's project on "Disarmament as Humanitarian Action: Making Multilateral Negotiations Work." Previously he worked for the International Committee of the Red Cross and, before that, was a disarmament negotiator for the New Zealand government from 1999 to 2002, based in Geneva, Switzerland.

Kerry Brinkert is manager of the Implementation Support Unit of the 1997 Mine Ban Treaty. From 1998 to 2001, he was the head of Research, Policy and Communications with the Mine Action Team of Canada's Department of Foreign Affairs and International Trade.

Tun Channareth is an ICBL ambassador who played a vital role in securing the 1997 Mine Ban Treaty. A founding member of the Cambodian Campaign to Ban Landmines, Channereth had both legs amputated in 1982 after he stepped on a landmine near the Thai-Cambodian border.

Robert Eaton is executive director of the Survey Action Center, established in 1998. He has over thirty years of experience in development and mine action working for United Nations agencies and nongovernmental organizations, including the Quakers and the Vietnam Veterans of America Foundation.

Peter Herby is coordinator of the Arms Unit in the Legal Division of the International Committee of the Red Cross and has represented the organization in arms-related negotiations since 1994, including those on landmines. Previously he directed the disarmament and arms control program of the Quaker United Nations Office in Geneva from 1983 to 1993.

Alexander Kmentt currently works for the Comprehensive Nuclear Test-Ban Treaty Organization (CTBTO). From 2000 to 2004, he was the deputy permanent representative of Austria to the Conference on Disarmament in Geneva, where he coordinated Austria's work on landmines, including facilitating Austria's presidency of the First Review Conference of the Mine Ban Treaty. Then, until 2006 he was head of the Nuclear Disarmament and Non-Proliferation Unit in the Austrian Foreign Ministry.

Kathleen Lawand has served as legal advisor for the ICRC in Afghanistan since January 2007. She was previously a legal advisor in the Arms Unit of the ICRC's Geneva-based Legal Division with key responsibility for landmines work. Lawand has also worked for the Organization for the Prohibition of Chemical Weapons, the UN High Commissioner for Refugees, and the International Criminal Tribunal for the former Yugoslavia.

Yeshua Moser-Puangsuwan is the ICBL's Landmine Monitor research coordinator on nonstate actors. He served as director of the Bangkok-based Nonviolence International from 1998 to 2006, providing field research into Burma's chronic landmine problem. Moser-Puangsuwan serves on the International Program Council of the Small Arms Survey.

Shannon Smith works on the Afghanistan files for the Policy Group of the Canadian Department of National Defence. Between 2001 and 2005, she worked for Canada's foreign ministry and chaired the Mine Ban Treaty's informal Universalization Contact Group.

Jerry White is a global activist who cofounded Landmine Survivors Network in 1995 to help war victims rebuild their lives and advocate for disability rights. He is a founder and president of Survivor Corps, with more than twenty years' experience in arms control, human rights, and survivor assistance.

Kirsten Young is Director of Advocacy and Rights for Landmine Survivors Network and the director of its Geneva office. She was a lead nongovernmental advocate in the Disability Rights Convention negotiations.